WOMEN WAGING LAW IN ELIZABETHAN ENGLAND

This book investigates the surprisingly large number of women who participated in the vast expansion of litigation in sixteenth and seventeenth century England.

Making use of legal sources, literary texts and the neglected records of the Court of Requests, it describes women's rights under different jurisdictions, considers attitudes to women going to court and reveals how female litigants used the law, as well as fell victim to it. In the central courts of Westminster, maidservants sued their masters, widows sued their creditors and, in defiance of a barrage of theoretical prohibitions, wives sued their husbands. The law was undoubtedly discriminatory, but certain women pursued actively such rights as they possessed. Some appeared as angry plaintiffs, while others played upon their poverty and vulnerability. A special feature of this study is the attention it pays to the different language and tactics that distinguish women's pleadings from men's pleadings within a national equity court.

Cambridge Studies in Early Modern British History

Series editors

ANTHONY FLETCHER

Professor of History, University of Essex

JOHN GUY

Professor of Modern History, University of St Andrews

and JOHN MORRILL

Reader in Early Modern History, University of Cambridge, and Vice-Master of Selwyn College

This is a series of monographs and studies covering many aspects of the history of the British Isles between the late fifteenth century and the early eighteenth century. It includes the work of established scholars and pioneering work by a new generation of scholars. It includes both reviews and revisions of major topics and books, which open up new historical terrain or which reveal startling new perspectives on familiar subjects. All the volumes set detailed research into our broader perspectives and the books are intended for the use of students as well as of their teachers.

For a list of titles in the series, see end of book.

Women Waging Law
in Elizabethan England

TIM STRETTON

CAMBRIDGE
UNIVERSITY PRESS

PUBLISHED BY THE PRESS SYNDICATE OF THE UNIVERSITY OF CAMBRIDGE
The Pitt Building, Trumpington Street, Cambridge CB2 1RP, United Kingdom

CAMBRIDGE UNIVERSITY PRESS
The Edinburgh Building, Cambridge, CB2 2RU, United Kingdom   http://www.cup.cam.ac.uk
40 West 20th Street, New York, NY 10011–4211, USA   http://www.cup.org
10 Stamford Road, Oakleigh, Melbourne 3166, Australia

First published 1998

Printed in the United Kingdom at the University Press, Cambridge

Typeset in Monotype Sabon 10/12 pt   [SE]

A catalogue record for this book is available from the British Library

Library of Congress Cataloguing in Publication data
Stretton, Tim, 1963–
Women Waging Law in Elizabethan England / Tim Stretton.
p.   cm.   – (Cambridge studies in early modern British history)
ISBN 0-521-49554-7 (hardbound)
1. Women – Legal status, laws, etc. – England – History.   2. Justice,
Administration of – England – History.   3. Trials – England.
I. Title.   II. Series.
KD734.S77   1998
346.4201′34–dc21   97–38679   CIP

ISBN 0 521 49554 7 hardback

For Pat and Hugh
For teaching me about history

CONTENTS

MAPS

FIGURE

TABLES

PREFACE

In Tudor England, 'to wage law' had a technical meaning akin to 'compurgation', a process that allowed defendants to defend certain legal actions on oath, supported by the oaths of neighbours or professional oath-takers.[1] In popular use, however, 'to wage law' meant simply to go to law, and it is women 'waging law' in this more general sense who are the focus of this book.[2]

During the reigns of Elizabeth I and James I, levels of civil litigation rose to unprecedented levels, directly or indirectly touching the lives of the majority of the population. Historians are familiar with the legal exploits of a select band of women at this time, including Anne Clifford, Bess of Hardwick and Lady Elizabeth Russell, but we know little about the legal experiences of the majority of women. What follows is a preliminary attempt to fill this gap through an analysis of women, law and litigation (as opposed to women involved in criminal prosecutions) focused around the sizeable number of women who put their names to lawsuits in the second half of the sixteenth century. It considers laws and the application of laws, estimates levels of female participation in different courts and assesses the attitudes of various individuals inside and outside the legal system to women who went to court. It also looks closely at the language of legal pleadings, comparing it with the language employed by moral commentators, satirists and playwrights. For, as the contributors to a recent study of law, literature and feminism in the twentieth century point out, it is useful to explore 'the multitude and complex ways in which women talk about themselves and allow others to talk about them, ways that are sometimes liberating and sometimes incriminating, but always fraught with questions of personal and therefore political power'.[3]

---

[1] 'Wager of law' remained part of English law until 1833, but it effectively fell into disuse after *Slade's case* in 1602; J.H. Baker, *An Introduction to English Legal History*, 3rd edn (London, 1990), pp. 6, 87–8, 395–6.

[2] For examples of this 'erroneous' popular usage, see Ben Jonson, *The Staple of News* (c.1626), V.i.117, D.R. Kifer, ed., *The Staple of News* (London, 1975); the *Oxford English Dictionary*, 2nd edn (Oxford, 1989), vol. 19, p. 804; *Thomas and Johanne Crace v. William Stokes*, PRO Req 2/188/62, B; *Richard Christopher v. William & Ellen Baylie et al.*, PRO Req 2/191/71, P; *Elizabeth Shipper v. Thomas Pury and Giles Danyell*, PRO Req 2/267/24, B.

[3] Susan Heinzelman and Zipporah Wiseman, eds., *Representing Women: Law, Literature and Feminism* (Durham and London, 1994), p. vii.

English law discriminated against women in the sixteenth century as it did in earlier and later eras, regularly failing to provide them with the same legal rights and opportunities as men. This study identifies that discrimination, but also reveals how significant numbers of Elizabethan women refused to be passive victims of a restrictive legal system and became active plaintiffs or vociferous defendants in a clutch of different law courts. It does so by looking not just at women, but at the men and the institutions they co-operated with or fought against, during a significant period in the history of English law.

The path this project has taken has been long and circuitous, inspiring friendships and levying debts on three continents. First and foremost I would like to offer thanks to Keith Wrightson. In overseeing the Ph.D. out of which this study has grown he showed patience and provided inspiration well beyond the usual supervisor's brief and I feel privileged to have spent time in his intellectual care. My thanks also go to Lynn Martin, who first set me on the path of women's history, to Wilfrid Prest, who encouraged me to look at the law (when my interests lay elsewhere), and to Chris Brooks who I was lucky enough to work alongside in Durham. All three have generously shared their expertise and enthusiasm, as well as countless references.

The shape this book has eventually taken owes much to the perceptive comments and suggestions of the examiners of my thesis, John Walter and J.A. Sharpe, and the editors of this series, especially Anthony Fletcher and John Guy, whose astute and rigorous criticism helped me to manage the difficult transformation from thesis to book manuscript. For references and advice I am indebted to Heather Kerr, Craig Muldrew, Grace Ioppolo and Lamar Hill. I also want to acknowledge the inspiration offered (either directly or through the example of their work) by Lyndal Roper, Laura Gowing, Bridget Hill, Martin Ingram, Amy Erickson, Patricia Crawford, Barbara Todd and Susan Staves, and the helpful comments of seminar and conference audiences in Cambridge, Durham, Oxford, Exeter, Adelaide and Sydney. Errors that remain owe nothing to these fine historians and everything to myself.

I am indebted to the following bodies for their financial support; the Association of Commonwealth Universities, the overseers of the Eileen Power Award, the History department at Durham University and the President and Fellows of Clare Hall, Cambridge. I would also like to express my thanks to the members of the British Council involved with administering Commonwealth Scholarships, and to the helpful staffs of the university libraries in Cambridge, Durham and Adelaide, the British Library, the New York Public Library, the Bibliothèque Mazarine in Paris and the Public Record Office (both at Chancery Lane and at Kew) in London. An earlier version of chapter 7 appeared in Jenny Kermode and Garthine Walker, eds., *Women, Crime and the Courts in Early Modern England* (London, 1994) and I would like to thank UCL Press for granting permission to reprint some of that material here.

During the writing of both my Ph.D. and this book, and during a year of unemployment in between, I have relied heavily on the hospitality and friendship, as well as the intellectual encouragement, offered by my family and a number of friends and colleagues. In a by no means exhaustive list, I would like to thank Paul Aiello, Mike Braddick, Sharyn Brooks, Elisabeth Citron, Gareth Edwards, Liz Foyster, Dagmar Freist, Anne Habiby, Steve Hindle, Mritiun Mohanty, Sarah Morgan, Martin Olin, the Harcourts, Sangeeta Pratap, Helen Sacharias, the Tewsons, Helen Weinstein and Andy Wood. Final thanks, for her patience in reading every chapter and for much else, are due to Lyndan Warner.

NOTES ON THE TEXT

Original spelling is retained in quotations, except that the letters u, i and the diphthong y have been modernised to v, j and th, where appropriate. Punctuation has also, on occasion, been modernised to aid clarity. Abbreviations have been expanded and additions or corrections appear in square brackets. The spelling of some names has been modernised in the text for ease of comprehension, but left in the original in footnotes for reasons of accuracy. Dates are Old Style, except that the year is taken to begin on 1 January. The dates of Renaissance plays refer to the date of composition or first known performance and are taken from the chronological table in A.R. Braunmuller and Michael Hattaway, eds., *The Cambridge Companion to English Renaissance Drama* (Cambridge, 1990). References to specific documents within Requests case files include a description of those documents, using the following abbreviations:

B	– Bill	A	– Answer
R	– Replication	Rj	– Rejoinder
I	– Interrogatory/ies	D	– Deposition/s
C	– Commission	CR	– Commissioners' Report
Dem	– Demurrer	mm.	– membranes
m.	– membrane*		

Note: *in instances where no membrane number appears on a document, I sometimes provide one, and this is indicated by the use of square brackets, e.g., '[m. 6]'.

ABBREVIATIONS

B.L.	British Library
Cal. S.P. Dom.	*Calendar of State Papers Domestic*
C.U.L.	Cambridge University Library
D.N.B.	*Dictionary of National Biography*
PRO	Public Record Office
S.P.	State Papers
S.T.C.	*Short Title Catalogue*

1

Introduction

The position of women is one thing in theory, another in legal position, yet
another in everyday life
Eileen Power, *Medieval Women*[1]

The law is a powerful determinant of status in any society. Laws establish the
age of legal responsibility, defining the point at which children become adults.
They permit individuals to act in certain ways and prohibit them from acting in
others and they set out the differing rights and responsibilities of women and
men. Taken together they provide a unique and highly visible embodiment of
the values, beliefs and prejudices of a given community. Feminist historians and
campaigners for women's rights have therefore looked to legal codes and legal
commentaries to learn the history of inequality between the sexes, and to consider directions for future reform. Theoretical notions about women's legal
position underpin many histories of women, however surprisingly little is
known about the full complexity of different women's (and indeed men's) relationships with the law prior to the modern period.[2] For while statutes and commentaries are revealing of attitudes to women and shifts in women's legal
status, they say little about the effect that laws had on women's lives. This study
seeks to address this imbalance, taking as its subject not women and the law, but
women and litigation, focusing predominantly (but not exclusively) on
Elizabethan England. Building on the work of other historians who have
analysed the law in practice, it seeks to raise, and where possible to answer, a
number of questions about the use English women made of legal institutions in
the sixteenth and early seventeenth centuries. For example, which women in this
period knew of their legal rights? To which social classes did they belong? How
many exercised their rights? In which courts? To what effect? How did commen-

[1] Eileen Power, *Medieval Women*, ed. M.M. Postan (Cambridge, 1975), p. 5.
[2] Janet Loengard, 'Legal history and the medieval Englishwoman: a fragmented view', *Law and
History Review*, 4 (1986), pp. 161–78; W.R. Prest, 'Law and women's rights in early modern
England', *The Seventeenth Century*, 6 (1991), pp. 169–87; a full discussion of the historiography
of women and the law follows in the next chapter.

1

tators, satirists, dramatists, judges, lawyers and opponents regard female litigants, and how did they characterise them in writings and in court?

The involvement of women in litigation has only recently begun to catch the eye of historians. Since breaking free from the long tradition of writing biographies of eminent women and searching for the roots of modern feminism, feminist historians have pursued two main lines of inquiry. Firstly, they have tried to determine the nature and extent of women's suppression in past times, identifying the agents, ideas and social mechanisms that consistently kept women from holding public office or exercising public power and restricted their authority within the household. Secondly, they have tried to ascertain how women lived, and the autonomy and independence different individuals achieved within a markedly patriarchal society. In recent years practitioners of the 'new' women's history have begun to concentrate attention on the latter, looking less at the impositions of the oppressors and more at the life and creativity of the oppressed. Having recognised the longevity of women's subordination, historians have realised that the ultimate origins and causes of inequality are destined always to lie outside the frame of a single study or period. Others have realised the limitations of casting women as victims of external forces in history, rather than as actors operating with or against those forces. Hence this shift in emphasis from tracing the causes behind women's suppression, to investigating the ways different women survived that suppression.[3]

Women found themselves excluded from most areas of government and administration, but they contributed to their communities and gained esteem in other ways. Studies of childbirth and household relations, of gossip and women's work have identified areas of female autonomy where women exercised authority over men or other women.[4] There has been a revival of interest in the history of women's work, one that has necessitated extending existing definitions of work to include the unpaid, informal and sporadic employment preferred by, or forced upon, women from all but the highest reaches of society.[5]

---

[3] In the concluding chapter of *Women in England 1500–1760*, for example, Anne Laurence explains that 'the purpose of this book has been to explore what women were able to do, not what they were prevented from doing'; Anne Laurence, *Women in England 1500–1760: A Social History* (London, 1995), p. 273; Judith Bennett, by contrast, has consistently focused on the causes of women's oppression; see Judith Bennett, 'Feminism and history', *Gender and History*, 1 (1989), pp. 259–63.

[4] Examples include Adrian Wilson, 'The ceremony of childbirth and its interpretation', in Valerie Fildes, ed., *Women as Mothers in Pre-Industrial England: Essays in Memory of Dorothy McLaren* (London, 1989); Diane Willen, 'Women in the public sphere in early modern England: the case of the urban working poor', *Sixteenth Century Journal*, 19 (1988), pp. 559–75; Laura Gowing, *Domestic Dangers: Women, Words, and Sex in Early Modern London* (Oxford, 1996).

[5] Studies include Lindsey Charles and Lorna Duffin, eds., *Women and Work in Preindustrial England* (London, 1985); Barbara Hanawalt, ed., *Women and Work in Pre-Industrial Europe* (Bloomington, Indiana, 1986); Susan Cahn, *Industry of Devotion: The Transformation of Women's Work in England, 1500–1660* (New York, 1987); Katrina Honeyman and Jordan Goodman, 'Women's work, gender conflict, and labour markets in Europe, 1500–1900', *Economic History Review*, 2nd series, 44 (1991), pp. 608–28; Bridget Hill, *Women, Work, and Sexual Politics in Eighteenth-Century England* (Oxford, 1989).

In all of these explorations of women's activities researchers find themselves having to compensate for layer upon layer of male bias, from the bias of the society under study and the bias of its male scribes and record keepers, to the bias of the generations of historians who largely ignored the experiences of women. The freshness and originality of a feminist-inspired approach to history is apparent in the diversity of the burgeoning list of topics of study, including sexual insult and political gossip, female and male conceptions of honour and reputation, histories of pregnancy and motherhood, and the influence of gender on education, marriage and household relations, to name but a few.

Feminist historians have generally characterised the law as belonging firmly in the first camp of women's history, seeing it as a key mediator of women's oppression. And in the rush to new pastures they have paid it less attention than the pioneers of the subject did a century ago, when women were struggling to achieve female suffrage and to overcome the worst impediments to legal equality.[6] Rarely have historians afforded it space in the second camp of women's history, as a forum where women could act independently and assert their rights.[7] Yet despite the paucity of rights they enjoyed compared to men, many Tudor and Stuart women went to law seeking redress for wrongs. In her 1974 study of women in the Elizabethan Chancery, Maria Cioni suggested not only that women regularly sued in Chancery, but that the claims they made influenced the development of particular equitable devices and forms of equitable relief.[8] Amy Erickson has added to Cioni's findings about women in Chancery and Laura Gowing has revealed the use female litigants made of London's church courts.[9] How women fared in other courts is yet to be seen, and there is a need to look at other legal institutions to meld an understanding of women's notional legal rights with an investigation of women's actual dealings with the law.[10] Litigation records can give an indication of the extent to which women

---

[6] For nineteenth- and early twentieth-century works on women and law, see Susan Staves, *Married Women's Separate Property in England, 1660–1833* (London, 1990), especially pp. 243–52.

[7] Exceptions for the periods preceding and following the sixteenth and seventeenth centuries include Judith Bennett, 'Public power and authority in the medieval English countryside', in Mary Erler and Maryanne Kowaleski, eds., *Women and Power in the Middle Ages* (London, 1988), pp. 18–36; Elizabeth Ewan, 'Scottish Portias: women in the courts in medieval Scottish towns', *Journal of the Canadian Historical Association*, new series, 3 (1992), pp. 27–43; Tim Meldrum, 'A women's court in London: defamation at the Bishop of London's consistory court, 1700–1745', *The London Journal*, 19 (1994), pp. 1–22; Margot Finn, 'Women, consumption and coverture in England, *c.* 1760–1860', *The Historical Journal*, 39 (1996), pp. 703–22.

[8] Maria Cioni, *Women and Law in Elizabethan England with Particular Reference to the Court of Chancery* (New York and London, 1985); Maria Cioni, 'The Elizabethan Chancery and women's rights', in D. J. Guth and J. W. McKenna, eds., *Tudor Rule and Revolution: Essays for G.R. Elton from his American Friends* (Cambridge, 1982).

[9] Amy Erickson, *Women and Property in Early Modern England* (London and New York, 1993), pp. 114–28; Gowing, *Domestic Dangers*.

[10] Ruth Kittel, 'Women under the law in medieval England 1066–1485', in Barbara Kanner, ed., *The Women of England from Anglo-Saxon Times to the Present: Interpretive Bibliographic Essays* (London, 1980), p. 125.

knew of their rights and exercised them, the types of actions they brought, the remedies they sought and the justice they received. They can also tell something of women's involvement in the activities which gave rise to law suits, providing an idea of their participation in trades, land ownership and commercial transactions, as well as their relations with neighbours and kin.

A stumbling block in this enterprise is the technical nature of the law and of legal records. Historians who lack legal training have often shied away from studying the law and litigation because of the difficulties of interpretation these subjects pose. John Baker has referred to the sixteenth and seventeenth centuries as 'the Dark Age of English legal history', observing that non-legal historians have often 'fled in despair from the mysteries of the law which permeates their history'. Lawyers, meanwhile, 'have always been bemused by the apparent continuity of their heritage into a way of thinking which inhibits historical understanding'.[11] In short, historians with the relevant expertise have tended to ignore the subject of women and the law, while historians blessed with a curiosity about these matters have lacked the training or the will to enter into a quagmire of technicalities and legal fictions regularly expressed in convoluted Latin or law French.

Feminist historians are not alone in having neglected the law in action. Partly as a result of these technical difficulties, social historians have only recently begun to realise the importance of studying private litigation. The pioneering researchers of 'history from below' tried to identify the notions of social hierarchy, the structures and the institutions which confined the lower orders in English society to a position below that of the ruling gentry and aristocracy. Like the feminist historians who followed in their wake, they viewed the law as an agent of control and regulation, and their interest in the imposition and maintenance of social and moral order led them to concentrate on criminal and ecclesiastical justice. The result is that the history of crime has grown into a recognised sub-discipline, while the social history of civil litigation, a sphere of law long dismissed as being the preserve of the wealthy, is only just beginning to be written.[12]

---

[11] J.H. Baker, 'The Dark Age of English legal history, 1500–1700', in D. Jenkins, ed., *Legal History Studies 1972* (Cardiff, 1975), p. 2.

[12] For the relative neglect of civil litigation, see C.W. Brooks, 'Interpersonal conflict and social tension: civil litigation in England, 1640–1830', in A.L. Beier, David Cannadine and J.M. Rosenheim, eds., *The First Modern Society: Essays in English History in Honour of Lawrence Stone* (Cambridge, 1989), p. 357; David Sugarman and G.R. Rubin, eds., *Law, Economy and Society, 1750–1914: Essays in the History of English Law* (Abingdon, Oxon., 1984), pp. 2–3, 59, 64; exceptions include C.W. Brooks, *Pettyfoggers and Vipers of the Commonwealth: The 'Lower Branch' of the Legal Profession in Early Modern England* (Cambridge, 1986); J.A. Sharpe, '"Such disagreement betwyx neighbours": Litigation and human relations in early modern England', in John Bossy, ed., *Disputes and Settlements: Law and Human Relations in the West* (Cambridge, 1983); J.A. Sharpe, 'The people and the law', in Barry Reay, ed., *Popular Culture in Seventeenth Century England* (London, 1985).

This concentration of attention on crime is understandable but it can be misleading. The difference between criminal and civil law is ultimately one of definition. Whether anti-social conduct was considered criminal, or actionable in civil courts, or both, or neither, depended on the rulings of judges and lawmakers. It was they who determined whether a cause would be tried, where it would be tried, who would try it and the punishment or penalty that would result. While it is important to know which kinds of behaviour early modern authorities labelled criminal and punished for reasons of public interest, it is wrong to assume that the overseers of criminal justice had a monopoly on the maintenance of public order. Criminal law obviously seeks to punish and limit acts of violence, but *all* law deals with the peaceable ordering of society, and civil litigation plays a significant role in defining acceptable behaviour and ensuring harmony within the community. In the words of C.W. Brooks, 'it is arguable that the civil law is even more important than the criminal law in maintaining the social and economic relationships in any society'.[13]

Implicit in social historians' relative lack of interest in non-criminal law is the idea that criminal justice was imposed and enforced from above, while private litigation, 'the squabbling of neighbours', was initiated by individuals, and therefore has little structural significance for historians. To take such a view demonstrates the danger of transposing modern definitions of crime, or indeed of any other aspect of the law, uncritically on to the past. As J.A. Sharpe pointed out in a review article on the history of crime: 'Suppressing modern assumptions is particularly important for a period which had an imprecise notion of the difference between sin and crime, when legal theory was only gradually achieving a clear distinction between tort and crime, and when legislative initiative might redefine previously licit behaviour as criminal.'[14] The bonds that knit a society together are as important as the forces that threaten to drive it apart, and evidence of both is exposed in the records of litigation.

Civil actions in the sixteenth century affected many more individuals than criminal actions or ecclesiastical actions, and they were certainly not the preserve of the rich. Brooks has demonstrated that even in the most important of Westminster's central courts, Common Pleas and Queen's Bench, the gentry and aristocracy were in a minority, and many litigants came from the middle ranks of society.[15] Even quite poor litigants waged law in these courts, petitioning to be allowed entry *in forma pauperis*, by which they would receive free representation by legal counsel and have their court costs waived.[16] Litigation in these courts was not particularly speedy or efficient, but it was relatively affordable, and large numbers of litigants from all over the country made use of their services.

[13] Brooks, 'Interpersonal conflict', p. 357.
[14] J.A. Sharpe, 'The history of crime in late medieval and early modern England: a review of the field', *Social History*, 7 (1982), p. 188.   [15] Brooks, *Pettyfoggers*, pp. 57–63.
[16] For a discussion of *in forma pauperis*, see chapter 4 below.

Historians have long been struck by the volume of litigation these and other courts handled and the extraordinary increases in business they experienced throughout the sixteenth century and into the seventeenth century.[17] The dramatic surge in central litigation has implications for historical subjects as diverse as the rise of central government, the extent of 'neighbourliness' and the growth of market capitalism, and it has yet to be fully mapped or adequately explained.[18]

Moreover, the central courts were only the tip of an extensive system of legal institutions spread throughout the country, a system which J.A. Sharpe and Martin Ingram have suggested catered for the popular classes as well as wealthy lords and landowners.[19] Marcus Knight has revealed the surprisingly egalitarian nature of the Durham Chancery in the seventeenth century.[20] Louis Knafla's project *Kent at Law 1602*, which plans to locate and record every action in every legal jurisdiction in Kent during the calendar year 1602, has already begun to reveal the scale of litigation and the relatively small proportion of cases handled by the central courts.[21] Craig Muldrew's work on debt litigation in King's Lynn in the later seventeenth century graphically reveals both the volume of local litigation and the participation of litigants from all but the poorest social groupings. At a time when business in the central courts was declining, the Lynn Guildhall court dealt with more than 1,000 suits a year, on average, in a town with an estimated population of no more than 8,000.[22]

England, it seems, was awash with law suits, and Muldrew's and Knafla's work suggests that historians have only scratched the surface of the subject of local litigation.[23] Many questions concerning the shape and significance of

[17] S.F.C. Milsom, *The Historical Foundations of the Common Law*, 2nd edn (London, 1981), pp. 30–1, 60; Marjorie Blatcher, *The Court of King's Bench, 1450–1550: A Study in Self-Help* (London, 1978), pp. 20–2, 154–5; E.W. Ives, 'The common lawyers in pre-Reformation England', *Transactions of the Royal Historical Society*, 5th series, 18 (1968); G.R. Elton, *England 1200–1640* (London, 1969), pp. 56, 65–6.

[18] On the causes of the increase in litigation and its significance, see Brooks, *Pettyfoggers*, pp. 75–111; Lawrence Stone, 'Interpersonal violence in English society 1300–1980', *Past and Present*, 101 (1983), pp. 22–33, especially pp. 28, 31; Sharpe, 'The people and the law'; J.A. Sharpe, 'Debate: the history of violence in England: some observations', *Past and Present*, 108 (1985), pp. 206–15, especially p. 213; Craig Muldrew, 'Credit, market relations and debt litigation in late seventeenth century England with special reference to King's Lynn' (University of Cambridge Ph.D., 1991), pp. 81–5, 87; and see Craig Muldrew, *The Economy of Obligation: The Culture of Credit and Social Relations in Early Modern England* (Basingstoke, forthcoming).

[19] Sharpe, 'The people and the law'; Martin Ingram, 'Communities and courts: law and disorder in early seventeenth-century Wiltshire', in J.S. Cockburn, ed., *Crime in England 1550–1800* (London, 1977).

[20] Marcus Knight, 'Litigants and litigation in the seventeenth century Palatinate of Durham' (University of Cambridge Ph.D., 1990).

[21] Louis Knafla, ed., *Kent at Law, 1602* (London, 1994).

[22] Muldrew, 'Credit, market relations and debt litigation', p. 58.

[23] Muldrew has compared C.W. Brooks' litigation estimates with population estimates and calculated that King's Bench dealt with just over 300, and Common Pleas just over 800, instances of litigation per 100,000 population; the equivalent figure for Lynn was nearly 20,000 instances per 100,000; Muldrew, 'Credit, market relations and debt litigation', p. 82.

litigation patterns remain to be answered, and it might seem premature to investigate the role of women in court actions before these general patterns have been established. Much feminist history has sought to provide balance, unearthing the female experience in situations where the male or general experience is already known. However, a feminist approach to history promises more than simply a history of women, it seeks to demonstrate the importance of looking at male and female contributions in any and every movement of history.[24] The sheer magnitude of the task of uncovering women's relationship with the law is daunting. As Bronwyn McIntyre commented in 1972, 'only a large-scale study of the records and judgments of the many courts of England could demonstrate the actual practice of the legal theories of special status for women'.[25] Such a study of every available court would take one or more lifetimes to complete, and this book takes a more modest approach, concentrating the bulk of attention on a single court, the Court of Requests, and comparing evidence from its records with current knowledge of women's experience in other courts.

Requests was the 'poor man's Chancery', a national equity court which flourished for just over a century and a half between the time of Henry VII and the onset of the Civil War.[26] In theory it was a court for poor litigants, entitled to hear 'poor miserable persons causes, as Widows and Orphans, and other distressed people, whose cases wholly rely on piety and conscience'.[27] In practice it entertained wealthy suitors in considerable numbers, but nevertheless it gave a hearing to a greater percentage of less well-off clients than any other central court. And among its poor and rich clientele were many women. On average one third of the cases that came before the 'Masters', or judges, of Requests involved a female plaintiff or defendant.[28] These women were not always litigating alone, many were joint parties suing with anything up to a dozen men, or wives suing or being sued with their husbands. But clearly the Masters of Requests were accustomed to dealing with women litigants in numbers every day the court was in session. Given that Requests was a central court many of these litigants travelled to London from distant locations, often staying for extended periods of time to have their cases heard or to answer the allegations of others. The resulting image, of women travelling to the capital in numbers to

---

[24] The history of industrialisation, for example, has been enriched by the identification of the importance of the increasing use of female and child labour in the nineteenth century; Maxine Berg, 'What difference did women's work make to the Industrial Revolution?', *History Workshop Journal*, 35 (1993), pp. 22–44; and see Christopher Hill, *History and the Present* (London, 1989), p. 13.

[25] Bronwyn McIntyre, 'Legal attitudes towards women in England 1558–1648' (University of New Brunswick M.A., 1972), p. 242.

[26] The precise origins of Requests, which George Spence argued lay in the fourteenth century, are unclear; see chapter 4 below.

[27] Thomas Ridley, *A View of the Civile and Ecclesiasticall Law* (London, 1607), p. 228.

[28] For detailed statistics of litigants in Requests and other courts, see chapter 3 below.

wage law, already challenges long-standing impressions of closeted female domesticity.

The records of Requests are particularly revealing because it was a court of equity. As William Lambarde explained in *Archeion*, equity 'doth not onely weigh what is generally meet for the most part, but doth also consider the person, time, place, and other circumstances in every singular case that commeth in question, and doth thereof frame such judgement as is convenient and agreeable to the same'.[29] The consideration of 'other circumstances' in pleadings, depositions and judgments translates into rich detail about litigants' backgrounds, and the backgrounds to their disputes. Furthermore, because Requests served the whole of England and Wales and acted in many instances as an appeal court, its records contain information about a range of jurisdictions, and concentration on this one organ of justice therefore provides information not just about women and equity, but about common law, custom and ecclesiastical law as well.

Social historians have dipped into the Requests archive to trace individual causes, or to shed light on certain types of action. R.L. Greaves used the records of the court to test ideas about marital behaviour found in literary sources.[30] Paul Seaver has used Requests records to investigate the character of master–apprentice relationships, while Alan Everitt sampled marketing disputes in the court to chart the growth of private marketing in the grain trade.[31] Historians have not ignored the court, but neither have they fully exploited its sizeable archive. As Lamar Hill lamented in his biography of Julius Caesar, the court's most influential Master, 'that the Court of Requests has not been thoroughly examined is unfortunate because of the wealth of social, legal, and political data its records contain'.[32]

Focusing the lion's share of attention on a single court like Requests leaves open the possibility that conclusions drawn from its records may not be representative. Maria Cioni, for example, made confident claims about changing attitudes to women in Elizabethan England on the basis of her study of women in Chancery. In her words, 'Chancery, like other courts, was a product and a reflection of the wants and needs of society. Therefore, the fact that Chancery was not only receptive of and attractive to women's plight but actually realized that

[29] William Lambarde, *Archeion or, a Discourse Upon the High Courts of Justice in England* (London, 1635), p. 69.

[30] R.L. Greaves, *Society and Religion in Elizabethan England* (Minneapolis, 1981), pp. 166, 171, 188, 273, 809; and see pp. 106, 598, 612.

[31] Paul Seaver, 'A social contract? Master against servant in the Court of Requests', *History Today*, 39 (September, 1989), pp. 50–6; Alan Everitt, 'The marketing of agricultural produce', in Joan Thirsk, ed., *The Agrarian History of England and Wales* (Cambridge, 1967), vol. 4, pp. 466–592, especially p. 544; see also Ann Haaker, 'The plague, the theater, and the poet', *Renaissance Drama*, new series, 1 (1968), pp. 283–306.

[32] L.M. Hill, *Bench and Bureaucracy: The Public Career of Sir Julius Caesar, 1580–1636* (Cambridge, 1988), p. 71.

they should be accorded some rights and duties indicates that social attitudes towards women were changing.'[33] Yet, as Clive Holmes has remarked, if attitudes were changing, 'one wonders why Chancery *alone* should have chosen to reflect the novel social attitudes'.[34] Given the fluid and changeable nature of all courts within the legal system, changes detected in one can never reliably be taken as marking significant developments in wider society. They are more likely to represent procedural ebbs and flows within the wider equilibrium of the central court system.

Most central courts underwent considerable change in the latter half of the sixteenth century as they expanded to meet growing demand, fought to secure jurisdiction, and competed with each other for business. In 1588, for example, Chancery Masters responded to increased pressure on their services by setting a minimum threshold for entry to the court, and from then on they referred cases worth less than £5 to Requests.[35] Overnight changes such as this were not uncommon, and they can distort impressions of the nature and popularity of courts if those courts are examined in isolation. Gaining as full an understanding as possible of the Court of Requests, its purposes, the methods its officials used to marshal evidence and to record pleas and decisions, and the language and conventions Masters and legal counsel used, can allow information from the Requests archive to be examined with some confidence. However, until more work is done on all the courts within the central system, conclusions about women's legal dealings, based on information taken from any single institution, obviously must remain tentative.

It may be hazardous to assume that Requests represents a perfect microcosm of Elizabethan society, but this does not mean that the court's records can only reveal information specific to this court. The archives of Requests, and of most courts, contain other information important for understanding women's experience of the law, in particular the attitudes of litigants, lawyers and judges towards women who came to court. The wording of decisions and the language that plea writers used to attack the integrity of male and female opponents harbour a wealth of information about contemporary perceptions. Consequently, a study of court records and women's relations with the law can contribute more than a fuller picture of how the legal system catered for, or failed to cater for, women. It has the potential to provide insights into a range of other questions which lie at the core of recent women's history.

The tension inherent in the two main strands of women's historiography, between the fact of women's subordination and the extent of women's inde-

[33] Cioni, *Women and Law*, p. 2.
[34] Clive Holmes' review of D.J. Guth and J.W. McKenna, eds., *Tudor Rule and Revolution: Essays for G.R. Elton from his American Friends* (Cambridge, 1982) in *Law and History Review*, 2 (1984), p. 156.
[35] For details of this and of other procedural orders in Chancery which affected Requests, see chapter 4 below.

pendence, has led historians to discern a number of apparent contradictions and paradoxes within early modern society which remain to be resolved.[36] Sixteenth and seventeenth century commentators repeatedly directed women to be passive, while at the same time society expected them to be active. Good wives were intended to remain silent and modest and obey their husbands, as they had obeyed their fathers, but the same good wives were under pressure to manage their households and govern their children. Widows were expected to remain unmarried and respect the memory of their husbands, yet those who complied threatened the perceived social order, by living outside the governance of a man. The refusal or inability of women to live up to prescribed ideals is evident in the gulf that existed between the advice directed to women in conduct books and sermons and found in intellectual debates, and women's actions in practice. Clearly maids did not always remain chaste and wives did not always remain silent. Widows remarried, women worked, they ran estates, they wrote books and they went to court. However, while many historians have recognised these gaps between attitudes and practice, few have tried to analyse them. To regard conduct books and sermons as prescriptive, rather than descriptive, because the gulf between advice and practice could be wide, is a significant step forward, but one that leaves many aspects of the dilemma unresolved.[37] For example, should we assume that few people were exposed to the ideas in these sources, or that these prescriptions were common knowledge amid a population who chose to ignore them?

Some feminist writers have set out to examine the dynamics of the relationship between prescriptive ideals and lived reality, to see whether women were aware of apparent contradictions, how men employed prescriptive literature and how individual women dealt with the demands of conflicting expectations. Alison Wall has shown how various women in the Thynne family mimicked published ideals of model female behaviour in their letters, while simultaneously playing an active part in the management of estate affairs. Joan Thynne's letters in particular show how a woman could combine 'the rhetoric of submission with independence of action'. Wall suggests that these women paid lip-service to the ideals that underpinned conduct book advice, but recognised them as being realistically unattainable, drawn more from fantasy than real life.[38] At the other extreme, as Laura Gowing points out,

---

[36] Kanner, *The Women of England*, p. 12.

[37] For an example of a historian who maintains that conduct books are more descriptive than prescriptive, see Kathleen Davies, 'Continuity and change in literary advice on marriage', in R.B. Outhwaite, ed., *Marriage and Society: Studies in the Social History of Marriage* (London, 1981).

[38] Wall points out that the majority of conduct books and exemplary sermons were produced by inexperienced 'boys and bachelors', very few by married men; Alison Wall, 'Elizabethan precept and feminine practice: the Thynne family of Longleat', *History*, 75 (1990), pp. 35, 37–8; but see Anthony Fletcher, 'The Protestant idea of marriage in early modern England', in Anthony Fletcher and Penny Roberts, eds., *Religion, Culture and Society in Early Modern Britain: Essays in Honour of Patrick Collinson* (Cambridge, 1994).

violent husbands appear to have used the rhetoric of household order to discipline their wives.[39]

Linda Pollock has stressed that most existing interpretations of these paradoxes are unsatisfactory because 'they restate the divide between prescription and actuality rather than resolve the enigma of that divide'. She has looked to the education of young men and women to see how parents and tutors instilled elements of masculine and feminine virtues into children of both sexes. Her conclusions support a view that stresses the flexibility of women's roles, recognising that while women were brought up to be deferential to men, they were also expected to develop a degree of independence and competence, both in thought and in action. Wives were not to challenge their husbands, but they had to support them, and be capable of managing their affairs in their absence. In other words, while society expected women to take on apparently contradictory roles, it provided them with a clear sense of which roles were appropriate for which moments.[40] Anthony Fletcher has recently endorsed this view and suggested that the importance of education in defining gender roles increased during the centuries following Elizabeth's reign.[41]

The urgings of clergymen and professional advice givers failed to convince every woman in society to live a life of docile obedience, but that does not mean the climate of expectation they created had no effect on women's lives and on men's behaviour. The chorus of advice counselling women to stay at home did not prevent them from going to court, but I will argue that it could make them warier litigants than men.[42] Courts like Requests formed a hinterland between what contemporaries considered to be the private and public spheres of life, and they provide interesting forums in which to compare expressed attitudes to women with women's behaviour in practice, not just on the simple subject of whether it was right for women to pursue actions in court on their own behalf, but of whether women went to court confidently or with some reluctance and how legal counsel, opponents and deponents characterised them in pleas and in depositions.[43]

To attempt to extract information about attitudes, expectations and social relations from central court records is an ambitious and some might say a foolhardy task. Many legal and administrative historians would regard the venture with suspicion, not just because they share different specialist interests and ask different questions of the past, but because they are aware of the limitations of legal records, in particular central court records, as a source of reliable histori-

---

[39] Gowing, *Domestic Dangers*, p. 27; and see the section on violence in chapter 8 below.

[40] Linda Pollock, '"Teach her to live under obedience": the making of women in the upper ranks of early modern England', *Continuity and Change*, 4 (1989), pp. 232, 246–7, 249.

[41] Anthony Fletcher, *Gender, Sex and Subordination in England 1500–1800* (New Haven and London, 1995), chs. 14, 15, 16, 18 and 19.   [42] See chapters 5, 6 and 9 below.

[43] For a discussion of the usefulness of the terms 'public' and 'private' in an early modern context, see chapter 9 below.

cal information.[44] The records of the central courts are incomplete, jumbled and inadequately calendared. In the sixteenth century cross-suiting, the entering of separate or counter-suits in the same or different courts, was common and actions confined to a single suit in a single court were surprisingly rare. Court officials had little success disentangling genuine actions from the mass of bogus or unnecessary litigation that contributed to the eventual choking of the courts and the decline in their business in the seventeenth century.[45] For modern historians the task is almost impossible, requiring the determined efforts of an army of researchers armed with computers. Once untangled, the documents of any case present a host of internal problems, discussed below, which compromise their reliability as historical sources. Yet, as J.A. Guy has said of Star Chamber records, the opportunities, as well as the pitfalls, are 'ubiquitous', as long as the documents are handled with the requisite care.[46]

Social historians have long looked to legal records for information about human relations and the material conditions of life. The Selden Society, and various county history societies have been publishing records for the use of social, economic and legal historians for more than a century. However, the past two decades have seen a quickening of interest, 'a stampede into the dossiers of justice', by practitioners investigating topics as wide-ranging as marriage, sexuality, honour, slander, literacy and orality, neighbourly relations, youth, old age, the emergence of a centralised state, master–servant relations, custom, and the enforcement of moral and social order.[47] The history of crime, mentioned above, represents a historical enterprise based almost exclusively on evidence extracted from legal records, and there are few bodies of legal records (many, like consistory court records, largely ignored or passed over by mainstream legal historians) that have managed to escape the inquisitive prodding of eager researchers.

---

[44] On the problems associated with interpreting central court records, see J.H. Baker, ed., *Legal Records and the Historian* (London, 1978), pp. 3–4; J.A. Guy, *The Court of Star Chamber and its Records to the Reign of Elizabeth I*, PRO Handbook No. 21 (London, 1985), pp. 26–7; W.J. Jones, *The Elizabethan Court of Chancery* (Oxford, 1967), pp. 1, 194; Elton, *England 1200–1640*, pp. 54–66; Christine Churches, '"The most unconvincing testimony": the genesis and historical usefulness of the country depositions in Chancery', *The Seventeenth Century*, 11 (1996), pp. 209–27; James Oldham, 'Truth-telling in the eighteenth-century courtroom', *Law and History Review*, 12 (1993), pp. 95–121; Tim Stretton, 'Social historians and the records of litigation', in Sølvi Sogner, ed., *Fact, Fiction and Forensic Evidence. Tid og Tanke. Skriftserie fra Historisk Institutt, Universitetet i Oslo, No. 2* (Oslo, 1997).

[45] In over half of Jacobean Star Chamber actions there is evidence that the parties were at law in other courts; T.G. Barnes, 'Star Chamber litigants and their counsel 1596–1641', in J.H. Baker, ed., *Legal Records and the Historian* (London, 1978), p. 12; for the decline in central court business see Brooks, 'Interpersonal conflict'; W.A. Champion, 'Recourse to law and the meaning of the great litigation decline, 1650–1750: some clues from the Shrewsbury local courts', in Christopher W. Brooks and Michael Lobban, eds., *Communities and Courts in Britain, 1150–1900* (London and Rio Grande, 1997). [46] Guy, *Star Chamber*, p. vii.

[47] Thomas and Elizabeth Cohen, *Words and Deeds in Renaissance Rome* (Toronto, 1993), p. 4.

Social historians' enthusiasm for legal records as a unique historical source grows with the emergence of each new study. For Lawrence Stone, legal records offer a rare chance to recover the thoughts and feelings of the vast sections of the community who left little trace of their lives, 'for here alone can the authentic voices of the poor be heard, if only as voluble witnesses, angry plaintiffs, and fearful defendants. Treated with care, these documents can act as "a point of entry into the mental world of the poor".'[48] It is certainly true that court records bring the historian closer to this lost mental world than other available sources. However, the distance that remains is still considerable. As Stone himself points out, litigation 'has a culture of its own, which shapes the nature of the evidence it produces'.[49] Pleadings in Requests bear more of the marks of the lawyers who framed them than of the litigants who initiated them. Given the obscuring filters created by male counsel, male scribes and male judges, it is unlikely that much survives in the records that could be labelled authentic female 'voices'. Consequently, for women's historians, as for other social historians, the growing interest in the potential of court records needs to be tempered with a sense of caution. In 1958 G.R. Elton wrote in the preface to *Star Chamber Stories* both of the potential and the pitfalls of using the records of that court: 'That they throw light on the lives, the habits and the speech of men and women in the sixteenth century goes without saying, though it may be as well to remember that evidence of life which is taken from legal records is always a little distorted.'[50]

Social and feminist historians who rush in where legal historians fear to tread need to realise that the 'little distortion' found in court records brings with it a host of problems of interpretation, and that extracting reliable information from legal records is rarely a straightforward task. Anthropologists understand the complexities of the relationship between litigated disputes and the events which give rise to them, where the arguments put before a judge, and sometimes even the dispute in question, can bear little or no relation to the incident which originally turned parties against each other. People sue their enemies over behaviour they would forgive in friends, and on occasions they use real or fabricated incidents as pretexts to dignify discord stemming from altogether different origins, so that as Simon Roberts has remarked 'the record of law may therefore provide an uncertain guide to the nature of social tensions'.[51] Social historians may query the narrowness of legal historians' approaches to court records, but they can learn from their informed awareness of the limitations of these records. W.R. Prest makes this point well: 'Historians who rush in to liberate the history of law from the constricting grasp of the lawyers, as religious

---

[48] Lawrence Stone, *The Past and the Present Revisited* (London, 1987), p. 241.
[49] Lawrence Stone, *Road to Divorce: England 1530–1987* (Oxford, 1990), p. 30.
[50] G.R. Elton, *Star Chamber Stories* (London, 1958), p. 10.
[51] Simon Roberts, 'The study of dispute: anthropological perspectives', in John Bossy, ed., *Disputes and Settlements: Law and Human Relations in the West* (Cambridge, 1983), p. 22.

history has been rescued from the theologians, run the opposite risk, of super-
ficiality and error in the treatment of major questions, arising from ignorance of
those very features which give the law and lawyers a claim to their own
history.'[52]

While most of the current generation of social historians are cautious in their
use of records, some have been guilty in the past of taking court records at face
value, without giving due concern to the purposes of the institution that produced them, the intentions and ambitions of the competing parties, and the
nature of the records themselves.[53] W.J. Jones, by contrast, began his administrative history of Chancery with a warning about the contents of the court's
records: 'It cannot be assumed that reasoned arguments always held sway over
human outburst, just as it should not be assumed that those who were believed
had told the truth or that witnesses whose version was rejected should be
counted as perjurers.'[54]

In any adversarial legal system, where conflict and debate are at the heart of
the settling of disputes, the truth can be an elusive commodity. In the civil
courts of sixteenth century England disagreement was ubiquitous; opposing
parties exchanged volleys of assertions, denials and counter-assertions in their
attempts to convince judges and juries of the superiority of their case. Then,
as now, judges were asked to choose between two or more conflicting representations of the truth, rather than to attempt to reconstitute the truth itself,
as they might under an inquisitorial system. They relied on the arguments and
evidence presented by each party, and rarely cross-examined witnesses to
establish points not already raised by counsel. In short, they lacked the
resources, and to some extent the desire, to discover a definitive, 'historical'
version of events, and restricted themselves to deciding which of the versions
offered to them by competing lawyers was more compelling. Litigants and
their counsel tailored their depictions of events carefully, selecting certain facts
while discarding or playing down the importance of others, expressing the
results in convenient, often formulaic, legal language.[55] In courts like Requests
lawyers often challenged their opponents' assertions as 'matters untrue and
imagined', and were reluctant to concede even those facts which seem to us to

---

[52] W.R. Prest, ed., *Lawyers in Early Modern Europe and America* (New York, 1981), p. 13.
[53] A good example is Gene Brucker's *Giovanni and Lusanna: Love and Marriage in Renaissance
Florence* (Berkeley, 1986) which uses litigation records uncritically to construct the narrative of a
love story; for a critique of Brucker's use of legal records see Thomas Kuehn, 'Reading microhistory: the example of Giovanni and Lusanna', *The Journal of Modern History*, 61 (1989), pp.
512–34 (I would like to thank Lynn Martin for this reference).   [54] Jones, *Chancery*, p. 1.
[55] For criminal cases see Brewer and Styles, who have written; 'those who find themselves in court or
before a magistrate are as likely to say what is expected of them, or what they think most
appropriate in the circumstances . . . as they are to blurt out the truth or reveal their true feelings';
John Brewer and John Styles, eds., *An Ungovernable People: The English and their Law in the
Seventeenth and Eighteenth Centuries* (London, 1980), p. 15.

have been immaterial.[56] Thomas Nashe recognised the polemical instincts of lawyers when in 1593 he urged his readers to take his recent invective against Gabriel Harvey, 'in that abject nature that you would doe the rayling of a Sophister in the schooles, or a scolding Lawyer at the barre, which none but fooles wil wrest to defame'.[57] The desires of litigants and lawyers to present their case in the best possible light means that, as a commentator on modern criminal proceedings has noted, 'in almost any trial there is the uneasy possibility that neither case captures the subtle reality of the incident'.[58]

The use of conditional pleas made inconsistency possible even within a single document. In a copyhold dispute in Requests from 1578, the complainants flatly denied that they had surrendered their estate in the manor court, as their opponents claimed. However, they then said, 'but if any such surrender were made, then the same was done by duresse of Imprisonment & threatenings of the said [defendant] to imprison & hange the said complainants uppon wrongefull & unjust accusacions'.[59] Did they make the surrender or not? Simple distortion could be partnered by blatant deceit. Parties entered bogus or insufficient suits to put opponents to great expense, to harass them or simply to delay them. Unsupported actions could cause delays of months or even years, time enough for unscrupulous parties to sell land to innocent third parties, to dispose of incriminating documents, or to wait for elderly witnesses or opponents to die. Other parties went further and sought to make illegal gains through court actions. Central court records are full of accusations of forgery and perjury, and Elizabethan parliaments were sufficiently concerned by the problem to pass a number of statutes dealing with both of these offences.[60] In his examination of marriage litigation, Richard Helmholz commented that 'one will not go far before finding some evidence of the use of suspect witnesses and false testimony'.[61] The mid sixteenth century bishop Hugh Latimer warned that the Devil himself was keeping truth out of the court room: 'If the Judge be good and upright, he [the Devil] wyll assay to deceave hym, eyther by the subtile suggestion of craftye Lawyers, or els by false wytnesse, and subtyle utteryng of a wrong matter.'[62]

The potential for this process to distort legal testimony made it difficult

---

[56] Pleadings contain various formulaic expressions which stress the falsehood of opponents' pleas. This particular example comes from *Robert Lyckbarrowe v. Thomasyne Thornebrugh*, PRO Req 2/159/99.

[57] Thomas Nashe, *Christs Teares Over Jerusalem* (London, 1593), preface 'To the Reader'.

[58] W.L. Bennett and M.S. Feldman, *Reconstructing Reality in the Courtroom* (London, 1981), p. 93.

[59] *Clement & Johan Nutt v. Nicholas Nutt*, PRO Req 1/17, p. 719.

[60] For example, 5 Eliz. I c. 9, updating and extending 32 Henry VIII c. 9, *Statutes of the Realm* (11 vols., London, 1810–28), vol. 3, pp. 753–4, vol. 4, pp. 436–8.

[61] Richard Helmholz, *Marriage Litigation in Medieval England* (Cambridge, 1974), p. 156.

[62] Hugh Latimer, *Twenty Seven Sermons Preached by the Ryght Reverende . . . Maister Hugh Latimer* (London, 1562), fol. 53.

enough for judges to reach a decision.[63] As an early seventeenth century commentator explained, 'in *foro conscientie* [forums of conscience] there is never any doubt or question concerning the fact being truly and sincerely discovered by the voluntary confession of the partie but in *foro contentiese* [forums of contest] the judge dothe often erre and is deceaved by presumpcion and probabilities'.[64] Modern onlookers, who lack the privileged access of the original judge to courtroom evidence and the demeanour of the parties, face a harder task separating fact from fiction, even in the rare cases where every possible document is available for scrutiny. When the decisions and decree books are lost, as is the case with Star Chamber, or when only a solitary bill or answer survive, as is often the case in Requests or Chancery, the difficulties are multiplied. J.A. Guy has said of Star Chamber records that plaintiffs' bills must be evaluated in conjunction with defendants' answers, 'if anything resembling the truth is to be revealed'.[65] W.J. Jones has said the same about Chancery records, yet as Guy revealed in another context, two thirds of all cases in the Chancery proceedings provide no documents except a bill of complaint, 'and thus few means of finding out what is really going on'.[66] The implication is that the bulk of this substantial archive is historically unreliable.

Another problem with Requests materials, one common to most central court archives, is that the language used in pleadings is heavily formulaic. Lawyers arranged the necessary information in each case into conventional frameworks of legal argument, often using a stilted language of stock phrases which can serve to obscure original attitudes. Even witness depositions, which as direct transcripts of witness interviews might be considered free from the distortion caused by formulaic language and the lawyer's hand, show signs of external interference.[67] They were often brief, and different deponents' responses to the same questions were commonly identical, exactly mirroring the wording of the interrogatories they answered.[68] Furthermore, examples of regional dialect are few, suggesting that recording scribes 'translated' responses for the benefit of the judges or Masters of the court.[69] Scribes did not invent

---

[63] As will be seen in chapter 4, the Masters of Requests made comparatively few final decisions, preferring to refer uncertain cases to arbitration.

[64] C.U.L. Gg.2.31, fol. 14ᵛ.   [65] Guy, *Star Chamber*, p. 26.

[66] Jones, *Chancery*, p. 194; J.A. Guy, 'The development of equitable jurisdictions, 1450–1550', in E.W. Ives and A.H. Manchester, eds., *Law, Litigants and the Legal Profession* (London, 1983), p. 82.

[67] For critiques of deposition evidence see Kuehn, 'Reading microhistory'; Elton, *England 1200–1640*, pp. 60–1; Churches, 'The most unconvincing testimony'; Oldham, 'Truth-telling in the eighteenth-century courtroom'; Stretton, 'Social historians and the records of litigation'; for an example of allegations of 'coaching' of witnesses, see *Thomas Good v. Elizabeth Shipper*, PRO Req 2/163/61, I; PRO Req 1/19, p. 593.

[68] Jones, *Chancery*, pp. 238, 244; church court depositions are usually much richer; see Gowing, *Domestic Dangers*, pp. 41–8 and *passim*.

[69] Regional dialects and idioms do appear in slander and libel cases, where the exact form of words and expressions were in issue; see Laura Gowing, *Domestic Dangers*, p. 55.

responses, but it seems likely that they summarised long answers and transformed witnesses' language into the idiom of the court.[70]

The formulaic language of many of these records does more than filter the thoughts, speech and concerns of the litigants and their lawyers, it distorts the reality of people's causes and their personal circumstances. Requests was a 'poor man's' court, and as later chapters will show, even rich litigants protested their poverty in pleadings. Similarly, litigants hoping to have their cause heard in Star Chamber had to include an allegation of riot involving force of arms in their plea, regardless of whether or not the grievance complained of had been accompanied by violence.[71] Eric Poole has suggested that the frequently repeated description of documents or proofs coming into the hands of strangers 'by casual means' was another legal fiction, a device used to set up an equity.[72] Legal fictions like these were not uncommon, and they create still more barriers for historians to negotiate.

The result of all these factors is that while the records of a case can offer good evidence of legal procedure, the remedy requested and the decision given, on their own they remain poor evidence for the facts which they describe. This is not to suggest that all litigants were liars, or that most pleas were not based on genuine incidents; merely that it remains difficult for historians to be certain of the veracity of any particular statement, or reliably to interpret the information in a single bill, answer, or other lone document. The commonest method for tackling these problems is to use other evidence to corroborate court documents: private letters can reveal if litigants' real motives differed from the motives they expressed in pleadings; tax records, wills, inventories and probate documents can confirm whether litigants were as poor as they alleged; records from other cases, or even from the same case, can indicate which litigant's version of events court officials felt inclined to believe; and so on, and so on. However, checking documents against other sources can only compensate for some of the shortcomings of court records, and in many instances other sources simply do not exist.

Fortunately there are ways out of this tangled web of obscurity and unreliable

---

[70] In an interesting example from another court, three witnesses in a Chancery case from 1559–60 'did in open Court depose that the commissioners have set down their depositions otherwise than they did depose'; *Peacock v. Collens*, English Reports, 21, p. 25; see also Jones, *Chancery*, p. 241; consider also the English version of Emmanuel Le Roy Ladurie's *Montaillou*, which contains English translations of Le Roy Ladurie's French translations of Latin prose constructed from Latin notes recording responses in French dialect; Emmanuel Le Roy Ladurie, *Montaillou: Cathars and Catholics in a French village 1294–1324*, trans. Barbara Bray (Harmondsworth, 1978), p. xvii.   [71] Guy, *Star Chamber*, p. 26; Elton, *England 1200–1640*, p. 61.

[72] Eric Poole, 'West's *Symboleography*: an Elizabethan formulary', in J.A. Guy and H.G. Beale, eds., *Law and Social Change in British History: Papers Presented to the Bristol Legal History Conference, 14–17 July 1981* (London, 1984), p. 102; according to Poole, this equity later developed into the equity of redemption. In Requests, widows were often accused of having obtained documents 'by casual means' after their husbands' deaths.

evidence that make it possible to liberate records inhabiting the darker corners of archives. The temptation, when faced with incomplete legal materials, is to play at being magistrate, deciding which party to believe, which party was probably guilty, and most precarious of all, what actually happened between the combatants that led them to discard informal means of dispute settlement and seek redress in a national court. Elton openly admitted that he was taking this approach when he wrote in the preface to *Star Chamber Stories* that 'time and again we shall have to admit that we can only conjecture the truth of the statements recorded or guess at the court's decision'.[73] Others follow this course less openly, or do not give the subject much thought.[74] An alternative approach is to recognise the various problems associated with correctly identifying and recovering the truth from the stylised records of the central courts, and to shift the focus of attention away from the events they purport to describe and on to the manner of their description.

Natalie Zemon Davis has demonstrated how new insights can be gleaned from legal records by taking just such an approach to their interpretation. In her book *Fiction in the Archives* she looked at sixteenth century French letters of remission, classed by other historians as 'a tissue of counter truths', to examine the narrative skills of their authors. Rather than attempt to compensate for the distortion in these texts, to discern the truth it conceals, she focused on the distortion itself. The fictional elements in these letters provide evidence of how murderers told stories, and how, in Davis's words, 'the rules for plot in these judicial tales of violence and grace interacted with wider contemporary habits of explanation, description and evaluation'. This method of reading mercy pleas to gain an understanding of the dynamics of story-telling is limited in its wider application. Laura Gowing has employed similar methods to examine the narrative structures employed by deponents in the church courts in seventeenth century London, however studies of a creative process like story-telling depend on an accurate knowledge of authorship.[75] Davis selected pardon letters because they represent 'one of the best sources of relatively uninterrupted narrative from the lips of the lower orders . . . in sixteenth-century France'. While admitting they were produced in collaboration, she argued that the unusual criteria governing their production, which in effect demanded a first person

---

[73] Elton, *Star Chamber Stories*, p. 17.

[74] G.R. Quaife, for example, has made enthusiastic use of depositions presented to quarter sessions and the consistory court in the seventeenth century, which he says 'recapture (even through the legalistic verbiage) the atmosphere of the particular situation and of the period in general', and he goes further than most in accepting the word of witnesses as evidence of the behaviour and incidents they describe; G.R. Quaife, *Wanton Wenches and Wayward Wives: Peasants and Illicit Sex in Early Seventeenth Century England* (London, 1979), preface, *passim*; see also note 53 above.

[75] Laura Gowing, 'Gender and the language of insult in early modern London', *History Workshop Journal*, 35 (1993), pp. 1–21; Gowing, *Domestic Dangers*, pp. 41–58, *passim*; see also, Clare Brant and Diane Purkiss, eds., *Women Texts and Histories 1575–1760* (London and New York, 1992).

account, means that they 'can still be analysed in terms of the life and values of the person saving his neck by a story'.[76] In Requests, and in many other jurisdictions, the voice of the litigant is too bound up in the formulaic language of the lawyer to permit an analysis of the narrative ability of sixteenth century English litigants. However, it is possible to follow the example of Davis and to look not at the truth in each case, but at contemporary representations of the truth. It is both interesting and instructive to see how litigants and their lawyers fought cases, the lines of argument they pursued and the kinds of facts they chose to emphasise. Key aspects of women's experience can be revealed by observing how male and female participants represented themselves and their opponents in court, the manner in which they and their legal counsel dealt with questions of credit and reputation, and by examining the popular stereotypes parties drew on in their descriptions of individuals and their behaviour.

By focusing on the story-telling, rather than the story-teller or the factual integrity of the story, questions of truth, falsehood, and authorship become less critical. Once again, this is not to imply that litigants in Requests were all compulsive liars; when Davis wrote of 'fiction in the archives', she was referring to the creative element involved in the selection and ordering of facts into explanatory 'stories', not to fiction in the sense of outright fabrication. Nor is it to imply that authorship is not important at all. It is merely to recognise that the destination of ideas can be as important as their origins. Litigants and their lawyers believed that the arguments they presented would appeal to the reason and sensibilities of the Masters of the court. Consequently, the distortion inherent in one-sided pleas from this adversarial court can be examined in its own right, to determine what it reveals rather than what it might conceal.

The first third of this book, then, will consider the subject of women and litigation in general terms, analysing historians' views of women and the law, describing the legal options available to sixteenth and seventeenth century English women, and estimating how many women made use of those options. It will also survey contemporary responses to women going to law, from the advice of moralists to the heated outbursts of judges confronted by outspoken women, setting these alongside the treatment of the theme of women and justice in satire and drama. The remaining two thirds will look at the workings of these ideas in practice by examining in detail the Court of Requests. As well as discerning patterns of male and female litigation within this jurisdiction (and neighbouring jurisdictions such as Chancery and Star Chamber), and suggesting possible explanations for Requests' popularity among women, these chap-

---

[76] N.Z. Davis, *Fiction in the Archives: Pardon Tales and their Tellers in Sixteenth-Century France* (Cambridge, 1987), pp. 4, 5, 25; Davis reveals, for example, how knowledge of rhetorical techniques was not limited to the educated classes, and suggests that since women were considered to be less prone than men to violent outbursts when provoked, they had to go to greater lengths to explain passionate killings when relying on the defence of justifiable manslaughter.

ters explore the dynamics of legal processes, pointing out the similarities as well as the differences between male and female experiences of the law.

These questions are addressed by sampling the records of the Court of Requests in three different ways. A statistical survey of 2,000 document files, using information taken from modern manuscript calendars, provides a broad picture of the numbers of women who frequented the court and the sorts of actions they brought, as well as the business of the court more generally.[77] A careful analysis of the extensive decree and order books and books of affidavits that survive for Elizabeth's reign (the only records which retain their original chronology) provides more accurate statistical information than modern calendars, which are not always reliable, as well as invaluable information about court procedure and the decision making process. Most of all, these books provide detailed summaries of every case that progressed to an advanced stage or a final hearing. However, as will become clear, few cases proceeded to a binding court order, and working backwards from final decisions provides an imbalanced picture of the business of the court. Therefore, a study of cases recorded in these decree and order books is supplemented by a detailed examination of a series of case files from throughout the reign; 100 from Somerset, 100 from Middlesex, and 100 from the rest of the country, most, but not all, involving female litigants. This is a small sample of the total of more than 20,000 files that survive from Elizabeth's reign, but one which provides insight into the detail of disputes, as well as the language and arguments of pleadings.[78]

I mentioned at the beginning of this chapter that the aim of this study is to explore women's experience of litigation, as opposed to the status of women before the law. However, the one does not make sense without the other; legal rights cannot be exercised until they are held, and a study of women and litigation must therefore be prefaced with an examination of women's legal rights and status in theory, against which to compare the experience of women in practice. The following two chapters review the historiography of women and the law, highlight women's rights under different codes of law, estimate the numbers of female litigants in various jurisdictions, and look to modern, as well as early modern, opinions about the prospect of women asserting and defending their rights in Elizabethan courts of law.

---

[77] The four volumes of published calendars give names and dates but little indication of subject matter or the documents held in each file. Therefore, my sample of 2,000 entries was taken from the first volume of modern manuscript calendars; PRO 9, vol. 93 (Requests proceedings), piece numbers PRO Req 2/257/1–Req 2/167/37 (excluding entries without dates and incomplete entries: PRO Req 2/157/429–467, Req 2/159/159–175, Req 2/160/77).   [78] See chapter 9 below.

2

Women, legal rights and law courts

All offyces belongynge to the common weale be forbydden [women] by the lawes.
. . . It is not permitted to a woman, though she be very wise and prudent, to
pleade a cause before a Juge, furthermore they be repelled in jurisdiction, in
arbiterment, in adoption, in intercession, in procuration, or to be gardeyns or
tutours in causes testamentary and criminall.

Henricus Cornelius Agrippa,
Of the Nobilitie and Excellencie of Womankynde
(London, 1542)[1]

HISTORIOGRAPHY

The past hundred years have witnessed a see-sawing of historians' perceptions of
the legal status of women in early modern England. To Frederick Pollock and
F. W. Maitland, writing in the final decades of the nineteenth century, the position was clear. By the time of Edward I, 'a sure instinct has already guided the law
to a general rule which will endure until our own time. As regards private rights
women are on the same level as men, though postponed in the canons of inheritance; but public functions they have none.'[2] Charlotte Carmichael Stopes, Alice
Clark and other historians in the vanguard of feminist history in the late nineteenth and early twentieth centuries agreed that women enjoyed a degree of legal
independence in England prior to the seventeenth century, under customary law
at least. However, far from 'enduring until their own time', they suggested that
the combined influences of capitalism, industrialisation, the emergence of the
professions and the rise to supremacy of the common law steadily undermined
any independence women had once enjoyed.[3] Doris Stenton, writing in the
1950s, concurred. In *The English Woman in History* she described the rights

---

[1] Henricus Cornelius Agrippa, *Of the Nobilitie and Excellencie of Womankynde*, trans. Thomas
Clapham (London, 1542)(written 1509), sig. fviii[v]; Agrippa was lamenting, rather than endorsing,
the restrictions women suffered.

[2] Frederick Pollock and F.W. Maitland, *The History of English Law Before the Time of Edward I*,
ed. S.F.C. Milsom, 2nd edn (Cambridge, 1968), vol. 1, p. 485.

[3] Charlotte Stopes, *British Freewomen: Their Historical Privilege*, 3rd edn (London, 1907); Alice
Clark, *Working Life of Women in the Seventeenth Century* (London and New York, 1992), pp.
236–7.

women, especially widows, enjoyed under custom and law during the Middle Ages. She gave examples of women appearing in court in the absence of their husbands, behaviour inconceivable under the common law, and concluded that among the native peasant stock of Lincolnshire, 'the ancient tradition of the rough equality between men and women had not yet been entirely forgotten'.[4]

Modern feminist historians are sceptical about the existence in the past of a 'Golden Age' of equality between men and women. Most believe that 'the ancient tradition of the rough equality between men and women' could not have been forgotten, because it never existed. As a group, English women have enjoyed fewer rights, fewer privileges, less wealth, less influence in spheres of power and less control over domestic affairs, than English men. As Judith Bennett has argued, with reference to employment conditions and opportunities, women's rights fluctuated and changed over time but their general position relative to men did not.[5] In the words of Patricia Crawford, describing the constancy between 1500 and 1750 of the notion that women were weaker than men, 'it is fascinating to observe that although the *reasons* for women's necessary subordination might change, the axiomatic inferiority of women remained'.[6]

It is clear that legal institutions played a significant part in limiting women's freedom of opportunity, and researchers investigating disparities within the law between the rights of women and the corresponding rights of men have assembled a catalogue of the legal disabilities women endured in sixteenth and seventeenth century England.[7] The law prevented women from becoming judges, from serving on juries, from standing for parliament or voting in elections. In inheritance, the doctrine of primogeniture privileged sons over daughters and directed real property away from women's hands. In marriage, the doctrine of coverture removed from a wife her very legal entity, making it impossible for married women, *femes covert*, to enter contracts or to assert or defend their rights in court, except with the consent and assistance of their husbands. A woman who married lost her surname, her right to choose where she lived, her right to legal protection against her husband (except in the most extreme cases) and her ability to own property.[8] The moveable property (goods or chattels) she brought to marriage became her husband's forever.[9] Control of any real property (land) she possessed, and the profits accruing from it, passed to her husband for the duration of the marriage. Property that fell in between, 'chattels real' like leases, became a husband's during marriage, though if they

---

[4] Doris Stenton, *The English Woman in History* (London, 1957), p. 79.

[5] Judith Bennett, 'History that stands still', *Feminist Studies*, 14 (1988), pp. 269–83.

[6] Patricia Crawford, 'From the woman's view: pre-industrial England, 1500–1750', in Patricia Crawford, ed., *Exploring Women's Past* (Sydney, 1984), p. 63.

[7] McIntyre, 'Legal attitudes towards women'; Leonore Glanz, 'The legal position of English women under the early Stuart Kings and the Interregnum' (Loyola University Ph.D., 1973).

[8] McIntyre, 'Legal attitudes towards women', p. 84.

[9] If any of her chattels remained unalienated when her husband died, a widow could retain them; Baker, *An Introduction to English Legal History*, p. 552.

remained intact at the conclusion of the marriage they returned to the wife or her heirs.[10] A married woman could not independently inherit legacies, nor could she accept gifts, even from her husband. She could not make a will without her husband's agreement, and any existing will or testament became invalid on the day she married.[11] The doctrine of coverture epitomised the idea, and helped to sustain the belief, that men were, in Richard Hooker's words, 'Lords & lawfull Kings in their owne houses', by giving husbands power over the rights, property and bodies of their wives.[12]

Bias against women in English law can be found at every turn. In Elizabethan England a man who killed his wife was guilty of murder, but a woman who killed her husband was guilty of petty treason and could be burned at the stake.[13] Adultery by the king's consort was full treason, as the fates of Anne Boleyn and Katherine Howard testify, while adultery by the king went unpunished.[14] Other crimes generally associated with women, like witchcraft and infanticide, also attracted unusually severe penalties, and the option of claiming 'benefit of clergy' was refused to women until 1691.[15] Wives found guilty of adultery forfeited their rights to dower, but unfaithful husbands retained their rights to the male equivalent, the 'Curtesy of England'.[16] And so the list of examples goes on,

---

[10] Pearl Hogrefe, 'Legal rights of Tudor women and the circumvention by men and women', *Sixteenth Century Journal*, 3 (1972), p. 100.

[11] The Statute of Wills (34 and 35 Henry VIII c. 5) permitted married women to make wills, but only with the permission of their husbands, unless they had duties to fulfil as executrixes or administratrixes; *Statutes of the Realm* (11 vols., London, 1810–28), vol. 3, pp. 901–4; Erickson, *Women and Property*, pp. 139–40; McIntyre, 'Legal attitudes towards women', p. 119.

[12] Richard Hooker, *Of the Lawes of Ecclesiasticall Politie* (London, 1617), p. 26.

[13] See Edward III's Statute of Treasons (25 Edward III stat. 5 c. 2), *Statutes of the Realm*, vol. 1, pp. 319–20; T.E., *The Lawes Resolutions of Womens Rights* (London, 1632), p. 208; W.S. Holdsworth, *A History of English Law*, 3rd edn (London, 1923), vol. 2, p. 449; Pollock and Maitland, *The History of English Law*, vol. 2, p. 484.

[14] Henry VIII had Anne Boleyn condemned for adultery even though their marriage had been annulled, while Katherine Howard was condemned by Act of Attainder; Betty Travitsky, 'Husband-murder and petty treason in English Renaissance tragedy', *Renaissance Drama*, new series, 21 (1990), pp. 173, 188 n. 4; several of Katherine's confidants were also arraigned for treason for concealing her supposed crimes; Charles Wriothesley, *A Chronicle of England During the Reigns of the Tudors, from A.D. 1485 to 1559*, ed. William Hamilton, Camden Society, new series, vol. 11 (London, 1875), pp. 132–4.

[15] McIntyre, 'Legal attitudes towards women', p. 15; in 1624 parliament extended benefit of clergy to women convicted of larceny of goods worth not more than 10s. (21 James I cap. 6); Cynthia Herrup, *The Common Peace: Participation and the Criminal Law in Seventeenth-Century England* (Cambridge, 1987), p. 48, n. 8.

[16] The right of curtesy gave to widowers a life interest in all of the lands that their wives died seised of (not merely one third, as with dower), provided the union had produced a child; T.E., *The Lawes Resolutions of Womens Rights*, p. 146; Edward Coke disagreed with Glanvill's view that adulterous women forfeited rights to dower, so practice may have been different in the sixteenth and seventeenth centuries; Pollock and Maitland, *The History of English Law*, vol. 2, pp. 394–5, 414–20; Keith Thomas, 'The puritans and adultery: the act of 1650 reconsidered', in Donald Pennington and Keith Thomas, eds., *Puritans and Revolutionaries: Essays in Seventeenth-Century History Presented to Christopher Hill* (Oxford, 1978), pp. 267–9, 273; for further examples of legal discrimination against women, see Keith Thomas, 'The double standard', *Journal of the History of Ideas*, 20 (1959), pp. 199–203.

a telling refutation of William Blackstone's often quoted assertion that, 'even the disabilities which the wife lies under, are for the most part intended for her protection and benefit. So great a favourite is the female sex of the laws of England.'[17] Critics of English law have pointed out the failure of the crown, parliament and the judiciary to equip women with sufficient rights outside of the household, and their refusal to offer women adequate protection within the household.[18] The resulting picture of women's relationship with the law is harsh and unremitting. Where Pollock and Maitland could write that 'private law with few exceptions puts women on a par with men', Antonia Fraser concluded ninety years later that, 'under the common law of England at the accession of King James I, no female had any rights at all (if some were allowed by custom)'.[19]

Concentration on the underlying philosophy of the English legal system has produced a bleak view of the position of women at law to stand against the outmoded interpretations of Blackstone in the eighteenth century and Pollock and Maitland in the late nineteenth century. But the see-saw of opinion about women and the law has yet to come to rest. Now that the bias within English law has been identified, and the prescriptive beliefs and assumptions held by many of its judges exposed, various historians are turning to investigate the practical effects of that bias and those assumptions on the lives of individual women. Scholars such as Susan Staves, Eileen Spring, Amy Erickson, Margot Finn and Laura Gowing have begun focusing on the precise make-up of different laws affecting women and examining women's experiences inside and outside the courtroom.[20] Through close readings of statutes and published case law and studies of the records of property ownership and litigation they have confirmed that a discriminatory ethos underpinned many areas of law. However, they have also shown that discrimination against women was neither even nor universal, and that women could use the law as well as fall victim to it. Taken together, their findings add rare flecks of light to the previously gloomy picture of women and the law.

The range of divergent interpretations of the status of women that historians have produced over the past hundred years is somewhat surprising within a subject as intent on certainty and precision as the law. The divergence stems, of course, from the different values and priorities of legal, social and feminist historians and the differing approaches each group has taken to the subject over the years. But historians have been able to reach such varying, and sometimes incompatible, conclusions about the same issues because of the vast size and

---

[17] William Blackstone, *Commentaries on the Laws of England* (London, 1765), vol. 1, p. 433.

[18] See for example, Nadine Taub and E.M. Schneider, 'Perspectives on women's subordination and the role of law', in David Kairys, ed., *The Politics of Law: A Progressive Critique* (New York, 1982), pp. 117–39.

[19] Antonia Fraser, *The Weaker Vessel: Woman's Lot in Seventeenth-Century England* (London, 1985), p. 5.

[20] Finn, 'Women, consumption and coverture', pp. 703–22; the works of these other historians are referenced throughout this chapter.

complexity of early modern English law. The territory covered by 'the law' stretched from the highest royal decree to the humblest act of a local constable, from parliamentary legislation to the exercise of royal prerogative, from treason to debt, and from land tenures and property transfers to written indentures and bonds. In this vast and undulating landscape no single viewpoint can provide a complete and uninterrupted panorama of the whole, making premature generalisations dangerous.

Two aspects of the complexity of the law have particular bearing on evaluating women's legal lives. The first is the simple fact that the common law enjoyed no monopoly in sixteenth century England, even if at times it has monopolised the attention of historians of women's rights.[21] Undue emphasis on this one area of law reflects the influence of legal historians, who have been inclined to take a developmental view of the law, concentrating their attention on studying 'winners', influential legal ideas and ultimately successful institutions, while paying less regard to the legal bodies and elements of law that have made little impact on subsequent law. During the period of this study the common law shared its legal stage with a gaggle of other jurisdictions – Edward Coke recognised sixteen – each of which provided women with distinct rights and remedies and opportunities for litigation.[22] The existence of these alternatives means that bleak prognoses about women's legal position built around the doctrines of primogeniture and coverture need to be modified using news from other legal quarters. To illustrate this point, the following sections provide a brief survey of the more significant of those other quarters, namely equity, ecclesiastical law and custom, as well as the common law, and examine the second point highlighted by recent scholarship: the extent to which social and legal practice could differ markedly from legal theory.

EQUITY

Mary Beard, the author of *Woman as Force in History*, had no doubt that the alternative to the common law that offered the greatest benefit to women was equity; the body of principles applied and developed in the prerogative courts of Chancery, Requests, the equity side of Exchequer, and the equitable jurisdictions of the Palatinate of Lancaster, with its own chancery in Lancaster and court of Duchy Chamber in London, and the Palatinates of Chester and Durham.[23] Maria Cioni agreed, observing in her 1975 study of Chancery:

---

[21] As Ruth Kittel has written, 'the study of women and the common law seems to have captured the interest of both legal and social historians'; Ruth Kittel, 'Women under the law in medieval England 1066–1485', in Barbara Kanner, ed., *The Women of England from Anglo-Saxon Times to the Present: Interpretive Bibliographic Essays* (London, 1980), p. 129.

[22] C.W. Brooks, 'The common lawyers in England, *c.* 1558–1642', in W.R. Prest, ed., *Lawyers in Early Modern Europe and America* (New York, 1981), p. 42.

[23] Mary Beard, *Woman as Force in History: A Study in Traditions and Realities* (New York, 1946), pp. 136–44, 198–204; Beard's primary interest was America in the nineteenth century.

Chancery laid the foundations for married women's property rights, gave security to women who held real and personal estates by means of future equitable interests not recognised at the common law, granted protection to the estate of the jointress and accorded a right to separated or divorced women to take a share of their husband's estate commensurate with the portion which they brought into marriage; that is, they were allowed 'equity of a settlement'.[24]

The basis for Beard's and Cioni's optimism was the willingness of the judges in equity courts to allow exceptions to the doctrine of coverture. These men recognised the injustices that could flow from the common law fiction that a married woman had virtually no legal identity separate from her husband, and they oversaw the development of measures that allowed women to circumvent some of the restrictions that coverture imposed upon them. The chief of these measures was the doctrine of the 'separate estate'. In the latter half of the sixteenth century, equity benches were more at ease than their common law counterparts with the notion that the possession of property and the enjoyment of property (the two elements which together constituted full ownership of legal title) could be divided, and the interests of the person enjoying the property protected. One person could own the legal title to property, or have possession of property, while another could benefit from the 'use' of it.[25] This apparently simple concept lies at the heart of many of the most complex areas of early modern law, and indeed of modern law in the areas of trusts, succession and taxation. To the uninitiated, the mechanics of 'divided' and 'conjoined' uses, 'passive' and 'active' trusts, and the common law rules against perpetuities and against 'a use upon a use' are mystifying enough to induce an allergic reaction. Fortunately, it is not necessary to master the twists and turns associated with the principle of separating legal and equitable, or beneficial, ownership to be able to observe the benefits it could bestow on women.[26]

Deft employment of trusts (or uses) theoretically allowed a married woman to retain independent control of property and keep it from becoming her husband's. She might transfer ownership of her title to property to a third party before marriage, thereby separating herself from any interest that could pass to her husband on marriage. Yet the third party who was now the legal owner of the property (either a 'feoffee to uses' or a trustee) was obligated 'by the trust in them bestowed' to act on behalf of the woman transferring the property. This might mean managing lands and passing on rents to the woman, or simply

---

[24] Cioni, *Women and Law*, p. i; and see Maria Cioni, 'The Elizabethan Chancery'.

[25] The Statute of Uses (27 Henry VIII c. 10) exploded the fiction of the division of legal and beneficial ownership by deeming that legal title vested not in the trustee, or feoffee for uses, but in the beneficiary; *Statutes of the Realm*, vol. 3, pp. 539–42. As Neil Jones has persuasively argued, the statute applied to divided uses but not conjoined uses, which lived on after 1536 and increasingly became known as trusts; Neil Jones, 'Trusts: practice and doctrine, 1536–1660' (University of Cambridge Ph.D., 1994), pp. 8, 72–99.

[26] For analyses of the complexities of uses and trusts see Pollock and Maitland, *The History of English Law*, vol. 2, pp. 228–33; Jones, 'Trusts: practice and doctrine'.

retaining the interest for the duration of the marriage and then returning it to the woman or to her heirs. Couples often agreed the arrangement of separate estates and set down the details in marriage settlements, but many uses and trusts remained secret. Settlements could be as simple or as complicated as the parties desired, reserving to a wife a variety of different rights, for example the right to make a will of her separate property or of a specified proportion of joint property, or the ability to guarantee a portion for a daughter's marriage.[27]

Equity courts helped to protect the interests a woman wished to keep separate from her husband. As Cioni points out, they also helped safeguard the rights of the jointress who did not seek to keep her property separate. Women who contributed portions to their marriage expected in return to be maintained should they be widowed. By the sixteenth century fewer and fewer wives put their faith in the common law right of dower, enshrined in Magna Carta. Dower could be difficult to define. It offered widows a life estate in one third of their husbands' lands, but did this mean a third of the lands they held at marriage, those in their possession when they died, or those they controlled in between? Moreover, the right only applied to lands held in fee, and therefore excluded lands held by copyhold or leasehold, lands subject to entails, or lands tied up in uses. Dower could also be difficult and time consuming to claim, often requiring the co-operation of the inheriting heir (and failing co-operation, legal proceedings), and in light of these complications it is not altogether surprising that many women opted to ensure a financially secure widowhood by arranging a jointure instead.[28] In early jointures married couples held interests in lands in their joint names (often lands bought for the purpose using women's portions (or dowries) although men usually contributed to the purchase as well) with the intention that the survivor would enjoy a life interest in the profits accruing from them. Jointure lands were clearly identifiable and they (or more usually the right to rents from them) became a widow's on the day she was widowed, without the need for legal process. Later jointures specified a guaranteed annuity rather than specified lands, the amount often set down in a marriage settlement, and equity courts proved more willing than common law courts to enforce these arrangements.[29]

---

[27] Amy Erickson, 'Common law versus common practice: the use of marriage settlements in early modern England', *Economic History Review*, 2nd series, 43 (1990), pp. 21–39, especially p. 25; although see chapter 5 below for the theoretical and practical difficulties associated with enforcing arrangements in settlements.

[28] Baker, *Introduction to English Legal History*, p. 309; Staves, *Married Women's Separate Property*, pp. 95–130, especially p. 101; and see T.E., *The Lawes Resolutions of Womens Rights*, pp. 179–80.

[29] Common law rules deemed that contracts a wife made with her husband before marriage became void on marriage (contracts a woman made with a third person were merely voidable; that is, a husband could choose whether or not they should remain in force); Holdsworth, *History of English Law*, vol. 3, pp. 528–30; vol. 5, p. 311; McIntyre, 'Legal attitudes towards women', p. 115; for further discussion of jointure and dower, see chapter 9 below.

As we shall see in later chapters, on rare occasions the judges and Masters in equity courts even permitted married women to sue their own husbands.[30] Through rights to 'paraphernalia', which let wives retain at least some rights of ownership of their personal belongings, equity also attempted to alleviate the indignity, and the practical difficulty, of the strict position at law where husbands owned and could sell the very clothes their wives stood up in.[31] In light of these underminings of coverture, it is easy to see why Cioni and Beard saw courts of equity as women's allies. Allies they could be, but as later sections will argue it is misleading to represent equity as women's legal saviour, just as it is misleading to represent the common law as their legal downfall.[32] The measures outlined here applied only to married women, and most were available only to women who had the resources, the access to legal advice and the foresight to establish uses or trusts, or to negotiate marriage settlements or jointures.

Where equity courts did benefit women more generally was in their procedures. In the language of maxims, common law looked to the cause, while equity looked to the person. Common law judges asked whether or not an individual had performed a certain act, whether they possessed good title to property, whether or not they had met the conditions of an agreement and so on. Answers to these questions lay in the hard evidence of bonds, title deeds, indentures, promissory notes and the like. Equity judges, by contrast, looked not simply at the actions individuals had or had not taken, but took account of their resources and the circumstances surrounding their actions. If a debtor had not repaid a debt in full by the agreed date, they were willing to listen to that debtor's excuses. If litigants lacked the bonds, title deeds, indentures or other proofs necessary to ground an action at common law, judges in equity courts would let them explain why they lacked these documents and perhaps make orders for their recovery. This could be particularly useful for women, who often had less access than men, through the operation of coverture or their exclusion from areas of public transaction, to deeds, leases, uncancelled bonds and other proofs.

The remedies that courts of equity offered could also be especially attractive to female litigants. Unlike their common law counterparts, who in most cases

---

[30] The ability of wives to sue their husbands is explored in detail in chapter 6 below.

[31] The seventeenth-century Chancery deemed that a wife's 'paraphernalia', her clothes, jewels, bed linen and plate remained her property, if she survived her husband, and her heirs' property if she did not (as opposed to other moveable property which remained the property of her husband and his heirs). The right, which existed from medieval times, was originally recoverable in ecclesiastical courts; Erickson, *Women and Property*, pp. 62–3; Baker, *Introduction to English Legal History*, p. 552.

[32] For criticisms of Beard's optimistic description of equity, see Gwen Gampel, 'The planter's wife revisited: equity law, and the Chancery court in seventeenth-century Maryland', in Barbara Harris and JoAnn McNamara, eds., *Women and the Structure of Society* (Duke, North Carolina, 1984), p. 20; Berenice Carroll, 'On Mary Beard's *Women as Force in History*: a critique', in Berenice Carroll, ed., *Liberating Women's History* (Urbana, 1976).

restricted themselves to awarding damages to victorious litigants, judges in equity jurisdictions increasingly made use of injunctions, either preventing an activity from taking place (whether the sale of a farm, the committing of waste on a copyhold, or the bringing of an action at common law) or guaranteeing (at least temporarily) quiet occupation of an interest in land. As will be seen in chapter 4 on the workings of Requests, equity meant flexibility, and women often appreciated this flexibility more than men, due to the particular social and legal restrictions under which they laboured.

ECCLESIASTICAL LAW

The ecclesiastical jurisdiction was extensive but eclectic. As Martin Ingram has shown, it is possible to divide the operations of the church courts into three broad yet overlapping categories of business, 'record', 'office' and 'instance'; what modern critics might identify as administrative acts, criminal or disciplinary prosecutions and civil suits between parties. Administrative duties included overseeing the collection of tithes and church rates, regulating the formation of marriages and issuing marriage licences, and dealing with probate matters and intestate succession.[33] The ecclesiastical law of 'thirds' divided the moveable goods or possessions of someone who died without leaving a will into three, or into two. In London and York the customary rule of 'reasonable parts' applied up until the turn of the eighteenth century, even to those who had made a will, guaranteeing a widow who lived in these dioceses one third of her late husband's moveable goods on his death, or one half if the couple had no children, regardless of the provisions he might have made in his will (dower, it will be remembered, gave a one third interest in land).[34]

The second interest of ecclesiastical authorities, their concern with the moral well-being of communities, led them to initiate prosecutions of a range of offences including fornication, bigamy, bastardy, drunkenness and failure to observe religious observances.[35] Women were regularly presented for sexual offences, but in the context of this study it is law suits between parties that are of interest. These included matrimonial suits, in which spouses sought a divorce *a vinculo* (the dissolving of the marriage bond, by establishing that the marriage had been invalid from the outset) or a separation *a mensa et thoro* (separation from bed and board without the option of remarriage, in response to proven accusations of adultery or cruelty) and defamation actions. As Ingram, J.A. Sharpe and Laura Gowing have all shown, the willingness of church courts to entertain these types of suits was particularly important for women. Where equity courts recognised exceptions to the doctrine of coverture, the church

---

[33] Martin Ingram, *Church Courts, Sex and Marriage in England, 1570–1640* (Cambridge, 1987), p. 43.   [34] Erickson, *Women and Property*, p. 28.
[35] See Ingram, *Church Courts, Sex and Marriage*, pp. 219–91.

courts all but ignored the doctrine, and allowed married women to sue in their own names without their husbands. As a result, women predominated in certain church court actions to an extent they never achieved in other jurisdictions. As will be seen later in this chapter, the outstanding example of this is defamation, where women came to outnumber men as plaintiffs and defendants and to approach their number as witnesses.[36] Gowing suggests that women used church court actions, just as they used the insults of slander themselves, not simply to attack the sexual reputation of others or to defend their own reputations, but to settle older scores and to shape relations between neighbours. It is wrong, therefore, to see women merely as victims of these regulatory systems, for some individuals clearly used the power of language and the power of the courts to settle long-standing disputes and to manipulate community hierarchies.[37]

CUSTOM

The common law was national custom, customary law 'common' to all. However, in many localities the grassroots of the English legal system remained local custom, the traditional law of the manor and of the borough. Landholders and tenants who held their lands by customary tenures attended courts to enrol their interests or to serve on juries of copyholders. In larger towns inheritance and property rights were often governed by borough customs. In areas where it persisted, customary law was the law with which local inhabitants were most familiar, and it offered men and women yet more alternatives to the common law.[38] It is difficult to generalise about custom because it was local, differing from town to town, manor to manor, and sometimes even from tenement to tenement. However, one of the most widely observed customary rights was the right of widows of customary tenants to inherit their husbands' holdings. A widow's right to 'freebench' or 'widow's estate' was similar in concept to dower, but in most instances it was more generous. In many localities widows were entitled to a life interest in *all* of their husbands' holdings, not simply a third. Widow's estate on some manors was for life, but more often the right was extinguished if a woman remarried, and, as Barbara Todd has shown, in practice widows rarely enjoyed full control of their interest if they had sons who came of age and married.[39]

---

[36] Gowing, *Domestic Dangers*, p. 12; J.A. Sharpe, *Defamation and Sexual Slander in Early Modern England: The Church Courts at York*, Borthwick papers no. 58 (York, 1980), pp. 15, 27–8; Ingram, *Church Courts, Sex and Marriage*, p. 302.

[37] Laura Gowing, 'Language, power and the law: women's slander litigation in early modern London', in Jenny Kermode and Garthine Walker, eds., *Women, Crime and the Courts in Early Modern England* (London, 1994); and see Peter Rushton, 'Women, witchcraft and slander in early modern England: cases from the church courts of Durham, 1560–1675', *Northern History*, 18 (1982), pp. 116–32.   [38] Brooks, *Pettyfoggers*, pp. 34, 39, 73–4.

[39] Barbara Todd, 'Freebench and free enterprise: widows and their property in two Berkshire villages', in John Chartres and David Hey, eds., *English Rural Society, 1500–1800: Essays in Honour of Joan Thirsk* (Cambridge, 1990), pp. 188, 193.

The nature of customary law and the uses widows made of its provisions in rural areas are discussed at length in chapter 7 below. For now it is sufficient merely to recognise the broad range of assistance custom might offer to women, and the number of customs which sanctioned behaviour that was impossible at common law. Edward Coke described how a married woman could purchase a copyhold ('untill her husband disagreeth'), how a husband could pass a copyhold estate to his wife by surrender, and how a 'speciall Custome' allowed a wife to pass a copyhold to her husband during marriage, although he added that 'this Custome hath beene much impugned, therefore I dare not justifie the validity of it'.[40] In certain boroughs tradition allowed married women to run businesses in their own names and to trade, become indebted and appear in court as if they were *femes sole* rather than *femes covert*, although it is unclear how widespread these customs remained by Elizabeth's reign.[41] Under the customary law of Gavelkind in Kent, wives of convicted felons could receive their dower third after their husbands were executed. In York, custom allowed a man to convey land to his wife by deed during marriage, and in Taunton there was a custom that the survivor of a marriage, whether wife or husband, should inherit all of their partner's freehold land.[42] The list of variations is almost endless, and it is important to note that customs could also be more restrictive than the common law, especially when it came to the rights of husbands to alienate their wives' property during marriage.[43] With the incomplete survival of court rolls and borough records, the full range of customs affecting women across England may never be known. However, customary law demonstrates better than any other system of regulation the degree to which women's rights and legal options depended not just on their marital status, but on where they lived, on the types of property they controlled and the tenures by which they held that property.

COMMON LAW

Historians writing the history of women's rights in England regularly cast the common law as the villain of the piece. The foregoing discussion of rival jurisdictions commits the same sin, through its focus on the alternative rules women might use to mitigate the undeniable harshness of the common law. It is important, however, not to take this denigration of the common law too far. Certainly, the common law was guilty of denying some rights to women, particularly married women, but it never denied them rights altogether. It allowed single women and widows to sue, contract and write wills without restriction, and it gave married women dower rights if they outlived their husbands. In her book

[40] Edward Coke, *The Compleate Copy-Holder* (London, 1641), pp. 94–5.
[41] Mary Bateson, *Borough Customs*, Selden Society vol. 21 (London, 1906), pp. cxii–cxiii.
[42] *A Breefe Discourse, Declaring and Approving the Necessarie and Inviolable Maintenance of the Laudable Customes of London* (London, 1584), pp. 26–8.
[43] Bateson, *Borough Customs*, p. cii.

Law, Land and Family: Aristocratic Inheritance in England 1300 to 1800, Eileen Spring turns the orthodox feminist view of women's legal rights on its head. She argues that the history of aristocratic inheritance is one of male elites attempting to circumvent common law rules because they were too *favourable* to women, not too harsh, due to the regularity with which they allowed control of property to fall into women's hands. Under the rules of intestate succession eldest sons inherited real property, but in the absence of any sons, daughters inherited. In the average elite family in Tudor and Stuart England this meant that daughters were eligible to inherit in between 20 and 25 per cent of cases. Yet figures for the seventeenth century suggest that daughters of the elites inherited estates in only 5 per cent of cases. The inference is that anxious landowners who were determined to keep power and prestige in male hands managed to bypass daughters in favour of uncles or other collateral males. And landowners achieved this through provisions in wills and marriage settlements, and in particular through the development of so-called 'strict settlements'. In other words, they used courts like Chancery to *defeat* common law rules that were advantageous to potential heiresses, not to circumvent rules that discriminated against these women.

Spring outlines a similar pattern with respect to dower. She argues that the shift away from common law dower to jointure did not necessarily benefit widows. While dower promised a woman the profits from one third of her husband's interests in land for the duration of her widowhood, regardless of the dowry or portion she had contributed at marriage, the value of jointures was linked directly to the value of women's portions. Later jointures usually guaranteed a widow an annual income equal to a set proportion of her dowry, commonly one tenth. This meant that a widow had to outlive her husband by ten years simply to break even on her, or more usually her family's, investment. Spring concludes that if the value of family estates is taken into account, jointures did not come close to equalling the value of dower thirds.[44] As Susan Staves has remarked about the eighteenth century (and in the context of the development of a doctrine of 'equitable jointure' that circumvented many of the requirements for jointure laid down in the Statute of Uses): 'A widow's entitlement to a life estate in land was transformed by equity into an entitlement to a jointure that could be a smaller estate in less secure personal property for less than the term of her life'.[45] Many of Spring's arguments have yet to be conclusively established empirically. However, the logic of her approach is compelling, and it serves as an important reminder that the flexibility offered by rival jurisdictions to the common law could be used to thwart women's entitlements as well as to protect or extend them. For aristocratic women at least, the common law could sometimes be the lesser of two evils.

The common law's bad press arises from its restriction of women's rights in marriage and in inheritance. But as the chapters that follow show, female liti-

---

[44] Eileen Spring, *Law, Land, & Family: Aristocratic Inheritance in England, 1300 to 1800* (Chapel Hill and London, 1993), pp. 42–65.   [45] Staves, *Married Women's Separate Property*, p. 99.

gants went to court over other matters besides marriage and inheritance. In many, perhaps most, instances they pursued litigation not as women asserting women's rights, but as creditors, debtors, executrixes, administratrixes, lease-holders, tenants, midwives, servants or traders seeking redress for wrongs. In these guises the common law courts were often the most helpful organs of justice for women, more helpful at times than equity courts, as estimates of female participation in litigation set down in the final section of this chapter will demonstrate.

The law encompassed a range of different jurisdictions, including criminal, civil and ecclesiastical, customary, prerogative, conciliar and common law. Each of the non-criminal jurisdictions presented women with distinct rights and the mechanisms for exercising those rights. The choice of jurisdiction was in many cases out of litigants' control, determined by the nature of their suits, the nature and value of their interests, and the village, manor, town, city, diocese or county in which they and their opponents lived. However, in other cases litigants and their lawyers were able to select the jurisdictions they thought would be most beneficial to their cause and then do their best to manipulate proceedings to their advantage. Consequently, the legal system needs to be considered in its complex entirety, even if the only way to unlock its secrets is by examining its constituent parts. Not only do all of the available jurisdictions need to be understood, it is important to realise how informal or rough and ready certain arrangements could be; how often different jurisdictions might overlap and contradict each other; how they might co-operate at the same time as they com-peted for business and power; and how the best laid plans of lawmakers, judges and jurists could go awry.

LEGAL THEORY VERSUS PRACTICE

Susan Staves, the author of *Married Women's Separate Property in England, 1660–1833*, is just one of many historians to observe that 'in early modern English law, the gulf between obvious statutory and judge-made rules, on the one hand, and practice, on the other hand, appears to have been very wide indeed'.[46] Examples of the width of this gulf are plentiful, and not, of course, restricted to activities involving women. In the criminal law, debate still rages over why there was such a wide gap in this period between the harshness of legislation and the extent of known crime, on the one hand, and the dearth of successful convictions, on the other. Douglas Hay suggested in *Albion's Fatal Tree* that this gap represented a conscious use of discretion by the judiciary, in league, or at least in sympathy, with parliament.[47] His arguments challenged the

---

[46] Staves, *Married Women's Separate Property*, p. 206.
[47] Douglas Hay, 'Property, authority and the criminal law', in Douglas Hay, Peter Linebaugh, John Rule, E.P. Thompson and Cal Winslow, eds., *Albion's Fatal Tree: Crime and Society in Eighteenth-Century England* (London, 1975), pp. 17–63.

view that this gap represented no more than the inefficiency of the English justice system, and they stand in marked contrast to interpretations that stress the participatory nature of this system prior to the nineteenth and twentieth centuries, reliant as it was on the co-operation and participation of local inhabitants serving as informers, witnesses, jurors, churchwardens, constables, sheriffs and magistrates.[48] Whether the result of 'cock-up' or 'conspiracy', all parties to this debate concede the existence of this gap between intention and practice. Students of women and crime have shown that this gap could be particularly acute where female offenders were concerned.[49] Early modern parliaments showed little sympathy for female criminals. As already mentioned, crimes associated with women, such as witchcraft, infanticide and husband murdering, attracted particularly severe penalties, reflecting the horror with which legislators regarded these offences and their desire to deter potential offenders from committing them.[50] However, these crimes apart, women rarely figured in the statistics of prosecuted felons; they were far less likely than men to be accused of a felony at assizes or quarter sessions (unless the offence was witchcraft or infanticide), and according to one estimate only one fifth of convicted women suffered the full legal penalty.[51]

Discrepancies of this kind reflect one of the more visible paradoxes of the age, a paradox inherent in the simultaneous perception of women as being weak and impotent, yet capable of wielding mysterious power and posing a threat to those around them.[52] Lawmakers and pamphlet writers regarded criminal women as a fearsome and dangerous class.[53] The idea of women committing crimes that threatened household or social order outraged legislators, and some of those the courts convicted suffered horrific punishments and were

---

[48] Herrup, *The Common Peace*; Cynthia Herrup, 'Law and morality in seventeenth-century England', *Past and Present*, 106 (1985), pp. 102–4; see also V.A.C. Gatrell, *The Hanging Tree: Execution and the English People 1770–1868* (Oxford, 1996), p. vi.

[49] Herrup, *The Common Peace*, pp. 173, 175; on the reluctance of juries to convict for infanticide, see Susan Amussen, *An Ordered Society: Gender and Class in Early Modern England* (Oxford, 1988), p. 114.

[50] For the misogyny and double standards within the judiciary concerning women's testimony as accused witches or as victims of rape, see G. Geis, 'Lord Hale, witches and rape', *British Journal of Law and Society*, 5 (1978), pp. 26–44; see also Clive Holmes, 'Women, witnesses and witches', *Past and Present*, 140 (1993), pp. 45–78.

[51] J.M. Beattie, *Crime and the Courts in England 1660–1800* (Princeton, 1986), p. 438.

[52] J.A. Sharpe, 'Witchcraft and women in seventeenth-century England: some northern evidence', *Continuity and Change*, 6 (1991), pp. 185–6; Jan de Bruyn, 'The ideal lady and the rise of feminism in seventeenth-century England', *Mosaic*, 17 (1984), p. 20; for examples that reveal the supposed mysterious powers of women, see Robert Burton, *The Anatomy of Melancholy* (Oxford, 1621), pp. 84, 190; Edward Jordan, *A Disease Called the Suffocation of the Mother* (London, 1603), p. 19.

[53] Frances Dolan has detected in literary representations, 'an anxiety about murderous wives in inverse proportion to the actual threat they posed'; Frances Dolan, *Dangerous Familiars: Representations of Domestic Crime in England 1550–1700* (Ithaca and London, 1994), pp. 26, 89 and *passim*.

represented in pamphlets as evil personified.[54] However, the living, breathing culprits (or alleged culprits) who appeared in criminal courts did not always inspire fear, sometimes they attracted a measure of sympathy, sincere or paternal, from judges, magistrates and juries who avoided convicting them of crimes to which brutal penalties attached. This paradox suggests that the more general gap discernible within the criminal law can partly be explained by the differing functions and perspectives of parliament and judiciary. Parliaments in Tudor and Stuart England, as today, sought to govern the future behaviour of broad classes of, as yet, anonymous people. When governing entailed controlling or deterring aberrant or socially destructive behaviour, they were regularly authoritarian, setting severe penalties. Judges and juries, meanwhile, had to pass judgment on the acts of actual individuals. One group dealt with the future behaviour of many people, and could afford to be rigid in their approach, the other dealt with the past behaviour of a few, and had more regular need to exercise discretion or to show compassion.[55] Margaret Cavendish mocked court gallants in her diary by telling them 'be sure you raile of all Women generally, but praise every particular one', but her sentiments might describe parliaments who 'railed against all women generally' with repressive legislation, and constables, judges and juries who showed leniency towards 'particular' women.[56]

In civil law, discrepancies between rules and the implementation of rules could be wider still. Amy Erickson has found evidence in wills and probate documents of the gulf between theory and practice in the field of women's property rights. Noting how a concentration on the common law doctrines of primogeniture and coverture can produce an impression of 'relentless female subjugation', she reveals that will-makers below the level of the gentry in Yorkshire, Lincolnshire and Sussex did not strictly follow the practice of primogeniture. Consequently, it was not unusual for daughters to inherit real property, or more often moveable property, on a surprisingly equitable basis with their brothers. Similarly, not everyone observed or sought to enforce the doctrine of coverture. For reasons of practical convenience wives accepted gifts,

[54] The attitudes of lawmakers can be inferred from two extraordinary statutes; the infanticide statute of 1624 (which made concealment of a stillbirth by an unmarried mother a felony, and represents a rare reversal of the traditional burden of proof) and the 1650 ordinance that made adultery a capital felony for married women but not for married men; Sharpe, *Crime in Early Modern England*, p. 61; Thomas, 'The puritans and adultery', pp. 257–8, 261.

[55] This is reflected in the common practice of devaluing stolen goods to turn grand larceny into petty larceny, the extensive use of 'benefit of clergy' for men, and pregnancy for women, to have death sentences commuted, and in the relatively high rates of acquittals in English felony trials; see Sharpe, *Crime in Early Modern England*, pp. 65–9; Herrup, *The Common Peace*, pp. 165–6 and *passim*.

[56] As quoted in Sara Mendelson, *The Mental World of Stuart Women: Three Studies* (Brighton, 1987), p. 17; Beattie, *Crime and the Courts*, pp. 436–9; Herrup, *The Common Peace*, pp. 149–50, 153; Thomas, 'The puritans and adultery', pp. 257–8, 261, 278–9, 280.

engaged in financial transactions and treated as their own various items of personal property which strict law decreed belonged to their husbands.[57] Mary Prior has shown that married women, including labourers' and husbandmens' wives, made wills in Elizabethan Oxfordshire. Most had the consent of their husbands, either given at the time of writing or according to the terms of an agreement made on marriage, or they made wills in their capacity as executrixes or administratrixes, however a few appear to have made a will without gaining permission from their husbands. Others made bequests in their wills of freehold land, in direct contravention of statute. As Prior reflects, 'it would be quite impossible by induction from the wills themselves to reconstruct the law which governed their making', a sentiment that is valid for most manuscript records of the workings of coverture in practice.[58] These reflections do not prove that the prohibitions of coverture were ineffectual – whenever a husband felt threatened or vindictive, he could enforce them – they merely emphasise that while husbands could enforce the doctrine of coverture, that does not mean that every husband did enforce the doctrine.[59]

The relationship within the law between elite expectation and common experience, like the relationship between moralists' advice to women and women's response to that advice, was complex and defies over-simplification. It can be tempting, given the foregoing examples of primogeniture and coverture, to characterise the common law as being restrictive and repressive towards women in principle, but freer and more tolerant or realistic in practice. Fynes Moryson, for example, in his *Itinerary*, published in English in 1617, marvelled at the tolerance and respect husbands showed their wives in practice, 'notwithstanding all their priviledges', by which he meant the power the law gave to married men.[60] However, for other areas of the law the exact opposite seems to have been true. In many cases, as Pollock and Maitland rightly pointed out, the common law appeared to offer women the same rights and opportunities as men, or was simply ambivalent about distinguishing rights according to sex. Yet social pressure regularly intervened to ensure that women were excluded from,

---

[57] Erickson, *Women and Property*, p. 19 and *passim*; and see chapter 6 below.

[58] 34 & 35 Henry VIII c. 5, *Statutes of the Realm*, vol. 3, pp. 901–4. Mary Prior, 'Wives and wills 1558–1700', in Chartres and Hey, eds., *English Rural Society*, pp. 201, 213; William Gouge acknowledged in his dedication to *Of Domesticall Duties* that his Blackfriars parishioners took 'much exception' to his statement that a wife had no freedom to dispose of family property 'without, or against, her husbands consent'; William Gouge, *Of Domesticall Duties* (London, 1622) (facsimile edn; Amsterdam, 1976), pp. 3–4.

[59] For a fuller discussion of coverture, see chapter 6 below.

[60] Fynes Moryson, *An Itinerary Written by Fynes Moryson Gent. First in the Latine Tongue, and then Translated by Him into English* (London, 1617) (facsimile edn; Amsterdam, 1971), part 3, p. 221; Moryson went on to say of English husbands that 'no people in the World, (that ever I did see) beare more scornes indignities, and injuries, from the pampered sort of Women, then they doe'. Whereas German husbands, he argued, kept their wives firmly under control, despite enjoying less powers at law than English husbands.

or simply not encouraged to avail themselves of, those rights or opportunities. Examples of this abound in the public sphere, where nothing in the law prevented women from becoming justices of the peace, churchwardens or overseers of the poor, but in practice very few found their way into these positions.[61] A reader at Gray's Inn explained in 1622 that although women were not forbidden in law from serving as overseers, they were nevertheless unsuitable candidates because of the 'weakness of their sex', which made them 'unfit to travel', and because they were 'for the most part uncapable of learning to direct in matters of Judicature'.[62] With respect to women appearing on customary homages, Edward Coke observed that 'a woman may be a free suiter to the Courts of the Lord, but though it be generally said that the free suiters be Judges in these Courts, it is intended of men and not of women'.[63]

Another reason why the historiography of women and the law is uncertain is because early modern law was uncertain, by today's standards at least. The boundaries between different jurisdictions were often blurred. The consistory court in York, for example, heard actions for defamation which technically should have been heard as slander at common law.[64] Moreover, consistency within jurisdictions was never universal. To give one example, it was accepted in the court of Chancery that wives could not appear as witnesses in cases involving their husbands, yet a manuscript commentary which stressed this exclusion also described various cases where wives' testimony was taken. In one, *Heydon v. Yark* (1576), the reason given was that the wife 'wore the Breeches'.[65]

Inconsistency such as this can be obscured if a lawyer's approach to the history of courts is taken, one which strives to construct a coherent story by pulling single strands of doctrine from tangled skeins of litigation. Legal doctrine deals with generalities, and tracing its development can never embrace the breadth of possibilities produced by individual actions and circumstances. Furthermore, in an age when law reporting was in its infancy, when a host of courts operated side by side, and individual judges in those courts dealt with countless differently placed litigants arguing different fact situations, many questions of legal doctrine were neither fixed nor clear. Precedent was a loose concept indeed, invoked more commonly in terms of the deterrence of similar behaviour in the future, than in terms of consistency with similar decisions in the past, and it would be hard to argue that Elizabethan judges observed anything resembling the later

---

[61] J.H. Baker, ed., *The Notebook of Sir John Port*, Selden Society vol. 102 (London, 1986), p. 113; Stopes, *British Freewomen*, p. 63.

[62] As quoted in Glanz, 'The legal position of English women', p. 112.

[63] Edward Coke, *The Second Part of the Institutes of the Laws of England*, 3rd edn (London, 1669), p. 119; and see Stopes, *British Freewomen*, p. 81.

[64] Sharpe, *Defamation and Sexual Slander*, p. 11.

[65] Holdsworth, *History of English Law*, vol. 9, pp. 197–8; C.U.L. Gg.2.31, fol. 590; and see fols 231, 447ᵛ, 464.

principle of *stare decisis*.[66] In this climate doctrine did not develop as smoothly and was not as representative, especially in equity courts, as some historians suggest when they speak of gradual and even increases or decreases in women's legal status.[67] In his book on the Elizabethan Chancery, W.J. Jones cautioned legal researchers to retain a healthy scepticism about the course of law in the sixteenth century. As he wrote: 'The temptation is to think in terms of a developing law, but often the law just did not develop. Instead it happened.'[68] Amy Erickson has pointed out how the willingness of legal institutions to recognise and enforce separate estates and marriage settlements that allowed wives to retain control of their personal and real property during marriage was somewhat haphazard. She notes, as W.S. Holdsworth noted before her, that Chancery decisions protecting separate estates for women were sometimes inconsistent, and the development of equitable rights was not a uniform process.[69] All of these examples underline the need to examine all facets of women's dealings with the law, and in particular the variety of their day to day experiences in different courts within Westminster and throughout the rest of the country.

NUMBERS OF FEMALE LITIGANTS

Women, especially if they were *femes sole*, theoretically enjoyed a number of rights, but how many exercised or defended those rights in courts of law? As mentioned in the introduction, it is presently impossible to determine with accuracy the contributions women made to national patterns of litigation, because national patterns have yet to be fully identified. Furthermore, quantifying totals and calculating percentages on the basis of information recorded by individuals and institutions uninterested in such details is a risky endeavour, made worse by the haphazard survival of relevant records. Nevertheless, it is useful to estimate the general scale of women's involvement in litigation by making a quick count of samples in select Westminster courts and comparing these with the few existing figures that record the participation of female litigants in litigation totals.

[66] The principle of *stare decisis* demands that judges should be bound by, not just guided by, the previous decisions of higher courts in similar cases, unless the case before them is clearly distinguishable on its facts. Maria Cioni suggested that the Chancellor and Masters of Chancery were observing this principle in Elizabeth's reign, but D.E.C. Yale has argued that modern ideas about precedent cannot really be dated before the time of Lord Nottingham; Cioni, *Women and Law*, p. 12, n. 1; Edward Hake, *Epieikeia: A Dialogue on Equity in Three Parts*, ed. D.E.C. Yale (New Haven, 1953), p. xxxvii.

[67] Maria Cioni believed women's legal rights improved steadily from at least the mid sixteenth century onwards. Alice Clark and Charlotte Stopes suggested that women's rights declined over the same period. For further details and references, see chapter 9 below.

[68] Jones, *Chancery*, p. 2.

[69] Erickson, *Women and Property*, chapter 6, especially p. 151; Holdsworth, *History of English Law*, vol. 5, p. 311.

The court most frequently associated with women in this period is the Westminster court of Chancery. Maria Cioni gave no indication in her work of levels of women's participation (her interest was more in the courts' procedures, remedies and general outlook) except to suggest that numbers were increasing during the reign of Elizabeth.[70] Amy Erickson has verified this impression by taking samples from the manuscript calendars of Chancery proceedings. She found that during Elizabeth's reign women appeared, as plaintiffs or defendants, in a quarter of all suits commenced in the court, and judging by a sample taken by Wilfrid Prest, this proportion rose to 40 per cent during the reign of James I. The proportion of women plaintiffs commencing suits (on their own or with others) rose over this period from 17 per cent of cases during Elizabeth's reign to almost 26 per cent of cases during the period 1615–1715.[71]

Requests presents a similar, but slightly different picture. Women appeared as litigants in almost one third of cases commenced during Elizabeth's reign.[72] They appeared as plaintiffs in 20 per cent of cases, and as defendants in 16 per cent of cases.[73] Unlike in Chancery, where the proportion of women appears to have risen significantly, the proportion of women in Requests rose only slightly over the course of Elizabeth's reign. In 1562 they made up 12.4 per cent of the total litigant population (based on samples of cases in advanced stages), rising to 13.6 per cent in 1603.[74] By 1624 women were involved in more than a third of cases in the court, and they made up 18 per cent of litigants.[75] Women never litigated in the prerogative courts on the same scale as men, and those who did sue often appeared with others – of the 17 per cent of cases in which women appeared in Chancery as plaintiffs, just under 10 per cent involved wives appearing with their husbands – but women took part in the expansion of litigation in the central equity courts, and were familiar figures within the hubbub of Westminster Hall and the White Hall.

The involvement of women in common law courts is assumed by most historians to be negligible. The only published figures that exist for common law jurisdictions (for non-criminal law) are C.W. Brooks' estimates for the

---

[70] Cioni, 'The Elizabethan Chancery', p. 159.

[71] Erickson, 'Common law versus common practice', p. 28; Prest, 'Law and women's rights', p. 182.

[72] Six hundred and thirty five case files, out of a sample of 2,000 from the manuscript calendars of the Requests archive, involve at least one woman (31.8 per cent); PRO 9 vol. 93 (Requests proceedings) piece numbers 157/1–167/37 (excluding incomplete entries; 157/429–467, 158/196–208, 159/159–175, 160/77).

[73] Women occasionally sued other women, which explains why the percentages of female plaintiffs and defendants exceed the total percentages of cases involving women.

[74] In Hillary and Easter terms 4 Elizabeth I, women made up 139 out of 1,120 litigants (12.4 per cent), and in Hillary term 45 Elizabeth I, they made up 313 out of 2,308 (13.6 per cent); PRO Req 1/11; PRO Req 1/21.

[75] In Hillary term 22 James I, women made up ninety six out of 531 litigants (18.1 per cent) and were involved in eighty three out of 220 actions (37.7 per cent); PRO Req 1/32, pp. 399–428, 449–506.

participation of widows in the two largest courts in the land, Queen's Bench and Common Pleas. His figures, based on an analysis of the given status of litigants in cases in advanced stages, indicate that widows made up only 6 per cent of litigants in Queen's Bench and Common Pleas in 1560. By 1606 this figure had fallen to 2 per cent for King's Bench and 3 per cent for Common Pleas. In 1640, the figure for King's Bench rose slightly, and widows made up 3 per cent of litigants in both courts.[76] At first sight these percentages seem relatively low, when compared with the positions in Chancery and Requests, yet they actually conceal relatively high levels of overall participation by women. These estimates for the participation of widows, especially the 1560 figure of 6 per cent, compare favourably with the equivalent estimates for Requests and Chancery. In Requests in 1562, 5 per cent of litigants with cases in advanced stages were widows (in 1603 the figure was 6 per cent, by 1624 it had fallen to 4.5 per cent) and in Chancery widows accounted for less than 2 per cent of the 17 per cent of plaintiffs who were women.[77] The suspicion that a considerable number of single women and married women as well as widows were named in common law actions can be confirmed by re-examining the rolls of warrants of attorneys that Brooks used in his general study of litigant status. A quick sample of the rolls for 1560 reveals that women were named in forty six out of 150 actions in Common Pleas (31 per cent) and made up over 13 per cent of all litigants in that court.[78] In Queen's Bench they were named in seventeen out of seventy six actions (22 per cent) and constituted almost 10 per cent of the litigant population.[79] These samples are small, but the results are provocative, suggesting that women were as likely to litigate in courts of common law as in conciliar courts of equity during the early years of Elizabeth's reign; and logic suggests that in terms of numbers they were *more* likely, given the large size of both of these courts. Moreover, even in the central court with the smallest female presence, Star Chamber, women took part in just over 10 per cent of actions in Elizabeth's reign, falling to just under 9 per cent of actions in the reign of James I.[80]

[76] Brooks, *Pettyfoggers*, pp. 281–3.

[77] Source, PRO Req 1/11 (4 Elizabeth I) and PRO Req 1/21 (45 Elizabeth I/1 James I); in the Elizabethan Chancery, widows made up forty four out of a sample of 2446 plaintiffs (1.7%); Erickson, *Women and Property*, tables 7.1, 7.2, p. 115.

[78] The first 150 entries (ignoring double entries) on the first four membranes of the roll of warrants of attorneys for Easter term 2 Elizabeth I include six spinsters, twenty nine wives and twenty three widows out of a total of 431 named litigants (13.5 per cent); PRO CP40/1187.

[79] The names of three spinsters, seven wives and ten widows appear among the names of 204 litigants (9.8 per cent) in the roll of warrants of attorneys for Easter term 2 Elizabeth I; PRO KB 27/1194.

[80] A sample of calendar entries for Star Chamber suits initiated by individuals (as opposed to royal officials) reveals that women were involved in thirty six out of 346 suits (10.4 per cent); although women made up less than 5 per cent of all litigants listed (sixty six out of at least 1377); unpublished PRO calendar Star Chamber Proceedings Elizabeth I, vol. 4 (shelf no. 9.60); for the Jacobean period 657 of the 7,715 surviving records of person against person suits (as opposed to those initiated by royal officials) include the names of women (8.5 per cent)(8228 bills survive

For courts that operated outside Westminster few figures exist. In his study of the King's Lynn Guildhall court, Craig Muldrew calculated that 9 per cent of plaintiffs and 6 per cent of defendants in the mid to late seventeenth century were women appearing on their own.[81] The Lynn court dealt overwhelmingly with actions for debt, and Muldrew concluded that women did not play a significant part in the world of credit relations and business transactions which spawned actions in the local court, and that widows in Lynn rarely acted as moneylenders.[82] If women did not feature prominently in debt litigation, they did have a heavy involvement in litigation concerned with defamation of character.[83] J.A. Sharpe discovered, in his study of defamation causes in the York consistory court, that female plaintiffs brought just over half (51 per cent) of the 1,638 defamation actions which entered the court during the 1590s. In the 1690s, this number rose to 76 per cent.[84] Gowing has found that in the period 1572–1640, women brought between 70 and 75 per cent of the defamation suits entered in London's consistory court, and almost 85 per cent of suits from urban parishes. Women brought 31 per cent of all actions in the court in 1590, rising to 54 per cent by 1633.[85]

Viewing the available statistics from a range of different courts, it appears that the numbers of women active in litigation (expressed in percentages) were high, given the social and legal restraints women suffered during this period, but nevertheless disappointing for a group that made up at least half of the population. As Sharpe points out, 'apart from a few peculiar matters', women were unlikely to be involved as frequently as men in litigation.[86] However, when analysing women's involvement with the law during the sixteenth and seventeenth centuries it is worth looking not just at percentages, but at the numbers on which those percentages are based. The increase in litigation at this time was extraordinary, far outstripping the rise in population, with many courts inside and outside London more than doubling their business between 1550 and 1600. The York consistory court heard 213 causes in 1561–2, rising to 357 in 1591–2,

overall); T.G. Barnes, *List and Index to the Proceedings in Star Chamber for the Reign of James I (1603–1625) in the Public Record Office, London Class STAC 8* (Chicago, 1975), vol. 1; see also Barnes, 'Star Chamber litigants', p. 9.

[81] These figures therefore do not include wives who appeared in this court with their husbands; Muldrew, 'Credit, market relations and debt litigation', p. 69; and see chapter 9 below.

[82] Litigation is not necessarily a good indicator of women's involvement in moneylending and credit networks; see William Chester Jordan, *Women and Credit in Pre-Industrial and Developing Societies* (Philadelphia, 1993), especially pp. 59–78; for examples of women moneylenders in Requests records, see chapter 5, n. 54 below.

[83] C.A. Haigh, 'Slander and the church courts in the sixteenth century', *Transactions of the Lancashire and Cheshire Antiquarian Society*, 78 (1975), pp. 1–13; Ingram, *Church Courts, Sex and Marriage*, ch. 10; Gowing, *Domestic Dangers*; Gowing, 'Gender and the language of insult'; Sharpe, *Defamation and Sexual Slander*.

[84] Sharpe, *Defamation and Sexual Slander*, pp. 27, 28.

[85] Gowing, *Domestic Dangers*, table 2, p. 35, and see table 3, p. 37.

[86] Sharpe, 'The people and the law', p. 249.

while the York Chancery increased its business from twenty seven actions in 1571–2, to 134 actions in 1599–1600.[87] In Westminster, the court of Exchequer received an average of 84 bills of complaint each year between 1558 and 1587, and an average of 334 bills each year between 1587 and 1603. The point is that with levels of litigation on the increase, static percentages represent rises in actual numbers. Even the apparent decline in the number of widows appearing in Common Pleas and Queen's Bench, suggested by the fall in the percentage figures given by Brooks, from 6 per cent in 1560 to between 2 or 3 per cent in 1606 (see above), represented not a decrease, but a slight *increase* in the actual number of widows who entered these courts: the 6 per cent figure for 1560 represents 142 widows who appeared in Queen's Bench and Common Pleas in Easter term 1560 while the 2 to 3 per cent figure for 1606 represents 160 widows.

If the rates of increase were significantly high, total volumes of business were higher still. By the close of Elizabeth's reign, Common Pleas and Queen's Bench were dealing with well over 20,000 suits a year, and by 1640 this figure had climbed to over 28,000.[88] At this time, W.J. Jones has estimated, Chancery was hearing 1,600 cases per annum that reached advanced stages.[89] Calculating the exact volume of business in Requests is virtually impossible (as chapter 4 will show) but the records of between 16,000 and 19,000 suits that survive for Elizabeth's reign provide an indication of the minimum number of actions commenced during that forty five year period. C.W. Brooks' speculative estimate of 54,075 causes commenced in the central courts in 1606 gives some indication at least of the remarkable scale of legal activity among the larger courts in Westminster.[90] Even taking a conservative estimate of women's overall participation in central litigation of 8 per cent, this would still mean that at least 8,000 women connected themselves with actions in these courts in this year. As stressed in the introduction, the number of actions litigated in local courts was higher still, and whichever percentages are used it is clear that women went to law in England not in their hundreds, but in their thousands. These estimates bear witness to a steady stream of women participating in civil litigation in a variety of different courts, and the next chapter examines the responses of judges, moralists, satirists and playwrights to both the idea and the reality of women involving themselves in the processes of law.

---

[87] Ronald Marchant, *The Church Under the Law: Justice, Administration and Discipline in the Diocese of York, 1560–1640* (Cambridge, 1969), table 8, p. 62; table 9, p. 68; the number of actions in the Bishop of Chester's Consistory court doubled between 1544 and 1594; Haigh, 'Slander and the church courts', p. 2.

[88] Brooks, *Pettyfoggers*, appendix, pp. 281–2, table 4.1, p. 51; Brooks' figures are for cases in advanced stages, so the total volume of business was almost certainly higher.

[89] Jones, *Chancery*, p. 304, n. 1.

[90] Common Pleas, King's Bench, Chancery, Requests, Star Chamber, Wards, and the equity and common law sides of Exchequer; Brooks, *Pettyfoggers*, table 5.1, p. 78.

$\ll$ *3* $\gg$

Female litigants and the culture of litigation

When Women goe to Law the Devill is full of Businesse
John Webster (1623)[1]

CONTEMPORARY OPINION

During the reign of Queen Elizabeth the proportions of women litigating in central jurisdictions fluctuated, rising in Chancery, falling in Common Pleas and Queen's Bench, and remaining fairly constant in Requests. But the physical numbers of women involved in litigation increased steadily. This meant more women travelling to London, more women staying in London for extended periods, and more women milling around Westminster, visiting attorneys, appearing as witnesses and presenting evidence on oath.[2] Before examining the nature of women's involvement with the courts, the kinds of actions they brought, and the extent to which relatives, lawyers and other third parties influenced their legal dealings, it is helpful to consider the climate of opinion that surrounded women who contemplated going to law. How did different sections of society regard the idea of women possessing and exercising legal rights, and how did they react to the increase in the numbers of women going to court?

The sixteenth and seventeenth centuries witnessed a well-documented outpouring of writings on the subject of women. Contributors to the long running debate over female nature defended or attacked women's capabilities and character in works like *The Scholehouse of Women*, *The Praise and Dispraise of Women* and *The Women's Sharp Revenge*, reworking and reinforcing familiar stereotypes of the 'bad' woman and the 'good' woman as they went.[3] Medical

---

[1] John Webster, *The Devils Law-Case. Or, When Women Goe to Law, the Devill is Full of Businesse* (London, 1623), sig. A1.

[2] The question of women's appearance in court is examined in chapters 4 and 6 below.

[3] See Ian Maclean, *The Renaissance Notion of Women: A Study in the Fortunes of Scholasticism and Medical Science in European Intellectual Life* (Cambridge, 1980), pp. 91–2; Linda Woodbridge, *Women and the English Renaissance: Literature and the Nature of Womankind 1540–1620* (Urbana, 1984); L.B. Wright, *Middle-Class Culture in Elizabethan England* (Chapel Hill, 1935), pp. 117–18, ch. 13.

writers revealed in English the mysteries of the female body, describing in detail what they believed to be the unpredictability of women's autonomous, 'ravenous' wombs, liable at any moment to wander within the body, inducing fits of 'suffocation of the mother'.[4] Authors of conduct books and advice manuals depicted ideal standards of female behaviour, while many ballad writers preferred to shock or delight their audiences with the opposite, with tales of lusty widows and dominant wives asserting their independence and demanding satisfaction from the men around them.[5] Dramatists presented an even richer set of female characters, many of them outspoken and independent, like Shakespeare's Lady Macbeth or Webster's Duchess of Malfi, although as Linda Woodbridge warned in her excellent study, *Women and the English Renaissance*, 'despite the truly spectacular number of assertive women in Renaissance literature', writers and commentators nevertheless regarded female assertiveness as abnormal.[6]

Authors working within various genres concocted a variety of representations of women in print. The range was considerable, but a number of familiar themes recurred, whether expressed in jests to invoke laughter, or in sermons to instil guilt or encourage moral improvement. These included concerns about women's sexuality, modesty, independence and speech, each of which might have had a bearing on how onlookers regarded female litigants. All of these concerns, and the belief in women's subordinate position which underpinned them, were expressed to fiercest effect in the prescriptive literature of conduct in which authors strove to mark out a place for women within the strictly conceived hierarchies of Elizabethan society. The purveyors of this idealised world view expected women to stay at home, keep their talking to a minimum and leave the affairs of the world to men. In the English translation of his *Instruction of a Christen Woman*, the Spanish humanist and tutor at Henry VIII's court, Juan Luis Vives, explained that women should 'ever use the counsayle' of trustworthy men, reminding his readers of the Roman belief that women 'shulde ever be under the rule of theyr fathers, and brotherne, and housbandes, and kynsmen'.[7] Ministers reiterated this message from the pulpit whenever they read out the homilies on marriage and obedience. And Sir Thomas

---

[4] See, for example, Jordan, *Suffocation of the Mother*; Jordan's was one of the more enlightened medical treatises of the age; see Michael MacDonald, ed., *Witchcraft and Hysteria in Elizabethan London: Edward Jordan and the Mary Glover Case* (London and New York, 1991), pp. vii–lv; and see Fletcher, *Gender*, pp. 30–40, 48–50, 66–8.

[5] See Kathleen Davies, 'Continuity and change in literary advice on marriage', in R.B. Outhwaite, ed., *Marriage and Society: Studies in the Social History of Marriage* (London, 1981); Suzanne Hull, *Chaste, Silent and Obedient: English Books for Women 1475–1640* (San Marino, 1982); Elizabeth Foyster, 'A laughing matter? Marital discord and gender control in seventeenth-century England', *Rural History*, 4 (1993), pp. 5–21.

[6] Woodbridge, *Women and the English Renaissance*, p. 214; Kathleen McLuskie, *Renaissance Dramatists* (Hemel Hempstead, 1989) p. 225.

[7] Juan Luis Vives, *A Very Fruteful and Pleasant Boke Callyd the Instruction of a Christen Woman*, trans. Richard Hyrde (London 1541), fol. 136.

Smith, in *The Common-Wealth of England*, concluded his discussion defining the political nation by saying 'also we doe reject women, as those whom nature hath made to keep home and to nourish their family and children, and not to meddle with matters abroad, nor to beare office in a cittie or Common-wealth, no more than children and infants'.[8]

Attacking or answering an opponent in court clearly involved 'meddling with matters abroad'. Litigation was a combative act performed in public before an audience of lawyers, judges and witnesses and set down in ink by scribes. It is easy to imagine moralists wincing at the very thought of women going to law. Lucy de Bruyn has suggested that a number of writers believed the Devil preyed upon women who haunted public places, and that these authors looked upon the courts as especial 'Seates of Satan'.[9] As will be seen in a moment, some commentators did indeed hold strong opinions about women going to law, but views of women's legal rights and entitlements were not always straightforward. For alongside the ideal of 'correct' female behaviour existed the ideal of justice, and when these ideals came into conflict most members of the moralising elite believed the latter to be more important than the former. Who, after all, could condemn outright women who ventured into court to defend themselves against their enemies?

Everyone agreed that women should not 'beare office' within the legal system, as judges or attorneys, but even the most polemical critics of female capability did not consider women so inferior or unworthy that they should be excluded from possessing legal rights altogether.[10] In *The First Blast of the Trumpet Against the Monstrous Regiment of Women*, John Knox questioned the ability of women to succeed to public office, but he had no objection to them succeeding to 'possession, substance, patrimonie or inheritance'. His objection was to female, Catholic authority, not to women's general social or legal status. In response to the question, 'is it not lawful, that women have their right and inheritance, like as the doughters of Zapheed?', he answered, 'it is not onlie laufull that women possesse their inheritance, but I affirme also that justice and equitie require that they so do'.[11] All parties conceded women's right to inherit, even if some had their eye more on dynastic succession than on ques-

---

[8] Thomas Smith, *The Common-Wealth of England, and Manner of Government Thereof* (London, 1601), p. 28.

[9] Lucy de Bruyn, *Woman and the Devil in Sixteenth-Century Literature* (Tisbury, Wilts., 1979), p. 89.

[10] The author of *The Mirror of Justices*, for example, thought women made bad pleaders and summoners, but agreed that they could be plaintiffs; W.J. Whittaker, ed., *The Mirror of Justices*, Selden Society vol. 7 (London, 1895), pp. 45, 47, 82; Christine de Pisan acknowledged that women 'holde noo pleadynge in the courte of Justyce', nor they knowe not of the causes ne dothe no Jugement', but she firmly rebutted accusations that 'women have not suffycyent understandynge for to lerne the lawes', saying 'the contrary is made open by experyence'; Christine du Castel, *The Boke of the Cyte of Ladyes*, trans. B. Anslay (London, 1521)[*S.T.C.* 7271], sigs ff.i^{r-v}.

[11] John Knox, *The First Blast of the Trumpet Against the Monstrous Regiment of Women* (Geneva, 1558), fols 47^{r-v}.

tions of equity between the sexes, and even under coverture, as Margaret Sommerville rightly points out, 'a wife's property rights were submerged, not annihilated'.[12]

Rights are nothing if they cannot be exercised, and most commentators acknowledged that women should be allowed to go to law. Bishop Hugh Latimer was quite happy for women to protect themselves in court. He saw nothing un-Christian about litigation between neighbours, even if he was cynical about the Westminster courts, where he believed rich litigants could purchase speedy justice while the poor were ignored, and in the sermons he delivered to Edward VI in 1549 he made repeated references to women who pursued legal causes.[13] In his second sermon before the young king he counselled the Lord Protector and Lord Chancellor to 'hear poore menes sutes yourself', as Solomon had heard the suit of the two 'poor' women who both claimed to be the mother of the same child, and he illustrated his point by referring to two women he felt were being denied justice.[14] The first was a gentlewoman who had lost her lands in a court action to 'a great man' rich enough to employ 'a great syghte of lawyers for his counsaile' who managed to sway the judge in his favour. The second was a 'poore woman that lyeth in the fleate' prison who remained unable to have her cause heard, despite offers made on her behalf by allies to put in sureties or bail bonds worth £1,000.[15]

Latimer's warning to his audience took the form of the parable of the importunate widow (Luke 18: 1–8) who had begged a judge to hear her cause until finally he gave in, 'because of her importunateness', so that he might have some peace.[16] He repeated the parable in his third sermon, offering the story as comfort for any individuals denied justice in this life, encouraging them with the reassurance that the Lord would be their judge in the next life: 'You widowes, you Orphanes, you poore people, here is a comfortable place for you. Thoughe these judges of the world wil not hear you, there is one wil be contente wyth your importunity, he wil remeady you.'[17] Latimer saw no reason why widows or other women should stay out of court, he simply recognised how difficult it could be for them to fight their way in.

---

[12] Margaret Sommerville, *Sex and Subjection: Attitudes to Women in Early-Modern Society* (London and New York, 1995), p. 104.

[13] In his first sermon before Edward VI, delivered on 8 March 1549, Latimer related a story of a bargain for a horse which 'became a Westminster matter, the lawyers gote twyse the value of the horse, and when all came to all, two fooles made an end of the matter'; Latimer, *Twenty Seven Sermons*, fol. 25; and see fol. 73ᵛ.

[14] Latimer, *Twenty Seven Sermons*, fol. 37; the Protector Somerset is said to have responded to Latimer's exhortation by hearing suits in person in Requests; I.S. Leadam, ed., *Select Cases in the Court of Requests AD 1497–1569*, Selden Society vol. 12 (London, 1898), p. xvii.

[15] Latimer, *Twenty Seven Sermons*, fols. 37, 41 [sic, 38].

[16] Bartholomew Chamberlaine referred to the Judge and the importunate widow in his burial sermon for the Countess of Warwick; Bartholomew Chamberlaine, *A Sermon Preached at Farington in Barkeshire, the Seventeene of Februarie, 1587* (London, 1591), p. 23.

[17] Latimer, *Twenty Seven Sermons*, fol. 45ᵛ.

Legal writers also appeared happy to see women exercise their legal rights. Sample plea forms in William West's *Symboleography* and the books of precedents produced by Thomas Phayer and John Rastall include women's names as well as men's, indicating how routine it was for women to participate in legal actions.[18] The preponderance of cases involving women's rights recorded by law reporters such as Edward Coke and George Croke only confirms this impression.[19] More tantalising evidence that legal authorities regarded women as credible participants in the legal system comes in the form of *The Lawes Resolutions of Womens Rights*. This volume, published in 1632 but almost certainly written towards the end of the sixteenth century, is devoted entirely to women's legal identity and entitlements. The author, whose identity remains something of a mystery, expressed from the outset his intention to 'handle that part of the English Lawe, which containeth the immunities, advantages, interests and duties of women, not regarding so much to satisfie the deep learned or searchers for subtility, as woman kind'.[20] He reasoned that women were subject to laws so they should have access to knowledge of those laws. The sense that this was a practical handbook designed to instruct women is underlined by the running title of the work, 'The woman's lawyer'. Unfortunately, as a practical guide to the law this treatise had a number of shortcomings. It was first and foremost a common law text, and the author barely mentioned equity. He discussed at length the merits of jointures over dower, but without giving practical details, and he offered no guidance about how to draw up the marriage settlements which most usually contained them, or how to enforce them in Chancery, or in Requests (which he never mentioned). Furthermore, much of the book, with its references to obscure case law and treatises and its use of technical terminology and Latin and law French, 'that Hotchpot French, stufft up with such variety of borrowed words, wherein our law is written', seems to have been aimed more at lawyers than at women themselves.[21]

Some historians have mined *The Lawes Resolutions of Womens Rights* for quotes that demonstrate the repressive ethos of sixteenth century law and the sexism, or at least paternalism, of the work's author.[22] In fact by the standards of the day, and within the deeply male world of the common law, the author was

---

[18] Erickson, 'Common law', p. 26; at least one edition of Thomas Phayer's book was owned by a woman, Elizabeth Hulbert; Jones, *Chancery*, p. 4.

[19] I would like to thank Chris Brooks for drawing my attention to the high proportion of cases involving women in Coke's reports.

[20] T.E., *The Lawes Resolutions of Womens Rights*, p. 3; on the probable identity of T.E., see Prest, 'Law and women's rights', pp. 173–5.

[21] Abraham Fraunce, *The Lawiers Logike, Exemplifying the Præcepts of Logike by the Practise of the Common Lawe* (London, 1588), sig. q3; Prest, 'Law and women's rights', pp. 179–80; although see Stenton, *English Woman*, p. 61.

[22] K.E. Lacey, 'Women and work in fourteenth and fifteenth century London', in Lindsey Charles and Lorna Duffin, eds., *Women and Work in Pre-Industrial England* (London, 1985) pp. 29–30, 57; Antonia Fraser, *The Weaker Vessel: Woman's Lot in Seventeenth-Century England* (London, 1985), pp. 5, 10.

surprisingly moderate and open-minded in his vision of women and their entitlements. The tone of the book, as one historian has noted, 'is one of wry sympathy for women', and the sexism of the text stems less from the author himself than from the law he described.[23] His aim was to set out the law, not to critique it, although on occasions he did express his disquiet at particularly discriminatory legal principles. He admitted, for example, having searched the year books to find a justification to explain 'why things may not passe by gift betweene Baron and feme', but he could find nothing beyond the simple excuse of 'unitie of person'. And after acknowledging that 'a womans name of dignitie changeth with the degree of her husband' (as William Heale put it in 1609, 'the wife is only dignified by the husband and not anywaies the husband by the wife') he asked: 'But what though the scrupulositie of the Common pleas were observed throughout the Realme, that Esquires Ladies should be no Ladies in Court and Country, whereunto I will never give voyce what inequality were in this depressing; shall not likewise a knights widdow marrying with a Baron or Earle as be much exalted *verament*, yet you see the dignitie hangeth meerely on the male side, carrying the scepter of Wedlocke.'[24]

'The woman's lawyer' may not have been perfect as a comprehensive women's guide to the law. But its author presented complex information in an accessible form for 'women witty in themselves', to inform them of their rights and to help them decide whether they had a case to bring, and for 'crafty men', the male counsel who instructed them.[25] Whether the work was bought and read mainly by women or mainly by lawyers, the fact that its author and publisher felt that the laws affecting women warranted an entire volume (at a time when law books on single classes of litigant were rare or non-existent) remains significant.[26]

Women, then, were permitted to go to court and they went to court, apparently enjoying the support of men like Latimer and the author of *The Lawes Resolutions of Womens Rights*. However, if female litigants had allies, they also had enemies. While no critics openly denied women the privilege of possessing rights, some questioned whether women should have knowledge of their rights, and whether they should exercise them in person. This was particularly true in the case of married women. Sir Thomas Smith maintained that it was the business of the husband 'to meddle with the defence' of the household, 'eyther by lawe or force', and that wives should confine themselves to 'the charge of the house and householde', which he said was 'indeede the naturall occupation, exercise, office and part of a wife'.[27] In his *Instruction of a Christen Woman*, Vives quoted Cato to the effect that 'an honest wyfe shulde be ignorant, what

[23] Juliet Dusinberre, *Shakespeare and the Nature of Women*, 2nd edn (London, 1996), p. 101; and see Stenton, *English Woman*, pp. 61–4.

[24] T.E., *The Lawes Resolutions of Womens Rights*, pp. 122, 126.

[25] T.E., *The Lawes Resolutions of Womens Rights*, p. 315.

[26] I am indebted to Wilfrid Prest for this point.

[27] Smith, *The Common-Wealth of England*, p. 133.

lawes be made or anulled in her countrey, or what is done amonge men of lawe in the courte'.[28]

These and other writers advocated that wives remain steadfastly in the shadow of their husbands. What were widows to do? The thirteenth century jurist Henry of Bracton, still a potent authority in the sixteenth century, stressed that a widow's heir should defend her dower and attend county, hundred and seigniorial courts on her behalf, 'for she herself ought to attend to nothing except the care of her house and the rearing and education of her children, if any', although he added that 'she ought to have her own court for the determination of all pleas that belong to her'.[29] Vives expected widows to seek the counsel of wise old men, and if they could not find such men he believed 'it is better to be ignorant safely, than to know with jeoperdy. For in courtes and in resort of men, and gatheryng of people, a wydow shuld nat medle', for fear of endangering 'those thynges, that a wydow ought to set moste by'. In the opinion of Vives, widows should lay worldly business at the feet of Christ. Any who might object to this advice, those who would say 'My landes be in perill, I am sued', Vives answered with the words of Ambrose, 'Do nat complayne, that thou art alone: For chastity requireth solytarines.' If widows had business in court and feared their opponent's attorney, they should take solace from the fact that 'our lorde entreateth for the[e], sayeng: Gyve judgement for the fatherles childe, and justifie the wydowe'.[30]

The sentiments Vives expressed lasted into the seventeenth century, Richard Brathwait repeating them almost word for word in 1631. Brathwait maintained that a widow should not court society, 'for in such meetings she exposeth her honour to danger, which above all others she ought incomparably to tender', adding that: 'If you have businesse with the Judge of any Court, and you much feare the power of your adversary, imploy all your care to this end, that your faith may be grounded in those promises of Christ: Your Lord maketh intercession for you, rendring right judgement to the Orphane, and righteousnesse unto the widow.'[31] Where Latimer advised widows to seek justice from the Lord because of the imperfect state of the justice system, Vives and Brathwait counselled them to do so for reasons of modesty and decorum.

The reflections of Vives, Brathwait and Latimer suggest the existence of uncomfortable tensions within the idealised world view put forward by conduct book writers, ministers and jurists. On the one hand, writers suggested that women remain at home and let male accomplices shield them from legal activity, as from other areas of public life, to safeguard their modesty and chastity. On the other hand, these writers recognised that this seclusion helped make

---

[28] Vives, *Instruction of a Christen Woman*, fol. 99ᵛ.

[29] Henry of Bracton, *De Legibus et Consuetudinibus Angliae*, trans. Samuel Thorne, *Bracton on the Laws and Customs of England* (Cambridge, Mass., 1968), vol. 2, p. 281.

[30] Vives, *Instruction of a Christen Woman*, fols 137ʳ⁻ᵛ, 140 [sic 138].

[31] Richard Brathwait, *The English Gentlewoman* (London, 1631), p. 111.

women vulnerable to exploitation and chicanery. The very unworldliness moralists prized in women made them easy targets for the unscrupulous and consequently women, no less than men, needed the protection that courts of law offered. Similarly, the premium these writers placed on chastity and good reputation put pressure on women to protect their good names however they could, which in the later sixteenth century increasingly meant bringing an action for defamation in the church courts, or an action for slander in the courts of common law or equity.[32] The suggestion that women rely on fathers, brothers, husbands, sons or male confidants to do their legal work for them provided no real escape from this apparent impasse. Demographic realities meant that it was unlikely that women could always find a close male relative to assist them (asuming they wished to delegate their legal burdens) and the law did not always permit this kind of surrogacy. If a woman was of age, and unmarried or widowed, her male relations or acquaintances could not simply litigate on her behalf; in legal terms they lacked 'standing' to put their names to suits, because the matters in issue did not directly concern them.[33] Practicalities like these, and the spirit behind the desire to render 'right judgement to the Orphane, and righteousnesse unto the widow', meant that even begrudging writers such as Vives and Brathwait acknowledged (despite their reservations) that some women did indeed go to law and that it was right that these women should receive justice.

Other related tensions are apparent in the language authors used to describe women with legal rights. In their discussions of women and justice, writers often drew upon the imagery of vulnerability and sympathy for the impotent. 'For naturally we hate them that have gret power and riches, and helpe them that have lytel', argued Vives, who used this reasoning to advise widows with legal claims to seek out 'feble atturneyes, or none at all. For than shall the judges take on them the roume of atturneis, whan they withstande often tymes myghty defenders and advocates.'[34] Weakness and poverty were here equated with innocence, as they were in the recurring biblical motif of the lost and forlorn orphan and the vulnerable widow. In Thomas Lodge and Robert Greene's morality play *A Looking Glasse for London and England* (1588), for example, the character Oseas condemns the hateful practice of usury because it plagues London to the point where, 'The poore complaine, the widowes wronged bee.'[35] Brathwait asked of landlords:

---

[32] Gowing, 'Gender and the language of insult', p. 2.

[33] Male accomplices could, however, deal on a widow's behalf and shield her from lawyers, opponents and the courtroom until and unless judges required her to attend a hearing; see for example, *Thomas Davis* v. *Alice Stepneth*, PRO Req 1/11, p. 37; *Helen & Thomas Tan* v. *John Morrell*, PRO Req 2/276/2, A.

[34] Vives, *Instruction of a Christen Woman*, fol. 140[r-v] [sic 138[r-v]].

[35] Thomas Lodge and Robert Greene, *A Looking Glasse for London and England*, I.iii.420; George Clugstone, ed., *A Looking Glasse for London and England by Thomas Lodge and Robert Greene: A Critical Edition* (New York and London, 1980), p. 145.

Who in his mercy hares the widdowes crie,
And in his pitty wipes the orphanes eyes,
Which thou hast caust to think on, so much rather
Sith God's the Widdowes Judge, the orphans Father.[36]

By the tenets of the Christian faith and the principles of equity and good conscience, the powerless deserved protection from the powerful. But what if a woman was herself powerful and independent? A woman's right to bring a law suit against a malicious adversary was clear, but it raised the possibility of women bringing law suits against opponents who were not malicious. Admonitions that women live under the control of men were compromised if women could bring lawsuits against men, just as admonitions that women refrain from speaking were compromised if women could speak out against opponents in the courtroom. At this point the imagery of impotence clashed head on with long-standing concerns about female independence and female speech.

The prospect of independent women speaking their minds in court was too alarming for most moralists to contemplate, and their concern at such a possibility can usually only be guessed at from their fixation with women's modesty. Vives reflected that when a widow approached 'feble' attorneys, her cause 'shalbe so moche more recommended unto them, the lesse that she recommendeth it. And her cause shalbe more like to be good, whom men thynk so good and vertuous, that she wyll neither aske nor hold that is nat her owne.' If women had to go to law, they should stand 'humble and lowely' behind their male attorneys and hope that male judges would show them sympathy. In this view less was more and silence was golden, for 'she that is bablyng, and busy, and troublous must nedes wery men, and make them to loth her, and hindreth her of the succour that I spake of'.[37] An innocent woman could speak out in the pursuit of justice in the manner of the importunate widow in Luke 18. In one of his satires, Thomas Lodge related the story of 'a certaine innocent and guilt-lesse woman' whom Philip of Macedon condemned while he was the worse for drink. She cried out in his presence, 'I appeale from *Philip* drunken to *Philip* sober' and shamed him into seeing sense and acquitting her.[38] However, if anyone introduced a speck of doubt about a woman's innocence, this exception to the general distrust of women speaking could quickly dissolve.

The tension between justice and modesty, between women's right to legal process and the independence that could accompany that right, can be felt in the frustration certain judges expressed as they witnessed increasing numbers of

---

[36] Brathwait, *The English Gentlewoman*, p. 223.

[37] Vives, *Instruction of a Christen Woman*, fol. 140^{r-v} [sic 138^{r-v}].

[38] Lodge presented the story, taken from Valerius Maximus, to show that 'the shaking off of dronkennesse is the establishing of reason, and the custom thereof the destruction of honestie'; Thomas Lodge, *Wits Miserie, and the Worlds Madnesse: Discovering the Devils Incarnat of this Age* (London, 1596) (Menston, Yorks, 1971), p. 83.

women pass through the doors of their courts. In February 1595, Thomas Egerton ordered that an empty room at the east side of Star Chamber should be reserved for the use of gentlemen and 'men of good account in the country', and should no longer be plagued with 'base fellowes and women or other suitors, as it has been'. Eight years later he made his feelings known in another case, after 'a clamorous and impudent woman' who was not a party to a case insisted on troubling the court with impassioned arguments. The judges ordered that she should be 'whipped and made to confess her fault', and after fining her husband £20 'for the better government of his wife . . . it was moved by the Lord Keeper that no woman should be a suitor in any Court in her own person'.[39] Egerton's outburst, whether provoked by the increasing number of female litigants crowding into Westminster, or by his personal attitude to women, came to nothing.[40] The other members of the court, perhaps mindful of the fee income female clients produced, did not support his motion. In Chancery, Anthony Benn complained about the 'shifts and Importunytes of most weomen suitors', who 'would be thought wise in speaking and fayer to be seene'. In his opinion, 'it were not amisse yf now in theyse dayes they weare shutt out of all courts for their witt is so lyttell and theyr will so great that nothing is just with them but that which satisfyeth them'.[41]

Benn and Egerton did not express a desire to deny women rights, but they wished to exclude them from the courtroom and prevent them arguing their cases, or responding to accusations, in person. What concerned them was the deportment of women in court, and here we encounter once again the caricatures that dominated so many depictions of women in print. Prescriptive authors who wrote about women dealt largely in stereotypes, presenting stylised images taken from opposite ends of a wide spectrum. They depicted virtuous women as examples for female audiences to admire and emulate, or described wicked women for them to despise. Some did both. Bishop Aylmer argued in a sermon before Queen Elizabeth that women were of two sorts:

some of them are wiser, better learned, discreeter, and more constant than *a number* of men; but another and worse sort of them, and *the most part*, are fond, foolish, wanton, flibbergibs, tatlers, triflers, wavering, witless, without council, feeble, careless, rash, proud, dainty, nice, talebearers, evesdroppers, rumour-raisers, evil-tongued, worseminded, and in every way doltified with the dregs of the devil's dunghill.[42]

Female litigants, as a group, did not fit easily into this world of pits and pedestals. There was room within the law for both the virtuous and the vice-

---

[39] John Hawarde, *Les Reportes del Cases in Camera Stellata 1593 to 1609*, ed. William Baildon (Privately printed, 1894), pp. 39, 161.

[40] In June 1600 Egerton gave a 'very grave speach in the nature of a charge' to the Star Chamber bench, instructing them to remedy a number of abuses including 'the vanitie and excesse of womens apparell'; Charlotte Merton, 'The women who served Queen Mary and Queen Elizabeth: ladies, gentlewomen and maids of the Privy Chamber 1553–1603' (University of Cambridge Ph.D., 1992), p. 70.   [41] Prest, 'Law and women's rights', pp. 182, 187, n. 59.

[42] As quoted in C.L. Powell, *English Domestic Relations 1487–1653* (New York, 1972), p. 147.

ridden, and to most observers the act of a woman going to court did not, in itself, offend idealised notions of how women should live and behave. What mattered to onlookers, Egerton and Benn included, was the manner in which women went to law. Widows who quietly claimed their dower through male attorneys, women who defended their reputations when slandered, and widows who defended the reputations of their late husbands against the charges of unscrupulous creditors, usually upset no one, except for their rivals in the court-room. But women who litigated not to defend themselves but to attack others, widows who put in suit bonds for debts that their husbands had settled when they were alive, and women who doggedly refused to give up on matters which had been decided in their opponents' favour, upset litigants, judges and moral-ists alike. Women, more so than men, were judged not just on their guilt or innocence, but on the motivations behind their dealings. Take, for example, the Chancellor's view on the question of which transactions a woman made before marriage would remain binding after marriage; as a Chancery commentator explained in 1601:

If a widow for the advancement of her child or kinsman in bloud doe give a lease or make a Bond or gives goods & after takes a husband whoe knowes not of this gift, my Lord will uphold the guift for the concideracions sake being naturall affeccion. But if a widdow doe contract marriage with any man & before consumacion thereof doe secretly assigne Leases, make Bonds or deeds of guift to the end to cosen her new husband, this my Lord by noe meanes likes.[43]

A husband in a Requests case accused his late wife of just such a secret assignment, and he argued that even if she had made it during her widowhood for the benefit of her children, 'yeat was the same devised and contrived of mallice and coveyne to thintent to defrawde and deceive [him] of that which of right to him ought to appertayne'.[44]

Women had freedom to act on behalf of, or for the benefit of, dependants or close kin. They had freedom to defend their good name or secure rights in prop-erty that were legitimately theirs. But it will be argued in the chapters ahead that they were less free than men to indulge in business dealings, to press bond penalties or openly to seek gain for themselves. Just as the Lord Chancellor did not like wives who tried to 'cosen' or deceive their husbands, few judges or writers looked kindly on women who appeared to use the law to further their own ends, or who were seen to pursue litigation too aggressively. The decree books of Requests contain dozens of orders censuring 'clamorous' women, who had entered multiple suits against a single opponent in one or more courts, or who the Masters felt had pursued an action too vigorously or too loudly. To the example of the 'clamorous and impudent' wife who prompted Egerton to fanta-sise about banning women suitors from his court can be added a host of further examples. In January 1564 Francis, Earl of Bedford, wrote to one of the Masters

---

[43] C.U.L. Gg.2.31, fol. 471ᵛ.
[44] *Jane & Elizabeth Thompson* v. *William Bradley & Robert Powe*, PRO Req 2/276/33, m. 2, A.

with regard to a suit 'two poor women' were bringing against one of his servants. 'I pray you to show them favour', he began, 'that when the law has proceeded on their case, I may rid myself of the continual exclamations they make to me for the matter.'[45] The Earl of Huntingdon wrote to the Masters from York in October 1579 about 'the clamorous complainante' in a case before them, advising them to give consideration to her 'poore' adversary.[46] The Privy Council wrote to the Masters from Hertford Castle early in November 1582 concerning the behaviour of a particularly persistent plaintiff, Beatrice Lamb of Lincolnshire, who was troubling Queen and Council with her 'continual clamour'. They begged the Masters not to allow this woman to enter the castle, and if necessary to deliver her to the local constable, 'and command him to convey her to the next constable in her way homewards'.[47] It was not only women litigants whom the authors of letters, the Masters and opponents considered to be clamorous. However, the association of clamorousness with women is clear.[48]

There was a right way and a wrong way to go to law. The right way was for a woman to say little, leaving her counsel to argue all aspects of her case on her behalf, in other words to entrust her affairs to a man. The perfect model for such a woman might be Katherin Brettergh, who died in 1601, aged twenty two. According to the author of her memorial, Katherin chose never to 'gad abroad with wandring Dinah to dancing greeves, markets, or publike assemblies', and on her death bed she said to the Devil: 'Satan reason not with me, I am but a weake woman, if thow have anything to say, say it to my Christ; he is my advocate, my strength, and my redeemer, and he shall pleade for me.'[49] The wrong way was for a woman to break silence and speak vigorously, confidently, and like a man whenever the opportunity presented itself. Lady Russell might qualify for this latter category. She brought a suit in Star Chamber in May 1606 seeking to recover possession of certain lands, despite various attempts by James I to persuade her to settle her affairs away from the courts. According to the account in Hawarde's reports, the judges doubted her right to the premises in contention and they 'began to moove the Courte' to adjourn for lunch, 'but the Ladye, interruptinge them, desyred to be hearde, & after many denyalls by the Courte, vyolentelye & with greate audacitie beganne a

---

[45] *Calendar of State Papers, Domestic Series, Elizabeth, 1601–1603; With Addenda, 1547–1565,* M.A.E. Green, ed. (London, 1870), p. 546.

[46] *Margarett Watterson v. Eleanor Byrkbeck,* PRO Req 2/157/478, letter.

[47] As quoted in Leadam, *Select Cases,* p. xix, n. 6.

[48] For further examples of the denunciation of clamorous women see Julius Caesar, *The Ancient State, Authoritie, and Proceedings of the Court of Requests* (London, 1598), p. 92; *Mary Froome v. William Froome et al.,* PRO Req 1/19, pp. 618–19; *Magdalen Holland v. Thomas Wilford,* PRO Req 1/19, p. 827; *Thomas & Margery Beadell v. Freemon Jrishe et al.,* PRO Req 1/21, p. 61; for an example of a supposedly 'clamorous' man, see *Richard Collard v. Countess Dowager of Rutland,* PRO Req 1/21, p. 324.

[49] *The Christian Life and Death of Mistris Katherin Brettergh* (London, 1612), p. 10.

large discourse, & woulde not by any meanes be stayed nor interrupted, but wente one for the space of halfe an howre or more'.[50] The Lady Russell Hawarde described represented the epitome of the undesirable female litigant. She ignored the advice of the King. She ignored the opinions of the highest judges in the country. She talked for half an hour, 'vyolentelye & with great awdacitie', refusing at every stage to heed the advice of men or to bow to their authority. Loud and obstinate, she was the very antithesis of the meek and silent women, such as Katherin Stubbes or Katherine Brettergh, idealised in published memorials.[51]

The general mood displayed by concerned moralists and jurists might be summed up by reference to an episode in the life of Thomas Wotton, the father of William Wotton the playwright. In the 1560s, Wotton supposedly vowed as a widower that if he remarried he would avoid three kinds of women; those who had children, those who were 'of his kindred' and those who had law suits. His distrust of women with law suits probably stemmed from a recognition of the complications that legal entanglements could bring, but it is likely that he was also expressing a popular wariness of combative or outspoken women. Despite his strong feelings, while pursuing his own law suits in Westminster Hall he found himself moved by the dignity and grace of another litigant, a widow named Eleonora Morton. Although 'there were in her a concurrence of all these accidents against which he had so seriously resolved', he felt so attracted to her that 'he resolved to solicit her for a wife, and did, and obtained her'. Female litigants in general might be viewed with suspicion, but in Wotton's eyes Eleanora rose far enough above the throng to satisfy the criteria of the 'good' woman litigant.[52]

SATIRE AND DRAMA

Thomas Wotton was wary of female litigants in the 1560s. By the 1590s the numbers of women participating in central court actions had swelled sufficiently to prompt outbursts from Egerton and Benn, and also, it would appear, to offer inspiration to satirists. The character Nan in Robert Greene's *A Disputation Betweene a Hee Conny-Catcher and a Shee Conny Catcher*, published in 1592, argued that women made better pickpockets than men because they could pass 'under the couler of simplicitie to Westminster, with a paper in our hand, as if we were distressed women that had some supplication to put up to the judges, or some bill of information to deliver to our lawyers, when God

---

[50] Hawarde, *Les Reportes del Cases in Camera Stellata*, p. 275.
[51] Philip Stubbes, *A Cristal Glasse for Christian Women. Containing an Excellent Discourse of the Life and Death of Katherine Stubbes* (London, 1591).
[52] Izaak Walton, *The Lives of Dr. John Donne, Sir Henry Wotton, Mr. Richard Hooker, Mr. George Herbert, and Dr. Robert Sanderson* (London, 1825), pp. 95–6; I would like to thank Jason Scott-Warren for directing me to this reference.

wot, we shuffle in for a boung as well as the best of you all'.[53] In *Christs Teares Over Jerusalem*, an appeal to the decadent citizenry of London to mend their ways, published in 1593, Thomas Nashe described the excuses bawdy-house keepers gave out to explain the presence of strange women in their houses. Keepers introduced 'plain' women as their nieces, or a 'neare kinswoman'. Young gentlewomen became the daughters of fictitious knights, sent to the capital to be placed with a lady. But 'bee shee of middle yeeres, shee is a widdow that hath sutes in law here at the Tearme, and hath beene a long Counsaile table petitioner'.[54]

Playwrights were slower to incorporate the theme of women and litigation into their drama, but the results were longer lasting. Elizabethan plays are full of examples of women on trial, of female characters judged for crimes they did, or did not, commit, but few of them can be described as waging law. Some, like Alice Arden in *Arden of Faversham* (c.1591) are accused of criminal acts.[55] Most are accused, usually falsely, of sexual offences. In Nicholas Udall's *Ralph Roister Doister*, written a few years before Elizabeth came to the throne, the widow Christian is slandered, and her sexual honesty is confirmed by a trial (which takes place off stage).[56] In *The Commody of the Moste Vertuous and Godlye Susanna*, written and first performed in the 1560s and published in 1578, Thomas Garter reworked the biblical story of Chaste Susanna from the Apocryphal Daniel: 13. Two corrupt judges, Voluptas and Sensualitas, fail to seduce Susanna and then falsely accuse her of adultery with a stranger. Once in court she refuses to say anything, and in the absence of a defence the presiding judge sentences her to death. Having placed all of her trust in the Lord, the Lord duly saves her through the intervention of Daniel, posing as a child, who cross-examines the judges separately and exposes their false testimony.[57] Slandered or falsely accused female characters are common fare in Shakespeare, in both his Elizabethan and his Jacobean plays. Rosalind in *As You Like It* (c.1599), Juliet, Isabella, Marianna and Mistress Overdone in *Measure for Measure* (c.1603), Hermione in *The Winter's Tale* (c.1609) and Imogen in *Cymbeline* (c.1610) all

---

[53] In the same text a prostitute trying to steal from a Westminster Hall pickpocket arranged to be discovered in bed with him by friends. When asked by these accomplices who she was, she pretended 'shee was a poore Countrey mayde come up to the Tearme'; Robert Greene, *A Disputation, Betweene a Hee Conny-Catcher, and a Shee Conny-Catcher, Whether a Theefe or a Whoore, is Most Hurtfull in Cousonage, to the Common-Wealth*, (facsimile edn; Edinburgh, 1966), pp. 14–15, 22; and see Robert Greene, *The Second Part of Conny Catching* (London, 1592), p. 60.   [54] Thomas Nashe, *Christs Teares Over Jerusalem* (London, 1593), fol. 79ᵛ.

[55] See Frances Dolan, *Dangerous Familiars: Representations of Domestic Crime in England 1550–1700* (Ithaca and London, 1994), pp. 51–7.

[56] Christian's honour is restored in Act V between scenes iii and iv; Nicolas Udall, *Ralph Roister Doister* in William Tydeman, ed., *Four Latin Comedies* (Harmondsworth, 1984), p. 198; Lorna Hutson, *The Usurer's Daughter: Male Friendship and Fictions of Women in Sixteenth-Century England* (London and New York, 1994), pp. 189–90.

[57] Thomas Garter, *The Commody of the Moste Vertuous and Godlye Susanna* (London, 1578).

have false allegations made against them.[58] Hermia in *A Midsummer Night's Dream* (c.1595) is accused not only of adultery, but of high treason and attempted murder. Katherine of Aragon gives an eloquent speech in her own defence in *King Henry VIII* (1613) and then refuses to dignify her opponents' sham prosecution with her presence.[59] Shakespeare has some of his characters, for instance Hero in *Much Ado About Nothing* (1598), judged or accused within legal settings or else accused in explicitly legal terms, as in the case of Lear's mock trial of Goneril and Regan, while others, like Desdemona in *Othello* (c.1604), are put on trial without any recourse to law.[60]

It may be significant that depictions of slander and false accusation against women became prominent in dramatic works at a time when concerns about male and female sexual reputation were particularly prominent, when women were coming to dominate rising levels of defamation prosecutions in the church courts, and when the law of slander was in flux and undergoing rapid change.[61] However, the image of a woman on trial is one of the most persistent and enduring in literature – stretching from Homer to the Bible to the present day. Apparent parallels between patterns of litigation and depictions of women on trial may therefore be illusory, with these characters representing no more than variations on a timeless theme, a recurrent symptom of the centuries-old imbalance in power relations between men and women. Nevertheless, the sheer number of examples suggests that slander and female (and male) honour were sensitive subjects in this period which many Elizabethan and Jacobean playwrights felt drawn to explore.

In all of the examples listed here female characters find themselves put on trial. They are all accused, they are not themselves accusers, they are defendants in criminal or ecclesiastical actions rather than plaintiffs in civil cases. None of them, in other words, goes to law of her own volition. The one example in Shakespeare of a woman at law who is not herself on trial is Portia in *The Merchant of Venice* (1596). However, she plays a judge not a litigant, and she conducts her legal business in male disguise (a boy actor dressed as a woman dressed as a man). Furthermore, the character is not Shakespeare's creation, but originates in a fourteenth-century Italian *novella*, so the fantasy that he might

---

[58] Woodbridge, *Women and the English Renaissance*, p. 246; Joyce Sexton, *The Slandered Woman in Shakespeare*, English Literature Monograph Series, No. 12 (University of Victoria, 1978), pp. 11–12, 40.

[59] Campeius: The Queen is obstinate,
           Stubborn to justice, apt to accuse it, and
           Disdainful to be tried by't; 'tis not well.
           She's going away.
King Henry VIII, II.iv.122–4.

[60] *King Lear*, III.vi.20–80; I would like to thank Grace Ioppolo for this reference.

[61] See chapter 2 above; Daniel Kornstein, *Kill All the Lawyers? Shakespeare's Legal Appeal* (Princeton, New Jersey, 1994), pp. 165–9.

have modelled her on a prominent female litigant is, alas, difficult to sustain.[62] She remains a striking example of a woman exercising remarkable legal prowess and cunning in public, not all of it admirable, and literary critics argue still about how to interpret her legal role. Some see her as representing mercy, and therefore equity, in contrast to Shylock's insistence on the letter of the law. Or, in another formulation, Portia and Venice represent the justice of the New Testament and Shylock the justice of the Old Testament. Others, such as Alice Benston, have questioned this division – as she puts it: 'How is it that Portia, eloquent spokesman for mercy, is not given the role as dispenser of that heavenly virtue?' – and argued that Portia and Shylock are surprisingly similar in their commitment to the rule of law.[63] Whichever interpretation is favoured, it seems clear that Shakespeare intended Portia's association with the law to have symbolic as well as dramatic effect.

In Jacobean drama, female characters at the mercy of the law were joined for the first time by those who used the law, women who accused others not just answered accusations themselves. In short, Jacobean dramatists presented women not only as victims, but as customers, of the legal system. In doing so they developed a character type that was to reach its zenith in the Restoration, exemplified by the Widow Blackacre in Wycherley's Restoration comedy *The Plain Dealer* (1676), 'a petulant litigious Widow alwaies in Law'.[64] The plays of Francis Beaumont and John Fletcher (written together or alone) are full of scenes of women caught up in the law. In *The Woman-Hater* (1606) 'an old deaf countrey Gentlewoman' seeks aid in petitioning the Duke of Milan for justice.[65] In *The Nightwalker, or the Little Thief* (c.1611) a mother gets herself 'up to th' ears in Law' against the usurer Justice Algripe to recover her daughter's dowry. Various lawyers send her to and fro between each others' chambers to 'bounce her for more money', but 'she's the merriest thing among these Law-drivers' and spends whole half-days in their studies parrying their attempts to 'get her with *Magna Charta*'.[66] Jacintha in *The Spanish Curate* (1622) convinces a judge to confirm her illegitimate son rightful heir ahead of the boy's uncle.[67] In the tragicomedy *The Queen of Corinth* (c.1617) the Queen acts as judge in a double

---

[62] M.M. Mahood, ed., *The Merchant of Venice* (Cambridge, 1987), pp. 2–3.

[63] In Benston's reading of the play, the casket scene, Shylock's trial and the ring episode all deal with the law and with 'its complex relations to vice, virtue, and vicissitude', and it is Portia's attitude to the law and to the sanctity of contractual bonds that is central to each of these 'trials'; Alice Benston, 'Portia, the law, and the tripartite structure of *The Merchant of Venice*', *Shakespeare Quarterly*, 30 (1979), p. 369; see also Kornstein, *Kill all the Lawyers?*, ch. 4, especially pp. 66, 82–3.

[64] Arthur Friedman, ed., *The Plays of William Wycherley* (Oxford, 1979), p. 376; for depictions of widows in Elizabethan drama, see Linda Bensel-Meyers, '"A figure cut in alabaster": the paradoxical widow in Renaissance drama' (University of Oregon Ph.D., 1985).

[65] *The Woman Hater*, III., i, in *Fifty Comedies and Tragedies Written by Francis Beaumont and John Fletcher* (London, 1679), part 2, p. 481.

[66] *The Nightwalker, or the Little Thief*, IV.i, in *Fifty Comedies and Tragedies*, part 1, p. 220; Woodbridge, *Women and the English Renaissance*, p. 246.

[67] *The Spanish Curate*, III.iii, in *Fifty Comedies and Tragedies*, part 1, pp. 135–6.

rape case, and the two female victims debate before her like lawyers to determine the fate of their male assailant.[68] Violanta is sentenced to death under
statute by an Italian Duke in *Four Plays in One* (c.1613), and her life is saved
when Cornelia, the Duke's wife, intercedes to plead on her behalf.[69]

Other playwrights explored the theme of women at law, including John Ford,
author of *The Ladies Triall* (1638), Cyril Tourneur, author of *The Revenger's
Tragedy* (c.1606) and Thomas Middleton, co-author of *The Widow* (c.1616).[70]
However, the author who showed the most consistent interest in the character of
the female litigant was John Webster. As Carol Ann Blessing has pointed out,
Webster included a woman arguing or defending a cause in a legal setting (or
occasionally having a cause argued on her behalf) in virtually every play he
penned: Vittoria in *The White Devil* (c.1612), the Duchess in *The Duchess of
Malfi* (c.1614), Leonora in *The Devils Law-Case* (c.1617), Virginia in *Appius
and Virginia* (1624), and (assuming Webster had a hand in their writing) Urse in
A Cure for a Cuckold (c.1625), Mariana in *The Fair Maid of the Inn* (1626) and
Lady Jane Grey in *Sir Thomas Wyatt*.[71] In the tragi-comedy *The Devils Law-
Case* (c.1617), the widow Leonora sues her own son Romelio, attempting to
prove him illegitimate so that she can have him disinherited and make her
daughter heir in his place. The fact that she is willing to muddy her own reputation, in her endeavour to ruin his, helps to explain why Webster gave this play
the subtitle at the head of this chapter; *When Women goe to Law the Devill is
Full of Businesse*. Leonora's forceful and confident attempt to use the law for
her own ends disgusts the 'honest' lawyer Ariosto. He refuses to take her case,
asking the lawyer's clerk Sanitonella, are there not

> Oppressions of Widdowes or young Orphans,
> Wicked Diverses[Divorces], or your vicious cause
> Of *Plus quam satis* [more than enough] to content a woman,
> But you must find new stratagems, new pursuits
> Oh women, as the Ballet [Ballad] lives to tell you,
> What will you shortly come to?

[68] The brother of one of the women jests that 'Such pretty Lawyers, yet/ I never saw nor read of';
The Queen of Corinth, V.iv, in *Fifty Comedies and Tragedies*, vol. 2, pp. 21–2.

[69] *Four Plays in One*, 'The Triumph of Love', in *Fifty Comedies and Tragedies*, part 2, p. 538; this
list can be swelled by adding the characters of Maria in *The Coxcomb* (ca. 1607–10), Erota, a
woman condemned to death for ingratitude, in *The Laws of Candy* (1619–23) and Mariana in
The Fair Maid of the Inn [co-written with Ford, Massinger and Webster?](1626); it is likely that
Fletcher also had a hand in Thomas Middleton's and Ben Jonson's *The Widow* (ca. 1616) in
which the eponymous heroine Valeria uses legal means to free herself from a marriage contract
gained by trickery; Thomas Middleton, Ben Jonson and John Fletcher, *The Widow*, in W.R.
Chetwood, *Memoirs of the Life and Writings of Ben Jonson . . . to which are Added, Two
Comedies . . . The Widow, and Eastward Hoe* (Dublin, 1756).

[70] The authorship of *The Revenger's Tragedy* is debated, with some critics favouring Middleton as a
more likely author than Tourneur; A.R. Braunmuller and Michael Hattaway, eds. *Cambridge
Companion to English Renaissance Drama*, (Cambridge, 1970) pp. 329–30, 415.

[71] Carol Ann Blessing, 'Women and the law in the plays of John Webster' (University of California,
Riverside, Ph.D., 1991), p. 11.

The 'spruce' lawyer Contilupo, by contrast, is delighted to accept Leonora's action, and he provides a hint of what women will 'shortly come to', saying

> Tis a Case shall leave a President to all the world
> In our succeeding Annals and deserves
> Rather a spatious publike Theater,
> Then a pent Court for Aud[i]ence; it shall teach
> All Ladies the right path to rectifie their issue.[72]

Contilupo's sentiments resemble those expressed by opponents of women in real court actions. As will be seen in later chapters, litigants suggested to judges that allowing defiant women to triumph at law would create precedents and set examples that other women might emulate, although they did so with a sense of foreboding, rather than with Contilupo's glee.

Dramatic representations of women in court are notable not just because of their frequency, or for the appearance of female accusers alongside female accused, but because of the character of their roles. It is noticeable that playwrights who depicted women at law considered many of the same concerns about women, and the same paradoxes surrounding women's behaviour, that occupied the minds of commentators, judges and litigants. In particular, they focused on female modesty and female speech.[73] The issue of women speaking comes up time and again in these plays, whether playwrights depicted women who were passive victims or feisty protagonists, and whether they intended the effect to be comic, tragic, or ironic. At one extreme we have Garter's 'chaste Susanna', a woman who does not speak at all. She is fearful of ending her life 'in infamy', yet she says, 'Lorde I leave me to thy will, and I will say no more.'[74] Susanna's refusal to speak made her a model of feminine virtue in the eyes of conduct book writers such as Vives, who pointed out to his readers that 'Susan excused her selfe of the crime of adulterye with silence, not with words'. Yet as Heather Kerr has argued, the status of women who did not speak in court was ambiguous, for 'within one cultural framework, silence is a sign of feminine virtue, indeed of femininity itself, while from within the interpretative framework of the law silence is one of the more general signs that may be read as a token of possible guilt'.[75]

Those female characters who do speak in court often seek permission beforehand. Jacintha in *The Spanish Curate* asks: 'Grant to a much wrong'd Widow, or a Wife/ Your patience, with liberty to speak/ In her own Cause.'[76] In *The*

---

[72] Webster, *The Devils Law-Case*, sigs G3ᵛ–G4, H.
[73] This focus was not confined to women in court; Lisa Jardine, *Still Harping on Daughters: Women and Drama in the Age of Shakespeare*, 2nd edn (London, 1983), pp. 46–8.
[74] Vives, *Instruction of a Christen Woman*, fol. 123.
[75] Heather Kerr, 'Thomas Garter's Susanna: "pollicie" and "true report"', *Journal of the Australasian Universities and Literature Association*, 72 (1989), p. 197.
[76] *The Spanish Curate*, III.iii, in *Fifty Comedies and Tragedies*, part 1, pp. 135.

White Devil, the defiant 'courtesan' Vittoria makes clear the paradox of the position of the woman in court after one of the judges proclaims that 'she scandals our proceedings'. In response, she 'humbly' tells her audience that while she tenders her 'modesty and womanhood', her defence 'of force, like Perseus/ Must personate masculine virtue'. As a defenceless widow she should remain silent, but to answer the charges laid against her she must speak out like a man.[77] In *The Fair Maid of the Inn*, the Duke of Florence asks Mariana 'briefly' to

> Deliver those agrievances, which lately
> Your importunity possest our Counsel,
> Were fit for audience, wherein you petition'd,
> You might be heard without an Advocate,
> Which boon you find is granted.

Once more we have the importunate female petitioner, except that when she is granted a hearing Mariana opens her plea by expressing her disquiet at having to speak in the first place. She says 'Though divided/ I stand between the Laws of truth and modesty, /Yet let my griefs have vent.' Her miserable position as a widow leaves her with no alternative but to plead before the justices, 'Wherein', she says, 'if strict opinion cancel shame,/ My frailty is my plea.'[78]

Those women in plays who seem unmoved by the contradictory pressures facing women in court – the desire to be heard and the need to remain modest – risk condemnation. Various characters in *The Devil's Law-Case* express their horror at Leonora's willingness 'to publish her owne dishonour voluntarily' and at her unnatural use of such 'poysoned violence' to undo her son. Her confidant Winifred suggests she administer this 'poyson' privately, but Leonora will have none of it:

> Privacie? It shall be given him
> In open Court, Ile make him swallow it
> Before the Judges face

To underline her disregard for her own reputation she challenges that, 'if he be Master/ Of poore ten arpines of land fortie houres longer,/ Let the world repute

---

[77] John Webster, *The White Devil* (London, 1631), sig. E4; and see Bensel-Meyers, 'A "figure cut in alabaster"', pp. 194–5; Frederick Waage has suggested that Vittoria is making a plea for 'English' rather than 'Italian' justice, unsuccessfully attempting to prevent her arraignment being perverted into a trial; Frederick Waage, *The White Devil Discover'd: Backgrounds and Foregrounds to Webster's Tragedy* (New York, 1984), pp. 41ff; Kathryn Finin-Farber contends that Vittoria is 'working the crowd', both on and off stage; Kathryn Finin-Farber, '"Framing (the) woman": *The White Devil* and the deployment of law', *Renaissance Drama*, new series, 25 (1994), pp. 227–8.

[78] *The Fair Maid of the Inn*, III.i, in *Fifty Comedies and Tragedies*, part 2, p. 391; on the paradox of female characters speaking in court, see Dympna Callaghan, *Woman and Gender in Renaissance Tragedy: A Study of King Lear, Othello, The Duchess of Malfi and The White Devil* (London, 1989), pp. 75–7.

me an honest woman.'[79] Finally, in a similar display of comic irony, when in *Four Plays in One* Cornelia argues that Violanta should not be executed under statute, and the court officers (who fail to recognise that she is the Duke's wife) order their guards to attach, or arrest, her, she replies: 'You'd best/ Let them attach my tongue.'[80]

Women in plays, as in life, were able to go to law, but they had to overcome impediments to do so. Enjoying far less freedom than men in the same position, it is as if female litigants in plays stand illuminated under harsher light than their male counterparts, so that every action is more sharply defined, often to the point of exaggeration. Guiltless women such as 'chaste Susanna' seem more innocent than guiltless men, independent women more unseemly, vocal women more disruptive. Despite the adage that the goddess justice is blind, these theatrical courtrooms give the distinct impression that they are designed for men, arenas in which women ask permission to enter, apologise when they venture to speak, and where their words are rarely heeded or taken seriously.[81]

The appearance of so many female characters in legal situations is intriguing, but what is their significance? Linda Woodbridge has suggested that the plethora of women in court scenes in English drama may reflect interest in 'the sexual inequities of judicial proceedings'.[82] The widow in *Ralph Roister Doister*, for example, appeals to God, 'the deliverer of all innocentes' and says 'Thou didst helpe Susanna, wrongfully accused, And no lesse dost thou see, Lorde, how I am now abused.'[83] Certainly, placing women in the dock could produce good theatre and provide 'an opportunity for the embattled women's strength of character to shine forth'.[84] But if these explanations help to account for the appearance of so many innocent female defendants in plays, they do little to explain the emergence in Jacobean drama of strident and sometimes culpable female plaintiffs. Another possibility is that the creation of female characters who used the law may result from changes in genre. Most literary scholars agree that the nature and form of drama altered as the Elizabethan period gave way to the Jacobean, especially where female characters were concerned. Angela Ingram, for example, has argued that from around 1600 an increasingly sceptical view of morality led playwrights to depict more complex female characters than their predecessors, presenting women who were influenced more by their surroundings than by their innate morality. To put it crudely, while Elizabethan dramatists tended to depict female characters who were either unequivocally good or unequivocally bad, their early Jacobean suc-

---

[79] An arpent is an old French measure of land, roughly equivalent to an acre; Webster, *The Devil's Law-Case*, sig. G3.
[80] *Four Plays in One*, 'The Triumph of Love' in *Fifty Comedies and Tragedies*, part 2, p. 548.
[81] For further discussion of depictions of women in court in plays, see chapter 9 below.
[82] Woodbridge, *Women and the English Renaissance*, p. 247, and see pp. 38, 116, chs 10–12.
[83] Udall, *Ralph Roister Doister*, V.iii.1893–4, in William Tydeman, ed., *Four Latin Comedies* (Harmondsworth, 1984), p. 198.   [84] Woodbridge, *Women and the English Renaissance*, p. 247.

cessors devoted more time to exploring the ambiguous moral ground that lay in between, and therefore may have been more open to developing female characters who were active litigants.[85]

The complexities of such arguments about change are beyond the scope of this discussion. Playwrights explored the themes of women, law and litigation for an array of different reasons, symbolic, artistic and cultural, as well as for dramatic effect, and trying to determine their intentions and inspirations when they developed particular themes and characters can be a perilous undertaking.[86] As Woodbridge has shown in relation to Tudor and Stuart debates about the nature of woman, the rich seams of anti-female comment in these exchanges have led some historians to despair at the bitter misogyny of English society, while others have detected in the pro-female comment the origins of modern feminism. Both these approaches, Woodbridge warned, make the mistake of reading literature as history. In her view the exchanges represent a literary 'parlor game' rather than an earnest debate, for almost every participant adhered to specific rhetorical forms and some of them wrote on both sides of the debate.[87] The work of dramatists can be even harder to decipher, but the appearance of female litigants in plays at a time when more female litigants than ever before were appearing in court seems to be more than coincidental. Moreover, the manner in which playwrights explored the theme of women at law provides an interesting counterpoint against which to compare the words and sentiments found in court pleadings.

The existence of some kind of link, however complex, between life in the law courts and depictions of life on the stage is not confined to dramatic representations of women and justice. The drama of this age was inextricably infused with the law, with perhaps one third or more of Elizabethan and Jacobean plays including a trial, an arraignment or a law suit.[88] Dramatists depicted litigation not just because trials and court actions lent themselves to dramatic treatment,

---

[85] Angela Ingram, 'Changing attitudes to "bad" women in Elizabethan and Jacobean drama' (University of Cambridge Ph.D., 1977); Woodbridge, *Women and the English Renaissance*, pp. 249–50; Kathleen McLuskie, *Dekker and Heywood: Professional Dramatists* (London, 1994), pp. 2, 91, 95, 100, 106.

[86] Occasionally parallels between real and fictional characters can be suggested; see Sylvia Freedman, 'The White Devil and the fair woman with a black soul', in Clive Bloom, ed., *Jacobean Poetry and Prose: Rhetoric, Representation and the Popular Imagination* (Basingstoke, 1988); David Lindley, *The Trials of Frances Howard: Fact and Fiction at the Court of King James* (London and New York, 1993), pp. 78–9; Charles Sisson, '*Keep the Widow Waking*: a lost play by Dekker', *The Library*, 8 (1927–8), pp. 39–57, 233–59.

[87] These texts may have had a negative impact on attitudes to women, but Woodbridge argued that it is wrong to assume that authors subscribed to the beliefs they expressed, or that contemporary events inspired those beliefs; Woodbridge, *Women and the English Renaissance*, chs. 1–5; for a counter view, suggesting that the debate represented more than merely a rhetorical game, see Lyndan Warner, 'Printed ideas about "man" and "woman" in France, 1490–1610' (University of Cambridge Ph.D., 1995), ch. 4.

[88] Daniel Kornstein calculates that two thirds of Shakespeare's plays include trial scenes; Kornstein, *Kill All the Lawyers?*, p. xii.

but also because theatre audiences in London included large numbers of lawyers and students from the Inns of Court, where many plays were performed.[89] More than this, playwrights confronted themes of law and litigation because they had personal experience of them. Shakespeare's plays drip so heavy with references to 'remainders', 'reversions', 'leet courts', 'law days', 'distraint' and 'livery of seisin', as well as legal themes and dramatised trials, that some early twentieth century commentators presumed him to have been a lawyer's clerk.[90] Furthermore, it is difficult to bring to mind an Elizabethan, Jacobean or Caroline playwright or writer who did not possess a connection with the law or personal experience of the law courts. Some had legal training or were attached to Inns of Court. Francis Beaumont (who once described the Blackfriars playhouse as a court where 'a thousand men in judgement sit') was a member of the Inner Temple and his father was a judge in Common Pleas.[91] Thomas Lodge was a student at Lincoln's Inn, while John Marston, John Ford and Sir Thomas Overbury (as well as, almost certainly, John Webster) were members of the Middle Temple.[92]

Many more playwrights appeared on the other side of the law, as litigants in civil disputes or defendants in criminal proceedings. Shakespeare may not have been a law clerk, but he had extensive experience of litigation both as plaintiff and witness (he appeared in Requests as a deponent early in the seventeenth century), and his parents fought suits in Queen's Bench and Chancery in the 1580s and 1590s.[93] Webster involved himself in civil suits, as did Middleton,

[89] Philip Finkelpearl has described the members of the Inns of Court (including the Inns of Chancery) as 'the largest single group of literate and cultured men in London'; Philip Finkelpearl, *John Marston of the Middle Temple: an Elizabethan Dramatist in his Social Setting* (Cambridge, Mass., 1969), p. 5; in 1592, Thomas Nashe wrote; 'Men that are their owne masters (as Gentleman of the Court, the Innes of the Courte, and the number of Captaines and Souldiers about London) do wholly bestow themselves upon pleasure, and that pleasure they devide (howe vertuously it skils not) either into gameing, following of harlots, drinking, or seeinge a Playe'; as quoted in Andrew Gurr, *Playgoing in Shakespeare's London* (Cambridge, 1987), p. 54; and see pp. 5, 51, 67, 72, 76, 149.

[90] Shakespeare may have inserted lines taken from Plowden's report of a 1562 case, *Hales v. Petit*, into the gravediggers' scene in *Hamlet*, V.i; Kornstein, *Kill All the Lawyers?*, pp. 14–15; L.W. Abbott, *Law Reporting in England 1485–1585* (London, 1973), p. 226; and see W.M. Merchant, 'Lawyer and actor: process of law in Elizabethan drama', *English Studies Today*, 3rd series, 3 (1962), pp. 107–24; O.H. Phillips, *Shakespeare and the Lawyers* (London, 1972), ch. 12; Charles Ross, 'Shakespeare's *Merry Wives* and the law of fraudulent conveyance', *Renaissance Drama*, new series, 25 (1994), pp. 148–9.

[91] As quoted in Gurr, *Playgoing in Shakespeare's London*, p. 22; Lisa Hopkins, *John Ford's Political Theatre* (Manchester, 1994), p. 3; *Dictionary of National Biography* (*D.N.B.*), eds. Leslie Stephen and Sydney Lee (63 vols., London, 1885–1900), vol. 11, pp. 54–5.

[92] Clugstone, ed., *A Looking Glasse*, pp. 6, 10; Freedman, '*The White Devil* and the fair woman with the black soul', p. 152; for further examples, see Finkelpearl, *John Marston*, Appendix A, 'Some important figures at the Inns of Court (1590–1610)', pp. 261–4.

[93] Shakespeare's father supposedly appeared in court sixty seven times; Kornstein, *Kill All the Lawyers?*, pp. 15–20, 234; Mahood, ed., *The Merchant of Venice*, p. 16.

who perhaps was inspired by the litigiousness of his mother and stepfather.[94] Lodge, another active litigant, sued his own brother in a debt action.[95] Ford, Middleton, Dekker and Rowley were all sued for libel in Star Chamber after co-authoring *Keep the Widow Waking* (1624).[96] Ben Jonson was twice imprisoned for offending figures of authority with his plays, the second time after co-authoring *Eastward Ho* (1605) with George Chapman and John Marston, while Christopher Marlowe, who had to appear before the Privy Council, seemed to make a hobby out of being arrested.[97] And so the list goes on, such was the prevalence of the law and legal experience within the circles of London's play-wrights.[98]

This was an intensely legal age. Litigation touched the lives of a greater pro-portion of the population than ever before, whether as suitors, jurors, witnesses or deponents, and not just in London but elsewhere as well. And despite the best efforts of moralists it touched the lives of women as well as men, as the figures in the last chapter demonstrate. Elite women like Elizabeth Russell and Anne and Elizabeth Clifford not only funded suits and employed lawyers, they took an active interest in their legal affairs and gained considerable expertise in various fields of law, as had Margaret Paston before them.[99] Grace Mildmay was an experienced litigant, and it is clear from her autobiography that she had a precise understanding of women's property rights.[100] Joan and Maria Thynne, members of the Thynne family of Longleat, involved themselves in the legal affairs of their husbands while they were married (Joan not only advising her husband, but also chastising him for making incorrect decisions) and Joan became a keen litigant in her own right after her husband died. Women with knowledge of legal process also sought to intercede in Requests actions brought by others, by begging favours from the Masters. Lady Montague, the Countess of Derby, Anne Warwick, Lady Anne Glenham, Francis Hertford, Lady Elizabeth Lumley and Elisabeth Oxenford are just some of the women who wrote to Julius Caesar on behalf of litigants they wished to support.[101] Charlotte Merton has shown how the women of the Royal chamber during the

---

[94] David Frost, *The Selected Plays of Thomas Middleton* (Cambridge, 1978), pp. ix–x.
[95] Thomas Lodge and Robert Greene, *A Looking Glasse for London and England*, ed. Tetsumaro Hayashi, (Metuchen, New Jersey, 1970), pp. 17–18.
[96] Charles Sisson, *Lost Plays of Shakespeare's Age* (Cambridge, 1936), pp. 80–124.
[97] Chapman was also imprisoned, but Marston managed to evade capture; W.D. Kay, *Ben Jonson: A Literary Life* (Basingstoke and London, 1995), pp. 74–5; Rosalind Miles, *Ben Jonson: His Craft and Art* (London and New York, 1990), pp. 102–3; Clifford Leech, *Christopher Marlowe: Poet for the Stage* (New York, 1986), p. 6.
[98] For further examples, see Gerald Bentley, *The Profession of Dramatist in Shakespeare's Time 1590–1642* (Princeton, New Jersey, 1971), pp. 24, 68, 87.
[99] Stenton, *The English Woman in History*, p. 93.
[100] Linda Pollock, *With Faith and Physic: The Life of a Tudor Gentlewoman Lady Grace Mildmay 1552–1620* (London, 1993), pp. 14, 33.
[101] BL Additional MS 12,506, fols. 49, 81, 89, 173, 175, 186, 187, 197, 219, 269, 319, 331, 341.

reigns of Mary and Elizabeth were active in representing and advancing the claims of suitors, both legal and non-legal, exercising power and influence and displaying expert legal knowledge; enough for Anthony Standen to complain to Anthony Bacon in 1595 about 'this Ruffianery of causes I am daylie more and more acquainted with, and see the maner of dealinge, whiche growethe by the Quenes strayghtnes to gyve these women wherby they presume thus to grange and hucke cause'.[102]

It is striking how often the language of law found its way into letters, diaries, pamphlets, books and ballads as well as plays. Maria and Joan Thynne not only discussed legal matters in their correspondence, they peppered their writings on all manner of topics with legal language and metaphor. In a letter to Joan headed June 1602, Maria wrote, 'My good mother, having so good an advocate as your own son to plead for me, I think it needless at this present to trouble you with long petition for your favour.' In May of 1603 she asked Joan to judge her character as if she were in a criminal court: 'but because the best proof comes by trial, try me as you please, and if you find my words and actions differ, let me be punished'.[103] The author of *Jane Anger Her Protection for Women* hoped that the Gentlewomen of England 'will rather shew your selves defendantes of the defenders title, then complainantes of the plaintifes wrong'. Doubting judgment before trial, 'which were injurious to the Law', she craved pardon 'committing your protection, and my selfe, to the protection of your selves and the judgement of the cause to the censures of your just mindes'.[104]

Anger was entering the fray in the debate about women, and Woodbridge has shown how frequently the participants in this enterprise made reference to law, whether presenting their contributions as judicial orations modelled on Quintilian, or letting elements of judicial rhetoric enter into epideictic orations of praise and blame. Joseph Swetnam, one of the most infamous anti-women writers in the English version of the debate, titled his venomous attack *The Araignment of Lewd, Idle, Froward and Unconstant Women*. His opponents replied in kind, Esther Sowernam (a pun on 'Sweetnam'?) titling her response *The Arraignment of Swetnam the Woman Hater*, followed by the anonymously published *Swetnam the Woman-Hater Arraigned by Women* (1618), a play in which the main character is made to answer for his misogyny before a jury of women.[105] The preponderance of legal and judicial forms in this genre is

---

[102] Merton, 'The women who served Queen Mary and Queen Elizabeth', pp. 177, 181.

[103] Alison Wall, ed., *Two Elizabethan Women: Correspondence of Joan and Maria Thynne 1575–1611*, Wiltshire Record Society vol. 38 (Devizes, 1983), pp. 26, 31.

[104] Jane Anger, *Jane Anger Her Protection for Women. To Defend Them Against the Scandalous Reportes of a Late Surfeiting Lover* (London, 1589), preface to the Gentlewomen of England, title page verso.

[105] Woodbridge, *Women and the English Renaissance*, pp. 41, 95–6; as Kathryn Finin-Farber has reflected, 'The spectacles enacted on the early modern stage often reflect the highly litigious society from which they emerge'; Finin-Farber, 'Framing (the) woman', p. 219.

explained partly by the decision of many contributors to utilise judicial rhetoric, however, it seems likely that the popularity of legal language and legal arguments and settings also reflected the more general saturation of English Renaissance culture with litigation and law.[106]

The place allowed to women within legal settings was carefully circumscribed by rules and by the opinions of observers. Women could be litigants, but they could not be judges or jurors. And what is more important for this discussion, they could not be lawyers. The author of *The Mirror of Justices* made it clear that women could not plead cases at the bar. They could bring cases as plaintiffs, as long as they were not 'lepers, idiots . . . criminals, outlaws, exiles' or 'married women without their husbands', but 'no heretic, nor excommunicate, nor criminal, nor man of religion, nor woman' could plead on behalf of another before a judge.[107] The character Soranso in Whetstone's *Heptameron* reflects that 'although there hath bene women learned and experienced in Mecanicall craftes, yet to heare a woman plead at the barre, preache in a pulpit or to see her build a house is a wonder and no example in use'.[108]

The frequent shunning of female pleaders reflected not just women's exclusion from positions of authority, but the widespread distrust and dislike of women speaking in public. Thomas Nashe questioned the wisdom of allowing women to speak in court actions in his satirical tirade against womanhood, *The Anatomie of Absurditie*, when he asked: 'Did not Calphernias impudancie (who was so importunate and unreasonable in pleading her own cause) give occasion of a law to be made that never woman after shoulde openly plead her owne cause in courts of judgment [?]'[109] In *A Curtaine Lecture*, published in 1637, Thomas Heywood passed on the following observation about women:

> Of their wrangling and litigiousnesse Juvenal thus speaketh: Nulla ferè causa est in quam non fæmina luem &c.
> There is no cause in Court, nor act in State,
> From which a woman cannot ground debate.
> And to that purpose hee introduceth one Manilia, a bold fac[ed] Roman Matron, who being full of controversie and through her wrangling having many suits in agitation,

---

[106] Studies exploring the links and the crossover of ideas (in both directions) between law and literature are burgeoning; see, for example, the contributions to Frances Dolan, ed., 'Renaissance drama and the law'; *Renaissance Drama*, new series, 25 (1994); Lisa Jardine, *Reading Shakespeare Historically* (London and New York, 1996), especially chs. 1, 2; Kornstein, *Kill All the Lawyers?*, pp. 3–11, 239–45; Hutson, *The Usurer's Daughter*; Susan Heinzelman, 'Women's petty treason: feminism, narrative, and the law', *The Journal of Narrative Technique*, 20 (1990), pp. 89–106.   [107] Whittaker, ed., *The Mirror of Justices*, pp. 45, 47.

[108] As quoted in Woodbridge, *Women and the English Renaissance*, p. 115; compare the situation in Scotland, where women could act as procurators, and wives could argue cases without their husbands; Elizabeth Ewan, 'Scottish Portias: women in the courts in medieval Scottish towns', *Journal of the Canadian Historical Association*, new series, 3 (1992), pp. 35–9.

[109] Thomas Nashe, *The Anatomie of Absurditie* (London, 1589), in J.P. Collier, ed., *Illustrations of Old English Literature* (New York, 1866) (reprinted 1966), vol. 3, p. 16.

blusht not in open Court to bee her owne Advocate and plead her own causes in publike assemblies.[110]

This was the divide along which authorities and commentators emphatically drew the line marking the behaviour they deemed acceptable for women and behaviour they felt was unacceptable. The apparent paradoxes explored in this chapter caused difficulties for those judges, lawyers and moralists who were unsure how to accommodate and protect the 'poor honest widow' without giving free reign to the 'boisterous, unruly wife', but these difficulties partially dissolved as long as women followed the advice of conduct book writers and let qualified lawyers plead on their behalf. Women who did this protected their modesty by placing their trust in reliant males (although in comedies and satire, lawyers were often depicted as lecherous men intent on despoiling female virtue) and they maintained silence by having those males speak on their behalf.[111] It was only when women ignored this script and stepped out from behind their counsel to speak on their own behalf that the idealised picture was upset. For those women in effect 'pleaded their case at the bar'. They moved away from playing an acceptable role as female litigants dependent on male counsel, and towards assuming the unacceptable role of female lawyers dependent on no one and acting on an equal footing with men.[112]

The following chapters will show that in the day to day running of their lives many women ignored this script, just as they ignored much of the other unwieldy, paternal and patriarchal advice directed at them by moralists; they suffered wrongs like any other litigant and like other litigants they went to court to have those wrongs redressed. However, these chapters will also give an indication of the abiding strength of that script, and show how difficult it could be for individual women to overcome the array of social, cultural and economic, as well as legal, impediments which stood between them and justice. Impediments which most men simply did not have to face.

Having investigated women's legal opportunities, calculated rough estimates of how many women took up those opportunities and seen how observers regarded their passage through the courts, it is time to investigate women's experiences in Requests. To make sense of women's dealings with the court it is first necessary to gain an understanding of the court itself, its history, purposes,

---

[110] T[homas] H[eywood], *A Curtaine Lecture: As it is Read by a Countrey Farmers Wife to Her Good Man* (London, 1637); Patricia Parker, *Literary Fat Ladies; Rhetoric, Gender, Property* (London and New York, 1987), pp. 106–7.

[111] E.F.J. Tucker, *Intruder into Eden: Representations of the Common Lawyer in English Literature 1350–1750* (Columbia, South Carolina, 1984), pp. 90–1; and see Beaumont and Fletcher *The Woman Hater*, II.i, in *Fifty Comedies and Tragedies*, part 2, p. 474.

[112] In Thomas Elyot's *The Courtier*, the character Julian suggests that it does women well to 'have a tendernes, softe and milde, with a kinde of womanlie sweetnes in everye gesture . . . that in goyng, standinge and speakinge . . . may alwayes make her appeere a woman without anye likenes of man'; Woodbridge, *Women and the English Renaissance*, p. 55.

administration and procedures. And to extract information from the court's records it is first necessary to understand the purposes for which these records were produced, and the circumstances of their production. Therefore the following chapter takes as its themes not just women, but court records, court officials and the business and custom of Requests.

4

The Court of Requests

The Angel Raphael . . . was both a Physitian in restoring his sight, and a
sollicitour, or Maister of requests in preferring his suites, to the throne of
Almighty God
(A.G.), *The Widdowes Mite*
(London, 1619)[1]

The Court of Requests appears to have admitted a higher proportion of female
plaintiffs and defendants during the reign of Elizabeth than any other
Westminster court. This chapter examines the workings of the court to discover
why it was popular with women. It also considers the court's business and clientele to determine the kinds of women who went to law and the matters they litigated. And it provides necessary background for the more detailed
examinations of female litigation that follow.[2]

BACKGROUND AND HISTORY

The Court of Requests has received mixed attention from historians. Legal historians have devoted little time to the court, because of its modest stature, its
failure to survive beyond the first half of the seventeenth century, and the belief
that it operated in the shadow of Chancery and provided no innovation in the
fields of equity or law.[3] Social and economic historians have dipped into its
archive to investigate specific causes, but as L.M. Hill recently observed, the

---

[1] (A.G.), *The Widdowes Mite, Cast into the Treasure-House of the Prerogatives, and Prayses of
Our B. Lady, the Immaculate, and Most Glorious Virgin Mary, the Mother Of God* (London,
1619), p. 4.

[2] For a more detailed account of Requests and its jurisdiction, see Tim Stretton; 'Women and litigation in the Elizabethan Court of Requests' (University of Cambridge Ph.D., 1993), pp. 67–123.

[3] Charles Gray, for example, suspected that Requests was 'probably ancillary to the Chancery and
of little importance for the fundamental legal change'; Charles Gray, *Copyhold, Equity and the
Common Law* (Cambridge, Mass., 1963), p. 3; John Baker has said of the demise of the court,
'Since it had developed no distinct equity jurisdiction of its own, nothing substantial was lost';
Baker, *An Introduction to English Legal History*, p. 139.

court and its Masters have 'been in a historiographic backwater since the six-teenth century', despite the thousands of case files in its archives that document the legal battles of a broad cross-section of the population.[4] A comprehensive history of the court has yet to be published, nevertheless enough information exists in print and in unpublished dissertations to ground a study of the role women played as plaintiffs, defendants and witnesses.[5]

The history of Requests, by its very nature, is uncertain. Neither crown nor parliament ever formally established the court; instead it simply evolved, growing out of the willingness of English monarchs to entertain, in person or by proxy, the complaints of poor subjects. What began as a series of *ad hoc* committees made up of councillors assigned to deal with 'requests' from sub-jects for justice, over time developed into a recognisable court dispensing equi-table justice to the poor (and the not so poor). The early Masters travelled wherever the monarch travelled, but some time in the reign of Henry VIII the court took up permanent residence in Westminster.[6] By the start of Elizabeth's reign Requests was firmly established as a central conciliar court headed by two Masters, one civil lawyer and one common lawyer, the two men alternating between hearing causes and personally attending the Queen to receive petitions from subjects.[7]

The character of the court can be discerned from the names by which it was known. Statute writers referred to it as 'the Court of Whitehall', indicating its physical position within the White Hall beside the Palace of Westminster.[8] The Masters spoke of 'the Counsell', or 'the Counsell in this court', an acknowledgement of the court's links with the Privy Council. Requests, like Star Chamber, began life as a judicial arm of the King's Council, but by

---

[4] Hill, *Bench and Bureaucracy*, p. 71.

[5] Apart from works cited in footnotes, see J.H. Baker and D.E.C. Yale, *A Centenary Guide to the Publications of the Selden Society* (London, 1987), pp. 72–4; A.K.R. Kiralfy, ed., *Potter's Historical Introduction to English Law and its Institutions*, 4th edn (London, 1958), pp. 168–70.

[6] Masters and the clerk of the court continued to follow the royal court dispensing justice and issuing writs, but hearings were held in the White Hall; on the origins and early history of Requests see D.A. Knox, 'The Court of Requests in the reign of Edward VI, 1547–1553' (University of Cambridge Ph.D., 1974), chs. 1, 2; A.F. Pollard, 'The growth of the Court of Requests', *English Historical Review*, 56 (1941), pp. 300–3; G.R. Elton, *The Tudor Constitution: Documents and Commentary*, 2nd edn (Cambridge, 1982), p. 187; J.R. Tanner, ed., *Tudor Constitutional Documents A.D. 1485–1603 with an Historical Commentary* (Cambridge, 1951), p. 229; see also, J.A. Guy, *The Court of Star Chamber and its Records to the Reign of Elizabeth I*, PRO Handbook No. 21 (London, 1985), p. 6.

[7] Leadam, *Select Cases*, pp. xii–xiii; as business increased, Elizabeth appointed 'Masters extraordi-nary' to assist the existing 'Masters ordinary', and the number of civilians and common lawyers in charge fluctuated between two and four. The new Masters received no pay, merely the expecta-tion that they would eventually succeed to an ordinary Mastership, which paid £100 per annum; W.B.J. Allsebrook, 'The Court of Requests in the reign of Elizabeth' (University of London M.A., 1936), p. 10.

[8] For evidence about the location of Requests, see H.E. Bell, *An Introduction to the History and Records of the Court of Wards and Liveries* (Cambridge, 1953), p. 167.

Elizabeth's reign connection with the Privy Council was more theoretical than actual.[9] To litigants and commentators it was the Court of Requests, the 'Poor Man's court' or the 'Court of Conscience', a forum where officials might be expected to consider the merits of plaintiffs' claims regardless of their means, and to favour justice ahead of procedural rigour.

Operating as a 'poor man's Chancery' the popularity of Requests increased dramatically during Elizabeth's reign, and with success came controversy. During the last decades of the sixteenth century, common lawyers and judges attacked the authority of the court, questioning the Masters' ability to issue injunctions 'staying' or delaying actions in other courts and to delegate decision-making powers to local commissions. In a string of actions, beginning in earnest in 1590 with *Locke* v. *Parsons*, common lawyers convinced judges in Common Pleas and Queen's Bench to issue prohibitions against the court, curbing the Masters' powers to make orders and decrees.[10] The decision in the Common Pleas case *Stepneth* v. *Floud* in 1598 went further, calling into doubt the very legitimacy of the court. Stepneth was a sheriff the Masters sent to arrest a recalcitrant defendant named Floud. He managed to persuade Floud to sign a bond ensuring his attendance in court, and when Floud defaulted he sought to recover the penalty on this bond at common law. However, the presiding judges in Common Pleas declared the Masters' writ of attachment invalid, saying that Requests 'was no court that had power of judicature, but all the proceedings thereupon were *coram non judice*, and the arrest of Flood was false imprisonment'. Anticipating Edward Coke's argument that Requests 'had neither act of parliament, nor prescription time out of minde of man to establish it', the Common Pleas judges in this case reasoned that the Masters had no authority to issue process and therefore the bond was unenforceable.[11] Women's rights were at the centre of this case, and it is discussed in further detail in chapter 6 below.

---

[9] The Lord Keeper of the Privy Seal was the *ex officio* head of the court (and all process was issued under the Privy Seal) but he did not sit in the court during Elizabeth's reign (although he appears to have done so during the reign of Charles I); PRO Req 1/19, p. 342; C.G. Bayne, *Select Cases in the Council of Henry VII*, Selden Society vol. 75 (London, 1958), p. xxxii; *Cal. S.P. Dom. Edward VI 1547–1553*, revised edn, ed. C.S. Knighton (London, 1992), item 812, pp. 290–1; G.R. Elton, *The Tudor Revolution in Government: Administrative Changes in the Reign of Henry VIII* (Cambridge, 1969), p. 134; PRO Req 1/34, p. 76.

[10] L.M. Hill, *The Ancient State Authoritie, and Proceedings of the Court of Requests by Julius Caesar* (Cambridge, 1975), pp. ix–xi; for an example of unease earlier than 1590, see J.H. Baker, ed., *Reports from the Lost Notebooks of Sir James Dyer*, Selden Society vol. 109 (London, 1993), pp. lxxx–lxxxi; vol. 110 (London, 1994), pp. 312–13.

[11] Edward Coke, *The Fourth Part of the Institutes of the Laws of England* (London, 1797), pp. 96–7; George Croke, *The First Part of the Reports of Sir George Croke*, Harbottle Grimstone trans., (London, 1661), pp. 646–7; Hill, *Bench and Bureaucracy*, pp. 45–6, 73ff; Hill, *The Ancient State*, pp. ix–xxi; Allsebrook, 'Requests', pp. 150–61; attacks like these continued, inside and outside the courtroom, as Requests became embroiled in the wider crisis over the royal prerogative, which culminated in James I's famous pronouncement in 1611 in favour of Chancery; for accounts of the controversy, see Brian Levack, *The Civil Lawyers in England 1603–1641: A Political Study* (Oxford, 1973), pp. 72–85; Jones, *Chancery*, pp. 490–4.

The decision in *Stepneth* v. *Floud* led one of the Masters, Dr Julius Caesar, to publish a defence, *The Ancient State, Authoritie, and Proceedings of the Court of Requests*, in which he sought to establish, by weight of example, the court's legitimacy as an independent judicial entity.[12] As a result of rulings like those in *Stepneth* v. *Floud* and *Locke* v. *Parsons*, Caesar lamented, Requests had come to be considered 'a generall and publique disgrace amongst the vulgar sort', and the court's orders 'scorned & publiquely slandered'.[13] Another commentator reflected how, 'the great and maine blemish of this Courte is the frequencie of Prohibitions which are graunted against the orders and Decrees of this Court'.[14] Despite the challenge of prohibitions the court soldiered on (its popularity actually increasing under James I) hearing actions brought by wronged women and men for at least another forty years. It survived the 1640 statute that sought to abolish Star Chamber and other 'misuses' of the royal prerogative, but became hamstrung in 1642 when the Privy Seal on which it depended for the effective issuing of process moved to Oxford, and sometime in 1643 it simply ceased to exist.[15]

VOLUME OF LITIGATION

The popularity of Requests, and the effect prohibitions and other outside forces had on its fortunes, can be observed in the fluctuating levels of business the court processed. W.B.J. Allsebrook demonstrated the swelling of Requests litigation when he revealed that 72 cases survive from the fourth year of the reign, rising to 264 for the forty fifth year.[16] However, his findings underestimate the scale of Requests business and can create a false impression of an even increase over time. Looking at the archive as a whole, just over 20,500 piece numbers or case files survive in the 174 bundles identified as coming from Elizabeth's reign in the class PRO Req 2.[17] The documents from a single case can be spread between more than one file, but these 20,500 piece numbers may

---

[12] Caesar based his defence on the association of Requests with the Privy Council and therefore on its existence from time immemorial; see Hill, *The Ancient State*, pp. ix–xxi.

[13] BL Additional MS 25,248, fols 57ᵛ–58; see also Leadam, *Select Cases*, p. xliii.

[14] C.U.L. Gg.2.31, fol. 27; and see, H.S. Scott, *The Journal of Sir Roger Wilbraham*, Camden Miscellany vol. 10 (London, 1902), p. 95.

[15] See 16 Charles I cap. 10, *Statutes of the Realm*, vol. 5, pp. 110–12; Knox, 'Requests', pp. 6–9; the office of Master of Requests resurfaced throughout the century, and the eighteenth century saw local courts of requests established in regional centres, but the court itself was never re-established; Allsebrook, 'Requests', p. 8.   [16] Allsebrook, 'Requests', p. 187.

[17] The Requests holdings in the PRO are divided into four classes; Req 1, which includes manuscript books; Req 2, the main body of proceedings; Req 3, uncalendared and unidentified loose documents; and Req 4, 'documents of interest to Shakespearean scholars'; 20,529 piece numbers for Elizabeth's reign from the class Req 2 are listed in the published calendar, *Public Record Office Lists and Indexes*, no. 21, 'List of proceedings in the Court of Requests preserved in the Public Record Office' (New York, 1963) (discounting bundles 1–25) and the unpublished manuscript calendars held in the PRO itself (shelf mark 9, vols. 93–99).

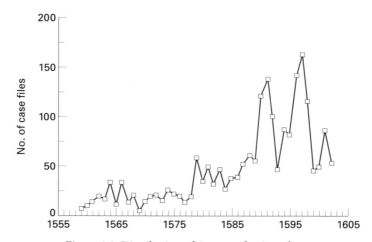

Figure 4.1 Distribution of Requests business by year
Source: PRO 9, vol. 93 (Requests proceedings) piece numbers PRO Req 2/157/1–Req
2/167/37 (excluding entries without dates and incomplete entries: PRO Req
2/157/429–467, Req 2/159/159–175 and Req 2/160/77). The sample represents about 10
per cent of the class PRO Req 2.

represent upwards of 16,500 separate actions initiated over this forty five year period, or an average of about 370 a year.[18] Plotting a sample of 2,000 calendar entries of case files on to a graph according to their year of commencement, reveals that the forty fifth year of Elizabeth's reign was by no means the busiest (see figure 4.1).[19]

Two thousand case files represent a relatively small sample, spread as they are over nearly half a century, and some of the peaks and troughs in this graph may owe more to statistical aberration than to actual shifts in patterns of litigation. However, the shape of the graph is broadly consistent with what we already know about the court's history. The steep rise in business it indicates after 1589 may have resulted from an order which Lord Chancellor Hatton made in Chancery the year before, as part of his overhaul of procedures for dealing with admissions *in forma pauperis*. On 30 November 1588 he directed that in future Chancery plaintiffs worth less than £5 in goods or 40s. per annum in income

[18] Of the 480 case files from Somerset listed in modern calendars, 340 contain original bills of complaint (not paper copies), suggesting that the ratio of case files to separate suits was 81 per cent; and 81 per cent of 20,529 is 16,628; D.A. Knox identified 677 suits among 729 surviving files belonging to the reign of Edward VI, so the real ratio may be nearer 93 per cent (representing 19,063 suits, or an average of 424 per annum); these figures, it should be emphasised, take no account of the store of documents in the uncalendared class PRO Req 3, or of the proportion of the archive which has been lost; Knox, 'Requests', pp. 63–4.

[19] For this graph to be accurate it is necessary to assume (as Knox assumed) that the loss of documents has been random; Knox, 'Requests', p. 67.

should take their cases to Requests, 'where in trothe they are most aptleye to be relieved'.[20] The equally sudden drops in business between 1591 and 1593 and again between 1598 and 1600, coincide with the years of fiercest competition from common lawyers, and almost certainly represent a loss of faith in the court in light of common law prohibitions of the kind already described.[21] The general trend, however, points to a steady increase in the popularity of the court among its litigants, an upward trend which continued into the seventeenth century.[22]

<h2 style="text-align:center">JURISDICTION</h2>

Most sixteenth century courts had jurisdiction over specified classes of actions or a code of law. They can be distinguished as common law, equity (preroga-tive), ecclesiastical or customary courts, and their business (whether it was civil or criminal) understood accordingly. The jurisdiction of Requests, by contrast, was defined largely in terms of classes of plaintiffs. As Julius Caesar reflected:

> The persons plaintiffs and Defendants . . . were allwayes either privileged as officers of the Court, or their servants or as the King's servants, or necessarie attendants on them; or else where the Plaintiffs povertie or mean estate was not matchable with the wealth or greatness of the Defendant; or wheare the cause meerely conteined matter of equity and had no proper remedy at the Common law.[23]

Requests was a court of equity, in the sense that it operated according to equi-table principles. Edward Coke described three matters that courts of conscience or equity should deal with; frauds and deceits for which there was no remedy at common law, breaches of trust or confidence, and accidents (if, for example, someone was meant to repay a debt by a certain day, but was robbed on the way to pay it, then they should be given relief from the penalty for non-payment).[24] The Masters did all of these things, but they did not restrict themselves to

---

[20] G.W. Sanders, *Orders of the High Court of Chancery* (London, 1845), vol. 1, part i, p. 61; evi-dence that this policy was carried out can be found in C.U.L. Gg.2.31, fol. 373; Francis Bacon made a more formal order in 1619, directing plaintiffs seeking entry into Chancery *in forma pau-peris* to take their plaints instead to Requests, or to the provincial Councils, or to have them settled by local gentlemen, 'except it be in some special cases of commiseration or potency of the adverse party'; Jones, *Chancery*, pp. 324–5, n. 2.

[21] It will be interesting to compare levels of business in other courts at this time, to see the extent to which these harvest failures and other economic upheavals of this decade affected legal activity.

[22] W.R. Prest counted 183 cases in entry books for Easter term 1616, and 641 cases for Easter term 1638, suggesting that this trend continued into the seventeenth century; W.R. Prest, *The Rise of the Barristers: A Social History of the English Bar 1590–1640* (Oxford, 1986), table 3.1, p. 60, and see pp. 64, 79; 199 bundles of case files survive in the class PRO Req 2 for the reigns of Henry VII, Henry VIII, Edward VI, Philip and Mary and Elizabeth I, yet 622 bundles survive for the reigns of James I and Charles I.   [23] BL Lansdowne MS 125, fol. 12; Knox, 'Requests', p. 346.

[24] Coke, *The Fourth Part of the Institutes*, p. 84; to give an example from Requests, when a man died unaware that his wife was pregnant, and his executor refused to make provision for the newborn child, the Masters ordered this man to supply a fourth part of the deceased's goods and chattels, as if the child had been alive at the time of his father's death; *John & Elizabeth Blake v. Richard Sandell et al.*, PRO Req 1/20, pp. 779–80.

matters of equity. They dealt with almost any matter if litigants could show themselves unable to pursue their claims in local or common law courts, due to their small means or the power and influence of their opponents.[25] From its inception the crown intended Requests to be an organ of simple and efficient justice, free from the procedural constraints and complexities that characterised the common law, and while its chief aim was to hear 'all poore mens sutes', it made a convenient clearing house for the resolution of any number of urgent, trivial or special cases that came to royal attention.[26] The theoretical breadth of the jurisdiction was wide, with Caesar noting that causes in Requests 'are of all sorts; as Maritime, Ecclesiasticall, Temporall . . . ', but it had limits. The Masters regularly dismissed actions because they were determinable at the common law, and because 'the sayd parties be men of wealth and abilitie to sue & prosecute the same there', or because parties lived within the boundaries of other equity jurisdictions, such as the Council in the North, the Durham Chancery, the Chester Exchequer, or the tribunals within the franchise and liberties of the Cinque ports.[27] They were also quick to dismiss cases that parties were fighting simultaneously in other courts, or that other courts had already decided, if they felt these cases contained no new matter.[28]

The geographical area the court served was as broad as its jurisdiction. Requests was a national court, with a brief to cater for '*all* poore mens suits' regardless of origin, and litigants from every region of England and Wales found their way into the White Hall.[29] A disproportionate amount of the court's business originated in London or the south east of England, with one fifth of all actions coming from London and Middlesex alone, and a further two fifths (38 per cent) from the counties of the Norfolk and Home assize circuits (see Map 4.1).[30] In part this bias towards the south east reflects no more than the concentration of population and wealth in this area; five of the six wealthiest counties in England, London and Middlesex, Norfolk, Essex, Suffolk and Kent,

---

[25] Knox, 'Requests', p. 306.

[26] The quote comes from Smith, *The Common-Wealth of England*, p. 129; although Smith himself made no mention of Requests in his original 1583 edition; Leadam, *Select Cases*, p. xv, n. 4.

[27] Caesar, *Ancient State*, p. 111; the Masters referred cases to ecclesiastical courts; PRO Req 1/17, p. 370; to the Marches of Wales; *Margaret Leicester* v. *Peter Leicester*, PRO Req 1/11, p. 239; to Star Chamber; *Eleanor Palmer* v. *Richard Jagger et al.*, PRO Req 2/56/62, Dem (and see PRO C3/247/62); to Chancery, because the defendant claimed privilege; *John Shawe* v. *John Wepey*, PRO Req 1/21, p. 63; to Durham; *Ellionor Madocks* v. *David Edowe*, PRO Req 1/17, p. 278; to Chester; *John Hallidey* v. *Thomas Gibson et al.*, PRO Req 1/17, p. 129; *Julyan Middleton & Agnes Bailiffe* v. *Edward Middleton*, PRO Req 1/13, fol. 29ᵛ; *Isabell Moreton* v. *George Moreton*, PRO Req 1/20, p. 794; the Masters declined to refer cases if plaintiffs requested remedies that these courts could not provide, such as injunctions staying actions at common law; see *Thomas Killingbeck* v. *Margaret Ellwick*, PRO Req 1/17, pp. 432–3.

[28] See, for example, *Elinor Norton* v. *William Henborowe et al.*, PRO Req 1/21, p. 92.

[29] In a sample of 2,000 case file entries in modern calendars which describe the origins of litigants, only the Isle of Man (which had its own jurisdiction) is not represented.

[30] Norfolk, Suffolk, Cambridgeshire, Huntingdonshire, Bedfordshire, Hertfordshire, Essex, Kent, Sussex and Surrey.

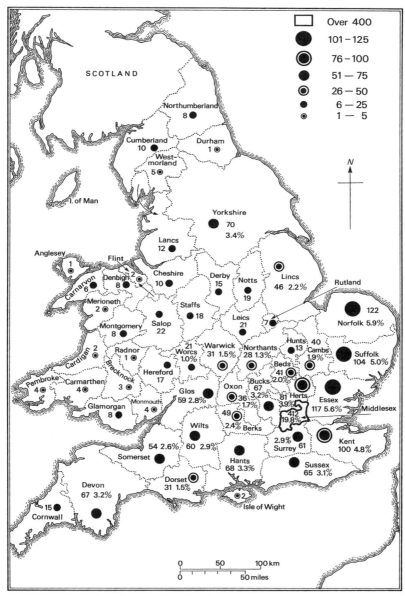

SCOTLAND

Northumberland
8

Cumberland
10

Durham
1

West-
morland
5

I. of Man

N

Yorkshire
70
3.4%

Anglesey
1

Flint

Lancs
12

Carnarvon
6

Denbigh 2
8

Cheshire
10

Derby
15

Notts
19

Lincs
46 2.2%

Rutland

Merioneth
2

Staffs
18

Leics
21

7

122

Norfolk 5.9%

Montgomery
8

Salop
22

Radnor
1

Cardigan 2

Worcs
1.0%
21

Warwick
31 1.5%

Northants
28 1.3%

Hunts 40
13

Cambs
1.9%

Suffolk
104 5.0%

Pembroke
4

Brecknock

Carmarthen
4

Hereford
17

Beds
41
2.0%

Glamorgan
8

Monmouth
4

Glos
59 2.8%

Oxon
67

Bucks
36 3.2%
1.7%

Herts
81
3.9%

41
19.8%

Essex
117 5.6%

Middlesex

Wilts

49
2.4% Berks

2.9%
Surrey 61

Kent
100 4.8%

54 2.6%

60 2.9%

Somerset

Hants
68 3.3%

Sussex
65 3.1%

Devon
67 3.2%

Dorset
31 1.5%

2

Isle of Wight

15

Cornwall

Over 400
101 – 125
76 – 100
51 — 75
26 — 50
6 — 25
1 — 5

0   50   100 km
0   50 miles

Map 4.1 Geographical distribution of Requests actions
Source: Two thousand consecutive entries in MS calendar PRO 9, vol. 93 (Requests
proceedings) piece nos. Req 2/257/1–Req 2/167/37 (excluding incomplete entries Req
2/157/429–467, Req 2/159/159–175, Req 2/160/77); because single actions could involve
litigants from more than one county, the sum of county totals exceeds 2,000.

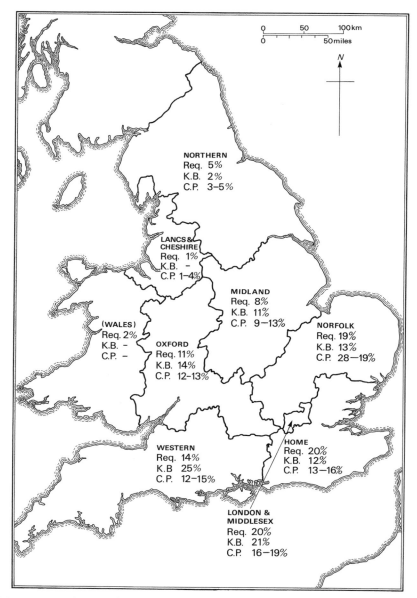

Map 4.2 Distribution of Requests, King's Bench and Common Pleas actions by assize circuit.
Source: For Requests, see Map 4.1; for King's Bench (1606) and Common Pleas (1560 and 1606) see Brooks *Pettyfoggers*, table 4.4, p. 64; the Requests figures are an average for Elizabeth I's reign.

were also the five largest producers of Requests' business.[31] However, population and wealth were not the only factors responsible for concentrating the
catchment area of Requests around London. Distance from the capital was
clearly a critical factor in determining whether a plaintiff thought it worth his
or her while to sue in Requests, for incidental expenses such as travel,
accommodation, and messengers' fees could be substantial, and most of these
increased with each mile travelled from the capital.[32] Given the limited resources
of most Requests litigants, and the poverty of many of their claims, it is hardly
surprising that the majority of Requests custom came from counties in the
vicinity of London.[33] Comparing the catchment area of Requests with the
catchment areas of Common Pleas and King's Bench (using C.W. Brooks'
calculations for the years 1560 and 1606) confirms the disproportionate
concentration of Requests business around London, although the similarities
between these three courts were more pronounced than the differences (Map
4.2).[34] Requests, then, was a national court with an equitable jurisdiction, established to process cases brought by the poor and by servants of the court and the
crown.

PROCEDURE

Procedure in Requests was all but indistinguishable from procedure in
Chancery, except that plaintiffs addressed their pleas to the Queen, not to the
Chancellor, and the Masters issued process under the Privy Seal not the Great
Seal.[35] Process began with a plea for assistance which plaintiffs made either in
person, or more usually in a written bill of complaint drawn up by a lawyer or
an experienced scrivener.[36] Most bills began with a description of the complainants' circumstances, including their names, occupations or status and
place of residence, and went on to describe the nature of their complaints and
to establish their eligibility to sue in Requests, providing reasons why they could
not pursue their causes at common law. After describing the nature of the com-

---

[31] Compare, for example, John Sheail's maps of the distribution of wealth and population throughout England based on the lay subsidy returns of 1524 and 1525; John Sheail, 'The distribution of
taxable population and wealth in England during the early sixteenth century', *Transactions of
the Institute of British Geographers*, 55 (1972), pp. 111–26.

[32] It is significant that the rich and populous county of Devon was only the ninth largest supplier of
Requests business.

[33] Districts with their own equitable jurisdictions, like Durham, Lancashire, Cheshire and the
Marches of Wales were also poorly represented; for the contribution of Durham to Chancery
business see Knight, 'Litigants and litigation, p. 108.   [34] Brooks, *Pettyfoggers*, table 4.4, p. 64.

[35] 'For so is the form of the Chancery and this courte', explained the defending counsel on a point
of procedure in a case from 1589; *John Walgrave v. Anne Nash*, PRO Req 2/291/5, A; Thomas
Powell observed of the two courts that 'the forme of their proceeding is generally alike'; Thomas
Powell, *The Attourneys Academy or, the Manner and Forme of Proceeding Upon any Suite*
(London, 1623), p. 87.

[36] For an example of pleas made to Elizabeth in person, see Leadam, *Select Cases*, p. xix, n. 6.

plaint, they ended with a request that process be issued (usually a writ to summon the defendant to make answer, or a suitable injunction) and a promise that the complainant would daily pray for the continued health of her Majesty. Qualified legal counsel signed the bill (whether or not they had been its author) confirming that the matter contained was fit to be heard in Requests, then one of the court's three attorneys 'exhibited' or entered it, after which the Masters issued process.[37] Once process was served, defendants answered the bill of complaint, or if they felt they had good reason not to, they demurred.[38] The court expected defendants to attend in person to make their answer, but if they were unable to attend, because they were old, sick or pregnant, or because they were busy with the Queen's business, the Masters might permit them to make answer on oath before a local justice of the peace, under a commission of *dedimus potestatem*.[39]

Defendants' answers entered the court in the same way as bills of complaint, engrossed on parchment and signed at the bottom by counsel. Most began with a token demurrer, usually an assertion that the allegations, if true, were determinable at the common law, followed by a full response to each of the plaintiffs' claims, and ending with an expression of the defendants' willingness to appear in person before the Masters to swear the truth of their answer. The ability to have defendants answer on oath was a major attraction of process in Requests. This option did not exist at common law, and common lawyers regularly criticised the use of oaths in prerogative and spiritual courts for its potential to contradict the common law rule against self-incrimination.[40] However litigants who could not muster the evidence necessary to mount an action at the common law welcomed the opportunity to have their opponents give sworn answers in a court of equity.[41] The Somerset widow Agnes Nowell felt that a public oath would reveal her right to justice because her opponent was 'a man reputed honest'.[42] Jane Lambert was reputed anything but honest, but Thomas Reader nevertheless believed that in Requests the truth 'by the oath of herself is lykely to bee in some parte syfted furth'.[43]

---

[37] C.U.L. Gg.2.31, fol. 25; for a brief period between 1598 and 1599 a fourth attorney, Damien Peck, managed to have himself admitted to practice; see PRO Req 1/19, p. 707; Allsebrook, 'Requests', pp. 48–9; most bills were endorsed on the reverse with a direction for process under the Privy Seal, written in Latin and signed by the attending Master, the majority calling for the defendant or defendants to appear and give answer by a certain date, on pain of a money fine.

[38] A defendant might demur because the plaintiff was *feme covert* or excommunicated and therefore lacked standing, or if they believed Requests lacked jurisdiction.

[39] Older women ranked highly among defendants excused appearance; see, for example, *Roger Jones* v. *Jone Jones*, PRO Req 1/39, 2 May; *Robert Garth* v. *Benjamin Titchborne & Elizabeth Garth*, PRO Req 1/21, p. 323.   [40] Holdsworth, *History of English Law*, vol. 1, pp. 609–10.

[41] In the absence of other evidence, personal testimony on oath alone could persuade the Masters to reach a decision; *Robert Gomersall* v. *Elizabeth Watkinson*, PRO Req 1/19, p. 638; Marcus Knight found the same to be true in the Durham Chancery; Knight, 'Litigants and litigation', p. 156.   [42] *Agnes Nowell* v. *Thomas Hall*, PRO Req 2/166/134, B.

[43] *Thomas Reader* v. *Jane Lambert*, PRO Req 2/262/20, B.

After a defendant had filed an answer, it was open to the complainant to respond with a replication, which the defendant in turn could answer with a rejoinder. Pleading complete, the next stage in the process was the gathering of proofs. It was at this point that litigants could seek to recover documents no longer in their possession, or to get copies of documents they had a right to see. Female litigants made frequent use of this facility, to recover proofs relating to interests that should have come to them when they were under age, or documents withheld from them by trustees or the administrators or executors of their late husbands' estates. They did so either to bolster their Requests suits, or to equip themselves to mount actions at common law.

As well as written proofs, parties could gather the testimony of witnesses by preparing interrogatories that selected deponents answered on oath.[44] The contents of interrogatories remained secret until the day of interview, but parties had to inform each other of the names and addresses of the witnesses they planned to call, and this might provide opponents with some idea of the matters that would be in issue. The court's recorder took depositions in Westminster, while outside London the Masters appointed a commission of justices or other senior inhabitants to interview witnesses and record their testimony.[45]

DETERMINATION AND REMEDIES

After parties had gathered witness depositions and other proofs, such as deeds, promissory notes, account books, copies of court rolls or bills of exchange, arrangements could be made for publication (when these documents and depositions became available to both sides) and a date set for a court hearing. At the hearing attorneys appeared, with or without the parties they represented, carrying relevant documents and pleadings. They argued the case afresh, reading out key passages from pleadings or drawing the court's attention to particular depositions. The Masters questioned those present and attempted to bring them to agreement or, when that proved impossible, to discern which party had presented the most convincing case and what orders they should make on their behalf. The only records of these hearings are the brief entries in the decree and order books, which say little except that 'upon openinge and debatinge thereof', it 'appeared to the council in this court' that one or other party had the better case. The nature of that 'debatinge' and the reasons why matters so 'appeared' are rarely described in any detail, but the orders and

---

[44] The procedure for gathering the testimony of witnesses was the same as in Chancery; see Jones, *Chancery*, pp. 237–45; Christine Churches, '"The most unconvincing testimony": the genesis and historical usefulness of the country depositions in Chancery', *The Seventeenth Century*, 11 (1996), pp. 209–27.

[45] Westminster depositions were written on paper and bear the signatures or marks of each deponent; depositions taken by commission were written on parchment and rarely included deponents' signatures.

decrees the Masters made are recorded in full. While common law judges could decide legal title and award money damages, the Masters had access to a more imaginative and expansive array of remedies. As well as ordering that defendants and their lawyers stay actions in other courts until matters of equity could be considered, the Masters issued injunctions preventing parties from engaging in certain behaviour, or ordering them to behave in specified ways. Occupiers of disputed lands or tenements, for example, could seek injunctions allowing them to keep possession of their interests while a dispute was being litigated, or after it had been settled. This mechanism proved particularly useful to widows struggling to keep control of their late husbands' holdings, for whom the alternative of an award of damages and the uncertainty of a protracted common law suit held little appeal.

CONCILIATION AND ARBITRATION

This, then, was the course that suits followed if they progressed to final decision, but the successful resolution of suits did not always require the making of decisions or the granting of decrees. In Requests, as in other Elizabethan courts, few cases stayed the distance to a final court order. The Masters dismissed a significant number in their initial stages, because they fell outside the remit of the court. Others lapsed because plaintiffs lacked the funds to continue, or because the issuing of process had induced defendants to settle matters outside the court.[46] Whenever they could, the Masters encouraged alternative methods of settlement that did not rely on decrees made under the authority of the Privy Seal. They referred cases to arbitration, often at the request of one or more of the litigants.[47] Alternatively, they appointed commissions to settle matters locally. They either directed those commissioners appointed to take depositions to try and bring opposing parties to agreement, or they formally appointed a commission of *oyer* and *terminer*, and delegated to commissioners the power to hear and determine the case before them. In 1523 they referred a dispute to the local abbot, requiring him to deal with it 'as he tendreth the good advancement of Justice, and the quietnesse of his poore neighbours, to Gods pleasure and the kings'. Throughout the life of Requests, the Masters were aware that court decrees were often a poor guarantee of lasting peace and 'the quietnesse of poore neighbours'.[48] As J.F. Philips has argued in a modern context, 'the system

---

[46] Caesar, *Ancient State*, pp. 86–7, 111, 120, 124–5; *Johan Cobbe* v. *John Johnson*, PRO Req 1/21, pp. 85, 199–200; the Masters often prefaced the arrangements they made for hearings with the words, 'if in the meane time the same matter be not ended by arbitrement'; *Thomas Reade* v. *Jane Reade als Lambert*, PRO Req 1/18, p. 15.

[47] Parties who agreed to submit to arbitration became bound to each other with money bonds to ensure that they would abide by the arbitrated decision; arbitrators might be named by the parties themselves, by the Masters, or might be the lawyers for both sides; *Nicholas Dotting* v. *Johan Shorte*, PRO Req 1/19, p. 901.

[48] Caesar, *Ancient State*, p. 77.

of settlement of disputes by arbitration is sometimes seen as contrasting with litigation, whereas in truth it is part of the same method. . . . It is generally not competitive with but rather complementary to the national and public judicial process.'[49]

The Masters' preference for extra-curial solutions and their reluctance to grant decrees is clear not only from the willingness with which they referred cases, but also from the conditional nature of many of these referrals. In 1557, for example, they directed a cause, 'to the arbitrament of *Sir William Cecill*, Knight, *Valentine Dale*, Doctor of the civill law, *Gilbert Gerard*, and *Roger Manwood*, Esquiers they to determine the same if they can, & if they cannot, then *Joh. Boxall* clerke, one of the Queen's honorable counsell of the court of Requests to be umpire, and if he can make no order &c. then the cause to be heard estsoones openly in this Court'.[50] A hearing in court was clearly the least desirable of the three options.

COSTS

Richard Robinson wrote of Requests in 1589 or 1590 that poor suitors 'do find in this Court great right for Little Monye, and also speedy redresse in their Causes'.[51] What passed for 'Little Monye' and 'speedy redresse' in the late sixteenth century? The cost of initiating a suit in Requests was high, 6s. 8d. for a writ of appearance under the Privy Seal directed to a defendant (compared to 1s. 6d. for an initial writ in Chancery) and a further 10s. for the drawing, engrossing and signing of each pleading.[52] However, while initial costs in Requests were higher than in Chancery, legal costs for completed actions were relatively modest. Calculating the average cost of a suit is difficult because the length and complexity of suits varied so widely, and because listings of actual costs are rare, but in most cases legal costs can be counted in tens of shillings rather than in tens of pounds. When the Masters awarded costs they almost invariably chose the figures 20s., 30s. or 40s. 'in part payment' or 'in part satisfaction' of monies expended. Occasionally they used the award of costs almost as the equivalent of a fine, ordering defeated parties to pay £20 in costs to compensate their opponents for excessive trouble or delay.[53] Yet even these extraordinary awards left Requests ahead of Chancery, where W.J. Jones has estimated that most suits cost between £50 and £400.[54] An early Jacobean critic of

---

[49] J.F. Philips, 'Arbitration', *Litigation*, 1 (1982), p. 239.

[50] Caesar, *Ancient State*, p. 116.

[51] Richard Robinson, *A Briefe Collection of the Queenes Majesties Most High and Most Honourable Courtes of Recordes*, ed. R.L. Rickard, Camden Miscellany vol. 20 (London, 1953), p. 24; for the dating of Robinson's essay see Knox, 'Requests', p. 304.

[52] The Masters later lowered the cost of a writ of appearance to 3s. 4d.; Allsebrook, 'Requests', p. 44.

[53] *Thomas Hathway v. Samuel Cocke*, PRO Req 1/21, pp. 68–9; *Henry Palmer v. Ruth Oxenbridge et al.*, PRO Req 1/21, p. 70.   [54] Jones, *Chancery*, p. 309.

Requests procedure conceded that costs in the court were lower and fairer than those in Chancery. He explained how Chancery clerks were supposed to 'rank their Clyents cawses for hearing Accordinge to their Dependencies in Court', but having paid high prices to obtain their positions they 'now sell their hearings at excessive rates, Whereas in this Courte [Requests] the Clyent hath his cawse heard att the mocon of his Attorney or Councell which is but a small Charge to the subjects'.[55]

Legal costs in Requests were modest, but in most actions the expenses associated with litigating a suit, including travel, accommodation and sustenance for litigants, messengers, witnesses and commissioners, regularly dwarfed purely legal costs. A plaintiff in 1533 claimed 20s. for legal charges but £6 10s. 8d. in total costs. In other cases legal costs amounted to only 8s. 8d. in a claim for 58s. 8d. (plus 20s. tax), and 23s. 4d. in a bill totalling £4 12s. 8d.[56] A married couple who alleged costs of £22, wanted £12 for accommodation alone and in a case from 1598 the Masters ordered a defendant to pay £14 to a messenger.[57] Claimants with modest means could gain entry into Requests because individual charges were cheap, but in long actions legal costs and incidental expenses could mount up. However, where the expense of a suit stood between plaintiffs and their access to justice, the option existed of gaining entrance to the court *in forma pauperis*.

IN FORMA PAUPERIS

By statute, poor litigants with just complaints could apply to have counsel and attorney assigned to them and their court fees waived.[58] This precursor to the modern legal aid system (the statutes allowing pauper admissions were only repealed in 1883) offered assistance to litigants who could show that they were worth less than £5 in goods, or owned land worth less than 40s. per annum.[59] The Masters of Requests rarely interpreted the requirement strictly, and in most cases they accepted the claimants' word that they were poor enough to be eligible.[60] A critic writing in the early seventeenth century complained that 'Licences to sue in forma pauperis are there [in Requests] twoe frequent before the Court to be sufficiently enformed of the just cause of their Complaint', and clearly not everyone who gained 'pauper' admission was a pauper.[61] Maudlen Hollande,

---

[55] C.U.L. Gg.2.31 fols 27$^{r\text{-}v}$; see also Leadam, *Select Cases*, p. xcix.

[56] Leadam, *Select Cases*, pp. 38, 91, 188.

[57] *Edward More & Frances Stourton* v. *Mary Sturton*, PRO Req 2/239/67; PRO Req 1/19, p. 225.

[58] See, for example, 11 Henry VII c. 12, *Statutes of the Realm*, vol. 2, p. 578.

[59] Forty shillings per annum was the standard measure of secure subsistence, marking as it did the upper boundary for entitlement to relief under the Poor Laws, and the lower boundary for the entitlement to vote, but it was a somewhat arbitrary figure, given that it was impervious to inflation.

[60] It was to be calculated, 'all debts having been paid', a condition that allowed much leeway at a time when credit played a dominant role in personal finances.

[61] C.U.L. Gg.2.31, fol. 27; but see *Thomas & Jane Day* v. *Robert Flick et al.*, PRO Req 1/19, p. 638.

for example, gained entry *in forma pauperis* in 1598 to recover a legacy worth £38 6s. 8d.[62] Clearly, the poverty of the claimant was at issue, not the poverty of the claim. A widow secured on her farm might be a rich woman. The same woman denied access to her farm might have nothing. Joan Lewis, for example, stressed in her bill of complaint that 'she is a very pore woman and hath all her goodes and cattall wrongfullie taken from her', leaving her with no means of funding a suit to gain remedy by the 'long tracke and course of your comyn lawes'.[63]

Sampling admissions to Requests *in forma pauperis* that have left a record, it seems that about 10 per cent of plaintiffs succeeded in having their court costs waived. The average was higher among those who lived within easy reach of London, for small matters were worth taking to Westminster only if Westminster was close at hand.[64] It also appears that the proportion of litigants gaining free entry to Requests increased over the course of Elizabeth's reign.[65] This would suggest that while the average wealth, or at least status, of plaintiffs in Requests rose over Elizabeth's reign (see below), so too did the proportion of plaintiffs who succeeded in persuading the Masters to waive their court costs.[66] Sir Thomas Smith believed that Requests was a court for the poor that had become corrupted over time, but on the evidence of pauper admissions Requests was as much a court for the poor at the end of Elizabeth's reign as it had ever been.[67]

Even with their legal costs waived, anyone who was literally worth less than 40s. per annum would have been hard pressed to meet the extra costs and expenses associated with litigation. For this reason the Masters occasionally heard causes summarily, either in court or in their chambers, to save expense.[68] Or they might refer poor litigants to a cheaper court, or to an understanding individual, so that matters could be settled locally. When Anne Ford brought an action in Requests, claiming a third of her late husband's lands in Colchester by right of dower, the Masters, 'having regarde & consideracon of the poore estate

---

[62] *Maudlen Hollande v. Thomas Wilford & Robert Holland*, PRO Req 2/47/25.

[63] *Johan Lewis v. Thobye Pleydell*, PRO Req 2/164/103, B.

[64] Six out of eighty one cases in the sample from Somerset were pauper admissions (7 per cent), while thirteen of the seventy one cases from Middlesex (18 per cent) involved plaintiffs admitted *in forma pauperis*.

[65] Judging from samples taken by W.B.J. Allsebrook, the proportion of *in forma pauperis* admissions rose from under 3 per cent in 1562 (two out of seventy two), to 5 per cent in 1568 (five out of 100), to just over 10 per cent in 1581 (nine out of eighty four), to 11 per cent in 1598 (twenty nine out of 264); Allsebrook, 'Requests', pp. 112, n. 2, 128, 201–40.

[66] This was partly due to orders in Chancery that encouraged plaintiffs with small claims to choose Requests; in 1565, for example, Sir Nicholas Bacon dismissed from Chancery all suits that concerned less than six acres of land, unless the lands were worth at least 40s. per annum; by comparison, D.A. Knox found virtually no record of admissions *in forma pauperis* in the Edwardian Requests; Knox, 'Requests', pp. 318, 321, 325, 340.

[67] Knox argued that Requests was never a poor person's court except in name, and that it accepted plaints from wealthy litigants in 1530 as well as in 1630; Knox, 'Requests', pp. 303–4, 308.

[68] Knox, 'Requests', pp. 328–9, 333; Allsebrook, 'Requests', p. 104.

of the said complainant, do order that the same matter shalbe referred to the hearing order and final determinacon of . . . baylifs of the towne of Colchester'.[69] As will be seen later in the chapter, Requests was not a court for paupers, but the Masters did what they could to provide justice for plaintiffs with modest means.

SPEED OF PROCESS

Process in Requests was relatively cheap, but costs mounted with each term that a case was on the court's books. Was process in the court 'speedy', as Richard Robinson suggested? Measuring the duration of suits in Requests, or in any sixteenth century court, is made difficult by the incomplete survival of records, the absence of dates on some pleas, and the difficulty of tracing actions from bill to decision. It can also be a rather artificial exercise, given the small percentage of cases that ended in a final court decree. However, despite these obstacles, it remains possible to estimate the length of time litigants could reasonably have expected their cases to last. Looking at all of the cases in the decree and order books that reached decisions (and can be dated) in Hillary and Easter terms 1562 the shortest time from commencement to final decision was two months and four days, the longest three years, three months and a day, and the average was just over ten months.[70] In Hillary term 1603 the fastest decision took just over a month and the slowest took one year, eleven months and thirteen days.[71] Once again the average time was about ten months, suggesting that the Masters were coping well with the large increase in their case load. Most cases, of course, did not last to the final decision stage. Taking a sample of eighty four cases with clearly dated documents, it appears that the average time it took defendants to answer bills of complaint was about two months and two days, and the average time between the first dated document and the last was about eight months.[72] Extraordinary cases could linger for years or even decades, but these figures suggest that the majority of plaintiffs and defendants could expect to be in and out of the court within a year.[73]

The record of Requests compares well with Chancery, where Jones estimated that actions took between two to five years to reach final resolution, with three

---

[69] *Anne Forde v. John Mills & John Andrews*, PRO Req 1/17, p. 688; *George Stokes v. Robert Till et al.*, PRO Req 1/21, p. 210.   [70] PRO Req 1/11, pp. 24–39, 75–95.

[71] PRO Req 1/21, pp. 47–105.

[72] This sample of eighty four cases with decipherable dates from across the period (that proceeded further than an initial bill) comes from the main sample of 300 case files described in chapter 1 above; times varied according to how far litigants lived from London, so that bills from Middlesex received an answer after an average of one month and twenty four days, while the equivalent average for cases from Somerset was two months and twenty seven days.

[73] Their causes, however, are likely to have lasted considerably longer, perhaps having progressed through at least one other court before reaching Requests; see Allsebrook, 'Requests', p. 149; for the speed of process in Requests in the reign of Edward VI, see Knox, 'Requests', pp. 332–3.

years the average; long enough to have Phillip Stubbes complain in *The Anatomie of Abuses*, 'sometimes you shall have a matter hang in sute after it is commenced a quarter of a yeare, half a yeare, yea a twelve month, two or three years togither, yea seaven or eight yeeres now and then, if either friends or money can be made'.[74] It also compares well with the present day, when civil actions in England and Wales take an average of two years from commencement to final decision.[75] Litigants in Requests complained that their suits had been 'long depending' in the court, but they were more likely to receive 'speedy redresse' there than in most other Westminster courts.

EFFECTIVENESS

These statistics suggest that for a busy central court, Requests was a relatively efficient organ of justice, an impression that is backed up by the experiences of the fortunate litigants who saw their actions proceed swiftly through the court to a final decision.[76] Richard Christopher entered a bill of complaint in Requests two weeks after his wife died, against defendants he alleged had spirited away her moveable goods, and he received judgment within three months. However, fast settlements like this were exceptional, and swift results were not always lasting or effective results.[77] In 1596 Anne Garforth saw her action pass through all of the usual procedural stages, from the entry of her bill to the taking of depositions and the issuing of an injunction, in only thirty three days. But her opponent ignored the injunction and she had to return to the court two months later to ask the Masters to issue a subpoena of contempt against him.[78] Joan Hurford, a widow from Somerset, enjoyed quiet possession of a copyhold interest thanks to a Requests decree issued in 1556, until her adversary decided to re-encroach on her lands in 1565. She entered a new bill in Requests, sparking off a protracted dispute marked by a succession of inconclusive commissions. When the Masters finally gave judgment in her favour in 1568, her opponent immediately launched a counter-suit.[79] Clearly, victory in Requests could be tenuous in nature, and the ability of the court to reach decisions needs to be measured beside its ability to enforce those decisions.

Requests relied for its authority on the Privy Seal. The Masters issued writs under the seal, demanding that defendants answer bills, appear in court or

---

[74] Jones, *Chancery*, p. 306; Phillip Stubbes, *The Second Part of the Anatomie of Abuses* (London, 1583), p. 9; the situation in Chancery went from bad to worse, George Spence warning in 1839 that 'No man, as things stand, can enter into a Chancery suit with any reasonable hope of being alive at its termination, if he has a determined adversary'; as quoted in Sugarman and Rubin, eds., *Law, Economy and Society*, p. 17.

[75] Frances Gibb, 'Lawyers criticise slow arm of the law', *The Times*, 14 January 1992, p. 5.

[76] *Richard Christopher v. William & Ellen Baylie et al.*, PRO Req 2/191/71; Req 2/163/20.

[77] Allsebrook, 'Requests', p. 98.

[78] *Anne Garforth v. William Shipman & Thomas Higgens*, PRO Req 2/212/8; Req 2/214/6.

[79] *Erasmus Pynne v. Joan Hurford & Henrie Hurford*, PRO Req 2/105/16; Req 2/25/26.

observe decrees or orders, with penalty clauses threatening fines for non-compliance. The standard penalty was £100 (where wealthy litigants or weighty matters were involved it could be £200, £500 or even £1,000) although there is scant evidence that the court ever levied fines from defaulters.[80] There is plenty of evidence, however, that defendants ignored writs of Privy Seal. In 1590 the court granted an injunction ordering various defendants to vacate contested premises until the question of title could be settled at common law. The person who fixed the injunction to their door described in an affidavit how they 'doe in very terrible & contemptuous manner keepe the possession [from] the said complainant, And have given threatening words, & have with gunnes, pistolls & other warlike weapons offred violence to such as have demaunded possession of the said howse'.[81] William Cartwright accused Sir John Burdett of causing the maidservant serving process on him 'to ete a pece of the seid wax And made here to swalow it doon' which apparently left her sick in bed for four days.[82]

The court's response when parties repeatedly ignored its process was to issue writs of attachment to local sheriffs (and within London to the warden of the Fleet) ordering them to apprehend offending individuals and to commit them to prison or safe custody for their contempts. Litigants might choose to ignore the Privy Seal (or to tear it up, tread it into the dust or throw it back in the face of the process server) but sheriffs, who could be fined if they failed adequately to carry out their duties, had less freedom to ignore the commands of a central court.[83] Attachments were common in Requests and appear to have brought many recalcitrant defendants to heel, but they were not always successful.[84] In 1603 the Masters had two women, Anne Mirrill and Mary Rokeby, attached and imprisoned in the Fleet for contempt after they disobeyed a Requests injunction ordering them to stay their suits at the common law. The two quickly escaped from custody and commenced actions in another court for false imprisonment. They ignored further writs from Requests and gave forth 'diverse, undecent and unfitt speeches against his majesties Counsaill of the same Court'. All the Masters could do was to issue a further injunction and a further attachment.[85]

If attachments were unsuccessful, parties seeking relief could ask the Masters to issue a proclamation of rebellion, and if that failed, a commission of rebel-

[80] A commentator on Chancery explained how the subpoena got its name from the penalty of £100, 'but the [£100] is never levied but incerted only *ad terrorem*'; C.U.L. Gg.2.31, fol. 347.
[81] *Thomas Cartwright* v. *Susan Ashley et al.*, PRO Req 1/16, p. 669; for further examples of defendants ignoring process under the Privy Seal and assaulting process servers, see subpoenas of contempt in PRO Req 3/33; Allsebrook, 'Requests', pp. 63–4.
[82] *William Cartwryght* v. *John Burdett*, PRO Req 2/4/337.
[83] D.E.C. Yale, *Lord Nottingham's 'Manual of Chancery Practice' & 'Prolegomena of Chancery and Equity'* (Cambridge, 1965), p. 29.
[84] The Masters also issued attachments against witnesses, enforcing them to appear and give evidence; *Snowball* v. *Snowball*, PRO Req 1/14, fol. 352.
[85] *Andrew Broome* v. *Thomas & Mary Rokeby et al.*, PRO Req 1/21, pp. 190–1.

lion.[86] A commission of rebellion led to the capture of Suzan Cole in 1599, but accomplices used force to help her escape from the arresting commissioners: 'And thereupon diverse violences and outrages unto them offred & uppon their persons executed.' The Masters reacted to this news by ordering a messenger of her Majesty's chamber to personally apprehend Suzan and her husband.[87] The frequency with which the court ordered writs of attachment, and proclamations and commissions of rebellion, is evidence of the fragile nature of the court's authority and of the problems the Masters faced ensuring that their will was done.

THE MASTERS OF REQUESTS AND THE ETHOS OF THE COURT

If the measure of an efficient court is taken to be its ability to make concrete decisions and have them emphatically enforced, then Requests was not, after all, an efficient court. Few of the cases it heard progressed to a final decision, and it found the orders it did make difficult to enforce. In 1517, long before common law prohibitions compromised the court's authority, the chronicler Hall wrote of Requests (and of other prerogative courts): 'These courtes were greatly haunted for a tyme, but at the last the people perceaved that much delay was used in these courtes & few matters ended, & when they were ended, they bound no man by the law; then every man was wery of them & resorted to the common law.'[88] Hall's obituary for an early incarnation of Requests was clearly premature. However, to judge the efficacy of Requests in this way is to misunderstand the function of the court and the nature of the justice system in which it operated. Original writs outnumbered final judicial decisions in *every* Westminster court (as they do in most modern jurisdictions), usually by ratios of more than ten to one.[89] An analysis of the success of Requests therefore needs to take account of the cases that left the court's books before the decree stage, not just those that remained. As this chapter has shown, not every plaintiff who entered Requests wanted the Masters to issue a decree; many desired temporary assistance that would help them mount or defend actions in other jurisdictions. Others appear to have shared the Masters' conviction that a final decree was not the only, or indeed the most satisfactory, route to achieving a

---

[86] *Robert Gibbes* v. *Mildred Maxfield*, PRO Req 1/19, pp. 527–8; for the text of such a proclamation, see *William Swayne* v. *Nicholas Sherewood*, PRO Req 2/267/58, m. 6, letter.

[87] *Roger & Suzan Hill* v. *Richard & Suzan Cole*, PRO Req 1/19, p. 908.

[88] As quoted in Leadam, *Select Cases*, p. xiv; it is likely that the target of Hall's criticism was Wolsey, often credited with creating or revitalising these courts.

[89] Completion rates in civil courts have never been high. In 1978, for example, of the 143,577 civil cases commenced in the Queen's Bench Division, only 1,793 came to trial; *Royal Commission on Legal Services*, Final report, vol. 1, part 1 (1979), p. 14; and in sixteenth-century Castille, Richard Kagan has calculated that the ratio of unfinished cases to finished cases in the chancilleria of Valladolid was fifteen to one; Richard Kagan, *Lawsuits and Litigants in Castile 1500–1700* (Chapel Hill, 1981), p. 84.

lasting settlement, and welcomed the resort to arbitration and to local commissions.[90] The court's books contain dozens of entries ordering that moneys, obligations or proofs held for safekeeping should be returned to parties now that they had reached agreement, suggesting that pragmatic, if not always amicable, out of court settlements were fairly common.[91] The archive also contains dozens of sealed commission reports that commissioners returned to Requests and which remain unopened to this day, again suggesting that parties settled or discontinued actions.[92] To fully appreciate the effectiveness of the Masters, it is best to see them as umpires overseeing non-legal methods of settlement and lending their authority to compromise solutions made by third parties, rather than simply as judges who made firm and final decisions.

The Masters' preference for arbitrated solutions, and their reluctance to make final orders, were inextricably linked to the notions they held about equity and about the proper functions of a court charged with making equitable decisions. The subject of equity is a vast and complex one. As a sixteenth century maxim explained: 'There is nothinge more usuall then the name of equitie and scarce any thing more obscure and Difficult then the matter it selfe.'[93] The Masters viewed equity as a means to bring justice to individuals denied it by their particular circumstances. Their primary concern was not with doctrine, the strict application of rules, or the fostering of consistency. In fact they were anxious to alleviate the injustice that 'consistent' legal rules could create in specific instances. Their concern was with the particular needs of particular parties, and on occasions this led them to engineer flexible equitable solutions that to modern eyes appear more capricious and arbitrary than legal and objective.

Take, for example, the case of a complainant from Essex who sought the help of the Masters to keep control of a life interest in a tenement he had purchased for £10. His opponent managed to convince the Masters that a condition of the original sale allowed him to buy back the interest at any time by returning the £10; in effect it was not a sale, but a secured loan or a mortgage. The Masters found for the defendant and ordered the complainant to accept his offer of £10 and surrender possession, but they did not leave the matter there. They ordered the defendant to assign a suitable replacement dwelling to the complainant by deed for a period of forty years, 'for that the said complainant is a poore aged man & haithe longe dwelte upon the said tenement, and havinge none other staie of living but onelie the said tenement . . . wherein he accounted hymself under collour of suche promys as was made unto hym to have his dwelling and abode there as longe as he livied'. The complainant was to be responsible for the upkeep of the alternative building, but the defendant was to charge him no

---

[90] *William Kingswell v. Richard Kingswell*, PRO Req 2/231/42; Jones, *Chancery*, p. 287.
[91] See, for example, PRO Req 1/17, pp. 435, 531; PRO Req 1/19, pp. 487–8, 628, 631, 709.
[92] PRO Wards 16, Knox, 'Requests', p. 65, n. 3.   [93] C.U.L. Gg.2.31, fol. 12.

rent.[94] To break a stalemate in another case, the Masters ordered that two defendants should pay to the complainants, 'in respect of their povertie, the some of ffortie shillings'. The only consideration for this arbitrary payment was that the complainants never again sue or vex the defendants in relation to this matter.[95] These and many other similar orders would have been impossible under the common law (or in Chancery after the Restoration). Lawyers are quick to condemn this liberal use of judicial power, because it produces uncertainty and unpredictability in the legal system. However, most of the men and women who sought relief in Requests (those who were not benefiting from patronage or favouritism that we would label corrupt) did not desire from the Masters consistency with precedents recorded in the dust of court records, but rather compassionate justice based on 'good conscience'.[96]

The flexibility that the Masters exercised and the peculiar brand of equity they dispensed made them popular with plaintiffs, even if it made them unpopular with defendants and their lawyers. As the following chapters will show, it made Requests particularly attractive to two overlapping categories of female plaintiffs; those who found their legal options and independence, or their access to documents, restricted by the workings of the doctrine of coverture; and those who saw Requests as their only, or their final, option. This was not because the Elizabethan Masters of Requests consciously set themselves up as champions of women's rights (except, as we shall see, in the exceptional case of wives who sued their husbands). Rather, that their mutual concern to offer justice and equity to the poor, to those who lacked the ability to sue at common law, and to those who were disadvantaged by the power of their opponents, proved useful to a larger proportion of women than men (compared with other courts), simply because women more often fell into these categories. If the Masters can be described as sharing a common commitment, then it was to the poor and the disadvantaged. Thomas Wilson, for example, actively campaigned against usury in parliament (and in print in his *Discourse Upon Usury*), while 'charitable Sir Julius Caesar' was so well known for his generosity that in his last years it was believed that he was 'kept alive beyond Nature's course, by the prayers of those many poor which he daily relieved'.[97] The association of poverty with

---

[94] *Giles Houlden v. Raffe Greneaker*, PRO Req 1/11, pp. 234–7.

[95] *John & Agnes Wadington v. Thomas & Ursula Sheffeld*, PRO Req 1/18, p. 353.

[96] On 'corruption' in Elizabethan law, see Prest, *Rise of the Barristers*, pp. 303–8.

[97] Wilson, in common with numerous plaintiffs in Requests, also complained about unscrupulous creditors who put bonds in suit at common law to claim extortionate penalties for late payment; Thomas Wilson, *A Discourse Upon Usury: By Way of Dialogue and Orations, for the Better Variety and More Delight of All Those that Shall Read this Treatise*, ed. R.H. Tawney (London, 1962); Walton, *Lives*, pp. 130–1; of the other Masters, Thomas Sackford founded and endowed almshouses, and Ralph Rokeby left £100 to Christ's hospital, £100 to the poor in Greenwich, and £100 to prisoners in the Fleet, Newgate, Marshalsea and other prisons (although to put his largesse in context, Lord Chancellor Egerton is said to have made £10,000 from being Rokeby's executor); *D.N.B.*, vol. 49, p. 152; vol. 51, p. 174.

widowhood remained strong in the public imagination, and as I will show in later chapters, litigants and lawyers played upon this association in pleadings, and the court's reputation as a haven for poor widows and orphans may well have drawn certain individuals to its doors.[98] The language of a letter that a former Bishop of Exeter, Miles Coverdale, sent to the Masters in June 1564 on behalf of a distressed woman certainly does nothing to dispel this impression:

As this poor widow, the bearer, came to me with weeping tears, praying me to direct a letter to you in her favour, having heretofore enjoyed some fruits of your charitable and godly inclination, in the lawful furtherance of such as have right and are no dissemblers, I am the bolder to beg so much of your favourable help as may comfort the said poor desolate widow, within the limits of equity and conscience. I have commended my humble suit to writing after this homely sort, not mistrusting your godly sincerity in your office, but rather desirous to see the heavy-hearted widow helped and relieved.[99]

The Court of Requests had many shortcomings, but the Masters offered justice that in most cases was cheaper, quicker and simpler than the justice dispensed by their rivals. This helps to explain its popularity with women and with men. But who used the court, and what manner of things did they litigate?

THE STATUS OF LITIGANTS

Dame Eleanora Zouche (wife and then widow of Edward Lord Zouche), the Archbishop of Canterbury, Sir Thomas Egerton and Ursula Walsingham, the widow of Sir Francis, all petitioned the Masters of Requests asking for relief.[100] Clearly the 'poor man's court' did not deal solely with the poor. However, an analysis of the status of litigants in Rèquests shows that elite plaintiffs, those who gained entry because they were 'privileged as officers of the Court, or their servants or as the King's servants, or necessarie attendants on them', were always in a minority, and that the litigant population in general was surprisingly mixed.

Determining the backgrounds of Requests litigants, especially female litigants, using records that they themselves helped to create is a risky endeavour.[101] Plaintiffs invariably exaggerated the extent of their poverty and inflated the values of their claims, prompting defendants to respond in kind with their own sets of twisted truths. In 1591 the servant of a member of the Inner Temple swore to the court that her former employer was withholding her goods, two

---

[98] See chapters 5 and 8 below

[99] Miles Coverdale, late Bishop of Exeter, to Dr Haddon and Mr Sackford, 7 June 1564; *Cal. S.P. Dom. Elizabeth Addenda 1547–1565*, p. 548.

[100] PRO Req 1/17, pp. 284, 310; Req 1/18, p. 883; Req 1/20, p. 773; *Elionora Zouch v. Elionora Zouch*, PRO Req 2/93/59; Req 2/252/99; Req 2/157/506; Req 2/159/200; PRO Req 1/15, fols 405–407ᵛ; it is ironic that one of the ways in which Julius Caesar sought to establish the credentials of the Poor Man's Court was to list the eminent people who had acknowledged the court's legitimacy by suing there; Caesar, *Ancient State, passim*.

[101] For the difficulty of accurately identifying litigants' status from court records, see Brooks, *Pettyfoggers*, pp. 61–2; Barnes, 'Star Chamber litigants', p. 10.

Table 4.1 *Litigants above and below the rank of gentleman*

	1562/3		1603	
Litigants below the rank of gentleman or lady	874	(84%)	1,817	(79%)
Litigants ranked gentleman or lady or above	166	(16%)	491	(21%)
Knights	25		55	
Esquires	81		184	
Dames/ladies	4		25	
Gentlemen	56		227	
Total	1,040	(100%)	2,308	(100%)

Source: Decree & Order books PRO Req 1/11, pp. 1–243; Req 1/21, pp. 1–325.

chests and 'divers gownes, petticots and kyrtells and divers parcells of apparell both of lynnen and wollen', worth a total of £70, and owed her thirteen years' wages at 40s. per annum. He replied that the goods were not hers, and that she had already received her wages (which amounted to 16s. a year).[102] Was this woman worth almost £100, or was she barely able to scrape together 16s. a year? Precision is impossible without reference to other evidence such as wills, inventories, probate accounts, hearth tax returns, manor court rolls and the like (records that are largely unavailable for poorer individuals in the sixteenth century). However, the 'additions' or labels of status and occupation litigants gave in pleadings, and the values they put on contested interests or goods (however exaggerated), provide some guide at least to the nature of the Requests clientele, and how it changed over time.[103]

Beginning with the gentry and the aristocracy, evidence from the decree and order books suggests that only about one fifth of Requests litigants styled themselves 'gentleman' or better. The proportion of high-born litigants rose slightly over Elizabeth's reign, from around 16 per cent in the regnal year 4 Elizabeth (1562/3) to around 21 per cent in 45 Elizabeth/ 1 James 1 (1603), a rise that might suggest that the status of Requests as a pauper's court was indeed becoming compromised (see table 4.1).[104] However, the increase was confined largely

---

[102] *Elizabeth Bankes* v. *Thomas Gowen*, PRO Req 2/182/11, B, A, B.

[103] Dowzabell Burton, for example, appeared in records three times over a six month period, first as 'spynster', then as 'servant' and finally as 'singlewoman', similar but distinct titles; *Margaret Smith* v. *Mary Lockett*, PRO Req 2/43/34; *David Gittins & Dowzabell Burton* v. *Mary Lockett*, PRO Req 2/129/24; for the inadequacy of additions as evidence of social status see Amussen, *Ordered Society*, p. 78; Keith Wrightson, 'Estates, degrees, and sorts: changing perceptions of society in Tudor and Stuart England', in Penelope Corfield, ed., *Language, History and Class* (Oxford, 1991), p. 44.

[104] Unfortunately, modern calendars record labels of status inconsistently, and are therefore unreliable sources for charting the given status of litigants.

Table 4.2 *Relative status of plaintiffs and defendants*

Case types	4 Eliz. I	45 Eliz. I/ 1 James 1
Plaintiffs suing opponents of **the same status**	224 (61%)	588 (63%)
Plaintiffs suing opponents of **higher status**	123 (34%)	156 (17%)
Plaintiffs suing opponents of **lower status**	20 (5%)	181 (20%)
Total no. of cases	367 (100%)	925 (100%)

Source: Decree & Order books PRO Req 1/11, pp. 1–243, PRO Req 1/21, pp. 1–325.

to the ranks of gentlemen, and more likely reflects the growing number of people who styled themselves 'gent' during this period.[105] A more suggestive indicator of change is the shift (once again slight) in the relative status of plaintiffs and defendants. At the beginning of Elizabeth's reign, 34 per cent of Requests plaintiffs sued defendants of a higher status than themselves (table 4.2). At the close of the reign only 17 per cent of plaintiffs sued defendants a clear level above them on the social scale.[106] Conversely, the proportion of plaintiffs who brought suits against their social inferiors rose from 5 per cent to 20 per cent over the same period. Members of the gentry increasingly sought to take advantage of the court's efficient process, most of them entering the court under the expanding category of 'in the royal service'. The exact opposite was true in the common law courts, where the likelihood of litigants suing their 'betters' in Common Pleas or Queen's Bench increased over the same period.[107] In Star Chamber, judging by evidence from the Jacobean period, plaintiffs almost always sued defendants of lower status than themselves.[108] The inconsistency of experience in different courts underlines once again the danger of reading widespread social change into shifts within any one jurisdiction. However, it remains possible to speculate that the Masters of Requests' championing of the right of weak subjects to seek justice against stronger opponents may have encouraged litigants of low status to bring suits against their social betters in the common law courts as well.

The presence of *any* titled plaintiffs in Requests does not sit well with the court's standing as a court for the poor. But more remarkable than the gentry's presence in the court was their relative absence. The fact that upwards of 80 per

---

[105] Brooks, *Pettyfoggers*, pp. 61–3.
[106] These figures refer to non-gentry plaintiffs suing defendants of gentle or aristocratic status.
[107] Brooks, *Pettyfoggers*, pp. 61, 281–3.
[108] Steve Hindle, 'Aspects of the relationship of the state and local society in early modern England, with special reference to Cheshire c. 1590–1630' (University of Cambridge Ph.D., 1992), pp. 113–14, table 2.8, p. 178.

cent of the litigants using a national prerogative court were *below* the rank of gentleman or gentlewoman sheds interesting light on the character of Tudor government, and on the workings of the central courts. C.W. Brooks has shown how legal process in early modern England was surprisingly inexpensive, and how a broad spectrum of litigants utilised the largest common law courts. His calculations show that between 70 and 75 per cent of litigants in Common Pleas, and between 75 and 80 per cent of litigants in Queen's Bench, came from outside the ranks of the gentry and the aristocracy.[109] Even in Star Chamber, 46 per cent of Jacobean plaintiffs lacked gentry status, and while powerful litigants enjoyed the advantage of good counsel (and the unscrupulous among them used their money and influence to buy favours, to delay cases, or to bankrupt opponents) wealth alone could not always buy justice.[110]

The Court of Requests was less a court for knights, dames, ladies and gentlemen and more a court for yeomen, merchants' wives, haberdashers and leather workers. The indexes to modern calendars identify nearly 3,000 individuals by their trade or occupation (excluding those who worked the land) and linen and woollen drapers, haberdashers, grocers, mercers, goldsmiths, merchant tailors, tailors, clothiers, cloth workers and inn keepers between them account for almost half of this number.[111] A few professionals used the court, but shoemakers, bakers, butchers and their wives or widows far outnumbered doctors of physics, surgeons, or attorneys. Along with men and women of yeomen or husbandmen status, these were the classes of individuals who provided the court with most of its business. The character of the litigant population is reflected in the status of the witnesses parties called to testify on their behalf. In a largely rural county like Somerset the majority of witnesses were husbandmen and yeomen called in to pronounce on local customs and usages (table 4.3). It is striking how few women appeared as deponents (only nine out of a sample of 211), and I will consider possible reasons for this paucity of female witnesses in chapter 7.[112] In Middlesex, by contrast, disputes were more various and the mix of witnesses far greater (table 4.4).[113] Gentlemen and women and yeomen predominated, but a whole panoply of traders also

---

[109] Brooks, *Pettyfoggers*, p. 59; in Chancery, between 50 and 68 per cent of litigants were of non-gentry status in 1627; Henry Horwitz, *Chancery Equity Records and Proceedings, 1600–1800: A Guide to Documents in the Public Record Office* (London, 1995), pp. 37–8.

[110] Barnes, 'Star Chamber litigants', table 1, p. 10.

[111] Linen and woollen drapers (186), haberdashers (159), grocers (149), mercers (146), goldsmiths (145), merchant tailors (141), tailors (134), clothiers (107), cloth workers (100), inn keepers (83), totalling 1,350 out of a total of 2,908 (46.4 per cent); *Public Record Office Lists and Indexes* (supplementary series), no. 7, 'Proceedings in the Court of Requests' (New York, 1966), vol. 1, pp. 700–1; vol. 2 (subject index), pp. 19–21; vol. 3, pp. 554–60; for details of the other trades listed in modern indexes, see Stretton, 'Women and litigation', table 3.3, p. 92.

[112] The sample of 211 deponents from Somerset comes from the sample of 100 case files from the county.

[113] The sample of 224 deponents from Middlesex is taken from the cases within the larger sample of 100 case files from the county which include depositions.

Table 4.3 *Status of Somerset deponents*

Men		Women	
Husbandmen	110	Wives	5
Yeomen	29	Widows	2
Tenants/homagers	26	Unstated	2
Gentlemen	18		
Esquires	4		
Weavers	3		
Tailors	2		
One each of: labourer, cordwainer, miner, clerk, roper, baker, shoemaker, tucker, vicar, servant-at-arms of her Majesty.			
Total	202		9

appeared, as witnesses to will-signings, leases, contracts, bonds and bad debts, and women appeared as deponents in roughly the same proportions as they appeared as litigants.[114]

The status of women in Requests is hard to determine, because the labels they supplied are even less enlightening than men's labels.[115] Widows tended to supply information about their late husbands' status and occupations not their own, wives gave their husbands' details and single women often supplied no information at all about their social background. The value of the claims women made provides some guide. The scope for inflating or deflating the value of debts, wages, moveable goods, marriage portions and jointures was large, in a court where litigants and their opponents rarely agreed on the value of any-thing. However, where lands were in issue, parties were more likely to agree their value; they merely disputed rights of ownership and possession. Turning, therefore, to a sample of eighty three Somerset women, it is possible to map out in very broad terms the minimum wealth of those who brought suits in Requests.[116] The richest women to enter the court were ladies of the manor or widows of wealthy men who claimed to control (or have rights to control) inter-ests in up to 300 acres of copyhold.[117] One woman said that her merchant

---

[114] It is important to remember, however, that this sample is not fully representative because it is made up almost exclusively of cases that involved female plaintiffs or defendants; it is possible, for example, that women involved in court actions were more likely than men to call on female witnesses.

[115] Michael Roberts, '"Words they are women, and deeds they are men": images of work and gender in early modern England', in Charles and Duffin, eds., *Women and Work*, pp. 138–41.

[116] For details of the sample, see chapter 7 below.

[117] *Agnes Grove* v. *John Thynne & William Goolde*, PRO Req 2/35/50.

Table 4.4 Status of Middlesex deponents

Men		Women	
Gentlemen	50	Wives	28
Yeomen	24	Widows	14
Haberdashers	7	Spinsters	5
Grocers	6	Servants (widow)	1
Carpenters	4	(single)	1
Goldsmiths	4	Unknown	1
Brewers	3		
Bakers	3		
Servants	3		
Clerks	3		
Pewterers	3		
Merchant taylors	3		
Two each of: esquires, apprentices, painters, embroiderers, tailors, inn-keepers, drapers, mealemen, parish clerks, sadlers, skinners			
One each of: fletcher, vitler, fisherman, waterman, gardener, bricklayer, locksmith, dicemaker, ropemaker, cook, glasier, topster, citizen joiner, tallow chandler, founder, servant-at-arms of her Majesties Chamber, Clerk of Lord Mayor's Court			
Total	153		50

husband had left her a bequest worth £165 in his will, while a widow executrix valued the estate she was administering at £200.[118] Below these women came a large grouping of copyholders who can be ranked according to the size of their holdings. One married woman shared an interest in a tenement and eighty acres (the equivalent, elsewhere in the country, of two yard lands).[119] A dozen or so women held interests of between twenty seven and thirty seven acres (the equivalent of one yard land). The majority, however (about twenty), held interests of less than twenty three acres (the equivalent of half a yard land), many claiming rights over a single tenement or messuage and between three and ten acres of copyhold. Below these women can be found an 'orphan maiden', a servant, and

[118] *Mary Thorne* v. *Erasmus Prynne & Nicholas Thorne*, PRO Req 2/39/90; *Johane Uphill* v. *Richard Hole et al.*, PRO Req 2/281/16.
[119] *Thomas & Agatha Townsende* v. *Thomas Wake et al.*, PRO Req 2/278/48.

the widows of shoemakers and labourers. In a county like Middlesex the spread of wealth was much wider. The rich were richer, and because of the county's proximity to Westminster, the poor were poorer. Where Thomas Barnes found in the Jacobean Star Chamber that female litigants tended to be wealthier or of higher status than male litigants, the opposite seems to have been the case in Requests.[120]

The evidence of litigant status, costs, *in forma pauperis* admissions, and the value of matters at issue in Requests cases confirms the initial impression that Requests was not a court for the genuinely or habitually poor. The genuinely poor, after all, did not normally possess the kinds of property that other parties could possess or damage on a scale that warranted a central court action. The poor who sought benefit in Requests were the temporarily poor, individuals recently dispossessed of their substance or in imminent danger of dispossession, or the powerless poor such as orphans. Plaintiffs might be 'poor' copyholders kept from their interests, but they were not in general the under-tenants of such copyholders.

WOMEN'S LITIGATION VERSUS MEN'S LITIGATION

The 'mixed bag' nature of the Requests jurisdiction, and the fact that the Masters did not work with any strict categories of subject matter (like the forms of action at common law), make it difficult to categorise the litigation it processed.[121] Suits for the recovery of evidence might relate to interests in land, to debts or to the rights of beneficiaries under wills. Disputes over bonds could relate to the ownership of chattels, to interests in land, or to the performance of promises. Definitive categorisation is difficult, but it is nevertheless possible to make a general division of Requests business during Elizabeth's reign. Judging from an analysis of modern calendar entries, it appears that an average of about 45 per cent of Elizabethan Requests actions concerned interests in land (including copyholds, leases, rents and customary rights), 31 per cent involved monetary matters (debts, bonds, promises, sale of goods and so on), 10 per cent comprised requests to 'stay' actions in other courts, 7 per cent concerned testamentary matters (wills, legacies, administration), while the remaining 7 per cent dealt with subjects as diverse as piracy, wardship, assault, theft and the selection of officers.[122] These average figures mask changes in the subject matter of suits over time. Samples collected by W.B.J. Allsebrook show that in 1562/3 over three quarters of actions concerned land tenure, commons, enclosure or rents, and less than a quarter involved debts, bonds and contractual relations. In 1598, only just over a quarter of actions related to land tenure and rents, while more

---

[120] Barnes, 'Star Chamber litigants', p. 9.   [121] Brooks, *Pettyfoggers*, p. 68.
[122] In the sample of 2,000 consecutive entries from manuscript calendars, 1,587 give an indication of the primary subject of the cause.

Table 4.5 *Nature of business according to sex of plaintiff*

	Male plaintiff		Female plaintiff		Male and female joint plaintiffs	
Land	537	(43%)	76	(58%)	102	(52%)
Debts and bonds	427	(34%)	29	(22%)	38	(19%)
Stay common law actions	144	(11%)	3	(2%)	8	(4%)
Wills and estates	69	(5%)	8	(6%)	42	(21%)
Other	81	(6%)	16	(12%)	7	(4%)
Total	1,258	(99%)	132	(100%)	197	(100%)

Source: PRO 9 vol. 93 (Requests proceedings); piece numbers Req 2/157/1–Req 2/167/37, excluding entries without dates, and entries where the sex of the plaintiff or the subject of disputes is unspecified or unclear.

than half involved debts, bonds and contractual relations.[123] In Requests, as in almost every civil jurisdiction in the land, debt actions were on the rise.[124]

This was the general picture, but how did women's litigation differ from men's? Table 4.5 distinguishes women's and men's litigation by subject. Once more, the categories are somewhat arbitrary and the calculations are based on calendar entries that are not consistently reliable, but they provide a useful overview of women's litigation. The first thing to note is that women, as a group, were more likely than men to bring actions in Requests concerning interests in land (58 per cent compared with 43 per cent). This may appear surprising, given the extent to which interests in 'real property' were a male prerogative, as exemplified by the rules of primogeniture. However, as Amy Erickson has pointed out, while it is undeniable that land 'pulled inexorably towards males', it 'spent a good deal of time in female hands along the way'; and the time it spent in female hands was often contested.[125] Women rarely 'owned' land in the modern sense of holding unencumbered freehold title, but they often held life interests in lands or possessed interests tied to lands, and they regularly went to law to claim or protect them.

Women, then, were more likely than men to litigate matters relating to inter-

[123] In the regnal year 4 Elizabeth I (1562/3) fifty seven cases out of seventy two concerned land tenure, commons, enclosure, or rents and the remaining fifteen cases concerned debts, bonds and contractual relations; in 40 Elizabeth I (1598) seventy three out of 264 related to land tenure and rents, 157 related to debts; of the remaining thirty four cases, twenty nine involved executors and administrators, three the possession of goods and chattels, one the custody of documents, and one unjustified ejection from office; Allsebrook, 'Requests', p. 187.

[124] See, for example, Brooks, *Pettyfoggers*, p. 74; Muldrew, 'Credit, market relations and debt litigation', p. 34.   [125] Erickson, *Women and Property*, p. 5.

ests in land, but they appear less likely to have brought actions involving bonds, debts and other financial transactions. This tendency is significant, given the increasing predominance of debt-related actions in the expansion of litigation, and it may help to explain why the proportion of actions brought by women appears to have fallen in common law courts like Common Pleas over the course of Elizabeth's reign. Widows with capital acted as moneylenders, but not on a grand scale, and perhaps not at the speculative ends of the credit market more prone to failure and breakdown. Women sued to recover debts they had inherited, and claimed the penalties for non-performance attached to contracts to marry, but as the next chapter will argue, they were less active than men in litigation arising out of wholly commercial enterprises.

Another discernible difference between male and female patterns of litigation is that men more frequently sought assistance from the Masters of Requests to 'stay' or postpone actions in other courts such as Common Pleas and Queen's Bench. This could mean one of two things. Either women were not being sued as often as men in common law courts, and so had less reason to seek relief in Requests.[126] Or they were being sued in these courts, but they lacked the knowledge, opportunity or the resources to come to Requests to have the Masters stay their opponent's actions.

This general sketch of women's legal dealings can be supplemented by considering the figures for 'mixed' alliances of plaintiffs, where women and men brought actions together, figures that include the sizeable number of suits initiated by husbands with their wives. The pattern for joint actions brought by female and male litigants is closer in shape to the pattern for female litigants than the pattern for male litigants, but it remains noticeably distinct. Men and women jointly litigated more suits concerning land and significantly fewer suits concerning money matters than men litigating on their own. However, joint male and female plaintiffs were more likely than any other group to bring actions over contested estates (21 per cent of cases, compared with 5 per cent for men and 6 per cent for women). The reason for this is the numbers of brothers and sisters, and the even greater number of husbands and wives, who sued together to claim legacies and contest wills.[127]

This overview raises interesting questions. To answer those questions, and to pursue the implications of the figures for female participation in court cases, it is necessary to examine in detail the records of individual actions. The Court of Requests was a relatively cheap and accessible court offering procedures and remedies that attracted a considerable number of women. It remains to be seen how those women made use of the court and how the Masters of Requests, and opponents, regarded them.

---

[126] To turn this around, women may have been suing men *more* often than men sued them; see chapter 5 below.

[127] For the reasons behind the high number of married couples suing together, see chapter 6 below.

5

Unmarried women and widows

Widow Blackacre: You shall hear me, and shall be instructed. Lets see your Brief.
Mr Petulant: Send your Solicitor to me, instructed by a Woman! I'd have you to
know, I do not wear a Bar-gown – –
Widow Blackacre: By a Woman! And I'd have you to know, I am no common
Woman; but a woman conversant in the laws of the Land, as well as your self,
tho' I have no Bar-gown.
William Wycherley *The Plain Dealer* (1676)[1]

In the eyes of the law, single women and widows had full legal capacity. When considering women's rights it is consequently a mistake to study only those areas of the law obviously associated with women, such as jointure, dower, marriage settlements and separate estates. Such a focus can be misleading, for two reasons. First of all, it ignores the fact that(in theory adult women without husbands were litigants like any others, free to go to court over the same issues as men.)In practice this meant not just dower and jointure, but debts, bonds, contracts, property transactions, inheritance and a host of other matters. Secondly, for reasons connected with the legal restrictions wives suffered during marriage, women in sixteenth century England rarely played as dominant a role in litigating their own marriage settlements and separate estates as logic might suggest. They took part in marriage negotiations, but only occasionally did they participate in court actions when negotiated agreements failed. Concentrating solely on marriage settlements, or even on dower or jointure, produces a distorted picture of women's participation in court actions, one that can underestimate women's actual involvement in the arrangement of marriage, and ignore their involvement in other legal affairs.

It was noted in the previous chapter how patterns of female litigation were distinct from patterns of male litigation. Women were more likely than men to sue over interests in land and matters connected with wills and estates, and less likely to sue over bonds and written agreements. These differences are intri-

[1] *The Plain Dealer*, III.i.202–20, in Friedman, *Plays of William Wycherley*, pp. 436–7.

Table 5.1 *Nature of business according to sex of Defendant (in actions brought by men)*

	Male defendant(s)	Female defendant(s)
Land	448 (43%)	89 (43%)
Debts and bonds	365 (35%)	62 (30%)
Stay common law actions	124 (12%)	20 (10%)
Wills and estates	42 (4%)	27 (13%)
Other	71 (7%)	10 (5%)
Total	1,050 (101%)	208 (101%)

Source: PRO 9 vol. 93 (Requests proceedings); piece numbers Req 2/157/1–Req 2/167/37, excluding entries without dates, and entries where the sex of the plaintiff or the subject of disputes is unspecified or unclear.

guing, and are explored within the pages that follow. However, more striking than the discernible differences between the actions male and female plaintiffs initiated is the broad conformity of their habits. On the basis of the comparisons made in the previous chapter, it would be difficult to argue that women stood out as a unique class of litigant with particular grievances and needs. This assumption is bolstered if reference is made to the sex of defendants, for the differences between suits against women and suits against men were even less marked (see table 5.1). The only significant divergence between the two groups is that men were more likely to sue women (on their own or with other men) than men over testamentary matters and contested estates, perhaps a further reflection of the prevalence of widows as executrixes and administratrixes of their late husbands' estates.

Observing the rough equivalence between the legal activities of women and men indicated by the figures in table 5.1, and table 4.5 in chapter 4, a student of jurisprudence might conclude that these results provide confirmation of the highest ideal of the law, that it was blind; that the Masters regarded the parties who came before them simply as litigants, regardless of their sex. Yet this was clearly not the case. The method of analysing litigation according to broad subject categories is insufficiently sensitive to uncover the undoubted differences between the experiences of the two groups. To appreciate the particular character of litigation involving women in Requests, it is necessary to sharpen the focus of attention, to look not simply at the subject of disputes, but at the background to disputes. In particular, it is important to consider women's status as litigants, for, as the past chapters have shown, what made the uniqueness of women's experience before the law undeniable was the uniqueness of their status. Therefore, to appreciate fully the use women made of the law it is essential to take account of the shifting sands of their legal personas. The author of *The Lawes Resolutions of Womens Rights* recognised this fact when he chose to organise his description of women's legal rights around the life cycle of marriage, looking in turn at 'maids, wives and widows'. Following his lead, the remainder of this chapter will concern itself with *femes sole* – unmarried women and widows who sued or were sued in Requests – and the following chapter will consider *femes covert* – married women who generally had to live their lives in the legal shadows cast by their husbands.

UNMARRIED WOMEN

According to the author of *The Lawes Resolutions of Womens Rights*, the law assumed every woman 'either married or to bee married'.[2] In fact a significant proportion of women in sixteenth and seventeenth century England never married, and those who did tended to marry relatively late.[3] The combination of these tendencies meant that at any one time during this period the number of unmarried women in English society exceeded the number of married women and widows combined. Peter Laslett has calculated that over the period 1574–1821 just under 60 per cent of females in society were single, about 32 per cent were married and just under 9 per cent were widowed.[4] More than half of the female population were 'maids' or 'spinsters', a higher proportion than at any time since, and while many were children, a considerable proportion were of legal age, yet we know less about this group of women than we know about either married women or widows.

Historians have studied the escapades of the minority of unmarried women accused in the ecclesiastical courts of sexual misdemeanours and bastard bearing, or found guilty of the crime of infanticide.[5] They have also uncovered information about unmarried women's employment. The majority of female workers were unmarried, employed in domestic and agricultural service, in cloth making, brewing, in retail trades and in countless other areas of employment. Those who were able to put aside some of their earnings saved for their futures, and there is evidence that single women lent out, at interest, money they had saved or inherited.[6] A number of occupations were closed to them, because many guilds opened their doors only to freemen or occasionally to freemen's widows, with the result that daughters working in the same trades as their mothers or fathers might have to cease their employment when their parents

[2] T.E., *The Lawes Resolutions of Womens Rights*, p. 6.
[3] Erickson, *Women and Property*, pp. 48, 83.
[4] Peter Laslett, 'Mean household size in England since the sixteenth century', in Peter Laslett and Richard Wall, eds., *Household and Family in Past Times* (Cambridge, 1972), table 4.7, p. 145.
[5] See, for example, Ingram, *Church Courts*, pp. 219–81; Keith Wrightson, 'Infanticide in earlier seventeenth-century England', *Local Population Studies*, 15 (1975), pp. 10–22.
[6] Erickson, *Women and Property*, p. 81.

died. Some independent spinsters managed to thrive in business, but unmarried women faced many more barriers in the workplace than unmarried men, and Mary Prior found in her study of female traders in Oxford that 'the independent spinster had no place in the Oxford commercial community'.[7] In legal terms, many historians have assumed that single women lived under the protection and control of their fathers until they married, after which the reins of control passed to their husbands.[8] Amy Erickson has pointed out the insufficiency of this interpretation. It ignores the high number of women who never married, estimated to range between 10 and 20 per cent of the female population. It also assumes that paternal influence was strong, when in fact it could be quite weak, given the number of young women who lived and worked away from home, and the number (within a society where late marriages and early deaths were common) whose fathers died before they came of age or decided whether to marry.

Many aspects of the lives of single women and spinsters remain unclear, but current knowledge suggests that unmarried women inherited legacies, ran businesses, held and invested moneys, controlled and leased lands, and entered contractual bonds with men they had agreed to marry.[9] In short, they participated in a range of activities that might give rise to legal wrangling. At the same time, unmarried women were regularly denied access to formal education (beyond rudimentary schooling), refused entry to apprenticeships and trades and barred from holding positions of authority, so that while they might be active within 'informal' areas of the economy and society they were often excluded from more 'formal' areas. The records of the Court of Requests go a long way to confirming this view. Descriptions within pleadings, interrogatories and depositions refer to unmarried women working, handling money, living independently, and exercising responsibility within family structures. A London haberdasher, for example, described how he made his daughter, rather than his apprentice, responsible for all of his moneys.[10] Only on rare occasions, however, did single women initiate court actions on their own behalf. The largest grouping of women in society, single women made up the smallest contingent of female litigants in Requests, around 10 per cent of the female litigant population and no more than 1 or 2 per cent of total litigant numbers.

That single women should be under-represented in the lists of plaintiffs in Requests is not at first sight surprising, for two areas of law likely to affect them, inheritance and the negotiation of contracts to marry, technically lay

---

[7] Robert Tittler, 'Money-lending in the west Midlands – the activities of Joyce Jefferies, 1638–1649', *Historical Research*, 67 (1994), pp. 249–63; Mary Prior, 'Women and the urban economy: Oxford 1500–1800', in Mary Prior, ed., *Women in English Society, 1500–1800* (London, 1985), p. 110.

[8] Fraser, *Weaker Vessel*, p. 164; Travitsky, ed., *Paradise of Women*, p. 69.

[9] Erickson, *Women and Property*, pp. 81, 91.

[10] *Walter Cope v. Henry Archer*, PRO Req 2/51/41, D, deponent William Goughe.

outside the normal Requests jurisdiction. What is surprising is the *extent* of single women's under-representation in the court. The scarcity of unmarried women in the records obviously resulted from something more than jurisdictional boundaries. Lack of adequate resources, as well as social pressures of the kind outlined in chapters 2 and 3, appear to have deterred single women from seeking relief not just in Requests but in other courts as well.[11] When examining court actions that involved unmarried women it is therefore worth keeping in mind that these women were far from typical in their displays of legal independence.

Despite the Masters general reluctance to deal with wills and legacies, the lion's share of single women's litigation in Requests concerned claims to recover or to protect interests due to them by inheritance, and undelivered gifts promised by fathers, mothers, uncles, brothers, masters, employers, friends and other kin. The Masters referred many such claims to the church courts, but they heard a significant number which involved matters of equity, usually relating to fraud or the withholding of evidence.[12] As the previous chapter intimated, the kinds of assistance Requests offered plaintiffs could be particularly useful to unmarried women. Daughters who had been under-age when their inheritance fell due, or when other arrangements were transacted on their behalf, often lacked precise knowledge of the interests owing to them. As adults they could seek help from the Masters to discover exact details of interests or to recover leases, indentures, bonds or other proofs from whoever was withholding them, enabling them to bring actions in the church courts or at common law.[13] Dorothy Cawtrell, for example, was convinced that under the terms of a deed she was the rightful inheritor of the lease of a messuage and seven acres of land her uncle had purchased twelve years before. However, without access to the deed itself she had no idea of the details of her uncle's grant, the conditions it contained or who had witnessed its signing, so she was unable to bring an action at common law to claim the reversion. She approached the Masters as her last and only hope, seeking to recover the deed or to have a copy made so she could proceed at law.[14] Joan Major made a similar plea in 1557, believing that a deed in her aunt's possession contained details of interests that should

---

[11] Robert Shoemaker found few unmarried women involved in the courts of London in the later-seventeenth century; Shoemaker, *Prosecution and Punishment*, p. 207, n. 13; Amy Erickson and Maria Cioni have found the same for Chancery in the sixteenth and seventeenth centuries: Erickson, *Women and Property*, table 7.2, p. 115; Cioni, *Women and Law*, p. 87; for a partial explanation for these low participation rates, see the next chapter.

[12] For examples of referrals to the church courts, see *John & Henry Crowe* v. *James & Margaret England et al.*, PRO Req 1/21, pp. 221–2; PRO Req 1/17, pp. 370, 408.

[13] For most legal purposes women became adults at twenty one; Blackstone, *Commentaries*, vol. 1, p. 451; and see T.E., *The Lawes Resolutions of Womens Rights*, p. 7; however some testators specified the age at which daughters would become eligible to inherit legacies or to receive annuities (for example, when they reached twenty five, or when they married).

[14] *Dorothy Cawtrell* v. *James Hooper & Richard Dibbell*, PRO Req 2/210/23.

now be hers. The Masters offered her assistance, but her simple plea grew into a complex battle over local custom and the terms of a disputed will that dragged on for more than five years.[15]

In contrast to women like Joan Major and Dorothy Cawtrell who were unaware of the exact details of their interests, other unmarried women knew precisely what they wished to claim, but had to wait until they became eligible to claim it. Joan Ford knew that she was named in a copyhold interest for lives (a customary tenure enjoyed for one, two or three lives, held by a copy of the entry in a manor court roll) and in 1566, as soon as she came of age, she sued her late mother's second husband to claim possession.[16] Her suit was successful, but her stepfather managed to transfer the copyhold to a third party, forcing Joan to bring a further action in 1567, and to defend herself when her stepfather counter-sued in 1568.[17] In 1562 Dorothy Roydon inherited an array of interests in lands and messuages from her father, all of them mortgaged for £20 to a Ralph Broughton, and when he refused to release them she immediately sued him in Requests. The Masters found in her favour and ordered Broughton to relinquish control of the identified interests, along with relevant deeds and evidences, in return for £20 and to sign a release promising never to trouble her over these interests in the future. Dorothy, for her part, had to agree not to expel any of the sitting tenants from these lands, without first informing the Masters and gaining their permission: the Masters appear to have been happy to restore a daughter to her birthright, as long as she did not plan to profit unduly from this recovery.[18] Not all single women waited until they were of legal age to sue. A number of orphans brought suits, on their own or with the assistance of guardians, against executors, administrators, close relatives or strangers who were fraudulently detaining from them moneys and goods due by descent.[19]

The other significant grouping of unmarried female litigants were female servants who brought suits in Requests to recover unpaid wages or to protect investments. Elizabeth Banks, the Bristol maidservant mentioned in the previous chapter, sued her employer to recover her possessions as well as her wages. Another servant, Elizabeth Watkinson, made a successful claim in the Mayor's Court in London's Guildhall against the son and executor of her dead employer for £10 in unpaid wages. Her opponent counter-sued her in Requests, alleging that his father had paid the sum while he was alive. However, after Elizabeth denied this suggestion on oath before the Masters, and described how her opponent was also troubling her with suits in Queen's Bench and Common Pleas,

[15] *Joane Major v. Margaret Major & Wylly Wever*, PRO Req 2/239/3.
[16] For more information about copyholds for lives, see chapter 7 below.
[17] *Johan Forde v. Thomas Wyllmott*, PRO Req 2/205/28; *Johan Ford v. Edward Gorge*, PRO Req 2/206/36; *Thomas Wilmot v. Johan Fourd*, PRO Req 2/155/58, Req 2/98/51.
[18] *Dorothie Roydon v. Raufe Broughton*, PRO Req 1/11, pp. 243–5.
[19] *Elisabeth Spenser & Elizabeth Spenser v. Jeames Mascall*, PRO Req 2/267/44.

they dismissed his action and awarded her 40s. in costs, the equivalent of a year's wages.[20]

Occasionally unmarried women were named as executrixes or administratrixes of the estates of their parents, and those who accepted these responsibilities dealt with these matters competently. On some occasions they may even have indulged in fraud. Sara Haselwood was made the administratrix of her deceased father's estate with the blessing of her mother Agnes. Apparently Agnes agreed to let her fulfil this role as long as she be allowed to retain the lease of the house in which she lived, along with certain goods, for the rest of her life. The two had set down this agreement in a bond with a penalty for non-performance of £100, but Sara later stole Agnes's copy of the bond and sold the lease to a third party for £30. After a protracted series of hearings and failed commissions the Masters found in favour of Agnes, and they labelled Sara a troublesome menace.[21]

Single women came to Requests to protect what was theirs. Heiresses sued to claim bequests, daughters brought actions to ensure the payment of annual or monthly allowances, servants sued to recover unpaid wages.[22] Unmarried women were far less likely than unmarried men to litigate business matters, to dispute purchases or sales of goods, or to claim the penalties on bonds for unpaid debts or unperformed promises they had negotiated themselves. It is interesting in this context to consider the case of the maidservant Alice Bawghes who sued her attorney William Knight for fraud. According to her bill of complaint she had made Knight responsible for all of her financial and legal affairs, entrusting him with sums of money to invest for her use and with uncancelled debts and forfeited bonds she wished him to pursue at law, worth a total of over £160. One of these bonds confirmed a promise of marriage, and since the promise had not been kept Alice wished to make a claim against her reluctant suitor for the £40 penalty for non-performance. According to Alice's story she was a working servant possessed of considerable resources who was not afraid to protect them; indeed she appears to have been active in seeking to enhance them. Yet she did so by delegating her financial, as well as her legal, affairs to an attorney. The world of bonds and deeds was not one she felt comfortable entering alone, and her bill described her as 'A verie simple and ignorante woman', in contrast to Knight who was said to be well versed in financial matters as well as 'haveing some experience in the lawes of this realme'.[23]

Unmarried women appear to have been reluctant plaintiffs, and the few who

[20] *Robert Gomersal v. Elizabeth Watkinson*, PRO Req 2/36/75, Req 1/19, p. 638.
[21] *Agnes Haselwood v. Sara Hazelwood et al.*, PRO Req 2/38/20, Req 2/225/10, Req 2/224/20.
[22] *Jane & Elizabeth Thompson v. William Bradley & Robert Powe*, PRO Req 2/276/33; *Jeane Goddarde v. William Goddarde*, PRO Req 2/210/47; Req 2/79/29; Req 2/81/18; *Edward & Mary Harden et al., v. Agnes Harvye et al.*, PRO Req 2/223/17; *Roger, Mawde & Johan Elys v. Thomas Chaffyn*, PRO Req 2/202/36.   [23] *Alice Bawghes v. William Knighte*, PRO Req 2/166/14.

went to court tended to enlist the assistance of intermediaries. It is not that daughters were kept under the firm control of their fathers, or as Antonia Fraser argued, that the legal rights of the *feme sole* 'were assumed to be swallowed up in those of her nearest male protector'.[24] Such a view is too simple. Rather, in a society that tended to equate female entry into adulthood with marriage, and in which the world of bonds and legal instruments was considered more a male than a female domain, it was often difficult for unmarried women to participate freely in legal and financial dealings. The distinction between assuming that unmarried women were restricted by convention and personal circumstance, and assuming that they lived under the control of their families and close kin is a fine one, but a distinction that is important to make. If families ran the affairs of younger women then we would find more cases in courts like Requests initiated by fathers, mothers and uncles concerning the rights and holdings of daughters and nieces. However, to make this distinction is not to deny that some daughters did live under the controlling hand of parents or kin. Opponents certainly alleged time and time again that this was the case, and the significance of their allegations will be considered in later chapters.[25]

Looking at the experiences of all of the unmarried women who found their way into Requests, it is possible to construct a hierarchy of the legal and financial independence single women exercised, or failed to exercise, in Elizabethan society. The resulting structure resembles a low, broad-based pyramid. At the bottom of this pyramid can be clustered the large group of single women who possessed interests, usually through inheritance, but who proved unable or unwilling to venture into court to claim or to protect what was rightfully theirs. The existence of this group can be deduced from the silent majority of unmarried women who never went to court, and from the actions of married litigants which will be examined in the next chapter. Above them can be grouped those single women who left responsibility for all of their monetary and legal interests to their families, either by choice or in response to family pressure. On the next level can be placed women with legal interests who were knowledgeable about their rights but who relied on attorneys, trustees or other intermediaries to look after the day-to-day running of their finances and legal battles. Finally, at the top stands a small but proud group of independent spinsters who managed their own finances and who used the courts without hesitation whenever the necessity arose.

WIDOWS

If single women were under-represented in Requests and other courts, widows more than held their own. Making up just under 9 per cent of women in society (according to Laslett's estimate) they constituted almost half of the female liti-

---

[24] Fraser, *Weaker Vessel*, p. 164.   [25] See chapters 6 and 8 below.

gant populations in Requests, Common Pleas and Queen's Bench, and around 5 or 6 per cent of the total numbers of litigants in these courts.[26] Widows, in other words, were the only class of women whose share of litigation came near to matching (and may at times have exceeded) the level of their presence in society. Commentators have long recognised widowhood as the time of greatest legal independence for women.[27] Women who outlived their husbands not only emerged from coverture and recovered their legal capacity, they tended to have more experience, greater self-confidence and greater resources than unmarried female litigants. That they enjoyed a visible presence in the courts is not surprising. However, what the Requests materials vividly demonstrate is how often widows had *cause* to go to court.

The death of a husband could prompt a woman to contemplate legal action for a variety of reasons. The most obvious of these, perhaps, was the need to secure the traditional widows' interests of dower, jointure and widow's estate, and widows litigated all of these interests in Requests, although to varying extents. Dower was a common law right, recoverable by writ of dower in a common law court, and the Masters tended to refer such claims to other courts. However, a small but steady stream of widows seeking dower gained access to Requests by raising questions of equity. When Anne Dowding tried to claim a third share of her late husband's manor on Anglesey, her opponent conceded that William Dowding had died seised of, or in control of, the title to the manor, but he refused to accept that Anne was William's widow. Anne established her marital status by referring the Masters to the parish book which recorded her marriage, and they ordered the recovery of her dower third as well as compensation for lost rents and profits.[28]

Jointure actions were more common than dower actions in Requests. 'Traditional' jointures, those in which a husband and wife jointly purchased an interest in land so that the survivor would assume sole ownership when one of them died, were predominantly common law matters because they concerned questions of title.[29] However, jointures set out in marriage settlements fell

---

[26] In the samples for 1560 described in chapter 2 above, widows made up 48 per cent of female litigants in Common Pleas (twenty three out of fifty eight) and 5.3 per cent of all litigants (twenty three out of 431); the first 150 entries (ignoring double entries) on the first four membranes of the roll of warrants of attorneys for Easter term 2 Elizabeth I; PRO CP40/1187; in Queen's Bench widows made up 50 per cent of female litigants (ten out of twenty) and 5 per cent of all litigants (ten out of 204); the roll of warrants of attorneys for Easter term 2 Elizabeth I; PRO KB 27/1194; according to C.W. Brooks' slightly larger samples from the same year, widows made up 6 per cent of litigants in both courts; C.W. Brooks, *Pettyfoggers*, p. 281.

[27] For example, Travitsky, *Paradise of Women*, p. 70; Fraser, *Weaker Vessel*, pp. 5–6.

[28] *Anne Dowding v. Robert Griffith*, PRO Req 1/11, pp. 27–8; for further examples, see *Florence Hall v. Giles Raimonde*, PRO Req 2/196/74; Req 2/197/66; PRO Req 1/11, pp. 28–30; *Elizabeth Fynche v. Thomas Raunce*, PRO Req 2/207/78.

[29] The Masters usually referred disputes over such jointures to the common law; see *Johan Cobbs v. John Johnson*, PRO Req 1/21, pp. 199–200.

within the purview of equity, and Requests and Chancery officials frequently dealt with them. Perhaps the most common dispute was over the identity of jointure interests, with parties arguing over the intentions of purchasers or donors, and whether they had meant to include particular lands or leases in jointure agreements.[30]

Causes involving widow's estate, or 'freebench', were more common again, although technically these matters also lay outside the Masters' jurisdiction. Customary rights attaching to customary tenures were matters for customary courts, and the Masters dismissed many cases from their court accordingly. However, in the sixteenth century, Requests, like Chancery, increasingly served as a court of appeal for customary actions whenever litigants could establish that they were unlikely, or had been unable, to gain a fair hearing in manor courts. The jurisdictional border between custom and equity proved weaker than almost any other, and a flood of customary cases came into Requests. The considerable numbers that involved the rights of widows form the subject of chapter 7 below.

Actions relating to dower, jointure and widow's estate could be fiercely contested. Given the nature of inheritance, widows often had to make claims against their late husbands' heirs, which might involve them suing (or being sued by) their own sons, particularly stepsons, or other family members or kin.[31] However, actions relating to these traditional entitlements did not dominate lists of widow litigation. This is partly because rights like dower and freebench were so prominent in the consciousness of many communities that widows often took up their entitlements without opposition. But it is mainly due to the array of other causes arising from the deaths of husbands that helped to make litigants out of a range of rich and poor widows.

In many instances husbands named their wives their executrixes, or if they died intestate their widows took on the administration of their estates. Women who accepted these responsibilities had to prove wills and enter inventories in the ecclesiastical probate courts, but their attempts to collect money from debtors, to satisfy creditors, or to claim ownership of disputed assets, often led them into the secular courts as well. They brought suits on their own behalf, and on behalf of their children or other beneficiaries. If their husbands had themselves been executors or administrators, or died with bequests owing to them, then widows might find their responsibilities banking up as they attempted at second or third hand to oversee, or make claims upon, the estates of individuals they might never have met.[32] Widow executrixes and administratrixes also had to defend themselves in suits brought by others. Heirs sued

---

[30] *Margaret Kempe* v. *William Franklin*, PRO Req 2/230/12.   [31] See chapters 6 and 7 below.
[32] *Mary Thorne* v. *Erasmus Prynne & Nicholas Thorne*, PRO Req 2/39/90; *Richard & Mathewe Goodall* v. *Marie Stubbes*, PRO Req 2/213/35; *Agnes, Edmond & Katherine Sheppard* v. *William Arnold*, PRO Req 2/159/138, R.

widows to claim legacies, impatient creditors sued them to recover unpaid debts or to claim the penalties for non-performance that attached to agreements in bonds, the beneficiaries of uses sued them to have those uses performed, and rivals for the loyalty or affections of widows' dead husbands accused widows of falsely procuring administration by concealing wills.[33] And as will be seen in a moment, widow executrixes and administratrixes were also counter-sued in Requests by individuals they were pursuing at common law. The preponderance of actions against widow executrixes and administratrixes is reflected in the figures in table 5.1, at the beginning of this chapter, which show that 13 per cent of actions brought against female defendants involved wills and estates, compared with only 4 per cent of actions brought against male defendants.

Widows who were not executrixes or administratrixes could also be active litigants. Like daughters and sons, they claimed legacies and contested wills. Others 'inherited' unresolved law suits from their husbands, which they continued in their own names by entering 'bills of revivor'.[34] An even greater number fought to retain control of their marital homes. Rival claimants brought actions to eject widows from houses, tenements and messuages on the grounds that these interests had belonged solely to these women's husbands, and therefore had expired when their owners expired, or else constituted part of their estates. Widows hurried to court to counter these suggestions, arguing, for example, that the interest they held in their family holding ran not for the length of their late husbands' lives, or the length of their own (chaste) widowhoods, but for their lives, or for a period of years which had not yet expired.[35]

The regularity with which widows asserted or defended their claim to houses, tenements, copyholds, or whole manors, helps to explain the high percentage of women's litigation that involved interests in land, 58 per cent compared with 43 per cent for men (see table 4.1). The ability of widows to assert an interest in land months or even years after their husbands had alienated it (because it had belonged to them before marriage, or was due to them under dower or jointure) led an early seventeenth century verse writer to warn those who 'wille be wise in purchasing' to check the ownership of the property interests they wished to buy:

Loke whether it movith of a weddyd woman
And ware well of Covert de baron.[36]

---

[33] *John & Agnes Greenewood v. Agnes Bishop*, PRO Req 2/38/57; *Richard Walker v. Elizabeth Kirkland*, PRO Req 2/165/232.

[34] *Margarett Haggott v. Thomas, Bishop of Bath & Wells et al.*, PRO Req 2/223/1; Req 2/96/42; Req 2/31/40.

[35] *Johane Wilcox v. Thomas Llewellyn et al.*, PRO Req 2/289/49, R, D, deponent Robert Lansdon; *Margaret Godfry v. Alman Mutton*, PRO Req 2/210/49, Req 2/214/18, Req 2/149/54, Req 2/149/78, Req 2/244/87.

[36] The author also warned buyers to check if the seller was of age, whether the lands were mortgaged and so on; C.U.L. Hh 2.6.(c), fol. 58ᵛ; see also Pollock and Maitland, *The History of English Law*, vol. 2, p. 411.

William Christmas failed to consider advice of this kind until it was too late. Only after he had agreed to purchase the lease of a manor did his legal counsel advise him that he should name the seller's wife Alice in the transfer. Unfortunately for William, this was something 'the said Alice was very unwilling to doe', and he was 'enforced to give her the some of one hundred pounds for her good will and consent thereunto'.[37] Women regularly, if unpredictably, gained possession of interests in land. They did not always keep control – husbands managed lands that belonged to their wives, and heirs sometimes took responsibility for a widow's interests if she became too old to manage lands herself. Nevertheless, interests came into women's hands, and women litigated to protect them.[38]

The onset of widowhood marked the opening of a new chapter in a woman's life, but as this expanding list of examples indicates, many individuals spent the first weeks and months of widowhood trying to clear up matters connected with the chapter of their life that had just closed. These women discovered that attached to their restored legal status came a whole raft of responsibilities, and shouldering these responsibilities turned many widows into litigants.[39] The time available for widows to adjust to their new situation and to mourn for their late husbands could be minimal. When John Lewis of Fernham in Berkshire (now in Oxfordshire) died in 1562, his widow Joan Lewis was appointed administratrix, and she immediately became embroiled in a bitter struggle to maintain control of his estate. Joan described in her bill how less than a week after John died his brother and another man, Toby Pleydell, came with accomplices and ransacked her house, carrying away goods, chattels and livestock worth £700. According to deponents, they removed everything except Joan's bed, and with bats, swords and staves expelled Joan from the house along with her children, one a baby at the breast of its nurse, 'who was kept without fier, bed or candle by the space of one day and one night'. Joan sued these men in Requests, but after Toby Pleydell produced a will and claimed to be executor, the case quickly descended into an unpleasant dispute over the legitimacy of the will, which some deponents alleged was made just a few hours before John's death, when he was 'past his memorie and could not tell what he did'.[40]

Taking charge of estate duties could be very rewarding – successfully managing an estate that was unencumbered by debt could leave a widow in possession of considerable assets, power and independence – but it could also produce

---

[37] *William Christmas v. George & Alice Poulett*, PRO Req 1/18, p. 882.
[38] Some widows agreed to release their rights to dower in return for an annuity or other money payment; *Florence Hall v. Giles Raimonde*, PRO Req 1/11, pp. 28–30.
[39] On the effects of widowhood on a woman's life, see Barbara Todd, 'The virtuous widow in Protestant England', in Sandra Cavallo and Lyndan Warner, eds., *Widowhood in Medieval and Early Modern Europe* (Longman; forthcoming).
[40] *Johan Lewis v. Thobye Pleydell*, PRO Req 2/164/103, B, A, R, Rj, D, deponents John Pyttman, Jane Tyndaill, Margarett Richardson.

hardship. In her capacity as the administratrix of her late husband's estate, the Kensington widow Alice Seller put up the lease of the family farm as collateral to raise £40 to settle some of her husband's debts. By the time she came to redeem the lease the due date had passed and her creditor evicted her. Having lost her only source of income, Alice was unable to pay her husband's remaining creditors and she was imprisoned in the Counter in London, where she languished for a year before bringing a suit in Requests to recover the leased farm.[41]

Widowhood acted as a catalyst for litigation because the death of a husband so often presented widows with duties to perform and interests to claim or to protect. In these instances external circumstances exerted pressure on widows to go to court, but in other cases widows embraced the opportunity that the resumption of legal status afforded them. They brought suits because they were able to bring suits, and their example marks yet another way in which widowhood could act as a spur to litigation. Agnes Nowell falls into this category. She sued Thomas Hall in 1591, immediately after the death of her husband. In her bill she described how she and her husband had separated, temporarily, fifteen or sixteen years before, and how he had given her £20 for her livelihood and maintenance. She had given the money to Thomas Hall, a neighbour and relative, to keep for her use, and he had retained the money ever since. In his answer, Thomas agreed that Agnes and her husband had separated (twenty seven or twenty eight years before, not fifteen or sixteen) and that he had kept £20 for her use. However, he alleged that he had repaid the sum immediately after the couple's reconciliation. The reason he had not given the money to Agnes was that, 'being a feme covert . . . all things which she possessed was her said husbands'.[42]

The Nowell case highlights various aspects of the unique position in which widows found themselves when it came to matters of law. Firstly, it is fascinating to observe how Agnes acted as soon as she was able (as soon as she emerged from coverture), bringing an action relating to a time when she had enjoyed independent, or at least quasi-independent, status in the past, even though between *fifteen* and *twenty eight* years had elapsed in the interim. The idea that she had harboured this legal grudge for so many years, unable or unwilling to enlist the support of her husband to sue Hall while she was married, provides a tantalising glimpse of the independent thinking of a married woman. The second thing to note is that the Masters allowed her to pursue her action despite its vintage, when in other circumstances they refused to hear cases that had lain dormant for just two or three years. Arguments of the type Hall presented – if it was true that he owed £20, surely Agnes and her husband would have sued him years before – usually found favour with the Masters and led them to dismiss

---

[41] *Alyce Seller* v. *John Blackeman & William Hunt*, PRO Req 2/271/20.
[42] *Agnes Nowell* v. *Thomas Hall*, PRO Req 2/166/134, m. 2, A; for details of coverture, see the next chapter.

many cases without a hearing. However, the Masters appear to have recognised the particular constraints that women endured under coverture, and showed themselves willing to make exceptions, presumably to prevent widows from being unduly prejudiced by their shifting status before the law. The sensitivity the Masters showed in these cases perhaps helps to justify Ridley's description of Requests as a court for 'Widows and orphans', but it is worth noting that the Chancellor permitted similar exceptions in Chancery, where widows can be found bringing actions after periods of fourteen, twenty and even thirty years.[43]

Thirdly, and finally, the Nowell case highlights a whole range of difficulties that widows might experience as a result of the oscillating nature of their legal status. Consigned to a curious legal limbo during marriage, wives might or might not be aware of the intricate details of their husbands' financial transactions, property arrangements and law suits. If they were unaware, this could leave them poorly placed to settle or conclude these matters if they became widows. What oral promises had their husbands made? Which deadlines for the payment of money had they met or failed to meet? Were there any witnesses to a transaction a widow could call upon in a legal action? If, on the other hand, a widow knew the answers to these questions and had precise knowledge of the matter in issue, opponents could nevertheless *claim*, as Thomas Hall claimed, that she was ignorant of these matters, that she had not witnessed the making of agreements, or that as a *feme covert*, 'all things which she possessed were her said husbands'.

The logic of coverture made it plausible for litigants to argue that widows remained unaware of their husbands' every legal and financial move in the past, in the same way that they might argue that executors or administrators were unaware of the undocumented promises, payments and actions of the deceased. However, the logic of marriage also made it possible for litigants to argue the exact opposite, that widows *had been* aware of their husbands' activities. Having shared a house and a life with their husbands it was natural to expect that they knew the details of their husbands' loans, debts and assets, and therefore in bringing court actions it was likely that they were feigning ignorance of these details to gain advantage. In 1599 John Aubrey complained to the Masters that the widow Parnell Smith was suing him at common law over an old obligation for a debt, owed to Parnell's husband, for which he had acted as surety, or guarantor. Parnell was her husband's executrix, 'and finding the said obligacion amongest other writings of her saide husbands uncancelled, althoughe the principall debte therein conteined were fully satisfied and payed, hath nevertheles putt the same bonde in sute at the common lawe, intending to recover the penaltie of the same'.[44] The clear implication was that Parnell was using her

---

[43] See Cioni, *Women and Law*, pp. 81–2, 111, 112.
[44] *John Aubrey v. Parnell Smith*, PRO Req 1/19, p. 796.

status as a widow to claim a penalty that she had no legal or moral right to claim. In similar circumstances John Leak complained to the Masters that the administratrix Elizabeth Hargrave 'givethe it oute that shee will sue and ympleade your said subjecte' upon several obligations belonging to her husband Henry, 'albeit shee well knowethe aswell by viewe of the daiebooke . . . of the saide Henry Hargrave as by suche notes as your subjecte hathe shewed unto her' that he had settled these debts.[45] Litigants accused widows of this kind of illicit double dealing on a regular basis.[46]

In these and in other cases, the extent of women's awareness of their husbands' dealings was a crucial issue, whether opponents contended that wives were ignorant (as Thomas Hall suggested of Agnes Nowell) or fully informed (as opponents said of Parnell Smith and Elizabeth Hargrave). Widows responded to these accusations by stating that they knew enough about the actions of their late husbands to know that alleged transactions had never taken place; that opponents had not settled debts, or negotiated oral promises that superseded written agreements. Or else they responded to accusations by asking their accusers for proof. If opponents had performed their promises, why had they let bonds remain uncancelled? If they had settled their debts, where were the acquittances? Some widows who used these tactics appear to have been calling their adversaries' bluff. Others seemed genuinely concerned to discover the truth about their late husbands' activities. Parnell Smith, mentioned a few moments ago, responded to the accusation that she was trying to collect a previously settled debt by saying that 'whatsoever shall credibly appeare in conscience or equitie to have been payed of the some aforesaide, she this defendant will most willingly allowe of & abate unto the said complainant'.[47] When a defendant answered Dame Margaret Stanhope's bill of complaint by alleging that her husband had granted him a lease of contested lands, she offered to settle their dispute if he could produce the lease. As her counsel explained, 'if it shall upon sight thereof fall out and appeare that the same lease was so made by the said Sir Thomas Stanhop . . . shee will permitt & suffer the said defendant quietly to enjoy the same for & under the rents . . . therein expressed'.[48]

The state of flux that surrounded a widow's recovery of status opened the way for unscrupulous opponents to make all sorts of allegations about double dealing and the unfair exploitation of out of date documents. However their accusations were plausible, because what they described was possible. Those widows who received anything from their husbands usually inherited more than a legacy, or control of lands earmarked for their jointure. They took into their hands the contents of their husbands' chests, closets and cabinets, which might

---

[45] *John Leake v. Elizabeth Hargrave*, PRO Req 2/165/135, m. 4, B.
[46] *William Posonbie v. Elizabeth Stagge*, PRO Req 1/18, p. 144; *James Buswell v. Anne Buswell*, PRO Req 1/17, p. 130.   [47] *John Aubrey v. Parnell Smith*, PRO Req 1/19, p. 796.
[48] *Margaret Stanhop v. Thomas Roe*, PRO Req 1/21, p. 26.

include bundles of paper and parchment including deeds, leases, promissory notes, bills of sale, indentures and other written instruments. A common euphemism in pleadings suggested that documents had come into the hands of the wrong person 'by casual means', a legal fiction suggesting theft or unauthorised possession that parties often levelled at widows, because of the unique access they enjoyed. The task of the widow, especially if she was executrix or administratrix, was to make sense of the documents now in her possession, and to pursue any matters that required resolution, which often meant putting obligations and other agreements in suit at common law. This could leave some widows in a quandary. Their duties as executrixes or administratrixes *obliged* them to put uncancelled bonds in suit.[49] Yet, as their husbands' widows, they might know that the debts or agreements in question had been settled. Double charging, whether malevolent or innocent, remained a distinct possibility. Alice Bishop sued her late husband's brother, William Bishop, for debt at common law, but William persuaded the Masters to issue an injunction against her to stop her suits after he produced a certificate from a minister confirming that he had repaid the outstanding sums.[50] Did Alice know that William had settled with her husband or not?

In other cases the time that elapsed between the date when a cause arose and when it reached the courts raised suspicions. The Agnes Nowell case demonstrated how a married woman could harbour a legal grudge for years, until widowhood gave her the freedom to go to law. Widow executrixes and administratrixes also resuscitated dormant causes, not their own this time, but their husbands'. In other words they sued opponents their husbands had failed or neglected to sue in the past. Maudlen Holland, for example, came to Requests to recover a legacy due to her late husband that she claimed her opponents, her husband's older brother and another man, had wrongfully detained for *thirty six years*. True to form, the Masters allowed her to pursue her action, despite nearly four decades of silence, and they made an initial order that the brother pay her the outstanding sum. When he refused to comply, Maudlen entered a fresh plea in which she described how the defendant, 'also did most cruelly beate her, contrary to his profession, he being a parson'. He and his co-defendant responded by arguing that Maudlen's husband had sealed a general acquittance, in the form of a deed, almost forty years before, releasing all claims and promising not to pursue legal action against them. Again questions arise; was Maudlen genuinely attempting to right an injustice done to her husband by his domineering brother? Was she merely fulfilling her duty as an administratrix to gather all of an intestate's interests? Or was she seeking to manipulate her status as a widow to make a claim that her husband had not, would not and

[49] I would like to thank Barbara Todd for reminding me of this point.
[50] *William Bishop* v. *Alice Bishop*, PRO Req 1/15, fol. 57.

could not have made himself, because he had indeed signed the alleged acquittance? To take one final example, the widow Margaret Togwell claimed a copyhold interest in Chancery after her husband died, but the presiding Master dismissed her suit almost immediately, after learning that her bill of complaint was identical to a bill her husband had entered in Requests seventeen years before. Was Margaret adamantly asserting a right now that she was no longer a *feme covert*, acting under the instructions of her legal counsel, or using her widow status to sue a defunct cause in a different court?[51]

Regardless of the truth or falsehood of the accusations litigants made about a widow's competence, integrity, and her knowledge of past events, these cases reveal the climate of confusion, real or imagined, that could surround the death of a woman's husband and her recovery of independent status. The death of any individual could create confusion about ownership and about the nature of past transactions, but the influence of coverture made this doubly true whenever a man was survived by his widow. Honest women might suffer, because they lacked the means to counter false allegations suggesting that they were manipulative profiteers. Dishonest or ill-informed women might benefit, falsely making claims at common law for debts and penalties their opponents did not legally owe.

Widowhood gave many women their first experience of litigation, whether in ecclesiastical probate courts, equity courts, customary courts or courts of common law. As this discussion has emphasised, widows were more likely to have dealings with the law in the first year of widowhood than at any other time (unless, of course, they became widows more than once). However, this does not mean that these women retreated from the courts after they had proved their husbands' wills and sued recalcitrant creditors. Widows litigated throughout widowhood, and they did not confine themselves to litigating matters connected with their husbands' estates. Some had independent wealth or trades, like the woman who explained how she had amassed £31 in gold 'by her greate labor and paynes takinge dyvers and many yeres by keepinge of women in child bedd'. She said she gave this money to her sister and brother-in-law to keep for her use, and when they detained it she sued them for fraud.[52] Those who inherited businesses sometimes carried them on, like Mary Cornwall, who was counter-sued in Requests for failing to deliver promised shipments of corn.[53] Those who inherited moneys often invested them, and those who inherited lands or estates sometimes took over their management. Looking after these investments and interests could induce independent widows to become prolific

[51] *Margaret Togwell v. Robert Penroddocke & Alice Johns*, PRO Req 2/279/28.
[52] *Johanne Swaynston v. Richard & Rose Atwyll*, PRO Req 2/274/75, m. 2, B; for further details of this case, see chapter 6 below; for another example of a widow midwife, see *Joan Frenche v. Alice Pynchback*, PRO Req 2/164/60, B.
[53] *Thomas & Danyell Burkingham v. Mary Cornewell*, PRO Req 1/18, p. 884.

litigants. Elizabeth Shipper, the widow of a prebendary of Gloucester cathedral, claimed to have inherited from her husband interests worth £300, and during her widowhood she leased some properties to tenants, sold or improved others, borrowed and lent money, and at one stage kept a victualling house. Between 1595 and 1601 she brought a series of suits in Requests against different defendants for fraud.[54]

The wealthiest grouping of independent widows to appear in Requests were those who controlled manors and oversaw manorial courts. Given the nature of Requests they usually appeared as defendants, answering suits brought against them by their tenants. Scattered through the court's calendars are the names of dozens of eminent widow landholders, including Dame Edith Horsye, Lady Isabel, Dowager Countess of Rutland and Dame Eleonora Zouche.[55] These women delegated responsibility to male stewards, but many kept a watchful eye on the management of their interests. When Agnes More took control of a manor in Wiltshire, the first thing she did was to 'take a knowledge' of all of her tenants to discover their interests, and then she disallowed all the grants of customary estates her husband had made without her consent.[56]

The London widow Dame Mary Cheeke, one of the few ladies of the manor to appear in Requests as a plaintiff, took a particularly active interest in the running of her manors. In her capacity as the administratrix of her late husband's estate, she possessed life interests in three Somerset manors, the management of which she left to her late husband's long-serving steward and his bailiff. However, when she began to suspect these two men of fraud, she dismissed them and began a series of actions against them, lasting from 1594 to 1600, to recover lost profits.[57] She was convinced that her steward had been accepting bribes, granting interests against custom for profit, and declaring only a proportion of the value of entry fines while pocketing the rest. He had been doing so even before her husband had died, and she calculated that his per-

---

[54] *Elizabeth Shipper* v. *Thomas Good & William Taylor*, PRO Req 2/39/60; Req 2/275/45; Req 2/157/382; Req 2/110/3; *Thomas Good* v. *Elizabeth Shipper*, PRO Req 2/123/53; Req 2/123/53; Req 2/163/61; *Elizabeth Shipper* v. *Thomas Pury & Giles Danyell*, PRO Req 2/267/24; *Elizabeth Shipper* v. *John Nicolls, Barnard Bennett et al.*, PRO Req 2/266/31; for details of Shippers actions against Thomas Good see chapter 6 below; for further examples of widow moneylenders see *John Courtman & Margaret Cutting* v. *Anthonie Hearing*, PRO Req 1/19, pp. 402–3; *Robert & Silvester Dackombe* v. *Phillippe & Jane Cottington*, PRO Req 2/197/2, B; *Johanne & John Littlejohn* v. *Anne Littlejohn et al.*, PRO Req 2/235/71, B; *Joan Frenche* v. *Alice Pynchback*, PRO Req 2/164/60, Rj; *Hugh Keyll & George Newbolde* v. *Richard Brooke*, PRO Req 2/85/52.

[55] *John & Agnes Larcombe* v. *Edith Horsye*, PRO Req 2/233/14; *Richard Collard* v. *Isabell Countesse of Rutland*, PRO Req 2/191/44; *Elionora Zouch* v. *Elionora Zouch*, PRO Req 2/157/506; Req 2/159/200.

[56] *Roger, Mawde & Johan Elys* v. *Thomas Chaffyn*, PRO Req 2/202/36.

[57] *Mary Cheeke* v. *John Whittinge*, PRO Req 2/188/23; Req 2/44/56; Req 2/57/13; PRO Req 1/18, pp. 24, 296, 818; Req 1/19, pp. 22, 203; *John Whyttyng* v. *Mary Chicke*, PRO Req 2/288/31; Req 2/157/91; *Mary Cheeke* v. *Christopher Symcocks*, PRO Req 2/47/36; Req 2/43/36; PRO Req 1/18, pp. 269, 544, 622, 631, 693, 824, 855, 860.

sistent frauds had netted him £1,000. Her meticulously detailed allegations resulted from a survey of her properties she commissioned from an attorney, and while Mary conceded that her knowledge of her husband's dealings could never be complete (one allegation, for example, she confessed 'she beleevith to be true because she cann fynd no such matter contayned in her booke of receipts'), she provides a fine example of a widow who actively monitored her business affairs, and was willing to expend large sums in court to protect them.[58]

MARRIAGE SETTLEMENTS, JOINTURES, USES AND TRUSTS

Marriage settlements, and the uses and trusts they often contained, involved the rights and entitlements of married women. Yet, most were arranged before women married, and most were litigated (if they were litigated at all) after they became widows. It therefore makes sense to discuss them in a chapter concerned with single women and widows, rather than in a chapter devoted to wives.

Marriage settlements continue to attract historical debate. A long list of historians, from H.J. Habbakuk, Lawrence Stone and Jeanne Fawltier Stone to Lloyd Bonfield and Eileen Spring, has argued about the purpose, significance and effectiveness of settlements, in particular strict settlements, and their influence on the size of landed estates in the later seventeenth and eighteenth centuries. Most agree that patriarchs saw the entails allowed in settlements as a useful means of shoring up family estates, preventing leaks of property to other families through the conduit of daughters, or wastage at the hands of spendthrift sons. They disagree about their application and effectiveness.[59] Susan Staves has warned students of strict settlement against assuming too male a view of the family by reifying the estate and regarding women merely as carriers or consumers of property. Perceiving daughters and widows as drains on family resources, because they consumed property at the expense of male heirs, is almost to deny to women a place within their own families. It suggests that male heads of households resented the women in their own families, while warming to daughters-in-law because their portions formed welcome contributions to family wealth.[60] Amy Erickson has taken this idea further, pointing out that concentration on the strict settlement has led historians to overlook other

---

[58] *John Whyttyng* v. *Mary Cheeke*, PRO Req 2/288/31 [m. 7], A.

[59] H.J. Habbakuk, 'Marriage settlements in the eighteenth century', *Transactions of the Royal Historical Society*, 4th series, 32 (1950), pp. 15–30; Lawrence Stone and Jeanne Stone, *An Open Elite? England, 1540–1880* (Oxford, 1984); Lloyd Bonfield, 'Affective families, open elites, and strict family settlements in early modern England', *Economic History Review*, 2nd series, 39 (1986), pp. 355–70; Eileen Spring, 'The heiress-at-law: English real property law from a new point of view', *Law and History Review*, 8 (1990), pp. 273–96; Eileen Spring, *Law, Land, and Family*; for a fuller list of contributors to this debate see Staves, *Married Women's Separate Property*, pp. 276–7, n. 5. [60] Staves, *Married Women's Separate Property*, pp. 202–5.

forms of settlement, which used trusts or conditions attached to jointures not so much to keep property within the family, but to guarantee the rights and property of women during and after marriage.[61]

These debates continue, and if historians are to resolve them it will be through the examination of settlement documents and family papers, rather than the records of the courts. But whether marriage settlements were designed to protect the interests of individual women, or to protect the interests of their families, the evidence in Requests suggests that women played a lesser role than might be expected in the negotiation and subsequent litigation of these arrangements. Women were active in the arrangement of marriage and in litigation connected with promises of marriage. Isabell Fretwell continued demanding payment from John Bawdy for non-performance of his contract to marry her even after she had married someone else.[62] However, *financial* arrangements were another matter, especially when women married for the first time. Parents made arrangements with parents and future sons-in-law or with trustees, and while daughters were consulted, their involvement was often circumscribed. When Maude Baber made plans to marry Andrew Lightfoote, her father set aside an interest for her, 'as in secreat use & confidence might remayne & be to & for the onlye behoufe, benefite & comoditye of the saide Mawde if she outlived her husband'. However all parties in this action, including Maude herself, agreed that she had not been 'acquainted with the course of proceedings therein'.[63] When Elizabeth Hall married John Wood, Elizabeth's father negotiated with John, and the two of them created a use for John's benefit during his lifetime and then for Elizabeth's benefit if she should survive him.[64] Having organised women's settlements, these other parties often sued each other if arrangements went wrong. When Margery Bolton married Thomas Mathew, the couple's fathers organised an elaborate settlement, and when the conditions of the settlement were not met it was the fathers who sued each other in Requests.[65]

We know from the evidence of letters, diaries, church court records and wills that women involved themselves in every aspect of the arrangement of marriages, including finances.[66] Amy Erickson has described how mothers in

---

[61] Erickson, 'Common law versus common practice', pp. 22, 24; compare this with Raymond Evershed's observation in the 1950s that the provisions in early trusts 'protected' women by preventing them 'under the impulse, (as it used to be said) of the kicks and kisses of their husband, from ever being able to touch any capital'; Raymond Evershed, *Aspects of English Equity* (Jerusalem, 1954), p. 4.

[62] *John Bawdye v. Thomas Wildsmyth, Stephen & Isabell Paynter*, PRO Req 2/173/30.

[63] *John & Maude Bluet v. John Baber*, PRO Req 2/178/55, m. 2, B.

[64] *Dorothie Hall's case*, PRO Req 1/17, pp. 127–8.

[65] *Thomas Boulton v. Walter Mathewe*, PRO Req 1/21, pp. 196–8; *Edwarde Haywarde v. Thomas Broughton*, PRO Req 2/220/29.

[66] Amussen, *Ordered Society*, pp. 71–3; Gowing, *Domestic Dangers*, pp. 141–8, 168; Ingram, *Church Courts*, pp. 200–5.

wealthy families negotiated on behalf of their daughters, trying to ensure that grooms possessed resources to match the resources of brides, and how poorer women, or women whose parents were no longer living, organised their marriages themselves.[67] However, when it came to signing documents or bringing a court action while a woman's husband was still alive, men tended to be involved far more often than women. The reasons for this are manifold. Part of the answer lies with coverture. Family members arranged financial settlements on behalf of their daughters or nieces because they considered themselves more experienced in financial matters and wished to ensure the best terms possible, especially if they had contributed money to the match. They also recognised the need to safeguard women from the influence of their husbands before marriage as well as during marriage. It will be observed in the next chapter just how difficult it could be for a woman to enforce her rights against her husband while she was married and why it was important that married women's rights not remain the sole responsibility or concern of wives. Mothers made arrangements as well as fathers, as Erickson points out, but when it came to the preparation of documents and the signing of agreements, men played a dominant role.

Susan Staves has observed about the seventeenth and eighteenth centuries, that 'the business of negotiating settlements and enforcing rights under them seems generally to have been left to men'.[68] The Requests evidence confirms her suspicion in relation to single women, but the experience of widows, by contrast, is very different. When it came to litigating settlements, a number of widows went to court to enforce agreements they had played no direct part in arranging (although to strengthen their arguments and to prove that they were eligible to sue, many went to lengths to suggest that they had contributed).[69] The situation with women contemplating second or third marriages was more complex. Widows marrying for a second time had the experience of their first marriage to draw on, and they were far more likely than single women to be supplying their own portions, or to possess other property, making them well placed to jockey for a good settlement. If they were executrixes or administratrixes they might have future obligations to fulfil. Widows facing remarriage were no more immune than single women to the impending limitations of coverture – if they wanted to preserve any property or rights to disposition during marriage, they could do so only by relying on trustees, family members or other allies – but they were far more likely than single women to make these arrangements themselves.

[67] Erickson, *Women and Property*, p. 96.
[68] Staves, *Married Women's Separate Property*, p. 205; *James Noble* v. *John Frenche*, PRO Req 1/19, p. 805.
[69] To bring an action an individual had to have 'standing', in other words be sufficiently connected with a case to be allowed to sue. To demonstrate this it was useful to show that they had provided something in return for the benefit they hoped to receive; in contractual terms, that they had provided 'good consideration' and therefore deserved to have a contract enforced.

Thomazin Buckford was the administratrix of her late husband's estate, worth an estimated £1,485, and when she remarried she asked her uncle to act as the 'instrument' of a trust. He was to arrange bonds and covenants with her new husband to ensure that he provided her with a reasonable jointure and did not interfere with her administration of her former husband's estate.[70] Christian Scott was her late husband's executrix, and she took care on the eve of her second marriage to pass the bonds, debts and other negotiable instruments in her possession to her son, in return for a general acquittance of the legacies owing to him, because she feared her new husband might take them from her.[71] Another executrix, Joan Mercer (one of the few women who managed to sue her own husband) was accused by her husband of dealing 'subtilye' with him before marriage, by assigning the lease of Brunden Hall to friends to hold for her use.[72] The widow Agnes Lee kept a London tavern, the King's Head, and when she agreed to marry William Rawlinson, a plasterer, he delivered to her an indenture, with an obligation ensuring performance of the indenture, which she passed on to 'one Lee in Fletestrete a cutler to be kept to her use'.[73]

Remarrying widows could be active in protecting their interests, but even the best laid plans could come adrift. Consider the action Sir George Norton brought against Edward Bosden in Requests early in the 1560s. In his bill, George alleged that his wife Margaret had, during her widowhood, 'in vearye secreate maner' passed goods by deed of gift to Bosden, her servant, for him to keep for her use. Under the terms of this arrangement Bosden was to let Margaret have use of her goods to pay her debts and to provide advancement for her kinsfolk if any of them chose to marry. If she decided to remarry, her new husband was to have thirty days in which to become bound to Bosden, or his executor or administrator, promising to observe these conditions, with a penalty for failing to do so of 2,000 marks. Margaret's arrangements seem admirable. However, according to her new husband George, Bosden ignored these agreed terms and had Margaret sign a false deed he had drawn up in his own favour. George uncovered this devious fraud soon after he married Margaret, and he set about recovering Margaret's interests by suing Bosden in Requests. The puzzle here is why Margaret herself was not a party to this suit. Was George genuinely coming to her aid, suing to recover her property when she had not realised that it was at risk? Or could it be that he was aiming to defeat the clever use she had constructed to keep her property safe from prying hands like his? Whichever alternative is correct, Margaret's plans went wrong, and she lost out either to a fraudulent trustee or to a domineering husband.[74]

---

[70] *Henry & Jane Trapp* v. *Thomazin Buckford*, PRO Req 2/277/54, A.
[71] *Bartholemew & Christian Scott* v. *Johen Land*, PRO Req 3/33.
[72] *Jhoane Mercer & John Walter* v. *Thomas(?) Mercer et al.*, PRO Req 3/33.
[73] PRO Req 3/32, deposition of Richard Nevile on behalf of Elizabeth Bolder.
[74] *George Norton* v. *Edward Bosden*, PRO Req 2/163/107, B.

If the defendant in an action from 1594 is to be believed, remarrying widows could go to fraudulent lengths to enhance their interests. Thomas Eyre defended himself in a debt action by alleging that his aunt Jane had concealed from her intended husband the fact that she had mortgaged her lands to her nephew as security for a £100 debt. She had deceived her husband in this way to 'make a greate shewie of her abilitie of her prefermente in maryadge'. And as Thomas was reliably informed, 'the sayd Jane hath obtayned of her husbande assurance of twenty Marks lande of yearelye inheritance to her and her heirs' in return for assigning her lands over to her husband (and to his heirs if the couple produced no children). To 'color her fraude herein' she had come to court with her husband, pretending to him and to the Masters that the £100 debt was a fraudulent invention.[75]

The picture that emerges from the Requests records suggests that the rights of women with access to equitable instruments like trusts and uses were many, but women themselves held no monopoly on the creation and exercise of those rights. The legal system joined with society at large to place pressure on women to make alliances with others, whenever they dabbled in matters of credit, property or law. Some resisted this pressure, others succumbed, but in understanding the full experience women had of litigation it is vital to consider the role of outsiders, whether fathers, mothers, husbands, brothers, sisters or other kin, trustees, agents, solicitors or attorneys in the management of women's property and affairs.

COUNSEL AND AGENTS

The level of participation of unmarried, married and widowed women in court actions varied from individual to individual. Some women appeared in person in London, others gave their answers to commissioners, and a number did not appear at all but relied on co-litigants or legal counsel to act for them.[76] Finding out from court records the precise part any individual played in proceedings is not always easy. Even more difficult to discover, however, is the role that counsel played in directing and perhaps instigating court actions. Did women with grievances always seek out legal counsel, or did lawyers sometimes approach women to persuade them to take actions to court (was there, in other words, a

---

[75] *Mathewe & Jane Graye* v. *Thomas Eyre et al.*, PRO Req 2/144/44, m. 2, A.

[76] Lady Lawrence described in a letter how she rode to London in 1570, after being summoned before Requests, only to find the court prorogued; E. Clerke to Richard Oseley, M.A.E. Green, ed., *Cal. S. P. Dom. Elizabeth I, Addenda, 1566–1579* (London, 1871), p. 208; when the Masters granted a commission in a case in 1587 they gave 'carriage' of the commission to the widow Barbara Shereman; *Shereman* v. *Shereman*, PRO Req 1/14, fol. 319v; in an Exchequer case against the widow Margery Thayer, the court accepted an offer made by Margery's seconds, 'without her privitie or consent to avoyde further expences in lawe & to purchase her quyetnes'; *William Webley* v. *Margery Thayer*, PRO Req 1/21, p. 80; for further examples, see chapter 6.

sixteenth century equivalent of 'ambulance chasing')? A common grievance of
the time, after all, was the 'lewd abuses of prolling solicitors and their great
multitude, who set dissension betwixt man and man, like a snake, cut in pieces,
crawl together to join themselves again to stir up evil spirits of dissension'.[77]

In most cases it is unclear how women got to court and the influence that
lawyers or other parties wielded in their causes, but accusations of external
manipulation in women's legal actions were rife.[78] Opponents suggested that
lawyers had encouraged women to sue, James Buswell arguing that the widow
executrix Agnes Buswell was suing him at common law over an old bond, 'not
without the privitie Confederacye & Complotte of one John Muscotte an
Attarnye at the lawe'.[79] Alternatively, they suggested that malicious strangers
had inspired widows to bring suits. For example, the defendant who alleged that
a widow's claims against him were 'devised only of malice and of a troublesome
minde by the instigacion of some busy . . . and perverse parsons', or the couple
who named a co-defendant in their counter-suit against a widow, because they
believed that he was 'a very busy fellowe and is th'onely cause or at the leste
wise a greate procurer of this trowble'.[80] Some opponents even suggested that
women were participants in court actions in name only, and that third parties
were hijacking actions without their consent or approval. When Anne Horne
sued William Hill at common law, Hill suggested that Horne's attorney had
instigated the action and was paying her costs and that he alone would benefit if
the suit was successful. The widow herself did not approve of the action, Hill
said, and in the nine years that she had held the disputed bond she had never
before thought to trouble him.[81] A woman in another action said that a man
named William Achym knew that a girl was under age, and he was bringing the
suit on her behalf without her consent.[82]

These examples raise the spectre of the professional litigant or legal barrator,
'A troblesome disturber of many persons' who funded and encouraged 'many
bad matters and wrongefull suits in lawe'.[83] Commentators regarded the solicit-

---

[77] Unnamed presenter of a bill to 'repress the multitude of common solicitors', 43 Elizabeth I, 1601,
The Parliamentary History of England, from the Earliest Period to the Year 1803 (London, 1806),
vol. 1, p. 918.

[78] The deponent John Tibbet recalled his neighbour Florence telling him that her counsellor from
Shepton, and 'one Heath of Wells', had told her that 'her writinge would not warrant her' her
claim of widow's estate in a farm; *Johane Wilcox v. Thomas Llewellyn*, PRO Req 2/289/49, D.

[79] *James Buswell v. Agnes Buswell*, PRO Req 2/115/29, B.

[80] *Johan Cosynes v. Richard Morgan & John Broderibbe*, PRO Req 2/187/49, m. 3, A; and see *John
& Agnes Larcombe v. Edith Horsye et al.*, PRO Req 2/233/14, R; *John Graye v. Thomas Spenser et
al.*, PRO Req 2/209/47, B; *Anne Garforth v. William Shipman & Thomas Higgens*, PRO Req
2/212/8, A.

[81] *William Hill v. Anne Horne & Robert Winniffe*, PRO Req 2/217/34; for another case, see *Elyanor
Brett & another v. Nicholas Sprakett*, PRO Req 2/179/67, A; in a different context, Clive Holmes
has revealed how male third parties could encourage women to make accusations of witchcraft,
or to appear as witnesses in witchcraft trials; Holmes, 'Women, witnesses and witches', pp. 53–4.

[82] *Elinor Rawlin v. William Achym*, PRO Req 1/14, fol. 103.

[83] *Michael Keynton et al. v. Alice Walley*, PRO Req 2/231/24, m. 3, A.

ing of causes as a key force behind the explosion of litigation, an evil they thought was poisoning the legal process and undermining relations between neighbours and there were calls in parliament to clamp down on the practice.[84] Most women strenuously denied suggestions that they were innocent, or willing, participants in other people's legal schemes. They either refuted allegations of assistance, or defended the people assisting them, like the plaintiffs who accused their opponent of trying to 'diswade the good intencion & devocion of any of the Replyants frendes shewed or meant towardes the Replyants in theyr extremityes'.[85] Yet women were open to these accusations because of the way that others perceived of their relationship with the law. As was noted in chapter 3, moralists advised women to leave legal matters to fathers, husbands, sons or trusted counsellors. In the case of widows, observers recognised the likelihood that widows would gain custody of bonds and indentures and other documents that might require action. Martin Billingsley, recommended in *The Pens Excellencie* (published in 1618) that no woman who survived her husband and inherited an estate ought to be without the ability to write:

For thereby she comes to a certainty of her estate, without trusting to the reports of such as are usually imployed to looke into the same: whereas otherwise for want of it, she is subject to the manifold deceits now used in the world, and by that meanes plungeth her selfe into a multitude of inconveniencies.[86]

Billingsley's advertisement for his wares implies that inheriting widows regularly sought assistance from others, and that they were open to manipulation when they did. Male executors and administrators faced similar problems, but the majority of commentators clearly assumed that men were more at ease than women in the world of bonds, finances and law suits.

The constraints of coverture made it practical for women to seek assistance from others if they planned to marry, and during marriage even the most independent women of property lived within a world of trustees and agents. And it seems that habits acquired in marriage often continued in widowhood. Jasper Moore, a yeoman, was 'a dealer & medler' for a woman named Joan in all her matters and legal causes during her widowhood.[87] Another widow made enquiry to a man 'who had the keeping of her money'.[88] We have already seen that Agnes Nowell 'for her better use and comoditie did comitt and deliver to the hands kepinge and direccion of . . . her neare kinseman' the money her husband gave her during their separation.[89] The fact that some women

---

[84] C.W. Brooks argues that this belief was largely unfounded; Brooks, *Pettyfoggers*, p. 137; see note 77 above.   [85] *Michael Keynton et al. v. Alice Walley*, PRO Req 2/231/24, m. 2, R.

[86] Martin Billingsley, *The Pens Excellencie or the Secretaries Delighte* [London, 1618], sigs Biv^v-C.

[87] *Thomas & Rachel White v. Phillip Onslowe*, PRO Req 2/27/1, B; see also *Griffin & Ellen Powell v. Joan ap John*, PRO Req 2/49/25, D, deponent Thomas Vere; *Margarett Smyth v. Mary Lockett*, PRO Req 2/274/37, A.   [88] *Jane Yates v. Edward Hynd*, PRO Req 2/293/9, A.

[89] *Agnes Nowell v. Thomas Hall*, PRO Req 2/166/134, m. 4, B; *Elizabeth Shipper v. John Nicolls et al.*, PRO Req 2/266/31; *Henry & Jane Trappe v. Thomasyne Buckford or Coyse*, PRO Req 2/280/30, D, deponent William Atwood.

entrusted all or part of their legal and monetary affairs to others allowed this claim to be directed against many more. An apprentice haberdasher explained how after the death of his master, his master's wife, 'beeinge then a widowe and wantinge one which shee might use and imploy in matters of importaunce greately concerninge her owne estate', had appointed him her agent, in return for £100 and the use of her husband's premises in St Lawrence Lane in London for the duration of her widowhood, 'and ffowres yeares after', at a rent of £16 per annum. The claim was a plausible one, yet the woman in this case (who had since remarried) denied the existence of any such arrangement with the plaintiff, or that she had needed to rely on anyone after her husband's death.[90]

Tacit assumptions about women's social position allowed litigants to suggest the involvement of third parties in women's legal affairs, whether or not outsiders were actually involved, a device that they employed for a variety of purposes. Some opponents used it to soften their attacks on female plaintiffs or defendants, or to deflect accusations women had made against them, by implying that the women concerned were not malicious, they had merely been misled by others. Christopher Symcocks explained that devious third parties had conspired to turn Mary Cheeke against him. Chief of these, he said, was an attorney, 'a notorious lewd factious and turbulent spirited fellowe', who had induced Mary to sue with wild promises of the profits he would recover for her in court.[91] Suggesting that Cheeke lacked worldly experience, and was open to manipulation by corrupt associates, allowed Symcocks to refute her accusations without appearing to attack Cheeke herself, and in doing so he utilised a condescending logic that he was far less likely to employ against a male opponent. Other protagonists asserted that women had accomplices to emphasise the power those women had at their disposal, and to counteract claims that they were weak creatures subject to victimisation, a theme that will be examined in more depth in chapter 8 below. In pointing out this discrepancy between accusations made against women and men, it is worth noting that the traffic was not all in one direction, and parties accused women as well as men of manipulating legal actions or of acting as accomplices. Sibell Ryder or Reader, for example, a widow from the parish of St Dunstan's in London, had to answer interrogatories in Requests which alleged that she had encouraged a married couple to sue and that she was funding their suits.[92]

The fact that women were more susceptible than men to accusations that other parties were aiding or manipulating them, or that they relied on other parties for their knowledge of key events, worked against many individuals.

[90] *Mathy & Jane Grey v. Jeffrye Roberts*, PRO Req 2/209/57, A; in an earlier case a defendant described Roberts as the 'cheif factor & solicytor of the buisyness & suits' of Jane; *Mathy & Jane Grey v. Thomas Eyre et al.*, PRO Req 2/144/44, [m. 2], A, the answer of Thomas Eyre.

[91] *Mary Cheeke v. Christopher Symcocks*, PRO Req 2/47/36, A.

[92] *James & Susan Aske v. William & Jane Paine*, PRO Req 2/172/25, D, deponent Sibell Ryder.

Some women, however, utilised the shared assumptions and logic behind these accusations for their own purposes. The widow Susan Ashley, for example, recovered a copyhold interest in her local Court Baron by arguing that she had been named in the copy, but her late father had surrendered it without her consent when she was only seventeen years old and powerless to oppose him. The court accepted that the surrender had taken place only 'by the procurement or rather enforcement of her said father' and they ejected the sitting tenant. The tenant went to Requests and persuaded the Masters to reverse this decision. He called Susan's neighbours, her wet-nurse and a woman who assisted at her birth to be witnesses, and they all deposed that Susan was born in 1562, 'the somer before the great plague in London and before the First going to new haven' and was therefore twenty one or older at the time of the surrender.[93] Susan then counter-sued in Star Chamber. In keeping with the conventions of that court, both sides related tales of guns and pitchforks, bailiffs in armour, violence against the person and the whole wall of a house 'accidentally' collapsing after a tug of war developed between those inside the house and those outside, as they vigorously pushed and pulled a loaded musket back and forth through a small aperture in the wall until it gave way.[94]

Who the victor was in this dispute is unclear, for decisions in Star Chamber actions do not survive, but what is significant is that both sides argued that Susan was victim to the controlling influence of others. She herself argued that her father had directed her affairs and sold her interest without her consent, while her opponents suggested that she had been induced to break the law, 'by the sinister meanes and practises' of three accomplices.[95] Either one man had misused his paternal authority to disinherit her, or three men and women had used their influence to convince her to perjure herself for profit.

Susan Ashley's protracted campaign of litigation usefully illustrates other themes that this chapter has sought to emphasise. Firstly, her legal dealings as a widow illustrate the competence of determined female litigants and their ability to target different jurisdictions; she made skilful use of a range of different courts, bringing actions in the Court Baron, to challenge the legitimacy of an initial surrender in the customary court, and in Star Chamber, to counter a suit in Requests. Her robust pursuit of justice suggests that she was a shrewd combatant capable of using the courts to recover an interest and then to protect it (making it even more poignant that she based her arguments on her naïvety as a single woman, subject to the controlling influence of her father). Secondly, the

---

[93] *Thomas Cartwright v. Susan Ashley als Waterworte et al.*, PRO Req 1/16, pp. 503–6; Req 2/157/85; Req 2/159/7.

[94] *Suzan Ashley v. George & Mary Mouse, Thomas Cartwright et al.*, PRO STAC 5/25/31; STAC 5/46/25.

[95] The Masters ordered that the tenant retain possession unless and until the defendants could establish their right to possession in any of the central courts; PRO Req 1/16, p. 505.

timing of her actions suggests that she suffered from the debilitating effect of coverture; why else did she wait until her husband had died before she sued to recover an interest that was seven years old? Her example not only confirms the importance of the life cycle of marriage for women's legal status, it serves as a reminder that women with *feme sole* status used the law (or failed to use the law) in very different ways according to how old they were, where they lived, whether their parents remained alive, whether they had been married before, and according to a whole list of other variables.

Widows were more likely than single women to have interests in property, and in most instances more able to manage and if necessary to fight to protect those interests. If that property, or indeed any other matter leading to litigation, was a legacy from their husbands, they might suffer the disadvantage of not being fully aware of the details. Alternatively they might take advantage of their supposed ignorance to double-charge creditors. But how involved were women with their husband's affairs during marriage, and to what extent did their involvement extend into the sphere of law? The next chapter examines married women litigants and suggests answers to some of the questions raised in this chapter.

—⟪⟫ *6* ⟪⟫—

Married women in requests

You [Mr Bumble] are the more guilty of the two, in the eye of the law; for the law supposes that your wife acts under your direction.'

'If the law supposes that,' said Mr Bumble, squeezing his hat emphatically in both hands, 'the law is a ass – a idiot. If that's the eye of the law, the law is a bachelor. (Charles Dickens *Oliver Twist* (1838))[1]

Elizabethan moralists encouraged unmarried women and widows to seek legal assistance from male kin or confidants, but the common law *demanded* that married women leave their legal affairs to their husbands. As described in chapter 2 above, the doctrine of coverture stripped married women of their legal entities and independence. It did not, however, remove all of their rights or all of their obligations. Moreover, while coverture theoretically barred married women from appearing in court alone, it did not bar them altogether, and the single largest grouping of women who involved themselves in Requests actions were married women appearing with their husbands. A far smaller, but more intriguing, group of women were the select band of wives who defied the rules and succeeded in suing their own husbands. Their experiences provide further evidence that the Masters recognised that women's particular legal status could sometimes require particular legal and equitable attention and assistance. However, before turning to examine married women as a class of litigant it is necessary to gain a fuller understanding of the theory and practical application of the doctrine of coverture.

COVERTURE

Technically, no married woman except for the Queen could sue or be sued apart from her husband, but as previous chapters have suggested, in practice exceptions to this and other rules of coverture are not difficult to find.[2] To begin with, the operation of coverture was not automatic. In common with so many other

---

[1] Charles Dickens, *Oliver Twist* (Harmondsworth, Middlesex, 1966), pp. 461–2.
[2] McIntyre, 'Legal attitudes', p. 85.

areas of early modern law, the day to day application of the doctrine to litigants depended on the diligence not of the courts, but of litigants themselves. Judges addressed the question of the competence of married women as litigants only when opponents brought the issue to their attention, and rules alone did not deter married women from attempting to bring suit. A ruling directing that 'noe woman being under Covert Baron' should be allowed to sue in Requests went on to suggest that such women should be sequestered, 'consideringe their importunacye and unreasonable requests *dayly used to the hinderance of good matters*'.[3] Furthermore, the theory of coverture was immensely complex. As the author of *The Lawes Resolutions of Womens Rights* explained, while the law regarded man and wife as one person for some things, 'in criminall and other speciall causes our Law argues them severall persons'.[4] The extent to which legal responsibility could practically be shared between husbands and wives created the greatest complications. If a married woman killed someone, was her husband liable for murder? If she stole property was he guilty of theft? The answer in these instances was no, but the fiction of 'unity of person' made similar questions difficult to resolve. In a case in Star Chamber in 1597, the assembled councillors dismissed a charge of riot against a married woman because there was no proof except for accusations against her husband, 'which, by the sentence of the Court, will not condemn the wife'.[5] If a married woman entered into a contract for good consideration, could her actions bind her husband?[6] Was the woman herself bound should her husband subsequently die? Lady Wakefield tried to confirm an agreement she had made while she was married, producing in Chancery a letter in which she had 'protested before God that noe want or necessitye should ever hereafter make her to alter her purpose'. However, the presiding judge dismissed her plea (for want of valuable consideration), saying that 'they were but the words of a feme coverte'.[7]

The author of a commentary on Chancery agreed that at common law a married woman who persuaded her husband to sell her land, 'and after of her own free will maketh an affidavit that if her husband dye, she shall never claime the lande', could always reclaim the land as a widow, despite her promises: 'For the lawe presumeth, that what is done by the woman coverte is done by the means of her husband.' However, while the woman could recover her land, the author stressed that she would be 'bounde in conscience', and therefore in

[3] Robert Dacre, 'Orders and rules in Requests', BL Additional MS 25,248, fols 32[r-v] [my emphasis].
[4] T.E., *The Lawes Resolutions of Womens Rights* (London, 1632), p. 4.
[5] Hawarde, *Les Reportes del Cases in Camera Stellata*, p. 74.
[6] For evidence of the complexity of the doctrine on this point, see *Manby v. Scott, English Reports*, 83, pp. 816–17, 823, 902–3, 980–82, 995–98, 1008–9, 1035–6, 1042–6, 1065–6.
[7] C.U.L. Gg.2.31, fol. 438; for fuller discussions of married women's rights at common law see Holdsworth, *History of English Law*, vol. 3, pp. 520–33; Baker, *An Introduction to English Legal History*, pp. 550–7.

equity, to recompense the buyer. Against the presumption of coverture 'shall lie no suite against her. And yet in hir own conscience she is bound to restitution.'[8] Married women were damned if they did and damned if they didn't.

Jurists struggled to find uniform answers to these perplexing questions, not just in the sixteenth century, but into the seventeenth, eighteenth and nineteenth centuries.[9] Legal minds were intrigued by the special nature of women's rights, and 'readers' and 'mooters' at the Inns of Court debated at length the paradoxes and inconsistencies inherent in coverture. Judges, in the meantime, had to deal with the stream of cases that came before them on the basis of the evidence presented. The flexibility they showed in dealing with individual cases invariably led to variations between cases, and doctrinal inconsistency, the bane of lawyers, was rife. It has already been noted how the doctrine forbade wives giving testimony against their husbands, yet in Chancery a woman was allowed to give testimony, 'because she wore the breeches'.[10] Similarly, in a Requests case from 1598 the Masters allowed a forty three year old wife to question the testimony of her eighty three year old husband.[11] However, variations within the courtroom were as nothing compared to the inconsistencies outside it, and the records contain plenty of evidence to suggest that in practice married women held property, accepted gifts, received payments, held money or goods to the use of third parties and made contracts, all without the permission and often the knowledge of their husbands.[12] A Bristol man admitted that his wife had been solely responsible for hiring and paying their servant, a woman he alleged still possessed the moneys 'his wife had in sekeret at her deathe'.[13] Silvester Dackombe supposedly lent £5 to Jane Cottington for the use of Jane's husband Phillipe Cottington, delivering the money 'seacrettlye and privilye'.[14] To borrow Margot Finn's phrase, in day to day life 'coverture is best described as existing in a state of suspended animation'.[15]

To be fully effective the doctrine of coverture had to be invoked, and before individuals could invoke it they had to understand it. There are numerous examples in the records of litigants who appear to have been uncertain about the workings of the doctrine until 'learned counsel' put them straight. Agnes Thompson had to ask various of her neighbours whether she could make a deed

---

[8] Francis Hargrave, *A Collection of Tracts Relative to the Law of England, from Manuscripts* (London, 1787), vol. 1, p. 346.

[9] I am currently researching a book on the history of married women and the law over the whole of this period.   [10] See chapter 2 above.

[11] *Jane Goddard v. William Goddard*, PRO Req 2/81/18, D, deponent Elizabeth Moore; although for an exception to the general rule in Chancery, see C.U.L. Gg.2.31, fol. 357[v].

[12] *Johanne Swaynston v. Richard & Rose Atwyll*, PRO Req 2/274/75, B; *Richard ffisher v. Anne Parkins*, PRO Req 1/19, pp. 499–500.

[13] *Elizabeth Bankes v. Thomas Gowen*, PRO Req 2/182/11, A.

[14] *Robert & Silvester Dackombe v. Phillippe & Jane Cottington*, PRO Req 2/197/2 [m. 10], B.

[15] Finn, 'Women, consumption and coverture, p. 707.

of gift to her children while she was married.[16] A defendant agreed to return to a widow property that had been hers before marriage, 'although the same by the strict corse of the comon lawes of this land (as this defendant is enformed) of right doth belong to this defendaunte'.[17] It is interesting to speculate how the majority of people who had not been so 'enformed' regarded married women's property in their daily lives.

In other cases it is hard to judge the knowledge of litigants. The records of a testamentary action from 1587 describe how an executrix refused to marry a suitor until he promised 'that he woulde not at any tyme duringe his lief soe alter the propertie' of her late husband, now in her control. In consideration, she promised the man he could have all of the rest of her goods. She was offering goods that under coverture would become his anyway, to prevent him interfering with property that the rules of coverture forbid him from touching.[18] In making this offer, was she ignorant of the workings of the doctrine? Or was she fully aware and offering him property she might otherwise keep to her own use in a trust, in the knowledge that it would be difficult in practice to prevent him interfering with her former husband's property? Or was her lawyer cobbling together a coherent story after the fact? Certainly, the defendant denied that the negotiations ever took place, pointing out how the rules of coverture made such an agreement unnecessary. He further argued that if the woman had in fact made such a promise, surely she would have made it formally and taken out assurances with her friends.[19]

Some litigants were ignorant of the details of coverture, others feigned ignorance. Others understood the doctrine only too well and tried to exploit this knowledge to advantage. The records abound with cases where plaintiffs and defendants attempted to use the doctrine to evade legal action by alleging that they or their opponents were *femes covert*.[20] Despite resistance from the Masters, certain litigants and lawyers succeeded by these means in having actions dismissed, but most individuals who raised the issue of coverture desired simply to delay proceedings.[21] In a case from Middlesex in 1592 the defendants argued that one of the complainants and one of the defendants had recently married and were now 'covert barron', but they had not corrected their pleadings to include the names of their husbands. The defendants did not

---

[16] *Jane & Elizabeth Thompson v. William Bradley & Robert Powe*, PRO Req 2/276/33, A.

[17] *Joane Frenche v. Alice Pinchbacke*, PRO Req 2/164/60 [m. 3], A.

[18] See Smith, *The Common-Wealth of England*, pp. 130–4.

[19] *Richard & Elizabeth (als Isabell) Browninge v. William Nelme*, PRO Req 2/166/33, B, A.

[20] *Johan Spragen v. Martyn Spraggyn et al.*, PRO Req 2/273/67, Dem, A.

[21] The Masters did dismiss cases brought by or against *femes covert*, but usually they let parties amend pleadings to include husbands' names; *Mary Cockrell v. Alexander & Thomas Taberer*, PRO Req 2/191/35; *Sara Baguley v. Nicholas Coleman et al.*, PRO Req 1/21, p. 52; *Agnes Sheppard v. David Birchett*, PRO Req 1/16, pp. 97, 142, 416; for Chancery see C.U.L. Gg.2.26, fols 130ᵛ-133, 139; Cioni, *Women and Law*, p. 35.

expect by this means to have the cause dismissed, but such a claim might buy time and prove a costly irritation to opponents.[22]

Other cases reveal how parties could manipulate the rules of coverture before they became embroiled in litigation, in one instance to get *into* court rather than to keep out of it. Joan Spragin brought an action in Requests against her husband Martin and a man named Richard Levens, explaining that Levens had commenced two actions on the case against her and her husband at common law. Both actions were directed primarily at herself, one accusing her of committing assault and battery, the other of uttering slanderous words, and her desire was that these actions be stayed. She explained that she and her husband had been separated (*a mensa et thoro*) by the Ordinary of the Diocese of London, and that her husband was acting in collusion with Levens. He intended to plead guilty to both of the spurious actions, Joan would be forced to pay damages, and he could thereby recover 'such goods as the said plaintiff now hath in her possession by the agreement of the said Martin', or else have the pleasure of seeing her imprisoned. The Masters accepted Joan's story and ordered Levens to stay his actions on pain of £200, and later that Martin pay Joan £10 in compensation. Depositions in the case tell a sorry tale of how Martin had viciously beaten Joan while they lived together. After they were separated he tried to exploit the rules of coverture in this other way, attempting to harass her and to avoid paying her alimony through deft and corrupt manipulation of the rigour of the common law.[23]

Women, too, were accused of manipulating the ambiguities of coverture to advantage. In 1587 Joan Swaynston brought a suit in Requests against Richard and Rose Atwell, claiming that Rose had agreed to hold a purse full of gold 'to her use', and that Richard had found it and taken the contents. Richard Atwell answered on his own, claiming that his wife and the complainant were sisters acting in collusion. Rose, he explained, had left him, and she and Joan had invented the charge between themselves, 'subtelly intendinge throughe some untrue confession of the said Rose' to defraud him.[24] In another case the widow Alice Gyles described to the Masters a story of assault and abuse similar to Joan Spragin's. She said that after refusing her husband's request that she surrender a life interest in a copyhold, he had 'most unconcionably' used force to compel her. According to her bill he 'did often beate and abuse' her, and 'so out-

---

[22] *Edward & Mary Harden et al.* v. *Agnes Harvye et al.*, PRO Req 2/223/17, A.

[23] Joan claimed that he had already succeeded, by similar means, in removing goods of hers worth 100 marks; *Johane Spraggen* v. *Martyn Spraggen et al.*, PRO Req 2/273/67, B; and see PRO Req 2/275/80, D; PRO Req 1/18, p. 913; Req 1/19, pp. 4, 138, 201, 209. 292, 301, 304, 405–6; for an example in Chancery of alleged collusion by a husband against his wife, see *Shilling* v. *Coole* (Michaelmas 38 Eliz. I), C.U.L. Gg.2.31, fol. 225ᵛ.

[24] *Johane Swaynston* v. *Richard & Rose Atwell*, PRO Req 2/274/75, m. 1, A; Richard suggested that for this reason the Masters should bar Rose from giving answer, and indeed no separate answer for her survives in the records.

ragiusly delte with your subjecte that he did breake one of your subjects armes and caused your subject to be impryssoned', until finally he succeeded in forcing her to make a surrender. The Masters, however, remained unconvinced. They appear to have accepted the contention of the defendant, John Bond, that Alice had fabricated stories about her late husband in the hope of recovering a copy-hold that was no longer hers. According to Bond, she had agreed to sell her interest after she and her husband fell into poverty, consenting to the surrender in private, when the steward examined her apart from her husband, as well as in public. The commissioners in this case reported that Alice 'very lewdly hadd practised to corrupt a witnes to speake in her behaulfe', while the year before they had written to the Masters saying 'we thinke the woman to be a very troblesome woman, and vexeth the foresaid defendant without any just cause'.[25]

Other women, either widows, or wives encouraged by unscrupulous second or third husbands, sought to manipulate the doctrine of coverture by dis-avowing transactions they had made while they had been married, or used the doctrine to explain why they had not acted or complained in the past.[26] Some husbands, meanwhile, disavowed transactions their wives had made. Anthony Compley told the Masters that while he had been away in Iceland his wife had sold his house to the defendant, and he wished to claim it back. The defendant replied that Anthony had instructed his wife to make the sale in his absence.[27]

The Masters met these claims and counter-claims as best they could, bringing principles of equity to bear as they gave emphasis to justice ahead of rigid rules. When Edward and Rose Reynolds brought an action in Requests against Lionel Ferrington and Edward Ross, the Masters ordered Lionel to pay Rose £7 15s. 1d. Subsequently, however, Edward told the Masters that he no longer wished to continue with the action, and he asked that they dismiss it. His actions provide a classic example of a husband exercising his power under coverture to prevent his wife litigating without his consent. However, Rose was able to produce an indenture establishing that she and her husband had been legally separated. On sight of this, the Masters ordered that Edward's call for a dismissal be ignored and the former decree ratified.[28]

In a case with perhaps greater significance, a married woman brought an action in the absence of her husband (but in the company of her father) against her father-in-law, claiming maintenance. The court heard how the mother and friends of Elizabeth Forth had delivered to the defendant a portion of £300 and given his son a further £100. Notwithstanding the advancement of these

[25] *Alice Giles* v. *John Bond*, PRO Req 2/157/191, letter; Req 2/144/19, CR; and see PRO Req 2/158/22; Req 2/158/93. [26] *John & Mary Fyppen* v. *Edward Nevell et al.*, PRO Req 2/207/82, R.
[27] *Anthony Compley* v. *The prior of St Peters, Ipswich*, PRO Req 2/8/84, B, A.
[28] *Edward & Rose Reignolds* v. *Lyonell fferington & Edward Rosse*, PRO Req 1/18, p. 881; for Chancery, see C.U.L. Gg.2.26, fols 130ᵛ-131.

moneys, the woman's husband had since abandoned her and gone overseas, leaving her without the means to keep herself and her children. The defendant had also taken pains to convey all of his lands to younger sons, thus defeating the jointure he had promised to make on behalf of his daughter-in-law. The Masters accepted these facts and could not see 'anie cause reasonable whie the said Elizabeth should be so abandoned, and lefte destitute of livinge and releife'. They ordered her father-in-law to pay her father, towards her maintenance, the sums of 100 marks for her expenses over the previous four years, £30 to cover the time since her husband fled overseas, and £300 for her and her children's futures (in effect a return of her portion given the failure of the jointure). If in the meantime the woman and her estranged husband should 'growe to good & perfect concorde and agreement, and be pleased & contented to live, cohabite and contynue together in love and amitie as man and wief should & ought', then the Masters would make further order. The woman brought her suit jointly with her father, and the Masters granted him the recovered moneys to hold for her use, but the case is still a fascinating example of the Master's willingness to see justice done in the case of a married woman.[29]

The evasion of coverture is always more fascinating than its observance, as an analysis of cases involving wives suing their husbands later in this chapter will show. However, it is important to consider such extraordinary cases in the light of their relative scarcity. Far more common, making up the largest grouping of cases involving women, were actions in which wives appeared with their husbands.

WIVES WITH THEIR HUSBANDS

Life beneath the cloak of coverture varied from wife to wife. Lady Anne Clifford owned and administered estates while she was separated from her husband Pembroke.[30] Other women owned little, controlled less and found themselves powerless to contradict or overcome the influence of their husbands. A significant number of wives, however, appeared in courts of law and equity alongside their husbands. The Court of Requests admitted thousands of married women as joint complainants and defendants, and their presence raises questions about why they appeared so often (why did husbands not litigate on their own?) and how active a part they played in joint actions.

In answer to the first question, wives so often appeared with their husbands because the conventions of law demanded their appearance. It has been observed how rules prevented wives from suing without their husbands. Rules also forbade husbands in certain situations from suing or being sued without

[29] *Henry Jernegan & Elizabeth fforthe* v. *Robert fforthe*, PRO Req 1/17, pp. 359–61; Robert Forth eventually paid the money but then brought his own counter-suit; PRO Req 1/17, pp. 492, 522, 752, 753.   [30] Lawrence Stone, *The Crisis of the Aristocracy 1558–1641* (Oxford, 1965), p. 661.

their wives, for example if they held the property at issue 'in right of their wives'.[31] Of course, not everyone obeyed the rules and in many cases husbands litigated their wives' rights without naming them parties to the action.[32] In one case the beneficiaries under a will chose to sue the husband of the executrix of the testator, but not the executrix herself.[33] Conversely, women often appeared as co-plaintiffs or co-defendants in actions which in strict legal terms did not involve their property or rights. Some married couples preferred to sue as a couple, as they would both be affected by the outcome. And plaintiffs named wives and husbands as joint defendants if they suspected complicity. In terms of procedure, rights obtainable in Requests were *in personam*, good against a named individual, rather than *in rem*, good against the whole world. Hence plaintiffs cast their nets wide, often naming wives as well as husbands, just as they might name tenant, steward and lord in a copyhold case, to ensure they named any and every opponent who might have a material connection with the interests they were claiming or contesting.

In answer to the second question, concerning the active involvement of married women named in suits, there is evidence that some married women participated in name only. The language of joint bills is often in the singular, 'he', with no mention of 'she' or 'they', as if the drafters and the court presumed the husband's dominance in the relationship. In a case that a husband and wife brought against another man, an agreement signed 'by assent of both parties' was signed only by the two men.[34] A blank space sometimes appears in the decree books where the name of a litigant's wife should be, which does little to suggest that scribes or Masters attached importance to married women's contributions to proceedings.[35] Despite these signs of a negligible role allowed to wives, other indications suggest a greater inclusion of married women in the business of litigation. To begin with, the procedures of the court preferred the appearance of plaintiffs and demanded the appearance of defendants, all defendants, to make answer.[36] Married women might ask to be excused from appearing; a common affidavit alleged that a party in an action 'is at this present greate

---

[31] Pollock and Maitland, *The History of English Law*, vol. 2, pp. 406, 408. Here, perhaps, is an explanation for the relatively high numbers of men and women joint plaintiffs who sued about land seen in table 4.1 (52 per cent compared with 43 per cent for men alone) and the relatively low numbers of men and women joint plaintiffs who sued about debts and bonds (19 per cent compared with 34 per cent for men alone). Under the rules of coverture husbands held land from their wives only in right of their wives, so had to sue alongside them. But debts and bonds were chattels, and therefore belonged to husbands alone, who could therefore sue without naming their wives.

[32] For an example of a plaintiff bringing an action 'in right of' his wife without naming her a party, see *Henry Penrose v. James Vyvian*, PRO Req 1/13, fols. 33ᵛ-34.

[33] *Katherine Knight v. David Jenkins*, PRO Req 1/21, p. 59.

[34] *Philip & Alice Carter v. Thomas Strowde et al.*, PRO Req 1/17, p. 415.

[35] See, for example, *Crowe v. ffraunc*s, PRO Req 1/21, p. 8.

[36] Dacre, 'Orders and rules in Requests', BL Additional MS 25,248, fols 29ᵛ-30; see also the wording of writs of Privy Seal; PRO Req 3/33; and Glanz, 'Legal position', p. 87.

with childe so that by meanes thereof shee cannot appeare'.[37] But even if women were excused from appearing, this does not mean they were excused from answering.[38] In the case of *Alice Pitt* v. *Simon & Margaret Jenks,* the Masters acknowledged that Margaret had a sick child and had 'necessarily to attend the same', but they ordered that a commission of *dedimus potestatem* be sent to take her answer.[39] Isabell Sadler, the Masters learned, 'hathe A yonge childe suckinge uppon her about the age of xvi weekes', and as her husband John was 'informed by his counsell', he and his son 'cannot convenyently Aunswer without the said Isabell'.[40] In another case they ordered that as the matter in the case 'dothe cheifly concerne the wyeves' of the defendants (two married couples), that *everyone's* answers should be taken by a commission of *dedimus potestatem.*[41]

The picture these and other examples paint is of a system lacking rigid rules, but not necessarily one lacking direction. The court demanded the participation of women when it was relevant to the case, and on occasion excused or over-looked it when it was not.[42] Once again, if opponents raised a fuss about this aspect of coverture then the court responded, but if no mention was made they were not so rigorous. In the main, however, married women appeared when instructed and played their part in proceedings. Joan and Richard Badger developed such a taste for litigation that after the Masters dismissed their case in Requests they were loathe to leave Westminster. The Master Alan Dale complained to her Majesty's Knight Marshall that the Badgers 'lye lyngering styll about the Court' where they walked 'Idely about as vagrant persons . . . (under color of having sute)'. He ordered that they be apprehended and punished as vagrants.[43] In a case where process under the Privy Seal was served on a married couple, it appears from the decree and order book that the woman travelled to Westminster on her own. She arrived to find no bill for her to answer, and the Masters dismissed the action against her and ordered that the plaintiff pay her 20s. in costs.[44] In 1582 at the summer assizes in Norwich, James Hayton showed in open court a Requests injunction against Thomas Weeche. Weeche's counsellors and attorneys agreed to abide by the injunction, 'but mistriss weeche, wyef

---

[37] See for example *Richard Browne* v. *Richard & Jane Ayers*, PRO Req 1/15, fol. 379.

[38] In a Chancery case against a married couple, the husband appeared but his wife neither came to court nor made excuse for her absence. The court issued an attachment against them both; *Monox* v. *Abell & wife*, C.U.L. Gg.2.26, fol. 115ᵛ; see also *Spicer* v. *Pakine, English Reports*, 21, p. 21.   [39] *Alice Pitt* v. *Simon & Margaret Jenks*, PRO Req 1/19, p. 839.

[40] *John Sadler* v. *Thomas Smythe et al.*, PRO Req 1/107, p. 800.

[41] *Edward Newgate* v. *Edward & Anne Taylor et al.*, PRO Req 1/40 [unfoliated], 10 June 28 Elizabeth I.

[42] In a case involving a married couple from Somerset in 1592, the husband made answer on 6 February, a commission was ordered on 22 May and the man's wife gave her separate answer on 21 June; *Robert & Silvester Dackombe* v. *Phillippe & Jane Cottington*, PRO Req 2/197/2.

[43] Alan Dale to her Majesty's Knight Marshall and his deputies, 6 November 23 Elizabeth I, PRO Req 3/33.   [44] *John Astell* v. *John & Mary Stone*, PRO Req 1/21, p. 263.

to the said Thomas, proceeded against this deponent and pleaded the cause her self'.[45] More general evidence comes from express references in pleadings to the opinions of wives, made explicit in phrases like 'she saithe that . . .', or 'the said Jane for her parte saith that she hadd never any purpose or will to persuade her husbond to so unreasonable a request'.[46] And a defendant whose wife was too ill to appear in person asked the Masters for an extension of time for himself, because 'hee cannot perfectly aunswere . . . before hee have had conference' with his wife.[47]

The involvement of husbands and wives in each others' legal affairs was frequently assumed, and the authorities in both Chancery and Requests considered that a subpoena served on a defendant's wife had effectively been served on the defendant.[48] When James and Susan Aske sued William and Jane Paine, they alleged that William, 'beinge combyned & confederated with the said Jane & by her procurement', consistently denied the feoffment of land that constituted their claim.[49] In a case where a man sued four married women, he only added their husbands' names to the bill 'for that alsoe your saide subject nothing doubtethe but that they the saide [defendants] have reveyled the trueth of the premisses unto their severall housebonds'. In the event, all but one of the wives answered on their own without their husbands, constituting yet another blemish on the copybook of coverture.[50]

Women's involvement in legal entanglements which bore their husbands' names could extend outside the courtroom. A deponent in the *Aske* v. *Paine* case suggested that Jane Paine had been the prime mover behind an enfeoffment. He reported that Jane had said to him: 'I have caused my husband to geve this house and land to my neece, Susan Reather And I praie you do the like to her.'[51] In 1568 a messenger swore on oath that he had served an injunction on a defendant who had then volunteered that he would be content to obey whatever decision the Masters had agreed upon. However, 'foorthwith the Lady his wife came to him and did stand with him, and immediately hee changed his former speaking, and saide that hee woulde pay no money'.[52] In another case a man allegedly asked if his wife could see an apprenticeship agreement, as she 'coulde better

---

[45] *James Hayton* v. *Thomas Weeche*, PRO Req 1/107, p. 1010; another possible example of a wife playing a leading role in a couple's law suits is the curiously labelled case, *Alice the wief of John Swanne* v. *Richard Fenton*; PRO Req 1/14, fol. 108ᵛ; and see Holdsworth, *History of English Law*, vol. 5, p. 315ff.

[46] For examples, see *Mathy & Jane Grey* v. *Thomas Eyre et al.*, PRO Req 2/144/44; *James & Susan Aske* v. *William & Jane Paine*, PRO Req 2/168/53, B.

[47] *Elizabeth Steward* v. *Thomas & Margerie Steward*, PRO Req 1/21, p. 6.

[48] PRO Req 1/107, pp. 721, 823, 835, 903, 967, 1100; C.U.L. Gg.2.26, fol. 107ᵛ.

[49] *James & Susan Aske* v. *William & Jane Paine*, PRO Req 2/168/53 [m. 8], B.

[50] *Richard Christopher* v. *William & Ellen Bailey et al.*, PRO Req 2/191/71.

[51] Jane supposedly wrote on the back of the deed of feoffment, 'To Suzan Reathers use There is two of these. The other is where my Joyncture is'; *James & Susan Aske* v. *William & Jane Paine*, PRO Req 2/157/20, D, deponents Sibell Reather, John Dryland; and see deponents Robert Smithe, Jane Reather.   [52] Caesar, *Ancient State*, p. 132.

reade the same then himself', whereupon 'she tooke the same and did teare it in many peeces'.[53] Women of gentle status often took an active interest in their husbands' legal affairs from home, and some ventured to the courts themselves. Elisabeth Oxenford wrote to Julius Caesar in November 1602 explaining that she had meant to deliver a request from her husband concerning one of his law suits, but a mishap with her coach prevented 'hope of any present opportunity to meete you at the court'. Unable to attend in person, she was forced to put her entreaties on paper.[54]

Married women, then, rarely participated in joint actions in name only. And most cases that bore their names involved causes or property in which they had an interest. Many of these interests had existed before these women married, which raises the interesting question of why they had chosen not to make claims at the time their interests first arose. As will be seen in a moment, marriage (or more often re-marriage) could be just as powerful a catalyst as widowhood for precipitating legal actions. In the normal course of events, when people were wronged they allowed their opponents reasonable time to make good. Then, if informal methods of persuasion and attempts at reconciliation or compromise failed, they went to court. The period of time between an event occurring and the commencement of an action in court could run into weeks or even months. In cases involving married women the time-lapse often involved years and sometimes decades.

We saw in the last chapter how Agnes Nowell waited two or three decades for her marriage to end before she was able to bring a suit.[55] Many single and widowed women waited similar lengths of time, bringing actions only once they had married or re-married. Soon after John and Joan Playse married they joined in putting an uncancelled bond in suit in Common Pleas against two defendants. Those defendants convinced the Masters in Requests to have that action stayed, persuading them that the debt in issue was twenty years old and had long since been settled.[56] Alice James and her husband sued for lands which they felt should have come to her *forty* years before.[57] John Hole enjoyed a copyhold interest under a series of grants and re-grants from Richard Buckland and his sons until Christmas 1567, when Buckland's widow Rose and her new husband recovered a third of the manor as dower, ten years after Rose's right to dower had fallen due.[58] In other cases the time between cause and action (following

---

[53] *Edmond & Anne Edwards* v. *John & Agnes Armiger*, PRO Req 1/19, p. 807.
[54] Elisabeth Oxenford to Julius Caesar, 20 November 1602; BL Additional MS 12,506, fol. 175.
[55] See chapter 5 above.
[56] *John Lowe & Richard Reades* v. *John & Johan Playse*, PRO Req 1/21, p. 98.
[57] *Roger & Alice James* v. *William Wyne*, PRO Req 2/226/25.
[58] *John Hole* v. *Richard & Rose Bewe & William James*, PRO Req 2/223/84; regardless of the time which elapsed before entry to court, a large proportion of women suing in Requests for their dower (most claimants sued at common law) sued jointly with new husbands; see, for example, *John & Elizabeth Blackborne* v. *Thomas Carter*, PRO Req 1/20, fols 32–33ᵛ.

marriage) was three years, four years or ten years.[59] That the Masters heard these cases is significant for, as we have seen, in other contexts they accepted delays in waging law as proof that no cause existed. In 1601 they ordered a man to cease his common law suit for debt against a woman because the debt 'hath continued in silence without demande thereof for the space of seaven yeares, whereby it seemeth that the same is satisfied'.[60] Clearly they recognised that married women, like widows, might have unique requirements when it came to the defence of their rights.

Why did women wait so long to sue? In most cases it is only possible to speculate about the reasons behind these delays, but four likely alternatives present themselves which might explain why marriage was so often a spur to litigation. The first possibility is that women lacked the resources to sue while they were unmarried or widowed. Taking a case to Westminster required not just money, but the ability to leave home, children and work to journey to local towns to visit solicitors, or to London to attend court. Many 'poor' widows and a number of 'poor fatherless maidens' gained entry to Requests, often suing *in forma pauperis*, but clearly many more found the demands of litigation in a central court beyond their reach until they could unite economic forces with a man.

The second possible explanation is that women lacked knowledge of their legal rights and entitlements. This accords with the view of Susan Staves that: 'Although some early modern women took an interest in their legal entitlements to marital property . . . most women appear to have been quite ignorant of the subject and inhibited about becoming informed or asserting legal entitlements of which they were aware.'[61] If women who were uncertain about their rights decided to marry, their husbands might investigate the history of their legal affairs and discover lands owing, legacies due, or other actionable causes ripe to be litigated. Just as widowhood could present widows with a rag-bag of their husbands' loans, debts and papers, marriage could bestow upon husbands an assortment of their wives' legal rights, causes and complaints. A father left his daughter Agnes money for her portion in his will, stipulating that she should receive it when she turned twenty two. She married and her husband joined her in a Requests action against the overseers of the will to claim her legacy. The overseers responded that she was not yet twenty two, but the Masters felt that this was 'no sufficient cause' for the defendants to deny the couple maintenance, given their poverty. They ordered the overseers to provide the couple with an allowance from the interest accruing on Agnes's portion until she turned twenty

---

[59] *Thomas & Agathe Townesende v. Thomas Wake et al.*, PRO Req 2/278/48; *Thomas & Maude Daniel v. Christopher & Margaret Rendal*, PRO Req 2/199/13; *Edmond & Anne Edwards v. John & Agnes Armiger*, PRO Req 1/19, p. 807.

[60] *Eden Curd v. William Alston*, PRO Req 1/20, fol. 36.

[61] Staves, *Married Women's Separate Property*, p. 205.

two. Only if she should die before then would her husband or heirs have to repay the money.[62] It is impossible in this case to know for certain which partner's knowledge or initiative brought the case to court, but it seems likely that the woman would not have chosen to challenge her father's will on her own.

Implicit in the doubts which surround the legal knowledge and motivations of husbands and wives lies a third possibility, that women with clear knowledge of their legal entitlements believed they had no actionable rights, or desired for reasons of conscience not to act upon rights they did possess, but their newly acquired husbands thought otherwise. In other words the prime movers behind many of these actions were greedy and opportunist husbands. As one litigant complained, if his recently married opponent possessed a legitimate right, 'it is very, verye like that she woulde have made Clayme to the sayde messuage or tenement at some tyme dureinge the space of these sixteene yeres'.[63] Allegations that greedy and opportunist wives were behind their husbands' actions were not unknown – in 1594 a couple accused the fifty year old widow Joan Jones of using corrupt means to entice a 100 year old widower to marry her, so she could get her hands on his property – but they were relatively rare.[64]

Other defendants whose peace was disturbed after an unlikely period of time also suggested that causes left dormant had been left dormant for good reason. In the case of *John Hole* v. *Richard & Rose Bewe*, mentioned above, in which the Bewes were claiming Rose's dower at common law after a decade, Hole (a defendant turned plaintiff) described how his friends had travelled to London on his behalf to seek the couple's goodwill, and had spoken to Rose on her own. She had said that 'by her goodwill the fatherlesse children shoulde have hit before any other' (in other words, John's grant should be honoured, despite the fact that it was voidable at law under the writ of dower), 'but of her selfe she woulde doe nothinge without the consente of her husbande'.[65] The successful opponents of John and Joan Playse, referred to above, emphasised in their pleadings that Joan's first husband had made no claim against them between the date of repayment and his death, and Joan had made no claim during her widowhood. It was only after she married her new husband, twenty years on, that the matter came to court.[66] When a newly wed couple, Albyn and Mary Willoughby, sued Mary's aunt to claim her inheritance, the aunt responded that Albyn had taken Mary away by unlawful means while she was still an infant and married her, 'much contrary' to the wishes of her aunt and all of Mary's

---

[62] *Richard & Agnes Smith* v. *Thomas Adowne et al.*, PRO Req 1/21, pp. 93–4.
[63] *Griffin & Ellen Powell* v. *Johan ap Thomas*, PRO Req 2/36/79 [m.3], A.
[64] *Thomas & Elizabeth Smythe* v. *Thomas & Joan Caton et al.*, PRO Req 2/266/57, B.
[65] *John Hole* v. *Richard & Rose Bewe & William James*, PRO Req 2/223/84, B, R, Rj, D, deponent Philip Bythesey.
[66] *John Lowe & Richard Read* v. *John & Johan Playse*, PRO Req 1/21, p. 98.

friends. Albyn may in fact have been liberating Mary's inheritance at her request, but the defendants went to lengths to paint him as an opportunist 'cradle-snatcher'.[67]

Defendants' accusations and insinuations are one thing, actual proof that a husband rather than his wife was primarily responsible for a suit is harder to find. For actions that defendants blamed on opportunism may have resulted instead from plain ignorance. John and Anne Whitebread sued Robert Noyes in Requests to recover title to five houses and land which had belonged to Anne's late father and therefore should have come to her as his heir. The Masters dismissed this action after Noyes produced proof that Anne's father had conveyed title to him during his lifetime.[68] Was John Whitebread calculating and fraudulent, or was Anne ignorant of the transfer? The unexplained postponement of actions can be suggestive, however, and so too can the logic of litigants' accounts of events. If, as a recently married couple alleged, a father-in-law had really withheld from his daughter-in-law her jointure despite her repeated pleadings and protestations, why had the woman then entrusted him with her other financial affairs throughout her widowhood?[69]

The fourth, and perhaps the most interesting, explanation for these delays is that some *femes sole* declined to go to law out of choice. Despite being fully aware of their rights, and in possession of the necessary resources to go to law, they consciously chose to wait until they married before pursuing legal causes. Maria Cioni noticed that heiresses rarely pursued causes in Chancery and suggested that 'the average girl would resign herself to the fact [that it was difficult for her to sue] and perhaps hope that when she married her husband might pursue legal action to obtain her rightful inheritance'.[70] Some defendants argued that this was indeed the case. When a newly married couple sued John Baber, he alleged that the woman had actually married her husband 'for the better Assistaunce & strengthing of her selfe in her said wrongfull attempte Against this defendant'.[71] Whatever the reasons that led some women to refrain from suing while they were *femes sole*, the fact that a certain number proved unwilling, or unable, to mount court actions until they married helps to explain why the numbers of unmarried women bringing actions in Requests remained relatively low. As well as confirming that the struggle to achieve justice could prove harder for women than for men, this evidence of postponed actions offers oblique evidence that the rhetoric encouraging women not to go to law alone may have had some effect. However, if a small group of women behaved as

---

[67] *Albyn & Marye Willoughby v. Elizabeth Earthe et al.*, PRO Req 2/283/59, A of Nycholas Wadham.   [68] *John & Anne Whitebread v. Robert Noyes*, PRO Req 1/21, p. 195.

[69] *Roger & Anne Litler v. Thomas Speight*, PRO Req 2/234/60, A.

[70] Cioni, *Women and law*, p. 87; Cioni, 'Elizabethan Chancery', p. 164; for a typical Requests case that may conform to this pattern, see *Thomas & Anne Hilsey v. John Maggs*, PRO Req 2/85/57, Req 2/158/107.   [71] *John & Maud Bluet v. John Baber*, PRO Req 2/178/55, m. 1, A.

moralists dictated, whether by default or out of choice, another group did no such thing. A select band of married women, wives like Joan Spragin, threw caution and coverture to the wind and brought actions against their own husbands.

In May 1587 Richard Puttenham, the brother of George, author of *The Art of English Poesie*, wrote to the Masters of Requests seeking respite from the demands of his estranged wife Mary. In his letter Puttenham complained that over a period of twenty years a succession of Masters had ordered him to pay between £20 and £30 a year, out of his 'poore livinge' of £100, 'to mainteine A proude stubborne woman his wief in unbrydled libertie from him'. Recently delivered out of prison, where his debts had forced him to spend four years, Puttenham argued that he was now a poor man, 'susteined onely by charitie and borrowinge of some pittifull men'. He beseeched the Masters to review his case and to end his molestation in their court. His reasoning was simple. Disagreements between husband and wife were a matter for the spiritual courts, not Requests. If the Masters nevertheless decided to persist with their intervention then they should recalculate the level of Mary's maintenance, taking account of his reduced circumstances. In his mind, the Masters had overridden the accepted authority of husbands over wives by allowing an exception to the doctrine of coverture impossible under the 'due course or Order of Lawe'. By recognising Mary's demands the Masters were allowing her 'this great prerogative in your Courte more then all other Waives on england have been accustomed unto'. The result of such recklessness, he argued, was that Mary was 'continually being boldened thoroughe sufferaunce'.[72] The rot, having been allowed a chance to set in, was spreading.

Puttenham's letter, like the pleadings prepared by his legal counsel, fell on deaf ears, and the Masters continued to enforce their original order. His outrage at their defiance of coverture indicates how controversial their decisions might seem to outsiders, and Puttenham was by no means alone in his disquiet. When Dame Elizabeth Stafford brought an action against her husband Sir Humphrey Stafford in 1562, he too complained that the Masters lacked jurisdiction to consider a suit between a wedded couple. He warned the Masters that any attempt to order maintenance for Elizabeth would have serious implications, asking:

---

[72] PRO Req 1/14, fols 279^{r-v}; Julius Caesar recorded a payment to Mary Puttenham in May 1576 of 13s. 8d., due to her for half a year's payment of her annuity, considerably less than the £30–£40 alleged by Puttenham; Caesar, *Ancient State*, p. 140; Mary continued to sue Richard for default while he was 'in the Gate House'; *Marie Puttenham v. Richard Puttenham*, PRO Req 2/256/75, D, deponent William Robinson.

What and how many worshipfull bloodes and goode howses within this Realme would or might be the rather overthrowne yf this Complainant, agenst whome so manyfest prooff of contynuall adultery ys to be shewed, shoulde escape cleare? What greater provucacon canne there be then to gyve bowldnes to all graceles and unshamefast women to Runne the lyke Base yf she the said Complainant shouldbe favored or spared?[73]

The language of pleadings is always exaggerated, but the suggestion that the Masters were inviting social revolution is remarkable.

Despite the teeth-gnashing of angry husbands, the Masters continued to allow married women access to justice and equity. The Requests archive contains at least a dozen petitions from wives suing their husbands (and very occasionally husbands suing their wives) from the early 1540s until the end of Elizabeth's reign in 1603.[74] Joan Morgan sought the assistance of Requests because she said her husband John Andrewes had 'fallen into a ffransey' and her life was now in danger. She pleaded with the Masters to restrain him from selling the couple's farm until she could discover whether or not she 'maie be lawfullie dyvorsed from hym'.[75] Far more extraordinary is the woman who defied the ecclesiastical law of bigamy as well as the rules of coverture by suing *two* former husbands, alleging that the first owed her an annuity of £20 a year and that the second had released the annuity without her consent.[76]

Taken together, these cases demonstrate the willingness of the Masters to hear the pleas of married women against their husbands, and their willingness to order maintenance and to ensure that maintenance was paid. The church courts had the power to free married couples from the obligation to live together, and to order that husbands continue to maintain their wives during the period of the couple's estrangement, but when it came to enforcing maintenance they could do little except threaten defaulters with excommunication. They might set out the conditions of separation in a bond with a penalty

---

[73] *Elizabeth Stafforde* v. *Humfrey Stafforde*, PRO Req 2/166/171.

[74] *Parnell Bowdo* v. *Peter Bowdo* [1542], *Margery Alcocke* v. *Nicholas Alcocke* [1544], in Caesar, *Ancient State*, pp. 96, 98; *Margary Acton* v. *Robert Acton* [1553], PRO Req 2/14/53 (mentioned in Caesar, *Ancient State*, pp. 109–10); *Issabell Osmoderley* v. *William Osmoderly* [1554], PRO Req 2/24/82; *Elizabeth Stafforde* v. *Humfrey Stafforde* [1561/2], PRO Req 2/166/171, Req 1/11, pp. 20–1; *Ellen Dumbrell* v. *Clement Dumbrell* [1567], PRO Req 2/196/96; *John Chapman* v. *Anne Chapman & Christopher Preston* [1588], PRO Req 2/193/16; *Marie Puttenham* v. *Richard Puttenham* [1591], PRO Req 2/256/75; *Jane Reade als Lambert* v. *Thomas Reade & John Jeffries* [1594], PRO Req 2/50/39; *Thomas Reader* v. *Jane Lambert* [1594], PRO Req 2/262/20; *Anne Lloyd* v. *Humfrey Lloyde* [1595], PRO Req 2/234/61 (reproduced in A.K.R. Kiralfy, *A Source Book of English Law* (London, 1957), pp. 301–8); *Johan Spragin* v *Martin Spragen & Richard Levens* [1596], PRO Req 1/18, p. 913; *Katherine Willoughby* v. *Kenelm Willoughby* [1601], PRO Req 2/286/45, Req 2/63/60, Req 2/31/3, Req 2/163/155; *Jhoane Mercer & John Walter* v. *Thomas(?) Mercer et al.* [1603], PRO Req 3/33; *Johan Morgan als Andrewes* v. *John Andrewes* [n.d.], PRO Req 2/166/129.   [75] *Johan Morgan* v. *John Andrewes*, PRO Req 2/166/129.

[76] The details of this extraordinary case are given in chapter 8 below; at this time bigamy could be prosecuted in the church courts. Only in 1604 did it become a criminal offence punishable in secular courts; Brian Outhwaite, *Clandestine Marriage in England, 1500–1850* (London and Rio Grande, 1995), pp. 9, 56; Ingram, *Church Courts*, pp. 149–50, 179.

attached, so that if a husband defaulted the bond could be put in suit at common law and he could be made to pay. However, bonds like this had to be arranged with third parties, because married women could not enter into contracts with their husbands, nor could they sue them at common law. Requests, by contrast, allowed separated wives to sue in their own names, either to claim maintenance, or to have existing orders of maintenance enforced or the levels of their maintenance recalculated. This was arguably the most innovative development within the Requests jurisdiction. The succession of maintenance cases, beginning with *Bowdo* v. *Bowdo* in 1542, appears to confirm John Baker's suspicion that the Court of Requests was at the forefront of the development of alimony.[77]

At first sight these cases seem to cut at the very root of coverture. However, it is doubtful that the Masters intended by their actions to subvert the doctrine altogether. On the contrary, their desire was to uphold it, although they were anxious to uphold its spirit as well as its form.[78] In most cases the Masters applied the doctrine without giving it a second thought. As earlier sections in this chapter have shown, they refused to hear actions that wives initiated without their husbands, or to enforce contracts or surrenders women made while married.[79] When they permitted exceptions, it was invariably because the couple in question had separated. In this sense, the cases fought between husbands and wives represent the exceptions which prove the rule. Coverture was designed to overcome (in the husband's favour) the dilemma of who should have legal responsibility within the partnership of marriage. If for any reason the relationship split asunder, then the doctrine no longer served its original purposes, and the Masters were no longer content to apply it without question. That they remained generally committed to the principle of coverture seems clear from the fact that they set it aside only a handful of times in sixty years. A similar picture existed in Chancery, where Maria Cioni has shown that the Chancellor was willing to let married women sue their husbands, but a glance at modern calendars confirms that examples of this happening were even rarer than in Requests.[80]

What made the approach of the Masters radical was not so much their attitude to coverture – even common law judges permitted limited exceptions to the

---

[77] Baker, *Introduction to English Legal History*, p. 562, n. 74.

[78] Janelle Greenberg has argued that the eighteenth century Chancery was similarly reluctant to subvert the rules of coverture, choosing instead to deem married women *femes sole* in certain specific circumstances; Janelle Greenberg, 'The legal status of the English woman in early eighteenth-century common law and equity', *Studies in Eighteenth-Century Culture*, 4 (1975), p. 178.

[79] The Masters dismissed the suit of Sara Baguley on the grounds that since the emergence of the cause in issue Sara had married Hughe Lee, who was 'yet in full lief' but not named in her action; *Sara Baguley* v. *Nicholas Coleman et al.*, PRO Req 1/21, p. 52; for Chancery, see C.U.L. Gg.2.26, fols 130ᵛ-133.

[80] I have found no examples of wives suing in their own names in published Chancery calendars, and Amy Erickson found only one; Erickson, *Women and Property*, p. 115; Cioni, *Women and Law*, p. 30.

doctrine in instances where a woman's husband had deserted her, was overseas or was in prison – but their definition of separation.[81] In almost every case of this type the couple in consideration had obtained a separation in the ecclesiastical courts. To accept this as grounds for restoring a wife's right to sue was a significant step forward, in comparison with the black-letter applications of the doctrine favoured by common lawyers, but it is difficult to describe it as revolutionary.[82] In other cases, however, the Masters took their commitment to equity further still, and entertained suits from women who had *not* gained an official separation, but whose marriages had effectively disintegrated. We have already seen how Joan Morgan sought interim help from the Masters while she waited to see if she could be 'lawfullie dyvorsed' from her frenzied husband. The language of her bill reveals the exceptional nature of the aid she and her counsel were seeking. Not only did it stress that she was without remedy unless the Masters 'movid with pittie take compassion on hir', but it asked them to provide assistance 'for the love of god' and 'in the waie of Charitie'.[83] It is unclear in this case whether the Masters responded to her plea, but the fact that she could make such a plea demonstrates their reputation for refusing to let the strict application of rules produce injustice. In other cases certain Masters did overstep this particular doctrinal mark, and by doing so they demonstrated the strength of their commitment to the protection of married women's interests and welfare.

Here we return to the Puttenham case, for Richard's major complaint was that he and Mary had not been separated, and therefore the Masters were usurping powers that he felt 'better pertained to the spiritual courts'. Puttenham was so incensed by the Masters' flouting of common law rules and ecclesiastical court powers that while in prison he petitioned the Privy Council. His petition, dated 1585, contained none of the polite restraint of his later letter to the Masters. Behind their backs he spoke his mind and made allegations that open up for scrutiny the way in which the Court of Requests functioned. Puttenham directed all of his accusations at one man, Thomas Sackford (or Seckford), Master from 1558. His catalogue of allegations of ill treatment and misuse of authority is astonishing, including suggestions that Sackford chased him out of doors threatening to strike him with his staff, took money from him without a court decree, refused to listen to his or other litigants' arguments, and contrived to strip him of his meagre funds in prison, so that he was forced to subsist on gruel. Puttenham suggested that Sackford was 'more lyke a madd

---

[81] See T.E., *The Lawes Resolutions of Womens Rights*, p. 157.

[82] Common applications of coverture could border on the ridiculous. Late in the seventeenth century, Mary Griggs married twice and was indicted in King's Bench under the Jacobean Bigamy Act. When she pleaded not guilty the prosecution produced her first husband in court to prove that she was already married. The court refused to admit his testimony, because husbands and wives were not allowed to plead against each other (except for treason) 'because it might occasion dissention'. Despite the presence in court of both of her husbands, the judges found Mary not guilty; *Mary Grigg's case*, *English Reports*, 83, p. 1.

[83] *Johan Morgan v. John Andrewes*, PRO Req 2/166/129.

man then Judge of a courte' and that if the Privy Councillors found his violent and arbitrary determination of cases without due process acceptable, 'then nedeth ther be no more courtes nor Judges in the Realme, nor yet so many men of lawe as ther be, for Mr Sackfords commaundement . . . is enough to dispatche all matters'. Puttenham claimed that never before had it been known 'that a Master of requests did appoynt men what stypende they shold allowe their wieves to spend at their liberte absent from their howsbandes', in other words without an official separation. He suggested to the Privy Council that should 'the sayd Sackforde mainteyn any mannes wief agaynst her howsbounde' in the future, then the Council should deem it 'right & reason that suche maintenance be don at his own costes'; Sackford alone was to fund all the alimony payments in England. To prove that Sackford's ruling was unprecedented and unwarranted, Puttenham stressed how the other Master, Dr Valentine Dale, 'in the open courte alwayes spook agaynst it'. Unfortunately, Puttenham explained, Dr Dale was 'Sackfords servant & not his fellow' and would say one thing in court and then 'consentethe afterwards to the contrarie' so as not to cross his senior colleague, or 'as they saye', he would 'holdeth with the hare & ronneth with the hownde'.

What the Privy Councillors thought of Puttenham's claims we shall probably never know, for the Lord Mayor of London, Sir Wolstan Dixie, intercepted his petition and 'supposing that it had conteyned some seditious matter' he opened it and sent it straight to Thomas Sackford.[84] Puttenham made more failed attempts to escape his obligation to support Mary and spent many of his remaining years languishing in prison for debt. However, his allegations highlight the peculiarities of Requests process. Given the nature of the court, its imprecisely defined jurisdiction, its philosophical objection to strict rules or procedural forms, and its ambivalent attitude to theories of precedent, it is quite conceivable that an individual Master could dominate proceedings or make arbitrary decisions. Given the tradition in the Elizabethan court of maintaining a balance between civilians and common lawyers, it is also plausible that while hearing a case like Puttenham's, the civilian Master in the White Hall might recommend relief for the victimised wife, while the common law Master vehemently objected to hearing the suit of an unseparated married woman.[85] The argument is hard to sustain in this instance, however, for Sackford was the common lawyer and Dale the doctor of civil law.[86] The possibility that some Masters were more receptive to cases involving married women, and more willing than others to overlook fixed rules, is bolstered by the fact that the cases

---

[84] Sir Wolstan Dixie to Thomas Sackford (enclosing Puttenham's petition), 30 October 1585, S.P. 12/183/66.

[85] The initials of the attending Masters are given in the Decree and Order books at the end of each day's sitting, so it is usually possible to determine who was presiding when particular cases were decided or orders made.

[86] It may be relevant that Sackford had been a commissioner for ecclesiastical causes and that Dale's brother was a common lawyer; *D.N.B.*, vol. 13, p. 387; vol. 51, p. 173.

between married couples were not evenly distributed over the decades, but fell into distinct clusters, one of the most noticeable coming in the 1590s.[87] Once again, this theory does little to vindicate the claims of Puttenham, for as the next case will attest, Mary Puttenham was not the only unseparated married woman who managed to bypass the spiritual courts and receive relief in Requests.

Litigation in lesser Westminster courts did not usually produce petitions to the Privy Council. The Masters were apparently sailing very close to the wind, and while they were left unscathed by Puttenham's challenge to their judgement and authority, they were not so lucky in a later case from 1595 (by which time Thomas Sackford was no longer Master). The case in question is *Anne Lloyd* v. *Humfrey Lloyd*, another suit between a married couple for maintenance. Anne argued in her bill of complaint that when she married Humfrey he had taken her portion and arranged a jointure of specified lands, but now he was trying to use violence to make her agree to surrender those lands. During their marriage she had, she said, 'lived free in the eye of the world from any suspicion of hard usage or cause of dislike between her and her said husband', but actually she had 'endured at her said husbands hands vile and inhuman maner of dealing . . . being day by daie . . . assaulted, beaten and wounded moste pyttyfully'. This mistreatment led her to escape with her child, 'for safeguard of her life', and she wanted the Masters to protect her jointure lands and order maintenance before Humfrey could flee the country to evade his obligations.[88]

In response to Anne's allegations Humfrey entered a demurrer, insisting that he did not have to answer her bill and that he desired 'nothinge more then the good of the complainant, and that she wolde live and remayne with hir husbande, as becoometh a wife to doo'. He demurred because he felt there existed no just cause why he should maintain Anne outside his house, and if her allegations were true then she could get a magistrate or assize justice to have him bound over to keep the peace ('a fitter and shorter course then to coome from thence two hundred myles, and here to complayne'), or she could seek a separation from bed and board at the church courts. He argued that Anne had left of her own free will, and that to grant maintenance without a separation by law or by his consent was 'against all justice and course of all laws, as this defendent taketh it'. Furthermore, he reasoned, if the Masters did order maintenance at equity, she could then come home and demand that he maintain her as his wife under common law, and he would be 'double charged'. He asked the Masters to dismiss Anne's action, and in a fascinating testament to the confusion surrounding coverture he also asked them to award him costs against Anne, 'if anie maie bee had agaynst his owne wyfe'.[89]

The Masters rejected Humfrey's demurrer and made him answer. He reiter-

---

[87] See note 74 above.   [88] *Anne Lloyd* v. *Humfrey Lloyde*, PRO Req 2/234/61, m. 1, B.

[89] *Anne Lloyd* v. *Humfrey Lloyde*, PRO Req 2/234/61, m. 3, Dem; in his answer Humfrey further argued that Anne could run up debts for clothing, food and lodgings, 'which by the Common Lawe of this Realme' he would be obliged to pay; *Anne Lloyd* v. *Humfrey Lloyde*, PRO Req 2/234/61, m. 2, A.

ated his former points and assured the Masters that Anne's jointure, worth £40 per annum, was safe. The Masters remained unconvinced, and they set a date for a hearing and demanded that he attend. Humfrey refused to come to Requests, but he agreed to come to London and appear with Anne before Lord Chief Justice Sir John Popham, the highest common law judge in the land, acting as arbitrator. He assented in writing to the agreement Popham worked out, which gave Anne the authority to receive rents from the lands she had orig-inally brought to the marriage (currently part of the disputed jointure).[90] However, when he failed to meet the conditions of this agreement it fell to the Masters to enforce them. With their patience clearly stretched to breaking point, they ordered one sheriff to arrange for Anne to receive the profits from her lands (in effect to sequester Humfrey's lands) and another sheriff to arrest Humfrey.[91] Once Humfrey was in custody, the arresting sheriff made him enter a bond guaranteeing his attendance at a second hearing and then released him. When he failed, yet again, to come to court the sheriff put the bond in suit at Common Pleas to recover the £100 penalty for default.

The sheriff's name was Stephens, or Stepney or Stepneth, and the Common Pleas action was *Stepneth* v *Floud*, described in chapter 4 above (the Lloyds came from 'Llandilo Tal-y-Bont' in Glamorgan in Wales, and English scribes often transcribed the Welsh 'Lloyd' as 'Flood' or 'Floud').[92] Anne Lloyd's case was therefore at the heart of the Justices of the Common Pleas' declaration that Requests had no jurisdiction, that it was *coram non judice*, and their instruction to sheriff Stepneth that in the future he should never again deliver Requests process.[93] It was the case that spurred Caesar to publish his defence of Requests, *The Ancient State and Authority of the Court of Requests*, and helped make the court a laughing stock. That the most controversial case in the history of Requests involved married women's rights is intriguing. Could it be that Justices Glanville and Anderson were outraged not so much by the Masters' exercise of powers for which they supposedly had no authority – arresting, imprisoning and sequestering the lands of a defendant – but their decision to award mainte-nance to a *feme covert* who had left her husband without his consent?[94] Even

---

[90] Julius Caesar's annotated copy of *The Ancient State*; BL Additional MS 25,248, fols 54[r-v]; PRO Req 1/19, pp. 116–17; after Anne collected rents under the authority of this indenture, Humfrey sued the tenants for non-payment of rents in Common Pleas, effectively double charging them; *Thomas Llewelyn et al. v. Humfrey Lloyd*, PRO Req 2/235/74.

[91] PRO Req 1/19, pp. 224–5; and see pp. 566, 612.

[92] See p. 72 above; Edward Coke referred to this case as *Stepney* v. *Flood*, Lamar Hill calls it *Stepneth* v. *Flood*, while George Croke and A.K.R. Kiralfy called it *Stepney* v. *Lloyd*; Edward Coke, *The Fourth Part of the Institutes of the Laws of England* (London, 1797), p. 97; L.M. Hill, *The Ancient State Authoritie, and Proceedings of the Court of Requests by Julius Caesar* (Cambridge, 1975), pp. x, xv, xxi; George Croke, *The First Part of the Reports of Sir George Croke*, trans. Harbottle Grimstone (London, 1661), p. 646; Kiralfy, *A Source Book of English law*, p. 308. [93] Kiralfy, *A Source Book of English law*, pp. 301–11.

[94] The fact that Lord Chief Justice Popham had arbitrated the agreement between Humfrey and Anne works against this possibility, although it is worth remembering that Popham was a former Master of Requests.

ecclesiastical courts balked at this possibility; in the Court of High Commission in 1632, for example, Sir Henry Martin refused to grant alimony to a woman until she proved that her husband had misused her, because he said that to grant it without such proof 'is the readie way to make every woman her husband's master'.[95] Alternatively, if the Common Pleas justices were solely concerned by the extent to which the Masters had exceeded their authority, why had the Masters chosen this particular occasion to take such unprecedented steps, if not out of recognition of the particularly difficult position facing a married woman seeking justice? *Anne Lloyd* v. *Humfrey Lloyd* certainly advances the credentials of Requests in general, and of Julius Caesar in particular, as a supporter of married women's causes. Caesar appears to have brought the couple together at an earlier stage and acted as an arbitrator negotiating an original settlement.[96] In *The Ancient State* he included details of three occasions when the Masters had granted maintenance (as well as numerous examples of defendants they had arrested, fined and imprisoned).[97] He was also active in organising marriage settlements for other women, and as mentioned in an earlier chapter, his correspondence contains dozens of letters from women seeking to advance their own or other people's causes.[98]

The cases that wives brought against their husbands in Requests provide revealing evidence of how much independence determined women could achieve despite the restricting bonds of marriage, and the lengths to which some Masters would go to support their causes, even if it meant putting the existence of their jurisdiction at risk. It is interesting to speculate whether the rhetoric employed by thwarted husbands held any truth, whether these cases did set an example for other women and led them to question any of the legal restrictions under which they lived. In other words, whether cases in Requests or Chancery demonstrated to women at large that actions previously considered impossible were now possible.

The Masters made various attempts to assist women while they were still married, but clearly they were pushing against the tide. The fact that married women could sue their husbands only in certain courts, and only in exceptional circumstances, highlights the precariousness of married women's rights at law, even as they were modified by equity. Once a husband died, his widow could disavow almost all actions done in her name while she had been his wife.[99] Similarly, in cases where a husband fraudulently alienated jointly held lands without gaining his wife's consent, she could fight to reclaim those interests

---

[95] Samuel Gardiner, ed., *Reports of Cases in the Courts of Star Chamber and High Commission (1631–1632)*, Camden Society, new series, vol. 39 (1886), p. 303.

[96] *Anne Lloyd* v. *Humfrey Lloyde*, PRO Req 2/234/61, m. 2, A.

[97] Caesar, *The Ancient State*, pp. 96, 98, 109–10.

[98] L.M. Hill, *Mistress Bourne's Complaint* (forthcoming).

[99] *Agnes Sheppard* v. *David Birchett*, PRO Req 1/16, p. 97; *Roger, Maude & Johan Elys* v. *Thomas Chaffyn*, PRO Req 2/202/36, D, deponent William Lucas.

after his death. But rarely could she do so before.[100] While their husbands remained alive, most wives were hamstrung. Short of seeking a separation there was little they could do on their own account to protect their interests while still married.[101] Earlier chapters have described how during marriage negotiations, a woman, or her family, could construct a variety of elaborate uses, trusts or jointures to safeguard property and other interests. If a husband breached the conditions contained in these arrangements, then the trustees, fathers, mothers or brothers who helped to establish these arrangements could sue him on his wife's behalf, but it could be extremely difficult for the woman herself to enforce them. These devices usually released women from the shackles of coverture only by transferring reliance on husbands to reliance on family members or trustees. If the terms of a marriage settlement gave a married woman the right to make a will and her husband refused her that right, how could the woman protest at law? In most cases a trustee or the holder of a bond ensuring performance had to sue on her behalf.[102] This point is conceptually important, underlining the power husbands had at their command and the extent to which married women's affairs were necessarily communal affairs, even if they only involved one other party, a professional trustee. Trustees, fathers, aunts and uncles could, like husbands, turn out to have self-interested motives. And if the men or women charged with overseeing married women's property or affairs turned out to be fraudulent, *femes covert*, unable to sue on their own, found themselves forced once more to rely on their husbands for support in recovering their interests.[103]

In practice, of course, many of these problems never materialised. Court records provide a distorted view of common experience, and for every marriage settlement, trust or use that went wrong and found its way into Requests, a larger and incalculable number went right. Husbands observed terms in written agreements. Families or trustees pressured husbands to honour their commit-

---

[100] *Johan Willyn* v. *Christopher Keny*, PRO Req 2/283/61, B; the law demanded that wives should be examined on their own to ensure that they were willing parties to any surrender, but in practice husbands achieved alienations without their wives' knowledge or authority; Pollock and Maitland, *The History of English Law*, vol. 2, pp. 409–10; *Elizabeth Eyer* v. *William Rowthe*, PRO C2 Eliz E/2/42; in Chancery a woman sued to recover her portion after obtaining a full divorce *frigiditatis*, and the Master of the Rolls accepted her suit (even though her father who had given the money was still alive) saying he would not be a 'formalist'; *Barrow* v. *Batten* (1594), C.U.L. Gg.2.31, p. 407.

[101] As a *feme covert* a married woman lacked standing to sue her husband in most jurisdictions, and given the theoretical bar on her ownership of property, she might also face difficulties funding any court actions.

[102] In *Avenant* v. *Kitchin* (1581–2) the court upheld a married woman's will after her death; Holdsworth, *History of English Law*, vol. 5, pp. 310–11.

[103] See, for example, *John & Margaret Gedney* v. *George Etheredge et al.*, PRO Req 1/21, p. 79; *John & Maude Bluet* v. *John Baber*, PRO Req 2/178/55; and see the arguments John Chapman made against his estranged wife's trustee; *John Chapman* v. *Chrystofer Preston & Anne Chapman*, PRO Req 2/193/16.

ments. As the work of Amy Erickson shows, many women managed to achieve the level of autonomy they desired despite their theoretical vulnerability at law.[104] But on the darker side, even women who made careful legal plans could face a difficult time. When the widow Ellen Cottingham married Clement Dumbrell, she made him agree to the terms of an elaborate marriage settlement. Under the conditions of this settlement, attached to a bond for £300 held by a London merchant for Ellen's use, Clement was forbidden from interfering with her lands or property without her consent. If he should die first, then Ellen was to recover the value of the moveable goods she had brought to the marriage (assuming his estate was worth that much) and in case she should die first, he was to allow her to make a will of *his* goods and money to the value of £20. However, once they married it appears that he beat her regularly, sold most of her goods and used force to confiscate her copy of the obligation containing the settlement. Under the name Ellen Dumbrell, she entered a bill in Requests (the source of these allegations) explaining that Clement had been imprisoned for his mistreatment of her. However, he was soon to be released and 'mindeth as he saith to sell awaie' both her lands and goods.[105]

Obstreperous husbands retained the power to sell the clothes off their wives' backs, and wives could face difficult choices between keeping their property interests intact and keeping their marriages intact. Social as well as legal pressures induced married women to rely on others to protect their interests. When Ellen Yelse agreed to marry Roger Harryyonge, it was her parents, William and Elizabeth, who oversaw Roger's conveyance of lands to establish a use and jointure for her benefit. And it was William and Elizabeth who took Roger to court years later when he broke the bargain and sold these lands, as well as other lands he held in right of Ellen, to fund his dissolute life and love of 'deise, cards and other unlawful games'. What is interesting here is that Ellen's parents argued that she had agreed to these surrenders. It was because she was 'obedient', they explained, that she had assented to her husband's request to sell, 'althoughe yt were to hire hynderance' and to the hindrance of the couple's eight children.[106] They were aware that married women could be placed in difficult positions if their husbands interfered with their interests. Such an interference threatened marital harmony, but in a society dominated by men, the 'disobedience' required by a wife to prevent such an interference with her property would have been regarded in most instances as a worse offence, and many wives suffered in silence.

In some cases the Masters observed married women's rights and needs even though the women themselves had made no direct claim. In 1599 Richard Jorden sued Thomas Burrowe and Hugh Elsworthy to recover £16 put in trust

---

[104] Erickson, *Women and Property*, especially pp. 224–8.
[105] *Ellen Dumbrell v. Clement Dumbrell*, PRO Req 2/196/96.
[106] *William & Elizabeth Yelse v. Roger Harryyonge*, PRO Req 2/293/13 [m. 4], B.

for his use while he was an infant. At the hearing, which Jorden failed to attend, the Masters began to doubt that the trust had been established for his benefit. They concluded instead that the donor had intended the money to be a portion for his daughter, Jorden's wife, to provide her with some maintenance during and after her marriage. Jorden had 'departed this realm' because of his lack of funds, and his wife was now 'in extreme povertie'. Although she was not a party to the action, the Masters ordered that the £16 in issue be delivered to her father to employ for her use and the use of her children.[107] In another case from the late 1590s, where a husband and wife brought a joint action against various defendants, the Masters effectively put the husband on trial. As a pre-condition to hearing the case they ordered him to deliver £100 to the court as security until he made a jointure for his wife, and co-complainant, Mary. Clearly they felt that Mary required support against her husband, as well as with her husband in their joint action, and they took care to specify that he make the jointure to the liking not just of Mary, but 'to the lyking of the freends of her the sayd Mary'.[108] The Masters enforced uses and trusts when trustees, or even beneficiaries, wished otherwise and in some cases they proved willing to act as trustees themselves.[109] In a case from 1591, for example, the Masters ordered a husband and wife to deliver deeds to court, where they would be kept for the woman's use for her life and then passed to the complainant.[110]

Women's legal and equitable fortunes, it would seem, were mixed. Significant numbers of women went to court, litigating grievances broadly similar to the grievances complained of by men. Women, in this sense, were litigants like any others, and the Masters who heard their causes concentrated on the guilt or innocence of the parties before them, rather than on whether they were male or female. However, the circumstances that gave rise to actions, and the allegations that parties made about each others' motives and capacities, could differ markedly in cases initiated by or against women. More importantly, women had to suffer dramatic changes in their legal status dependent on marriage, and despite exceptions in law and in practice coverture remained a potent doctrine. The many and various devices women (or their allies) could call upon to safeguard women's rights in marriage were often effective in cocooning a woman's interests during the period of her marriage, keeping them intact for her widowhood. However, they were less effective in guaranteeing her rights against the wishes of her husband while he was still alive. Husbands could be denied their wholesale rights of bounty and possession, but their position as masters of their own families was never seriously put under threat.

---

[107] *Richard Jorden v. Thomas Burrowe als Barbie & Hughe Elsworthie als Hole*, PRO Req 1/19, pp. 792–3.   [108] *William & Mary Palen v. Edward Mitton et al.*, PRO Req 1/19, p. 246.
[109] *Richard & Christian Marble v. Nil & An Kerkeke*, in Caesar, *Ancient State*, p. 76.
[110] *Peter Staple v. Agnes Staple*, PRO Req 1/19, p. 637; when Agnes died, in June 1603, the lease was duly returned to Peter; PRO Req 1/21, pp. 217–18.

The records suggest a complicated picture of women's independence and of forces inherent within the law and within society which resisted that independence. The language and imagery litigants and their counsel used is also revealing about the world in which these individuals lived. Some claimed the women they faced in court were shrewd, manipulative and well versed in the law. Others claimed that their female adversaries were ignorant, incapable and easily led. Women themselves claimed either that they were strong, independent and self-sufficient or that they were 'weak', 'impotent', ignorant or reliant on the generosity of kin and of the court. The truth or falsehood of these various depictions of litigating women, and the insights they can provide about actual women as well as gender stereotypes, are the subject of chapter 8.

This chapter and the last have looked at women from a range of social backgrounds from all over the country, litigating a variety of actions. Women could, and many did, overcome the pressures of law, society, family and kin to claim interests for themselves inside courtrooms as well as out in the world. The exploration of women's experiences in Requests has revealed something of the interaction, slippage and occasionally the confrontations between equity and the common law, and in the cases involving separations, the way Requests could operate as a court of appeal for ecclesiastical court decisions. The next chapter looks to a fourth form of law, local custom, and what it had to offer women. It examines how actions in Requests managed to bring the laws and traditions of ancient custom into confrontation, or at least dialogue, with equity, as it was interpreted and dispensed by the Masters. It does so by focusing on a specific grouping of women, the widow copyholders of rural Somerset.

Freebench, custom and equity

> We still understand only imperfectly the tenacity and force of local custom
> E.P. Thompson, 'The grid of inheritance' (1976)[1]

Scrutiny of the records of the Court of Requests has so far shed light on women's relationship with equity, with the common law and, if we include the scattering of separation and maintenance cases, with ecclesiastical law. It has become apparent that women suffered the ill effects of discriminatory rules in all of these systems, but that canny individuals who were aware of their rights, and who had access to the jurisdictions that best suited their needs, could and did use the law to advantage. Now it is the turn of custom. The Masters heard a considerable number of customary actions, brought by litigants from manors all over England. These plaintiffs used Requests as a court of appeal, arguing that they could not receive a fair hearing in their manor court, due to the power and influence of their opponents or the bias of the steward, the lord or the lady of the manor. And, as we shall see, many of these litigants were women. Lacking knowledge of every local custom, the Masters usually appointed commissioners to decide matters on their behalf, or else to equip them with the means to settle these deeply local conflicts from within the White Hall in London.[2] The surviving interrogatories, depositions, copies of documents and commission reports, along with case materials and the written decisions and orders of the court, provide a unique source for investigating customary disputes. They help to reveal how lords, ladies, stewards and tenants regarded custom and how different parties sought to prove unwritten customary law in a Westminster court. More specifically, they shed light on the quality of the rights women enjoyed under custom, and show the influence women wielded within the customary process.

---

[1] E.P. Thompson, 'The grid of inheritance: a comment', in Jack Goody, Joan Thirsk and E.P. Thompson, eds., *Family and Inheritance: Rural Society in Western Europe, 1200–1800* (Cambridge, 1976), p. 335.

[2] See Robert Dacre, 'Orders and rules in Requests', BL Additional MS 25,248, fol. 32ᵛ.

It was observed in chapter 2 that a number of historians interested in the history of women and law, from Mary Beard to Maria Cioni, have championed equity as the pre-eminent provider of rights to women in the sixteenth century. Many of their predecessors, by contrast, believed that women fared best under custom. Alice Clark, writing in 1919, was convinced that the slow passage from custom to the common law had a detrimental effect on the lot of women. She believed that women participated fully in the hearing and sanctioning of local customs, as members of local juries of tenants, or 'homages', and argued that 'the changes which during the seventeenth century were abrogating customs in favour of common law' had the effect of eliminating women 'from what was equivalent to a share in the custody and interpretation of law, which henceforward remained exclusively in the hands of men'.[3] Doris Stenton, writing forty years later, agreed that custom was superior to common law in the field of women's rights. She provided instances of married women appearing in court as their husbands' agents, and also in their own right, behaviour which was technically impossible at common law. In identifying 'rough equality between men and women' among Lincolnshire tenants, she observed that widows' rights to freebench meant that 'the wife of the unfree peasant farmer was relatively in a stronger position than the wife of her husband's lord'.[4] For many years Clark's and Stenton's beliefs about custom went largely untested (unlike their general interpretations of women's changing status which have been the subject of repeated criticism and reappraisal), but that is beginning to change. Amy Erickson has trumpeted the importance of custom as a source of rights for women, and Barbara Todd has compared the fortunes of widows in two neighbouring Berkshire villages, Long Wittenham, where custom still held sway in the seventeenth century, and Sutton Courtney, where it did not.[5] Todd's analysis examines customary property rights in practice, and her conclusions provide a more equivocal view of the benefits custom extended to women: custom could offer security to widows, but property rights alone did not guarantee good status.[6]

THE NATURE OF CUSTOM

Why did historians of women's rights, and indeed historians of class conflict, popular culture, crime and civil litigation in the sixteenth, seventeenth and eighteenth centuries, pay custom relatively little attention for so many years? R.H. Tawney regarded customary law as central to any debate about the sixteenth century, and today custom is receiving renewed attention from a range of different historians. However, with the exception of agricultural historians, Eric

---

[3] Clark, *Working Life of Women*, p. 237.   [4] Stenton, *The English Woman*, pp. 76, 79.
[5] Erickson, *Women and Property*, pp. 6, 29–30.   [6] Todd, 'Freebench and free enterprise'.

Kerridge's stinging attack on Tawney's interpretations, and some specialised ploughing in the sometimes heavy clay of the Brenner debate, few historians paid much heed to custom during the intervening years.[7] In part this neglect stems from the unforgiving nature of the sources. As F. W. Maitland observed a hundred years ago, court rolls 'are taciturn, they do not easily yield up their testimony', and custom is local, so that it can usually be studied 'only by watching some group of manors decade by decade and year by year'.[8] Custom can also be unobtrusive, because it is unwritten and based on common consent rather than on conflict. As C.K. Allen noted in *Law in the Making*, custom 'grows up by conduct, and it is therefore a mistake to measure its validity solely by the element of express sanction accorded by courts of law or by any other determinate authority'.[9] However, the relative neglect also reflects the tendency in the recent past for many social and legal historians to consider custom as being in decline by the sixteenth century, and to regard it as being immemorial; to see customary law as a backward looking and inflexible maintainer of continuities that was becoming increasingly out of place in an age of legal centralisation and change.[10]

Measured against the steady consolidation of the common law, custom was declining as a legal force in the sixteenth century. Yet for many communities customary law remained a significant force throughout the sixteenth and seventeenth centuries and beyond, with tenants attending manor courts to transfer interests in lands, to answer charges, to participate in the customary process as jurors on the homage, or simply to witness proceedings and to keep abreast of local affairs and gossip.[11] The number of customary actions that came to Requests (as well as to Chancery and to other Westminster courts) is itself evidence of the resilience of custom, and as E.P. Thompson argued, it is a mistake to judge the influence of custom by counting the number of acres of customary land. You must count the number of tenants.[12] A recent study of forty nine manorial surveys in seventeenth century Dorset, for example, revealed that 6

---

[7] Today, of course, custom has more than regained its position near the centre of historical debate, absorbing the attention of scholars interested in social protest, local identity and political consciousness, popular social and religious practices, and the spread and influence of literacy and print.

[8] F. W. Maitland, ed., *Select Pleas in Manorial and Other Seigniorial Courts*, Selden Society vol. 2 (two vols, London, 1889), vol. 1, p. xi.

[9] C.K. Allen, *Law in the Making*, 7th edn (Oxford, 1964), p. 70.

[10] This is a manifestation of the tendency to assume the dominance of the 'immemorial', 'ancient constitution' in English legal thought; see C.W. Brooks, 'The place of Magna Carta and the ancient constitution in sixteenth-century English legal thought', in Ellis Sandoz, ed., *The Roots of Liberty: Magna Carta, Ancient Constitution, and the Anglo-American Tradition of Rule of Law* (Columbia, 1993), pp. 57–9; Erickson, *Women and Property*, p. 29.

[11] Brooks, *Pettyfoggers*, p. 36; for the significance of custom to the free miners of ancient mining areas, see Andy Wood, 'Custom, identity and resistance: English free miners and their law c. 1550–1800' in Paul Griffiths, Adam Fox and Steve Hindle, eds., *The Experience of Authority in Early Modern England* (Basingstoke, 1996).

[12] Thompson, 'The grid of inheritance', pp. 328–9.

per cent of interest holders were freeholders, 5 per cent were leaseholders and 89 per cent were copyholders.[13]

On the question of the rigidity of custom, it is true that communities and courts alleged the existence of customs from 'time immemorial', and that some local usages persisted unchanged for centuries.[14] In the words of Bracton, 'the force of custom and long use is not slight'.[15] However the fact that customs *could* remain unchanged does not mean that they *did* remain unchanged. To quote E.P. Thompson again, 'so far from having the steady permanence sug-gested by the word "tradition", custom was a field of change and of contest, an arena in which opposing interests made conflicting claims'.[16] R.W. Hoyle has reached similar conclusions about custom in the north west of England, explaining that the tenure of 'Tenant right' was not 'a static entity, but . . . a flex-ible relationship between lords and tenants actively being moulded by the forces applied to it'.[17] For Thompson and Hoyle, the most important contests were the vertical contests between lords and tenants, the struggles between Thompson's 'patricians and plebs'.[18] Women were parties to these contests, as tenants and as ladies of the manor, but more often they were involved in horizontal contests with fellow tenants, which were just as susceptible to flexibility and change. The ability of communities of tenants and landlords to alter customary usages in response to changing circumstances gave customary law its enduring strength, and in analysing the rights of female tenants I intend to focus not just on the longevity of custom, but on the flexibility of custom, and to consider the implications of that flexibility for women.

WIDOW'S ESTATE

A number of different customs applied specifically to women, affecting, for example, the rights of daughters to inherit property from their parents and the rights of married women to trade within certain towns as if they were *femes sole*.[19] However, as the discussion of custom in chapter 2 made clear, the most significant and widely observed custom affecting women was the widows' right of freebench or widow's estate. In Somerset, for example (the county from which most of the cases discussed in this chapter are drawn), widow's estate was one of the commonest customs to produce litigation in Requests. Entries in

[13] J.H. Bettey, 'Manorial custom and widows' estate', *Archives*, 20 (1992), p. 208.

[14] Customary law still applies in England; see *New Windsor Corporation* v. *Mellor* (C.A.), [1975] Ch. 80, p. 386.   [15] Henry of Bracton, *De Legibus et Consuetudinibus Angliae*, vol. 2, p. 22.

[16] E.P. Thompson, *Customs in Common* (London, 1991), p. 6.

[17] R.W. Hoyle, 'An ancient and laudable custom: the definition and development of tenant right in north-western England in the sixteenth century', *Past and Present*, 116 (1987), p. 24.

[18] See also C.E. Searle, 'Custom, class conflict and agrarian capitalism: the Cumbrian customary economy in the eighteenth century', *Past and Present*, 110 (1986), p. 113.

[19] Bateson, *Borough Customs*, pp. cxii–cxiii.

modern calendars suggest that around 290 of the 750 Somerset Requests actions that survive for Elizabeth's reign, about 39 per cent, involved at least one woman litigant. Of these 290, I estimate that just under half involved disputes over copyhold, and a quarter, perhaps seventy or eighty, involved widow's estate.[20] In principle the custom of widow's estate was a simple right. It allowed the widow of any copyholding tenant who died in possession of a copyhold estate to enter and enjoy that estate, or part of it, for her life (or for as long as she remained chaste and unmarried) provided she paid the rents and performed the services due. In practice, the custom could be the subject of bitter disagreement and conflict, as the following example illustrates.

Joan Ellis brought a suit in Requests in 1558 against Humphrey Poole, his wife Margaret Poole, the steward of the manor and the steward's servant, claiming her widow's estate in a customary messuage in Baltonsborough. She described how after her husband died the steward and his men denied her any rights in the holding, and 'with vyolens dyd dryve oute of the said howse your said Subjecte & vii of her childer'. In asking for redress Joan argued that the custom of widow's estate in Baltonsborough was universal, giving a life interest to the widow of any copyholder who died in possession of a copyhold estate. The defendants suggested that the custom did not extend to every widow. It had exceptions. They alleged that previous estates in remainder granted to other tenants took precedence over widow's estate, if they had been granted before the date of the widow's marriage. In this case, they said, the local Abbot had granted the reversion of the property to the defendant, Margaret Poole, before Joan married her husband, and therefore she could not sustain a claim under custom.[21]

The Masters established a commission to gather evidence, and Joan called tenants from Baltonsborough and surrounding manors to answer interrogatories prepared on her behalf. All agreed that in principle every widow had a right to her husband's lands under custom. An eighty year old deponent from Glastonbury said that Joan should have her widow's estate, 'if old custumes shuld take place', and a husbandman who had lived in Baltonsborough for only six years said that although he was a newcomer, from what he had heard she should have her widow's estate. But they had different impressions, or were simply unsure, of the details of customary law and of Joan's particular circumstances. Few of the witnesses could remember whether Joan had married her husband before or after the granting of the reversion to Margaret. Some were unsure about which customs applied to which manors. One man said that he

---

[20] Entries for cases identified as originating in Somerset found in *Public Record Office Lists and Indexes*, no. 21, and manuscript Requests calendars housed in the PRO; the calendars do not always distinguish whether customary disputes involved widow's estate, so this estimate is consequently speculative.

[21] *Jone Eles* v. *Humphrey Poole et al.*, PRO Req 2/165/64, B, A; Req 2/23/94, B.

thought that the manors of Baltonsborough and Badcom shared customs, and in Badcom widows received their estates. Most deponents did not hazard opinions, but instead gave examples of widows whose rights had been recognised in the past. William Pypett told his examiners how 'the wydowes of them that have died tenants have had ther widowes astate in their husbands tenements that they have died possessed of', and he gave examples of two widows who had paid heriots to enter their widow's estate ahead of remainder holders, both of whom later agreed to give up possession in return for a money pension.[22]

A lone husbandman from the manor, John Rush, deposed on behalf of the defendants. He told his examiners that the disputed lands had been granted to Margaret Poole in remainder before Joan had married her husband. He had been present at court when the homage had been 'at variance' and unable to decide whether or not to vote Joan an estate. He said they had referred the matter to the Lord, who in turn referred it to the assizes at Chard, but the court admitted Margaret Poole tenant in the meantime. He alleged that the widows who had inherited interests ahead of holders of estates in remainder had all subsequently been evicted from their lands, and the pensions some of them had received were voluntary, and not linked to customary widows' rights, for the widows had not paid heriots after their husbands died.[23]

The defendants lost this case. As Joan narrated in a later case, the Masters decided this action in her favour, on the basis of deposition evidence, despite the fact that, 'there be divers wytnesses which have deposed that widowes shoulde not have theyr wydowes estate in the saide manor of Baltonsboroughe'. They ordered that Joan should have possession of the premises during her widowhood according to custom, until and unless the defendants could produce additional evidence to satisfy the court that Joan did not have good title.[24] The defendants duly produced new evidence, not the word of a husbandman this time, but the opinions of knights, squires and gentlemen who came from Glastonbury, and from manors up to twelve miles away from Baltonsborough. These men presented evidence of a more 'legal' nature than the opinions and anecdotes from memory favoured by husbandmen of the manor, and their views add weight to C.E. Searle's argument, concerning the eighteenth century, that the definition of local custom 'was highly variable in relation to class position'.[25] The local surveyor said that he possessed court rolls and books of record which proved that reversions took precedence over widow's estates by custom, and his gentleman assistant said that he had seen and kept the court rolls proving the same.[26]

---

[22] *Jone Eles* v. *Humphrey Poole et al.*, PRO Req 2/165/64, D, deponents William Hutchens, Edward Hebbar, William George, William Pypett.
[23] *Jone Eles* v. *Humphrey Poole et al.*, PRO Req 2/165/64, D, deponent John Russhe.
[24] *Johane Eles* v. *Humphrey Poole et al.*, PRO Req 2/23/94, B; Req 2/22/13, copy of order.
[25] Searle, 'Custom, class conflict and agrarian capitalism', p. 120.
[26] *Jone Eles* v. *Humphrey Poole et al.*, PRO Req 2/165/64, D, deponents Ralph Hopton, Richard Powys.

No other documents or a decision survive from this later case, suggesting that the new bill was dismissed without further process, that the defendants chose not to pursue their appeal, or that this information has been lost. Nevertheless, the surviving records raise interesting points about the mechanics of custom, as it operated on the manor and as it was dealt with in Requests, and about the intricate details litigants believed attached to the custom of widow's estate. First of all, they show the depth of uncertainty that could surround something as apparently certain as ancient custom. The confusion of Joan's deponents about the finer details of widow's estate and the suggestion that the homage had been 'at variance' (and had recommended the matter be referred to the assizes), all point to the fragility of custom in people's minds. Much of this fragility is of course artificial, caused by the distortion of the legal process. As should be clear by now, disagreement over matters of fact is an integral part of any adversarial legal system. But deep disagreement over matters of law was rare in Requests actions, and the fact that parties openly claimed incompatible customs, disagreeing over the form of custom, as well as its applicability, suggest that custom was sufficiently unclear to be included in the gamesmanship of the courtroom.

Customary law was uncertain because it was intensely local; the rules settled for one tenement might or might not apply to a neighbouring tenement. It was uncertain because it was essentially unwritten. Of course in practice stewards wrote down 'unwritten' customs in custumals and recorded customary transactions in court rolls. However, as E.P. Thompson reflected, customs as they were recorded in custumals could be very different from the 'denser reality of social practice'.[27] Most of all, customary law was uncertain because it was changeable. However timeless customs appeared to onlookers, customary law was fluid, and the form of customs could shift from generation to generation, or even from year to year. In a case from 1571, where the issue was whether customary courts could grant reversions without the consent of the current tenant, deponents on both sides agreed that according to ancient custom, reversions could *not* be granted without consent. But they also acknowledged that at least a dozen reversions *had* been granted without consent during the preceding thirty years. Supporters of the custom were adamant that it was still in force, but as many of them spoke in terms of 'the custom until 20 or 30 years ago', it seems that they had not been so adamant on previous occasions.[28] This was how custom worked: tenants fiercely asserting that custom in general was inviolable, but voting on the homage for, or turning a blind eye to, subtle shifts of custom in individual cases, according to their personal attitudes and current community norms.

---

[27] Thompson, 'The grid of inheritance', p. 337.
[28] *Thomas & Johanne Crace v. William Stokes*, PRO Req 2/188/62, D, deponents John Bydsham, William Myllard, John Kene, John Lewes.

The second, related, point that comes out of the Ellis case is the importance the Masters placed on oral testimony, and the tension that seems to have existed in their minds between the force of oral testimony and the authority of written evidence. Eric Kerridge argued that when faced with matters of custom, the Masters made judgments based solely on written proof. He quoted Alexander Savine, who wrote that 'the court of Requests looks for truth, not in the *Rechtsbewusstsein* [legal consciousness] of the local population, but in the dust of the manorial records'.[29] The Masters certainly took heed of written records when they were available. In a customary dispute from Oxfordshire in 1562 they dismissed a claim because the custom alleged by the complainants was not listed in the steward's book.[30] But it is also clear that they remained reluctant to pass judgment on the basis of documentary proof alone.[31]

In the majority of cases, rather than rely on dusty manorial records, the Masters chose to establish a commission, empowering commissioners to interview witnesses and arbitrate a local solution, or to supply depositions and a report to assist them in reaching a decision. The Masters appointed commissions for a number of reasons. To begin with, the integrity of documents could rarely be assured and allegations of forgery were rife.[32] Early in the seventeenth century, for example, the law reporter Richard Compton recorded details of an entire Latin custumal that had been forged.[33] Even where documents were genuine, they might not apply to the individuals or to the interests in question and the Masters were aware of the dangers of relying on uncorroborated documentary evidence, just as they were concerned that their equitable interventions to right local wrongs should not cause any further injustice. However, the Masters' frequent demands for local examinations of parties also stemmed from their recognition that customs were rarely fixed or immovable. They realised that for a custom to be valid, it had to have existed 'time out of the memory of man', and so considered it only right to consult the memories of local men and women. Under modern law, 'immemorial custom' means uninterrupted existence since before the third of September 1189 (a date set by the Statute of

---

[29] Eric Kerridge, *Agrarian Problems in the Sixteenth Century and After* (London, 1969), p. 67.

[30] *Richard & Agnes Jones* v. *John Golder*, PRO Req 1/11, pp. 201–4.

[31] On the general importance of oral authority over written authority, see D.R. Woolf, 'Speech, text, and time: the sense of hearing and the sense of the past in Renaissance England', *Albion*, 18 (1986), pp. 159–93.

[32] *Alice John* v. *George Hill*, PRO Req 2/226/48, R; *Elyanor Brett & William Walrond* v. *Nicholas Sprackett*, PRO Req 2/179/67; and see *John Browne* v. *Frauncis Whetstone*, PRO Req 1/21, p. 176. In a Chancery action from 1576/7, the plaintiff alleged that the court roll by which the defendant claimed title had been incorrectly entered by the steward's clerk. The defendant demurred 'for that the plaintiffe shall not be received by surmize to object against or impeach the said Court Rolles'. The Court rejected this demurrer as insufficient, and ordered the defendant to make a proper answer; C.U.L. Gg.2.26 fol. 108ᵛ.

[33] Richard Crompton, *Star-Chamber Cases. Shewing What Causes Properly Belong to the Cognizance of that Court* (London, 1630), pp. 37–8.

Westminster as a limiting date for writs of right).[34] There is no need to prove that a custom was in use before this date – demonstrating usage for a long period raises a presumption of immemorial existence – however, proof that a custom *did not* exist at this time can prove fatal. In a case from 1872, for example, a stall holder asserted his right to set up a market stall under an ancient custom linked to 'statute session' hiring fairs. His opponents defeated his claim by demonstrating that these 'statute sessions' had originally been authorised by the Statute of Labourers, passed in the reign of Edward III, and that therefore the custom had not been in existence in 1189.[35]

In the sixteenth century, when record keeping, the consultation of records, printed law reports, and modern ideas about legal precedent were just beginning to make inroads into a still largely oral society, 'time out of memory of man' was a far less definite concept, one which meant different things to different people. For Edward Coke and other Westminster jurists it meant outside the collective recollections, based on documentary records, of society in general. But for most people it meant outside the reliable memories of particular individuals. As Theodore Plucknett pointed out in *A Concise History of the Common Law*, 'in an age when custom was an active living factor in the development of society there was much less insistence upon actual or fictitious antiquity'. He went on to quote Azo (an author Bracton respected) who believed that a custom could be called 'long' if it was introduced within ten or twenty years, 'very long' if it dated from thirty years, and 'ancient' if it had existed longer than forty years.[36] The Masters of Requests were themselves Westminster jurists and they saw eye to eye with Coke on the general principle of immemorial custom, but as judges in a working equity court they remained sensitive to what immemorial custom meant to the tenants and lords who lived by it.[37]

To prove that the custom of widow's estate had existed, 'time out of mind or memory of man' in Baltonsborough, Joan Ellis called the oldest residents of the manor to depose on her behalf. The twenty two tenants who testified all said they were over forty years old, and eight claimed to be seventy or older. All of them asserted that widows had 'always' received widow's estate on their manor, but none of them gave examples from outside their own personal experience or memory. Memory of the memory of others could extend the period of recall by

---

[34] Lord Hailsham, ed., *Halsbury's Laws of England*, 4th edn (London, 1975), vol. 12, paragraph 407.

[35] *Simpson v. Wells* (1872) L.R. 7 Q.B. 214, as described in Allen, *Law in the Making*, pp. 134–5.

[36] Theodore Plucknett, *A Concise History of the Common Law*, 4th edn (London, 1948), pp. 290–1.

[37] It was noted in chapter 4 how in *The Ancient State, Authoritie, and Proceedings of the Court of Requests*, Julius Caesar attempted to justify the legitimacy of Requests by proving that the Masters were members of the King's Council, and therefore the court could be said to have existed since time immemorial.

a few decades. A sixty year old yeoman deposing in an action between Mary Palmer and Christopher Rolles described the details of widow's estate on his manor, 'the contynuance of which custom he knoweth to have ben observed by the space of [fifty] yeres and more and hathe herde by credyble reporte that the custom was suche afore the tyme of his knoledge'.[38]

'Credyble reportes' aside, 'time out of memory' effectively meant not much longer than the sixty or seventy years of living memory. Sometimes it meant an even shorter time. In the Palmer case, Mary called as a deponent the foreman of the homage that had voted to exclude her from her lands. He had been named foreman because at thirty seven he was the oldest customary tenant on the homage, and he explained how he and his fellow jurors had made a presentment against the plaintiff because her copy included three lives, whereas custom only permitted copyholds for two lives. The homage had believed this to be the custom, 'not knowinge of matter to the contrary', however the foreman had since discovered that his own tenement had previously been granted for three lives, 'to one Horlock, who quyetly enjoyed the same'. He now knew that another tenement had also been granted for three lives, and that the steward agreed that such grants were good. Learning of his mistake, he lamented to another witness that he was 'a younge man and knewe not what he did and was very sory for his so doinge and . . . that he thinketh in his consyence that the complainant hathe not made any forfeicture of her saide grounde'.[39] Westminster may have been having its memory unfettered by effective record keeping, but to tenants on Somerset manors, recent precedents were as important as ancient precedents, and while the age of customs was prized, the age of evidence was not. A widow from Kingston in Somerset made a claim under the 'anciente custome' of widow's estate, in which she challenged her opponent's evidence, a certificate of custom, alleging that the clerk of the manor court had prepared it by referring to 'ancient' court rolls.[40] Ancient court rolls and custumals made suspect evidence, it seems, because they might be out of date.

It is important not to underestimate the significance that individuals attached to the long heritage of custom, but it must also be recognised that despite the growing authority of written evidence, most people depended upon the finite time-scale of living memory. Keith Thomas has pointed out the consternation felt by Oxfordshire villagers when an epidemic ravaged the elderly population so that, as one Thomas Willis reported, 'there scarce remained alive any for

---

[38] *Mary Palmer* v. *Christopher Rolles*, PRO Req 2/33/108, m. 4, D, deponent John Willis; a deponent in another case said he had heard of custom 'by the report of old men'; *John Whyttyng* v. *Marye Cheeke*, PRO Req 2/288/31, D, deponent Arthur Dishe.

[39] *Mary Palmer* v. *Christopher Rolles*, PRO Req 2/33/108, m. 4, D, deponents William Byshoppe, William Wykes.

[40] *Alice John* v. *George Hill & Margaret Togwell*, PRO Req 2/226/48, m. 2, R, m. 4, B; Alice John alleged that the certificate had also been based on the presentment of a homage consisting of the 'dere frends' of the defendants.

upholding the customs and privileges of the parish'.[41] The dissolution of the monasteries provided another event which disrupted the unbroken lineage of custom in people's minds, creating a mood of anxiety that can be sensed in depositions and pleadings. Copyholders on defunct monastic lands began qualifying assertions that a custom had existed 'time out of memory of man', by saying that the customs on two neighbouring manors 'were all one in the Abbots time'.[42] Joan Ellis relied on the testimony of 'religious persons now in the monastery of westminster' who had formerly been monks in Glastonbury, and the drafter of one of her bills in Requests crossed out the word 'shall' from the phrase 'shall enjoye her wydowes estate' and replaced it with 'hathe used to enjoye' her widow's estate, in recognition that things were not as they had been.[43] In Worcestershire, the presumption that 'new' customs could not be created led manor courts to conclude that the widows of priests were ineligible for freebench; presumably because priests' wives, never having existed before, had never held copyholds in the past.[44] The Masters recognised the importance of living memory and went out of their way to ascertain local opinion, for they understood that while a written record might establish antiquity, it often said nothing about whether a custom had been, and remained, common practice. So, customary law was not so indelibly inscribed in the past that it could not change, and despite the attempts of common lawyers to bring it closer under the wing of the common law, in areas where it persisted it remained responsive to local pressures and needs.

When customs changed, the change could be sudden and involve the conscious decision of a community. An early seventeenth century commentator on Chancery described how lords and tenants could alter customs on their manors by indenture, providing that all affected parties consented to the change. He described a case in Chancery that involved such an indenture, and explained how the Lord Keeper had shown a willingness to recognise and enforce the new customs, 'because els all the Coppieholders of that Mannor or of any other Mannor of England which have altered their Customes in like Case by consent shalbe prevented & altered & nothinge wilbe certaine'.[45] More often change was gradual, and all but imperceptible to witnesses. Christopher Dyer described in his study of peasant holdings in west Midland villages how witnesses in an inheritance dispute in Whitstones in 1538 agreed that, 'they never knew any man's daughter was adjudged to any customary tenement . . . and that . . . [never]

---

[41] Keith Thomas, 'Age and authority in early modern England', *Proceedings of the British Academy*, 62 (1976), p. 234.

[42] For example, *Elizabeth Vale v. Hughe Smythe & Richard Cromewell*, PRO Req 2/281/23, m. 6, D, deponent John Whippey.

[43] *Johane Eles v. Humphrey Poole et al.*, PRO Req 2/23/94, B; for an example of a landlord unsuccessfully pretending a grant of former monastic lands by Henry VIII, see *John Tymewell v. Robert Isack*, PRO Req 1/11, pp. 89–93.

[44] *Agnes Arnet v. John Born*, PRO Req 2/157/19, letter.   [45] C.U.L. Gg.2.31 fol. 476ᵛ.

they had any such custom there used'. This was, as Dyer notes, 'in flat contradiction of the court rolls which show daughters inheriting as late as 1462'.[46]

COPYHOLDS FOR LIVES

With regard to the widows of Elizabethan Somerset, the fact that customary law was not rigidly fixed helps to explain why so apparently simple a custom as widow's estate could become the subject of intense litigation in manor courts and in Requests. For while widow's estate was one of the more constant of customs, the customary tenure to which it most commonly attached in the sixteenth century, copyholds for lives, changed markedly over time, as a brief review of its history will show. Copyhold, holding by copy of court roll, developed out of feudal villeinage some time in the fourteenth or fifteenth centuries. Originally, copyholds were granted for one life. If a male copyholder died leaving a widow, her claim to widow's estate (assuming the custom applied) could not interfere with the claim of another interest holder, because no other interest holder existed. Over time copyholds became heritable, and when a copyholder died, custom usually dictated that reverting interests be re-granted to his or her heir. This innovation gave security to families, but it did so by creating future interests, and with them the possibility of conflicting claims. Future interests became severable from the family with the advent of copyholds for lives, which allowed a copyholder to write into his or her copy the names of future holders.

This form of tenure was the subject of anything up to a half of Requests actions from Somerset, yet when Edward Coke wrote his influential work on copyholds, he neglected it almost entirely.[47] As Richard Fisher explained when he wrote on custom in 1794; 'in his excellent little Treatise, called "The Compleat Copyholder"', Coke 'treats only of pure and genuine Copyholds; whereas at this time of day, there is a sort of bastard species (if the expression may be allowed) of Copyhold Tenures; namely, Copyholds for lives.'[48] Copyholds for lives flourished when Coke wrote – future interests were the bane of the common law, and perhaps he hoped that by neglecting them they would simply go away – and despite this snub, they continued to develop. By the late eighteenth century a whole range of new forms had sprung up, including copyholds for three lives in being, where the persons named in the copy never enjoyed possession, but merely acted as trustees for unnamed tenants in possession. Charles Watkins tried to make sense of the shifting history of copyholding in his 1797 treatise, in the preface of which he explained:

---

[46] Christopher Dyer, 'Changes in the size of peasant holdings in some west Midland villages 1400–1540', in R.M. Smith, ed., *Land, Kinship and Lifecycle* (Cambridge, 1984), pp. 291–2.
[47] Coke, *The Compleate Copy-Holder*, p. 162.
[48] R.B. Fisher, *A Practical Treatise on Copyhold Tenure, with the Methods of Holding Courts Leet, Court Baron and Other Courts* (London, 1794), p. iv.

He [the author] has endeavoured to extract something at least like consistency from the crude mass of matter which the books afford. He has even endeavoured to reconcile the jarring and discordant cases on several points which he had to consider; but this, he must confess, sometimes appeared to be rather out of the reach of the powers usually allotted to humanity; and which he, consequently, could only lament.[49]

The course of change from copyholds for one life to copyholds as increasingly marketable interests, and copyholders as trustees, was of course slow and unpredictable. In Whitstones, Christopher Dyer found that dealings in interests in land were fluid, and reversions common, in the late fourteenth century and for much of the fifteenth century, but after 1500 copyholds tended once again to pass within families, as they had done prior to 1349.[50] However, the more fluid the land market, and the greater the number of remainders, reversions and other future interests, the more likely a widow seeking her widow's estate might face competition. The Requests records are full of 'jarring and discordant cases' that expose the clash of interests between widows and future-interest holders, as well as the changeable nature of copyholds for lives.

Sparring widows and their opponents alleged a startling array of different formulations of the custom of widow's estate, either asserting or contesting the right of a widow to 'jump the queue' and possess a copyhold ahead of the designated next holder. In 1573, Agnes Grove asserted that the right of widow's estate accrued to the widow of *any* copyholder named in a copy for three lives. Her opponent countered that *only* the widow of a purchaser could claim an estate, and then only if no other wife's name was in the copy and no reversion had been granted before the couple's marriage.[51] When the widow of a purchaser of a copy for three lives claimed her widow's estate in 1586, her opponent argued the exact opposite, saying only the widow of the longest liver of the three persons named in the copy had any rights to widow's estate.[52] Finally, a widow who tried to claim possession of the copyhold her husband had held for thirty years, on the grounds that widow's estate applied universally, was assailed with a barrage of counter customs. Her opponent said that if a man took a tenement by copy of court roll to himself and to his first wife, then any subsequent wife had no rights to an estate under custom. Further, if a widow took a customary tenement to herself and to her 'next marier' and then married, custom declared that her husband,

shalbe by the custome of the saied mannor adjudged hedd and cheffe holder of the tenementes purchased by his wiffe and shall hold the same during his liffe, and his wiffe who was the purchaser to have only an estate during her widow[hood] if she happ[en] to servyve her saied husbonde and shall not have an estate for the terme of her liffe notwithstanding she was purchaser.

---

[49] Charles Watkins, *Treatise on Copyholds* (London, 1797), p. vii; see also Brooks, *Pettyfoggers*, pp. 198–9.   [50] Dyer, 'Changes in the size of peasant holdings', pp. 285–6.

[51] *Agnes Grove v. John Thynne et al.*, PRO Req 2/210/118, B, A; Req 2/35/50, B, A.

[52] *William Allambrigge v. Anne Allambrigge*, PRO Req 2/168/19, B, A.

Moreover, if the purchasing widow died and her husband married again, as the steward alleged had happened in this case, then by custom this second wife had no claim to widow's estate.[53]

Two clear themes emerge from the mayhem of the cases. The first is the simple but important fact that interests in copyholds for lives offered widows a superior alternative to widow's estate.[54] If a wife was named in a copy there could be little doubt about her right to inherit. Furthermore, being named in a copy gave a woman an interest for life if she survived her husband, not just an interest for the duration of a chaste widowhood. This gave a widow the freedom to remarry without prejudicing her interest, and so provided her with security if she found herself widowed for a second time. For wives and widows, the relationship between copyholds for lives and widow's estate was akin to the relationship between jointure and dower. Jointure could offer a woman an interest that was superior to dower and easier to claim, *if* a jointure was arranged, whereas dower was an automatic right. Similarly, being named in a copy gave a widow a better interest than having to rely on widow's estate, but she had to be named. Widow's estate, by contrast, applied automatically.

The second theme that runs through these cases is the importance of individual and community expectations in widow's estate disputes. Most of the arguments that opponents conjured against widows, and most of the formulations of custom they enlisted to support these arguments, were strictly economic in nature. Individuals who purchased future interests expected to enjoy those interests. All purchasers of reversionary interests took a risk, banking on the life-span of the current holder. Most, however, did not wish to bank on the life-span of the holder's widow as well. Hence, all of the formulations of custom which specified that widow's estate applied only if no reversions had been granted before the woman's marriage. Concerns about money were behind other arguments and customs: that only the widows of purchasers of copies had widow's estate; that only the widow of the longest lived of the three named had widow's estate, if all three had contributed money to the purchase. Those who had paid felt they deserved to enjoy rights ahead of those who had not paid. Without limitations like these, opponents of widows seem to have been saying, the custom of widow's estate could turn copyholds for three lives into copyholds for six lives.

Not all widow's estate cases, however, can be characterised as simple clashes between traditional beliefs about the entitlements of widows and the economic concerns of other interest holders. Some revolved around the relationship between parties. As I have tried to demonstrate, changes in copyholding

---

[53] *Johan Cosynes* v. *Richard Morgan & John Broderibbe*, PRO Req 2/187/49 [m. 3], A; in this case, Agnes Grove's case and Joan Ellis's case (in which Cosynes appeared as a deponent), the plaintiffs and the defendants all asserted that the customs they alleged (which were all different and incompatible) applied to all of the manors of the barony of Glastonbury.

[54] Stenton, *The English Woman in History*, p. 103.

customs could exert pressure on widows claiming widow's estate by increasing the number of rival claimants they could expect to face if they were not named in copies themselves. However, the existence of a future interest did not in itself challenge a widow's rights. Widow's estate almost always delayed the interest of another interest holder, if only an inheriting son or daughter, and the possibility that a woman might outlive her husband and claim her widow's estate was to be expected. Conflict arose most often when the possibility that a widow might claim widow's estate was *not* expected, in other words when it disturbed the expectations of the next holder, as happened in the Ellis case.

As the cases show, a variety of circumstances could interfere with the expectations of holders of future interests, but the commonest trait shared by widows claiming or defending widow's estate in Requests was that they were second wives. Second or subsequent wives were disadvantaged twice over. Firstly, they were almost never named in copies, which meant that they had to rely solely on custom. Yet, as we have seen, many formulations of widow's estate barred women from making a claim if their copies contained the name of another wife. A tenant might make provision for his first wife, by naming her in a copy, but he was less likely to name his second or any subsequent wife, because this would entail surrendering his copy and paying an entry fine to take a new one. Secondly, a woman whose husband had been married before faced an expanded list of potential rivals, and in some cases a diminished list of potential supporters. Through no real fault of their own, second or subsequent wives could disturb community or family perceptions of the accepted sequence of copyhold inheritance. Children named in copies, for example, often resented the unexpected interruption to their plans that came when a stepmother claimed her widow's estate. Waiting for your natural mother to live out her years was one thing; waiting for a woman who was not a blood relation, and who might be close in age to yourself, was another. The result was dozens of instances of stepchildren suing stepmothers, when they would never have sued their natural mothers. Similarly, it was not uncommon for stepmothers to sue their stepchildren, and for other step-relations like brothers and sisters to sue each other.[55]

When cases of this type came to court, widows whose husbands had married before did not as readily command the support of the homage in customary courts, and of deponents in Requests actions, as widows who were first wives. To fellow tenants on the homage, a widow who had worked on a customary holding for decades beside her husband might have appeared a worthier recipient of widow's estate than a young second wife widowed after only a year, especially if her claim kept out her husband's adult son, or the purchaser of a remainder interest. In this sense custom could be normative, offering greater

---

[55] See, for example, *John Willet* v. *Johane Willet*, PRO Req 2/283/55; *Margaret Upham* v. *Richard Upham*, PRO Req 2/281/15; *Alice Gibbes* v. *Ambrose Butler*, PRO Req 2/209/18.

protection for conventional behaviour than for uncommon or less common behaviour.

Second wives regularly faced opposition from rival claimants among the tenantry and even from within their own families. However, when rival claimants were not fellow tenants but landlords, some second wives proved capable of exploiting the custom of widow's estate for profit. J.H. Bettey has found a series of cases from seventeenth century Dorset involving ageing tenants who married young brides to deprive lords and stewards of entry fines and the possession of customary interests. Some men who could not enter their children's names in copies because they were the last named, or who had failed to enter their names for reasons of expense, married young women after making them agree to divert a proportion of the profits from their widow's estate to specified individuals. In the 1620s, for example, a dying man married a young widow after making her sign an agreement that after his death she would permit his eldest son to farm the lands and share the profits with his siblings. In return, she was to get £5 a year, house room and fuel. Women in a position to bargain could make a profit from such deals, but others, girls as young as twelve years old, gained little from these arrangements except for a premature widowhood. Bettey suggests that 'frauds' like these may have been common in Dorset, and they were certainly long lasting. William Stevenson complained as late as 1812 of 'customary tenants marrying in the last stage of decrepit old age to very young girls'. Bettey's only example from Somerset demonstrates that this practice could be influential in encouraging landlords to try and extinguish copyholds and replace them with leaseholds. As a result of a survey conducted in 1674, a sickly tenant in his eighties was offered £150 if he would surrender his copyhold. He refused and married a young servant maid, leading the steward to advise the lord: 'I say have not anything to do with them except they will turne their Coppys into Leasehold.'[56] These cases confirm the power of custom in contests between landlord and tenant, but also show why universal rights to freebench could be unpopular with other participants in the land market.

Having examined the operation of widow's estate and observed the clutter of exceptions it could attract and the resentments it could arouse, the nature of the custom and its guiding ethos become a little clearer. It appears that in most instances community tradition did not intend freebench to provide every widow with a universal pension. If this had been the desire, why was freebench so rarely a life interest, and why did so many copyholders go to the trouble of naming their wives in copies? Rather, as Barbara Todd has argued, there was clearly a sense that widow's estate operated as 'a bridge between generations rather than an individual woman's right of ownership', with the result that only a minority of widows retained full control of their estates until they died. The custom gave widows a whole or a half interest, rather than a simple third, so

---

[56] Bettey, 'Manorial custom and widows' estate', pp. 210–14.

that they could not only keep themselves, but raise their children, if they had children, and manage the interest before it passed to the next heir.[57] The right was a compromise between the needs of widows and the needs and expectations of their children and of the land market, and this is reflected in the way the right worked in practice. In Long Wittenham, for example, Todd found that in many cases widows shared control of customary estates with their children, or passed control to their eldest sons when they came of age, or more commonly when they married.[58] In Requests the compromise is apparent in the numbers of widows who permitted the next holders of their interests to work their lands, in return for an annual pension.[59] These kinds of practical arrangements were particularly common when widows were stepmothers, for their presence so often interrupted existing family arrangements organised on the basis of trust and natural affection.

Naming a woman in a copy removed the possibility of ambiguity, and in some manors the custom of freebench appeared to demand that a woman be named in a copy. Joan Wilcox defended her life interest in a copyhold against claims that it was a right of freebench, and therefore had expired on her remarriage, by asserting that on her manor, 'hit hath not bynne seen within time of memorye of man that any widowe hath enjoyed wydowes estate in the same capitall messuage or farme by the custom of the said Mannor unles hit be soe graunted unto her expressely by the coppie thereof'.[60] However, naming a widow in a copy did not overcome the problems raised by the competing rights of mothers and children and other tenants. In fact, it often exacerbated them. Todd found that the majority of wives in Long Wittenham were named in copies until the 1580s, but then the landlord and tenants agreed to modify the custom to forbid naming, because it made it possible for widows to disinherit children from a former marriage in favour of children from their current marriage. Subsequently, widows were entitled to an interest only for their widowhoods, and not for life, with the result that remarriage by widows became less common.

Widow's estate had its limits. The right was subject to opposition, it did not always operate smoothly when the market in customary lands was active, and not all widows who received interests under the right controlled those interests until their deaths. However, it remained a formidable entitlement, and the level

---

[57] In parts of Staffordshire, widow's estate could be either a whole or a half interest, presumably varying according to the presence of surviving children; *Marie Taylor* v. *William Brown & Margaret Holway*, PRO Req 2/276/10.

[58] Todd, 'Freebench and free enterprise', pp. 184–7, 193.

[59] *Florence Hall* v. *Giles Raimonde*, PRO Req 1/11, pp. 28–30.

[60] *Johane Wilcox* v. *Thomas Llewellyn et al.*, PRO Req 2/289/49, m. 12, R; a defendant in another case argued that even if a woman was the purchaser of a copy, if she remarried then her estate for life would become an estate for her widowhood, and would be extinguished when her husband died, 'notwithstanding she was purchaser'; *Johan Cosynes* v. *Richard Morgan & John Broderibbe*, PRO Req 2/187/49 [m. 3], A.

of opposition it received should be regarded as a mark of its strength as much as its weakness. Clearly, some tenants were unhappy with the generosity of the custom and the quantity of customary lands it placed in widows' control. Todd found from her sample of twenty four holdings in Long Wittenham, from between the mid sixteenth century and 1700, that widows held title to around one fifth of the available holdings, a greater proportion than in Sutton Courtney where custom did not govern inheritance.[61] The cases which reached Requests were the exceptions, and it is likely that most widows of copyholders either possessed a life interest by copy, or claimed their widow's estate without opposition. They enjoyed the protection of custom, the support of the homage and the tacit approval of the next holder whose interest they were displacing. A significant number, those whose situations did not conform to expected patterns in ways that might upset the expectations of other interest holders, could face a challenging time, but they could appeal against local decisions, if they had the resources, by taking them to Westminster courts of common law or equity, such as Requests.

THE MASTERS' RESPONSE

The Masters dealt with customary disputes in the fashion already described, regularly enlisting local support from commissioners and encouraging local solutions. They restricted themselves to the unfair or immoral behaviour of individuals, not the possible unfairness of custom. If they decided that a claimant had a valid interest, they were willing to use the authority of equity to override the authority of local lords, ladies and stewards, but they went out of their way to avoid interfering with custom itself.[62] Employing their usual flexibility, they refused to allow technicalities to deprive individuals of their rights or livelihoods. When a customary court decided that a tenant's surrender and re-taking of his customary interest had been invalid, for example, they ordered that the man's widow should enjoy widow's estate in the lands despite her lack of a sustainable right. They argued that the man had made his surrender with 'thintent to have the same againe for the terme of his lief, whereby his widowe might also have the benefitt of her widowehed of & in the same according to the custome of the said mannor, as she ought to have had, if no such surrender had ben made'.[63] In another case a widow tried to claim an interest because she was named in a copy, but she was unsuccessful because her husband had surrendered and sold the interest before he died. The Masters expressed their doubt that a married woman's future life estate could be sold by her husband without her consent, and they ordered that 'in respect of the povertie of the said com-

---

[61] Todd, 'Freebench and free enterprise', pp. 178–82, 196.
[62] The Chancery bench took a similar view; Jones, *The Elizabethan Court of Chancery*, p. 264.
[63] *Agnes & Amyas Gaylard* v. *John Gaylard*, PRO Req 1/17, p. 72.

plainant' and 'by the consent of the said parties & of the learned counsaill of both sides', the defendant was to pay the widow £6 13s. 4d. In return she was to surrender her interest and permit the defendant to cancel her copy.[64]

On some occasions, however, the Masters went further, making equitable decisions in favour of litigants who appeared to have no claim sustainable in either law or equity. In 1562 a complainant successfully sued a widow, convincing the Masters that she could have no interest by copy in the lands she possessed because the lands were not copyhold. However, the Masters ordered, again with the consent of the parties, that the woman should surrender the copy by which she had claimed: 'And that thereupon the said complainant in consideracion of the greate Age and povertie of the saide Defendant shall by Dede Indented demise the premisses . . . to the saide Defendant for terme of fowertie yeres then nexte ensueinge (if she live so longe . . .).' The defendant had to pay rent for this land, 40s. a year, 'assessed by the saide Counsaill of the saide courte', and to maintain the house at her expense, but the grant is exceptional none the less.[65] In a similar case from the same year, a widow failed to establish her right to widow's estate in lands occupied by the defendant. Having respect 'that the said complainant ys a woman of grete age and verie poore' the Masters ordered that the defendant should continue in occupation, *but* that he should pay 'yerelie unto the said complainant [£30] . . . during her naturall lief, over and besides the lordes rente'.[66] These cases provide further evidence of the Masters' liberal perception of equity, and as Hoyle has remarked 'the tempering of strict law with such humanity appears to have been typical of early modern judicial practice'.[67]

The Masters did not restrict this extraordinary brand of equitable relief to the poor. In 1593 Lady Elizabeth Pawlett sued the new lord of the Somerset manor of Alundishay, Sir Mathew Arrundell, for the return of copyhold lands he had confiscated after she refused to appear in court in person when summoned. Sir Mathew had amerced her lands, notwithstanding that she was: 'A very aged gentlewoman, her majesties servant and dwelleth [120] myles distant from the saide mannor.' She argued, and the court accepted, that in the past she had instructed servants by writing under seal to do all suits and services due to the lords of the manor. The Masters ordered that this arrangement should continue for the duration of her widowhood, although they took pains to prevent this order setting any precedent, 'to any other tenante or widowe entitled to any widowes estate as aforesaid within the saide mannor to dispence with theire fealtie or personall apparance . . . at the saide mannor'.[68]

[64] *Isabell Gerrard v. Thomas Haufford*, PRO Req 1/17, pp. 125–6.
[65] *William Manner v. Joane Gregory*, PRO Req 1/11, pp. 155–6.
[66] *Elizabeth Prowse v. John Powe*, PRO Req 1/11, pp. 220–1.
[67] R.W. Hoyle, 'Tenure and the land market in early modern England: or a late contribution to the Brenner debate', *Economic History Review*, 2nd series, 43 (1990), p. 3.
[68] *Elizabeth Pawlett v Mathewe Arrundell*, PRO Req 1/17, pp. 320–1.

Over the course of Elizabeth's reign the Masters meddled less and less with the decisions of manor courts and made fewer, what to modern eyes appear to be, capricious or charitable orders. The increasing willingness of central common law courts to allow actions of trespass concerning copyhold land meant that the Masters were faced with fewer customary actions, and dismissed an increasing number without hearing, as 'matters best fit to be heard at the common law'.[69] However, this does not mean that the Masters washed their hands of customary actions, and when they referred cases to the common law they often directed the shape that common law proceedings should take, and reserved to themselves final judgment on any remaining matters of equity. In November 1597 the court made an order, in the case of *Alice Langton* v. *Thomas Fletcher*, that Thomas was to bring an action of trespass in Queen's Bench for the recovery of copyhold lands, after which the court would then make further orders for 'the releife of the said complainant as to them should seeme consonant to equitie & justice'. If he refused to bring an action, then he was to convey the disputed lands to Alice in return for £40. He refused. In February 1598 the court noted that Thomas's refusal to proceed at common law was 'to the prejudice & damage of the sayd complainant, being A poore aged widowe', and ordered that he pay Alice £20 before the first of March, in part payment of the sum they felt was due to her.[70] In other cases they ordered that defendants allow complainants on to disputed lands for one hour, so those complainants could ground a trespass action at common law and so (with luck) settle the question of title.[71] Or they referred cases to the common law but ordered defendants not to take advantage of the fact a complainant had never been admitted to an interest, 'but shall give unto her the benefit of admission in pleading'.[72]

Widows who turned to Requests when their interests were threatened found the court responsive to their claims. The court investigated their rights with diligence, and occasionally made equitable orders imbued with a considerable spirit of charity. Once again the actions of the Masters suggest that while it cannot be said that they showed favouritism to women in general, they consistently showed sympathy to the poor, the aged, and the intimidated, and widows fell into these categories more often than most. The Masters' compromise solu-

---

[69] According to Eric Kerridge, possession of a customary estate could be recovered at common law using personal trespass actions from at least 1499 (on manors where the custom allowed tenants to sub-let their interests for up to a year without the consent of the lord); from 1588 in the King's Bench; from 1596 in Exchequer; and from 1599–1610 in Common Pleas, where possession could be recovered for all manors, regardless of sub-letting customs; Kerridge, *Agrarian Problems*, p. 72; for an example of a referral, see *William Hammond* v. *Thomas Dockwra*, PRO Req 1/21, p. 186.

[70] *Alice Langton* v. *Thomas Fletcher*, PRO Req 1/19, p. 243; for another example, see *Thomas Bowdiche* v. *John Everie*, PRO Req 1/17, pp. 311–12.

[71] *Thomas, Margaret & John Childe* v. *John Richards & John Nickson*, PRO Req 1/15, fol. 105.

[72] *Ann Anncell* v. *Michael Anncell*, PRO Req 1/21, pp. 55–6.

tions brought a degree of equity to the manor, but as Tawney pointed out, through their overriding of manor court decisions, they were unavoidably undermining the integrity of customary law, and perhaps hastening its decline.[73]

CUSTOM VERSUS THE COMMON LAW

Alice Clark and Doris Stenton both believed that custom provided women with better rights and greater legal independence than they received under common law. There is much to recommend their interpretation. The Requests materials confirm that widow's estate was a powerful right that was widely observed, one that gave many widows a full interest in their late husbands' lands for the duration of widowhood, rather than the meagre third that came with common law dower. Custom offered advantages to many women because it was local: communities of tenants might extend help to widows in their midst which the more anonymous common law might deny. Widow's estate was regularly contested, but widows who had their claims rejected could appeal to the homage of the manorial court, or to Requests, Chancery and later the Westminster courts of common law. However, custom guaranteed women few rights apart from freebench – daughters, for example, did not always inherit equally with sons, and if a woman with a customary interest married, her husband took control of that interest for the duration of their marriage – and the Requests materials make it difficult to share Clark's and Stenton's optimism about women's participation in the customary process. Clark believed that women who possessed copyhold interests played a key part in the adjudication of custom because they served as jurors on homages, but this appears rarely, if ever, to have been the case. Barbara Todd could find no examples of women serving on homages in Long Wittenham, and I have yet to find mention of female homagers in any cases in Requests.[74] Women who held interests by copy may have arranged to send deputies to serve on the homage in their stead, but most manorial courts denied them the ability of serving in person, confirming Edward Coke's view, quoted in chapter 2 above, that 'a woman may be a free Suitor to the Courts of the Lord, but though it be generally said that the free suitors be Judges in these courts, it is intended of men and not of women'.[75]

The absence of women from homages was reflected in their rare appearances as witnesses in customary disputes. As was seen in chapter 3, in a sample of cases that directly involved women's customary rights, fewer than ten of the deponents who gave evidence before commissioners were female, compared with over 200 who were male.[76] Parties preferred to call male deponents to

---

[73] R.H. Tawney, *The Agrarian Problem in the Sixteenth Century* (London, 1912), p. 296; for an eighteenth century example of equity overriding custom to the detriment of a widow claiming widow's estate, see Staves, *Married Women's Separate Property*, pp. 103–4.

[74] Todd, 'Freebench and free enterprise', p. 185.

[75] Coke, *The Second Part of the Institutes*, p. 119.   [76] See table 4.3.

describe the experience of other widows than to call those widows themselves, suggesting that commissioners, lawyers and widow litigants regarded women's testimony as being somehow inferior to men's. The limited participation of women in the operation of custom is further confirmed by a Chancery case from the seventeenth century, in which a copyholder sought relief against a new custom set down in an indenture of alteration. He argued that his mother had not been a party to the alteration, and that as her heir, he should not be bound by it. However, the Lord Keeper ruled against him, on the grounds that his father had agreed to the change, despite the fact that his father had only held the interest through his mother, who had been allowed no say in the alteration of custom.[77]

It is clear from the Requests archive that custom continued to affect the lives of many people in many areas of England in the sixteenth century. The force of custom as a concept is also strongly apparent. All parties in customary actions repeated the same formulaic phrases, 'according to the custom of the manor', 'time whereof the memory of man was not to the contrary' and 'time out of memory of man', over and over, in their attempts to harness the almost spiritual authority of custom to their cause. But the strength of custom in people's minds stood in marked contrast to the malleability of customary law in practice, as Thompson, Hoyle, Searle and others have demonstrated with respect to long running confrontations between lords and tenants.[78] The slip between the illusion of the immutability of custom and its flexibility in daily use gave custom, as a system of law, its enduring strength. While common lawyers worried about 'jarring and discordant cases', under customary law such cases were simply forgotten.[79] However, acknowledging the flexibility of custom makes it dangerous to assume that women's lives would have been radically different if custom had not lost out to the common law. The ability of communities to alter customs over time meant that customary law was capable of absorbing, as well as withstanding, the prejudice against women which is so often associated with the common law. The lesson the records teach is that when comparing women's rights under custom with women's rights under the common law, it is important to realise that women's rights under custom were neither homogeneous nor static. They differed from manor to manor, they could shift and change on the same manor over time, and given their normative character, they could even differ, in terms of the strength of support they offered, from individual to individual.

Customs survived only when they were regularly asserted and etched into the memories of each generation. This was obviously more likely to happen when

---

[77] C.U.L. Gg.2.31, fol. 477.

[78] Thompson, *Customs in Common*; Thompson, 'A grid of inheritance'; Hoyle, 'An ancient and laudable custom'; Searle, 'Custom, class conflict and agrarian capitalism'.

[79] Jack Goody, *The Logic of Writing and the Organisation of Society* (Cambridge, 1986), p. 137.

customs reflected or expressed local feeling, when they tapped into or constituted part of a community's 'moral economy'. Put very simply, customs survived in localities when enough people wanted them to survive. Most people in communities agreed in principle that widows deserved support, and despite the fact that tenants often contested claims for freebench, where copyholding persisted widow's estate usually persisted, sometimes surviving into the eighteenth century and beyond. Where customs lacked this kind of deep local support, or were rarely asserted, they could quickly lapse. And customs which favoured women other than widows, by giving them property or independence, were probably less likely to receive such support. Therefore, when considering the resilience of enduring customs, it is important to recall the apparent amnesia of Christopher Dyer's Whitstone tenants, who in 1538 were unaware that daughters had regularly inherited on their manor until less than seventy years before. If this process of collective forgetting, as well as collective remembering, can be more precisely analysed, it may hold the key to how other ideas and beliefs changed and passed within communities. In particular, how restrictive, patriarchal attitudes to women passed from generation to generation, and how individuals and communities managed to adapt them in response to other changes in society.

The manner in which parties pleaded customary rights, and the ways they joined witnesses in repeating the stock phrases from which customary law derived much of its authority, show how various parties to Requests actions attempted to use the power of language to press their legal and moral claims. The next chapter explores the process of pleading in more detail, picking a path through a minefield of misrepresentation and falsehood to look at the ways litigants and their counsel presented themselves and their causes, and derided the character and claims of their opponents.

8

Pleading strategies in Requests

A Lawyer hath both authority and law to tell any lye, that his Clyent will informe
Barnabe Rich, *My Ladies Looking Glasse* (1616)[1]

In his 1975 study of the equity side of Exchequer, W.H. Bryson wrote in glowing terms about the advantages of using court records as an historical source: 'The records are free from ignorances, negligences, prejudices, opinions, and historians' purposes. They were made and kept for reasons other than to aid the uses to which they shall now be put; this assures their impartiality as sources of historical description.'[2] Bryson's words may have relevance for institutional historians, but from the perspective of social and feminist historians it seems clear that litigant pleadings from central equity courts are not free from, but rather brim full of, 'ignorances, negligences, prejudices and opinions'. The incomplete survival of records, and the fact that so many cases never proceeded beyond the initial stages of pleading, make it difficult to accurately determine even simple facts about the numbers of litigants who used different courts, the background of those litigants and the subjects of their actions. Yet even if archives were complete – if every case in a court had proceeded to a final decision and every document survived – historians interested in social relationships and attitudes would still face problems of interpretation: how best, for example, to classify cases when the grievances that set parties at odds could differ from the causes they brought to court? And how best to reconstruct disputed events from stylised pleadings produced by obviously self-interested parties? In other words, whose word to believe when opposing parties rarely agreed on anything?

I argued in the introduction that the adversarial nature of the legal system ensures that, without corroboration, court records remain a problematical

---

[1] Barnabe Rich, *My Ladies Looking Glasse* (London, 1616), p. 67.
[2] W.H. Bryson, *The Equity Side of Exchequer: Its Jurisdiction, Administration, Procedures and Records* (Cambridge, 1975), p. 2.

source for the facts that they describe.[3] And that in a court like Requests, the authentic voices of litigants and witnesses can be difficult to recapture, because they have passed through so many legal and institutional filters. I also argued that not all of these difficulties are insurmountable. For while opposing pleas repeatedly contradicted each other, and while the contributions to pleadings of lawyers and litigants can be difficult to distinguish, what remained constant at all times was the common desire of all concerned to convince the Masters. Therefore, by shifting attention from the origin of ideas in pleadings to their ultimate destination, this common desire can be made the focus of study, and the eternal problem of separating the contributions (and values) of litigants and lawyers can be set aside for a moment. As Clive Holmes remarked in his study of fenland disturbances in the seventeenth century, documents can often be more revealing 'about the writers' sense of the interests of the body they are address-ing, than about either the events they purport to describe, or the ideals which motivated those involved'. As he further pointed out, 'the concern for *audience* informs every aspect of the structure and substance' of petitions and letters. In his words: 'It is not merely a rhetorical veneer, but dictates the choice of inci-dent which is detailed, and of the language and actions of the rioters which are emphasized.'[4]

So it was with Requests pleadings. The authors of pleadings constructed nar-ratives to suit the prejudices of their inquisitors, and the facts they selected, the incidents or characteristics they chose to emphasise and those they chose to ignore, as well as the language they used, are all revealing.[5] The apparent defects in the records can therefore be exploited to advantage, by focusing on the incon-sistencies between accounts and on the resort to stereotyping, exaggeration and other methods of story-weaving that litigants and lawyers used to fashion their cases into convincing pleadings. In particular, in the context of the aims of this book, it is possible to examine the ways in which women's pleadings differed from men's, and the ways representations of male litigants differed from repre-sentations of female litigants.[6]

---

[3] Observe James Oldham's comments; 'The adversary system is commonly assumed to be designed to cope with the central supposition that many witnesses cannot be trusted to tell the truth, and as long as judges and juries produce results with which the public is generally comfortable, the systematic lying that takes place in the courtroom may not be socially destructive'; Oldham, 'Truth-telling', p. 117.

[4] Clive Holmes, 'Drainers and fenmen: the problem of popular political consciousness in the seven-teenth century', in Anthony Fletcher and John Stevenson, eds., *Order and Disorder in Early Modern England* (Cambridge, 1987), p. 168.

[5] On this point, see David Underdown, *Fire from Heaven: Life in an English Town in the Seventeenth Century* (London, 1993), p. 83.

[6] For an analysis of the ways women presented themselves in London's church courts, see Gowing, *Domestic Dangers*, especially chs. 4, 6, 7.

POVERTY

Past chapters have identified distinctive patterns of argument and representation in cases involving widows and unmarried women. It appears that single
women often played on their helplessness, especially if they were orphans.
Widows too, sought sympathy from the Masters for their impoverished positions, although they were quick to refute opponents' claims that they were
either 'simple' or calculating, by stressing their knowledge and competence and
by professing their innocence.[7] Exceptions abound, but the common emphasis
that many single women and widows laid on their vulnerability represents
perhaps the clearest distinction which can be identified between the pleadings of
women (excepting married women) and the pleadings of men. However, it is a
distinction which needs further substantiation and discussion.

All complainants in Requests, unless they were employed in the service of the
royal household, made reference in their bills of complaint to their inability to
gain justice in other courts, due to their poverty or to the power advantage
enjoyed by their opponents. The hollowness of these cries of poverty or
incapacity, when they sprang from the mouths of lords, ladies and wealthy
members of the gentry, has already been noted.[8] But while all manner of litigants cried poor or alleged injustice, the pleadings of women are marked by the
variety and the intensity of the imagery of weakness and poverty they contain.
Elizabeth Spenser and her sister, for example, told the Masters that they were
'pore orphanes destitut of frends, welth & other suplies and helpes to recover &
gett ther owne'.[9] Joan Major's counsel described her as 'a very poore and
symple mayden and not of habilitie to sue for her right' except in Requests.[10]
Joan Willyn's bill stated that she was 'devoid of any other staye of livinge unles
your highnes, of your accostomed & aboundant mercie beinge herin moved
with pitie, shall vouchsafe to extend and streche forthe your hand and helpe in
this behalfe'.[11] Other widows bemoaned that they were 'very poore and lyke to
famyshe and starve'.[12]

Women who stressed the weakness or poverty of their condition were clearly
doing more than attempting to satisfy the criteria for entry into Requests. Take,
for example, the case of *Mary Burges* v. *Andice Phillips*. Mary's bill described
how her first husband, John Cotton, died leaving her a life interest in various
goods and two dwellings. She then married a Frenchman named John Burges,
who 'beinge very perverce and maliciously disposed, within three or foure dayes

[7] See chapters 5 and 7.   [8] See chapter 4.
[9] *Elisabeth Spenser & Elisabeth Spenser* v. *Jeames Mascall*, PRO Req 2/267/44, m. 1, B.
[10] *Joane Major* v. *Margaret Major & Wyllym Wever*, PRO Req 2/239/3, m. 13, B.
[11] *Johan Willyn* v. *Christopher Keny*, PRO Req 2/283/61, B.
[12] *Agnes, Edmond & Katherine Sheppard* v. *William Arnold*, PRO Req 2/159/138; *Maudlen
    Hollande* v. *Thomas Wilford & Robert Holland*, PRO Req 2/47/25, Petition; *Elizabeth Vale* v.
    Hughe Smythe & Richard Cromewell, PRO Req 2/281/23, B.

after the mariage fledde awaye from youre sayde Oratresse and yet absentethe him selfe, of meer frowardnes withoute merite on the parte of youre sayde Oratresse, to hir great impoverishment and utter undoinge'. Burges's flight left Mary without support, forcing her to let the two houses to Andice Phillips for £7 a year. After gaining entry to the houses, however, Phillips refused to pay any rent and 'very injuriously & violently and uncharitably did thrust your Majesties sayde Oratresse out of the sayde howses' and 'with force keipethe hir oute of possession'. Furthermore, he 'nameth him selfe executor unto the sayde Cotton, hir late husband, and uppon the falce pretence thereof offereth to sell the sayde houses', having already sold or spoilt all of Mary's goods contained in the houses. The result of this appalling behaviour, Mary alleged, was that Phillips 'inforcethe youre sayde Oratresse to begge lodginge and releiffe of hir neighbors, and so lamentablye oppresseth hir that with out youre grace's spedie helpe herein she is lyke to remayne destitute of lawfull assistance ... to hir utter undoinge and to the great incouragement of suche lyke malifactors that take pleasure in the oppression of the poore'.[13]

Mary's desperate condition was not an incidental detail; it formed the backbone of her case. Her widowhood, her remarriage, her ruthless desertion at the hands of Burges, all had little obvious bearing on her suit against Phillips. But they provided the background to his mistreatment of her. Technically Mary was not a widow, but implicit in her narrative is the sense that her husband's desertion had left her as disadvantaged and exposed as a widow: after Burges exploited her, Phillips took advantage of her weakened state to deprive her of her possessions and livelihood. It is almost as if Phillips was in some way answerable for the crimes of the Frenchman, his actions marking him out not simply as a thief, but as a coward willing to gain from the plight of a deserted and therefore a defenceless woman.

Women and their counsel were aware of the Court of Requests' reputation as a haven for the poor in general, and for poor widows in particular. The 'poor' Spanish widow Eleanor Nanez claimed bonds worth thousands of pounds, telling the Masters that any failure to recoup her losses would be to her undoing, 'unless your highnes accustomed Justice to such poore widowes be herein extended'.[14] By accentuating their impoverished condition women hoped

[13] *Marye Burges v. Andice Phillipps*, PRO Req 2/26/151.
[14] *Elianor Nanez & Fardinando Alveres v. Andrew Browne*, PRO Req 2/245/67, m. 11, B; for further examples of women appealing to 'your Highness accustomed Clemencye and goodnesse', or 'accustomed pyttie and clemency', see *Ellen Dumbrell v. Clement Dumbrell*, PRO Req 2/196/96, B; *Ellen Greene v. Richard Norris*, PRO Req 2/26/38, B; *Margaret Smyth v. Mary Lockett*, PRO Req 2/247/37; *Elizabeth Vale v. Hughe Smythe & Richard Cromewell*, PRO Req 2/281/23; on the few occasions when men made such appeals they tended to speak of Elizabeth's 'accustomed Zeall to Justyce', or on one occasion to her 'accustomed goodnes to poore subjects'; *Wylliam Wyett v. Ellen Colle et al.*, PRO Req 2/104/5; *William Hill v. Anne Horne & Robert Winniffe*, PRO Req 2/217/34.

to attract maximum sympathy from the Masters, and to achieve this end they drafted into their accounts any detail they felt might help their cause. Widows emphasised the number of children they had to support. Rich women spoke of the shame they felt at having to beg relief from their friends and, in common with Mary Burges, a number of women emphasised their lack of male support-ers. Male plaintiffs sometimes lamented that they were 'without stay of frends' in their hour of need, but rarely did they emphasise their solitary state with the vigour most widows employed.[15] Agnes Greenland, for example, not only described herself as 'a verie poore & impotent creature without frends or abili-tie to sue or defende her right', to whom failure at law would result in 'the utter impoverishing of your said subject, her children and familie', she also empha-sised that she was an 'olde woman' and 'sole'.[16] Other women also stressed that they were *femes sole*, and their apparent attempts to associate the absence of a husband with vulnerability echoed, or perhaps exploited, the directions in advice literature (surveyed in chapter 3 above) calling on single women and widows to leave matters of property and law to male allies.[17] 'Poor' widows and single women regularly stressed that male or female opponents were taking advantage of their 'unpower povertie and indajence', as if spinsterhood and widowhood in themselves were sources of incapacity.[18]

Widow executrixes often presented the most powerfully argued cases based on their desperate circumstances, for not only might they be poor and have dependants to look after, but they carried the added responsibility of having to settle their husbands' financial affairs and administer their estates. Katherine Taylor and Marie Turnor both brought actions seeking relief from the penalties on bonds they had inherited as their late husbands' executrixes. Both said they were willing to pay their late husbands' creditors the original sums owed, plus reasonable consideration for forbearance, but they balked at having to pay double these amounts in penalties on agreements to which they had not been parties. Taylor described how her husband's death had left her with three chil-dren and 'great with childe of the [fourth], to the no small desolation and dis-comfort of your saide subjecte . . . beinge altogether unprovided where to bestowe herselfe and her children'. Her creditor opponent, she argued, sought to exploit her precisely because he had observed her 'great adversytie'. She had done her utmost to fulfil the disputed conditions and had assured her creditor that if he had lost a single penny contrary to her husband's agreement, she would recompense him 'accordinge to enye reason & conscience wherfore to

---

[15] In a 1568 case, Thomas Wilmot described himself as 'a poore simple man', but he did so primar-ily to explain why he had failed correctly to instruct his counsel, rather than to gain sympathy; *Thomas Wilmot v. Johan Fourd*, PRO Req 2/155/58, B, R.

[16] *Agnes Greneland v. Elianor Seward & John Stocker*, PRO Req 2/210/101.

[17] *John Browne v. Mary Sturton*, PRO Req 2/136/11, A.

[18] *Agnes Chicke v. Elizabeth Clifton*, PRO Req 2/190/27, B.

advoyde the daunger of the common lawe being stricte in thease cases'.[19] Marie Turnor told a similar story. Her husband's death had left her with five small children and debts which far exceeded the value of his estate. She had offered to assign to her opponent debts of an equivalent value, however 'well knowinge the premisses and the poore estate' of Marie, he had refused her offer, 'althoughe divers other of the credytors of your highnes said subjects husband have soe done'. His greed was such, she said, that he had threatened that he would 'have the uttermoste farthinge of the bonde and all his charges and by noe meanes wylle he be entreated to accept as aforesaid what ys reasonable at her handes (her poore estate consydered)'.[20] Both of these women, along with other executrixes, believed that by virtue of their status they warranted special equitable relief. However, in both cases their opponents demurred, claiming that there was no case to answer, Katherine Taylor's opponent suggesting that her bill contained 'more superfluos and vain matter then matter of substance'.[21]

How do the pleadings of male litigants compare? A number of features are common to the pleadings of both women and men. Male and female orphans presented themselves in much the same ways, and men concentrated on their incapacity if they were old. Richard Collard's lawyer, for example, drew attention to the 'decayed aged and myserable estate of your highnes subject', who was 'an aged and unlettered man'.[22] On the whole, however, men tended to refer to their poverty in slightly different ways, making less of their personal weakness.[23] Most claimed they could not sue at common law because they lacked the relevant evidence, not because they were poor.[24] If they were poor, the condition was usually temporary, linked directly to the losses about which they complained, not (as with single women and widows) to their marital state. Richard Walker admitted that he was 'a verie poore yong man', but he went to lengths to explain that he had just emerged from a nine year apprenticeship as a baker, and he was claiming disputed legacies 'minding by godes permission to provide him a stocke for his preferment in his said science'.[25] Men confessed the imbalance

---

[19] *Katherin Taylor v. Jonas Waters*, PRO Req 2/279/8, m. 2, B.

[20] Turnor said that in her capacity as executrix she had paid out £40 more 'than ever came to her hands'; *Marie Turnor v. Thomas Pye & John Franklyn*, PRO Req 2/276/75, m. 3, B; Pye's demurrer, dated 25 November 31 Elizabeth I, is signed by Edward Coke.

[21] *Katherin Taylor v. Jonas Waters*, PRO Req 2/279/8, D.

[22] *Richard Collard v. Isabell Countess of Rutland*, PRO Req 2/191/44, B, R; *Thomas & William Wyllyn v. Christopher Kenne et al.*, PRO Req 2/288/36, B, R; *John Hole v. Richard Bewe et al.*, PRO Req 2/223/84, B.

[23] Men were just as likely as women to emphasize their poverty and their inability to support their wives and small children in petitions for entry *in forma pauperis*. But having gained entry, they placed less emphasis on their material condition; *Richard Christopher v. William & Ellen Baylie*, PRO Req 2/191/71; *William Rigolts v. Peter Dormer*, PRO Req 3/33, letter from G. Perkham to Masters Sackford and Dale.

[24] *Henry King v. Eleanor Palmer & Millicent Mortymer*, PRO Req 2/165/131; *William Haydon v. John Hurd*, PRO Req 2/223/38, B; *John Hawker v. Alice & Thomas Hodges*, PRO Req 2/221/23, B.

[25] *Richard Walker v. Elizabeth Kirkland*, PRO Req 2/165/232.

of power they suffered in relation to their opponents, but rather than emphasise their own weakness or vulnerability they concentrated on the power, wealth or local influence of their opponents, which suggests they were perhaps more loathe than women to admit dependency on others.[26] They may also have lacked the vocabulary to do so, for while the expression 'poor widow' could conjure up a panoply of sympathetic imagery, the expression 'poor widower' was almost unknown.[27]

Joint pleadings, especially those entered by married couples, on the whole resembled men's rather than women's pleadings. Husbands and wives tended to concentrate attention on the power as well as the impropriety of their opponents, and few couples made poverty the mainspring of their actions.[28] However, it is interesting that a number of married plaintiffs drew attention to the supposed vulnerability of wives prior to marriage. A newly married husband and wife, Thomas and Maude Daniel of Ickford in Buckinghamshire, claimed dower in lands due to Maude from a previous marriage by stressing that this interest constituted, 'the onely thinge where upon she was to lyve and to maynteyne her poore estate withall'. It is as if they hoped to gain retrospective sympathy for Maude's poverty when she was widowed and *sole*, even though she was now married and supported by her new husband.[29] In another Ickford case, Thomas and Emma Blaggrove brought an action to recover from Thomas Tipping an indenture which gave Emma a life interest in lands in the parish. They described the fraudulent dealings Tipping had used to deprive Emma of her interest while she was a widow, and explained that Emma had accepted these arrangements, 'beinge a verey symple womann and verey fearefull to staund in sute and [contempte?] of Lawe with her Lorde'. Their depiction of Emma's fear and ignorance, and the fact that she waited until she married before suing, provide interesting collateral support for the observations about

---

[26] A Somerset tenant explained that he could not have 'indifferent tryall' in the manor court against his brother Peter because the 'offycers of the said mannor nowe beinge are the verye speciall ffrends and favourers of the said Peter and do not onelye further and ayde hym in hys said pretensed title But also do asmoche as in them ys to hynder and withstande the said title and intereste of youre highnes said subjecte'; *Alexander ffarthinge* v. *Peter ffarthinge*, PRO Req 2/207/6, [m. 9], B; male defendants, by contrast, sometimes accused their opponents of taking advantage of their poverty; *Alice Gibbes* v. *Ambrose Butler*, PRO Req 2/209/18.

[27] Whereas Alice Walley could argue that her opponents were seeking to weary, oppress and terrify her, 'being A widowe wantinge sufficient experience and capacitie to defend suche ynjurie', there was no obvious male equivalent; *Michael Keynton et al.* v. *Alice Walley*, PRO Req 2/231/24, m. 3, A.

[28] The Craces, for example, alleged they came to Requests because William Stokes was 'a man of greate welthe and greatlye ffrynded with dyvers of the Chapter of Wells and with the offycers of the same'; *Thomas & Johanne Crace* v. *William Stokes*, PRO Req 2/188/62, m. 13, B; for examples of couples describing themselves as 'verie pore people utterlie unable and insufficient to prosecute anie sute in law' against opponents 'of such grete might ritches & power', see *John & Mary Fyppen* v. *Edward Nevell et al.*, PRO Req 2/207/82, B; *Albyn & Mary Willoughby* v. *Elizabeth Earthe et al.*, PRO Req 2/283/59, R.

[29] *Thomas & Maude Daniel* v. *Christopher & Margaret Rendal*, PRO Req 2/199/13.

the apparent reluctance of certain women to litigate alone, identified in chapters 5 and 6 above. Although the defendants argued with equal passion that Emma was a capable woman who had surrendered her interest voluntarily for profit, and they cited a verdict against her at common law as proof.[30]

That women protested their poverty more often and more vigorously than men is not altogether surprising, given the numbers of women in Elizabethan England who lived in poverty.[31] But against the possibility that women's pleadings simply reflected actual conditions must be set the sceptical reception many opponents gave to women's tales of poverty and impotence. We have already seen in previous chapters how the opponents of Susan Ashley rejected her claims that she was an innocent victim manipulated by her father, and how Alice Gyle's tale of violent oppression was rebuffed with claims that it was she who had been the oppressor.[32] When a woman from Bath claimed that she was a poor widow 'wantinge sufficient experience and capacitie' to defend herself at law, her opponents insisted that she was a woman of considerable substance who could better serve God by relieving them.[33] The defendant John Drewe likewise refuted the claims of his widowed daughter-in-law, Alice Drewe, that she had no lands for the maintenance of herself or her children, by saying that *he* had maintained the children, and that Alice controlled a tenement and a lease worth £110.[34] In another case a defendant challenged a woman's bill of complaint for 'beinge drawen into a needlesse lengthe with vayne protestacions of povertie and other idle suggestions', while Humfrey Stafford accused his wife Elizabeth of attempting to 'hide under a surmysed pretence of symplycytye'.[35]

Defendants in other cases used simple economic logic to question women's assertions of poverty. In the claim Elizabeth Banks made in Requests for unpaid wages, mentioned in chapter 5 above, Banks' employer asked the Masters to consider that if, as she alleged, she had arrived at his house without a shilling and had never been paid a penny in wages during her long years of service, how then had she kept herself during those long years, and how had she acquired the considerable quantity of money and goods that she alleged he was detaining from her?[36] In a claim for widow's estate, Eleanor Harris described how the

---

[30] *Thomas & Eme Blaggrove als Osborne v. John Hubard & Thomas Typpynge*, PRO Req 2/174/33, B, A; I would like to thank Dr Tewson and Herb Dover for enlightening me about the Tippings of Ickford.

[31] Tim Wales found that up to 70 per cent of the recipients of poor relief in seventeenth century Norfolk were widows; Tim Wales, 'Poverty, poor relief and the life-cycle: some evidence from seventeenth-century Norfolk', in Richard Smith, ed., *Land, Kinship and Life-Cycle* (London, 1984), Table 11.3, p. 361.   [32] See chapters 5 and 6 above.

[33] *Michael Keynton et al. v. Alice Walley* PRO Req 2/231/24, m. 2, R, m. 3, A.

[34] *William Cattcot & Alice Drewe v. John Drewe*, PRO Req 2/189/18, B, A; William Cattcot was Alice's father.

[35] *Thomas Good v. Elizabeth Shipper*, PRO Req 2/123/53, m. 7, A; *Elizabeth Stafforde v. Humfrey Stafforde*, PRO Req 2/166/171.   [36] *Elizabeth Bankes v. Thomas Gowen*, PRO Req 2/182/11, A.

farmer of the manor forcibly kept her from her rightful inheritance under custom, to the detriment of herself and her eight children. The farmer, however, responded with a different story. He asserted not only that Eleanor had no right to the land, but that when he had offered her £60, 'for charyties sake', as a gift 'to the poore children of the said Harrys', on condition that she promise in writing to leave £40 of it to her children, she had refused him. Furthermore, according to witnesses she had twice come with men and illegally harvested his wheat, on one occasion assaulting a deponent with a corn pike. By his account she was not a poor widow anxious to support her hungry offspring, but a violent and unruly woman who put her own greed before the needs of her children.[37]

While some widows sought to gain mileage from the image of the poor deserving widow, appealing to the sense of Christian charity embodied in Latimer's cry of solace, 'you widowes, you Orphanes, you pore people, here is a comfortable place for you', many of their opponents offered a more cynical view, closer in tone to Thomas Overbury's jest that should a widow live to be thrice married, 'shee seldome failes to cozen her second Husbands Creditors'.[38] The accusations and counter-accusations parties presented add weight to Linda Pollock's contention that 'both men and women manipulated the ideology of women to achieve particular objectives', and demonstrate how opponents in legal actions did everything within their power to expose this manipulation.[39] It is interesting in this context to consider the advice of Leonard Cox in *The Art or Crafte of Rhetoryke*, a book 'very necessary to all such as wyll eyther be advocates and proctoures in the lawe'. In describing the attributes of the judicial oration, Cox reported that during the confirmation 'we must loke upon the sex/ whether it be man or woman that we accuse/ to se[e] yf any argument can be deducte out of it to our purpose, As in men is noted audacite/ women be comonly tymerouse'.[40]

It would seem, then, that genuinely poor women flocked to Requests, and not so poor women pleaded poverty and weakness more often and in different ways than men. The images of poverty they presented depended on their marital status; single women and widows, women 'without men' in a society dominated by patriarchs, made far more of their vulnerable states than married women. Men, by contrast, usually pleaded their impotence only if they were orphaned or aged, not if they were unmarried or widowed, and on the whole they tended

---

[37] *Eleoner Harris v. Hughe Rudge & John Graye*, PRO Req 2/218/14, B, A, D, deponent John Salmon.

[38] Thomas Overbury, *His Wife: With Additions of New Characters, and Many Other Wittie Conceits* (London, 1627), p. 205.   [39] Pollock, 'Teach her to live under obedience', p. 251.

[40] Cox (who based his work on Melanchthon's *Institutiones Rhetoricae* (1521)) illustrated his point with the following example; 'I am a woman and a yonge mayden/ mylde and gentyll/ both by nature and yeres. My softe handes are nat apte to fyers batayles [fierce battles]'; Leonard Cox, *The Art or Crafte of Rhetoryke* (London, 1532), sigs A2ᵛ, E1ʳ⁻ᵛ.

not to stress their own weakness more than was necessary, preferring instead to focus attention on the strength of their opponent. These reflections on the pleading styles of men and women are interesting, but necessarily impressionistic, and problems with deciphering formulaic language remain. Did practised ears hear, but take little notice of, phrases like 'to her utter impoverishment'? Did the concentration of half a dozen conventional phrases about poverty in a plaintiff's bill mean that the litigant was especially poor, that their counsel wanted the court to think that they were especially poor, or on the contrary, that they were in fact wealthy enough to afford a long and detailed bill? General patterns can be discerned in the records, but exceptions abound, and conclusions must remain limited. To determine with more certainty some of the other pleading strategies litigants adopted, it is necessary to alter the focus of study; to look not simply at men and women, but at specific groups of litigants, and to look not just at metaphors of power, but at the other kinds of information litigants and counsel marshalled to their causes.

MAPPING HIGH AND LOW MORAL GROUND

One of the major attractions of 'English bill' equity courts for litigants was the willingness of Masters and the Chancellor to look beyond the black letter of the law and the dry ink of conditions in bonds, leases and other written agreements, to the personal circumstances of individuals. What is surprising to modern onlookers is the diversity of the information that litigants and their counsel thought sufficiently pertinent to include in pleadings. As previous chapters have shown, in their efforts to provide context for their own actions, and to question the actions and motivations of their opponents, litigants ranged far beyond strictly legal arguments. The richness of the ensuing detail, and the uses to which it can be put, can best be illustrated by looking in detail at an example, in this case the rather extraordinary suit (mentioned in passing in chapter 6) in which Katherine Willoughby sued two of her former husbands, Kenelm Willoughby and Henry Fenner. The point at issue in this case was the status of a £20 annuity that Kenelm owed Katherine for maintenance since their separation: she claimed that he refused to pay it; he claimed that Henry Fenner, her second husband, had released it. However, details of the annuity barely featured in the extensive pleadings. In their bill, answers, replication, rejoinder, interrogatories and depositions, Katherine and Kenelm (and to a lesser extent Henry) concentrated their attentions on the general demeanour of each party. In effect they put each other's characters on trial, leaving the Masters to judge them on their performance of, or on their failure to perform, the duties expected of husband and wife. Katherine and Kenelm argued the worth of their own behaviour and the shortcomings of their opponent's, not just in the dealings which surrounded the creation of the annuity, but throughout their marriage and subsequent separation. The result is a revealing balance sheet of merit and worth, credit and reputation, which provides a valuable example of the way one couple presented ideal and flawed pictures of marital behaviour to the Masters of a central court.

Katherine kept her descriptions of her behaviour brief. She had brought Kenelm a dowry of £300, plus £100 in goods, and during their time together she had behaved 'in all dutyfull manner' towards him and had mothered thirteen children. A deponent said he had never heard that Katherine had ever 'used or behaved herself otherwise then well' during or indeed since her marriage.[41] Her descriptions of Kenelm's behaviour, by contrast, were extensive. She accused him of 'loose' living and claimed he beat her, and wasted his substance by spending more on women of evil fame than on her. He had fathered a child with his mother's maid and had made violent threats against Katherine until she could bear no more.[42] '[E]ntering into consideracion with hir selfe of the con-tynuall torments and daunger shee lyved in, [she] resolved with hirselfe rather to take some smale mayntenaunce of him, and so to lyve with some of hir owne kyndred, then to lyve still with him in discontent.' She moved to her brother's house, and had to rely on his support after Kenelm refused to honour his promise of maintenance. Kenelm, meanwhile, had approached an acquaintance, Henry Fenner, and convinced him that Katherine was divorced and that he should propose marriage to her. Fenner proposed and Katherine (believing herself to be lawfully divorced) accepted, regarding his apparent wealth as her salvation during her time of poverty and distress. Once married, Kenelm persuaded Fenner to sell Katherine's annuity for a small sum. To make doubly sure, Kenelm tricked his former wife into signing a release of her rights in the annuity, by convincing her she was signing an acquittance for a loan of 40s.[43]

Katherine presented herself as a model wife, one who had loved and respected her husband and blessed him with money and children. By reason of her dowry and exemplary behaviour she warranted maintenance, and she had done nothing that might bar her from receiving it.[44] Kenelm, meanwhile, was a base rogue. The subject of Katherine's plea to Requests was not the breach of any specific agreement, but the continuing failure of an immoral, deceitful husband to keep his wife.

Kenelm, not surprisingly, responded with a different story. He described how it had been his 'most myserable and unfortunate Chaunce, or rather the will and pleasure of god soe fair, to punyshe' him, that had led him to marry

---

[41] *Katheren Willoughbie* v. *Kenelm Willoughbie & Henry Fenne*, PRO Req 2/31/3, m. 1, D, deponent William Dutton.   [42] Kenelm's main threat is described in the next chapter.

[43] *Katheren Willoughbie* v. *Kenelm Willoughbie & Henry Fenne*, PRO Req 2/286/45, m. 4, B.

[44] Katherine even stressed that she and Fenner had spent the small amount of money which accrued from the sale of the annuity on medical treatment to save the life of one of Kenelm's sick children; *Katheren Willoughbie* v. *Kenelm Willoughbie & Henry Fenne*, PRO Req 2/286/45, B.

Katherine. He told the Masters that her dowry had amounted not to £300, but to £200, paid in lots of 20s., 30s. and 40s., 'and soe by dribletts' over ten or twelve years that it did the defendant 'lyttle good'. His contributions had far exceeded hers. He had brought up, educated, advanced and apprenticed five of their surviving children and paid for two daughters' weddings. He had maintained Katherine for twenty years, keeping her, in the words of one deponent, 'better than his estate and maintenance could beare', while she went out of her way to cost him money. Having dispatched Katherine's claims that she was a financial asset, he moved on to attack her credentials as a good wife, fixing on her sexual infidelity. '[A]s the voice of the cuntrey went shee lived Incontynently', declared one deponent. Another described how Kenelm had acquired letters Katherine had sent to London offering sexual favours to a new lover and demanding 50s. in wages from an old one, 'which shee pretended should bee paid her for spynnynge'. Servants reported that she left doors unbolted 'in the dead tyme of the night' and had installed a false window in her house, to form 'a previe passage for her customers to leap out at, if they shold bee suddenly surprised'.[45]

Kenelm painted a detailed picture of Katherine, representing her as the very antithesis of a model wife. According to his depiction, she was outspoken, disloyal, extravagant and so sexually incontinent that she resembled a common prostitute. To deliver himself of 'so great and cumbersome a burden', he had agreed to grant her an annuity. She then chose to marry Fenner, who had sold the annuity to fund his ailing business. In short, Kenelm argued, he had faultlessly performed his duties as a husband, while Katherine remained a dangerous, independent woman to whom it would be reckless for the Masters to grant maintenance.[46]

What is extraordinary about the pleadings of both sides in this case is the sheer weight of accusation they contain. Neither party was content simply to outline his or her claim to the annuity, and to describe the illegal or deceitful actions of their opponent. They went to lengths to amass volumes of claims and counter-claims, trying to better their opponent in the quantity as well as the quality of their allegations of proven immorality. Their aim was not so much to prove a single criminal or immoral act, but rather to demonstrate, by weight of example, that the other party had a deep-seated immoral propensity, an incurable 'criminal streak'.

Katherine and Kenelm achieved their ends by aligning themselves at opposite ends of a moral spectrum. They sought to show how their own conduct con-

---

[45] *Katheren Willoughbie* v. *Kenelm Willoughbie & Henry Fenne*, PRO Req 2/286/45, m. 3, A; Req 2/163/155 [mm. 3, 4, 5, 6], D, deponents Robert Feilder, Alice Woodgate, Mathew Waters, Richard Rogers.

[46] *Katheren Willoughbie* v. *Kenelm Willoughbie & Henry Fenne*, PRO Req 2/286/45, m. 3, A.

formed to standards of acceptable behaviour, and how their opponent's conduct fell short of these standards, and what emerge from the pleadings are four distinct character portraits: good wife; bad wife; good husband; bad husband. In a world where individuals commonly made sense of their surroundings by reference to social, moral and religious opposites, and regularly judged themselves, events and other people in terms of their relationship to ideal types, this sharp cleaving of personal morality and social behaviour into 'good' and 'bad' comes as little surprise. The tendency for people to organise their views of the world, and to structure arguments, in terms of antithetical extremes, whether good and evil, God and the Devil, Christ and Antichrist, order and chaos, heaven and hell or the elect and the damned, was becoming increasingly common in the later sixteenth century.[47] Within the pages of his popular rhetorical guide to letter writing, *The English Secretorie*, for example, Angel Day described 'the causes of praise and dispraise', explaining how people's deeds can be designated '*Honestum* or *Inhonestum*, under which is comprehended what is just or unjuste, godlye or wicked, direct or indirect'. In Day's careful division of society, persons were 'temperate & sober in demeanour, or otherwise accompted dissolute & wanton'. Deeds were either good or bad, there was no middle ground. Describing how best to depict a person's character in correspondence, he had the following to say: 'In commendation or vituperation of the deeds of any one we shall weigh with our selves what notable actions have been, wherein he or shee have honourably behaved them-selves, or by perpetuall infamye thereof have deserved in each posterity for ever to be remembered.'[48]

This, in effect, is exactly what the authors of pleadings set about achieving, marking down details of the honourable aspects of their own behaviour alongside the 'infamye' of their opponents. What is interesting is the extent to which all sides agreed on the standards expected of certain individuals. The Willoughbys, for example, were at one over the ideal roles of husbands and wives, their vehement disagreement was over whether either party had fulfilled their assigned role. Suddenly, from the cacophony of disagreement and contra-

---

[47] Karen Newman, *Fashioning Femininity and English Renaissance Drama* (Chicago and London, 1991), pp. 18–25; Richard Cust and Ann Hughes, eds., *Conflict in Early Stuart England: Studies in Religion and Politics 1603–1642* (London, 1989), pp. 17–18; Patrick Collinson, *The Birthpangs of Protestant England: Religious and Cultural Change in the Sixteenth and Seventeenth Centuries* (London, 1988), pp. 147–8; examples of this didactic thinking can be found everywhere, from ballads to borrowings from the bible; Tessa Watt, *Cheap Print and Popular Piety, 1550–1640* (Cambridge, 1991), plate 49, pp. 248–9; Christopher Hill, *The English Bible and the Seventeenth-Century Revolution* (London, 1993), pp. 284, 310, 322 and *passim*; and see Callaghan, *Woman and Gender*, pp. 10–13.

[48] Angell Daye, *The English Secretorie. Wherein is Contayned, a Perfect Method, for the Inditing of All Manner of Epistles and Familiar Letters* (London, 1586) (facsimile edition; Menston, Yorks., 1967), pp. 59–60; Day's book was one of the most popular sixteenth century guides to the rhetoric of writing, reprinted eleven times between 1586 and 1635, and was almost certainly read by lawyers.

diction it is possible to detect a clear note of agreement, one that can be amplified by considering and comparing other cases involving husbands and wives.[49]

The archive of Requests contains examples of cases covering the full range of human interactions within society. By focusing on the relationships of complainants and defendants (rather than just the subjects of their disputes) it becomes possible to build up an idea of the universally understood criteria by which litigants judged the behaviour of others within a whole variety of relationships, not just the intense, personal relationship of marriage. For example, how clients expected attorneys and solicitors to behave, the respect parents and children demanded of one another, the expectations apprentices had of their masters (and vice versa), and in light of the previous chapter, the obligations customary tenants and lords and ladies of the manor felt they owed each other.[50] For the purposes of this chapter, court materials can show how women described themselves and their place in relationships in different ways from men, and how male and female litigants were open to different accusations, and had different defences at their disposal. They can also reveal the special expectations that parties attached to dealings with close family and distant kin and the stress they placed on trust when dealing with strangers and professionals. Before considering these wider questions, it is worth looking more closely at what we can learn from cases fought between, or which made reference to the relationship between, wives and husbands.

The first theme that arises from the Willoughby pleadings, and from the records of other marital disputes, is the importance that wives and husbands placed on economic considerations in the making and breaking of marriage; firstly in the provision or acquisition of money and property, and secondly in the management and dispersal of money and property. Fierce disagreements about the value of dowries, the adequacy of maintenance and the desire for economic parity of resources are as revealing as they are predictable. It is interesting, for example, how often parties linked their arguments about the provision of property and funds to questions of social status and class. The Masters of Requests looked to Richard Puttenham's means when they calculated the maintenance he should pay to his estranged wife Mary. Richard, however, was adamant that they should calculate payments in accordance with *Mary's* means and the social status of her family. He said that she had brought nothing to marriage, not even 'a gallie halfepennie', and yet she 'impudently

---

[49] The fact that husbands and wives appealed to such stark and conventional images of good and bad behaviour suggests that they were distorting the truth. But the fact that they appealed to the *same* conventional images means that their pleadings provide useful examples of the use of ideal and defective types outside of a purely literary setting.

[50] Thomas Chaffyn, for example, denied the copyhold claim of Roger Ellis, saying that Ellis had failed to do suit to the courts held at his manor, 'nor had not behaved himself as A customery Tenante of the said Manor'; *Roger, Mawde & Johan Elys v. Thomas Chaffyn*, PRO Req 2/202/36 [m. 9], A.

craveth twise or thrise so much to lyve on alone . . . as her father, mother, brothers, systers and herselfe were wonte and fayne to lyve on all together'.[51] In marriage she had risen to his social level, but according to Richard's view of equity, in separation she should return to her own. Dame Margery Acton claimed maintenance from her husband by itemising everything that her husband had gained by marrying her. Almost all of it, from money, plate and property to the lucrative office of Her Majesty's saddler, came from her father.[52]

When Anne Lloyd sued her husband Humfrey, she went to considerable lengths to establish her social credentials, explaining how she was a gentlewoman of good birth and parentage, the sister of Leyson Evans Esquire, and had been married twice before, to gentlemen 'of speciall creditt, [worth], and estymacion in their countrey'. It was this background that had allowed her to bring to the marriage sixty cattle, 200 sheep, £400 in money and lands worth £40 per annum, and which made Humfrey's failure to keep her in a manner reflecting her status all the more unforgivable.[53] Battles of this kind took place up and down the social register. Joan Spragin said that she was 'descended of good parentage', while her estranged husband Martin was 'A man of base byrth and a bad condicion'. Martin responded by denying that there was any 'dyspargemente' for Joan, 'beinge a tapsters dawghter to be maryed to the sonne of an honeste yeoman', especially as she had '[not] one penny to her porcyon nor yet clothes worth the namynge to her backe at the tyme of her marryage'.[54]

Recent studies have contrasted male concerns about honour in the past, based on birth, wealth, demeanour, ideals of chivalry, occupation and creditworthiness, with far narrower concepts of female honour based almost exclusively on chastity and sexual reputation.[55] The importance of sexual reputation to women was undeniable, however the lengthy defences women constructed in civil actions present a more complex view of female honour and self-worth; depending on their social standing, women made much of their employment, their financial independence and their reputations as moneylenders. Married women like Katherine Willoughby emphasised their skills as household managers, as parents and educators of their children and as exemplary wives to their husbands even under the most trying conditions. In an inheritance dispute between Joan French, the widow of William French a London wine porter, and Alice Pinchbeck, William's sister, Joan described how she had advanced William financially, both before and during marriage, and had been such a model wife in all respects that he had named her his executrix. Alice

---

[51] PRO Req 1/14, fol. 279.   [52] *Margery Acton* v. *Robert Acton*, PRO Req 2/14/53, B.
[53] *Anne Lloyd* v. *Humfrey Lloyde*, PRO Req 2/234/61.
[54] *Johane Spraggen* v. *Martyn Spraggyn et al.*, PRO Req 2/273/67, m. 5, A, m. 6, B.
[55] Laura Gowing, for example, writes of sexual conduct being 'the entire foundation of women's honour' and 'the only measure of their marital conduct'; Gowing, *Domestic Dangers*, p. 180; although see Laura Gowing, 'Women, status and the popular culture of dishonour', *Transactions of the Royal Historical Society*, 6th series, 6 (1996), pp. 225–6, 234.

responded by saying that Joan had lived with her husband, 'very unquietly giveing the said William greate occasion of disquietnes, neither giveing [him] sufficient necessaries in the time of his sicknes and in such sorte as a good loveing and dutifull wief ought to have done', leading him to reconsider her appointment as executrix.[56] Exchanges like these suggest that women's self-respect and sense of reputation grew out of an expansive criteria of behaviour and demeanour, and that female honour, no less than male honour, was dependent to a considerable degree on social rank.[57]

So much for the provision of wealth and property, what of its spending? Parties in maintenance actions almost always depicted their partners as economic liabilities. According to the volleys of claims and counter claims in pleadings, bad husbands failed to maintain their wives and wasted family capital on gambling and other sinful enterprises, while bad wives squandered their husbands' substance and spent far more than they had brought with them to marriage. The arguments spouses directed against one another had a moral as well as a purely economic dimension, implicitly suggesting that financial profligacy was a mark of general degeneracy. According to Kenelm Willoughby and his witnesses, Katherine lived so wastefully, 'by rydinge and gaddinge abrode without his consent', that he was forced to spend 100 marks a year to keep her. She had sold household provisions to help fund her extravagant lifestyle, and had tried to persuade servants to tell lies on her behalf in the hope that Kenelm would increase her allowance. In reply, Katherine described how Kenelm returned from overseas, where he had fled to avoid prosecution in the church courts for fathering a child, and immediately resumed his former course of life, 'still spending & wasting his substance in maynteninge of them [his mistresses] and gevinge your subject lytle or noe mayntenance at all'.[58] Where husbandry and huswifery manuals urged frugal, sensible and sober management of farms, property, and household provisioning, husbands and wives in Requests accused each other of the opposite, of waste in all things.[59]

Wives and husbands used the logic and language of contract to express all manner of grievances, as if marriage and its obligations were conditions

---

[56] *Joane Frenche v. Alice Pynchback*, PRO Req 2/164/60 [m. 3], A.

[57] Faramerz Dabhoiwala, 'The construction of honour, reputation and status in late seventeenth- and early eighteenth-century England', *Transactions of the Royal Historical Society*, 6th series, 6 (1996), p. 208; Garthine Walker, 'Expanding the boundaries of female honour in early modern England', *Transactions of the Royal Historical Society*, 6th series, 6 (1996), pp. 235–45; for a broader view of male honour and reputation, see Elizabeth Foyster, 'The concept of male honour in seventeenth century England' (University of Durham Ph.D., 1996).

[58] *Katheren Willoughbie v. Kenelm Willoughbie & Henry Fenne*, PRO Req 2/286/45, m. 3, A; PRO Req 2/163/155, D, deponent Robert Feilder.

[59] A woman who married for the second time described how a use had been created for her benefit because her first husband had been 'but a yonge mane and unstayed and whose thryftinesse and frugallitye was uncertaine'; *John & Maude Bluet v. John Baber*, PRO Req 2/178/55, B; see also Foyster, 'A laughing matter?' pp. 8, 12–13.

attached to a bond. Joan French described how she had laid out money on her husband's behalf while he was sick, and in return she 'did assuredly hope and beleve to be recompenced & regarded by her said husband, not onely with [his] love & good opinion . . . but also accordinge to all equitie & good conscience with the best and greateste parte of his welthe & estate'.[60] Parties included anything they could within this currency of marriage, even their children. Warring spouses itemised the money they had spent on their children's maintenance, education, marriages and portions, and contrasted this with the inadequacy of their partners' contributions. When wives or husbands had been married before, they were quick to suggest that their spouses were unduly neglecting or favouring children from former marriages. Some parents depicted children not only as costs, but also as contributions. Mothers emphasised how many children they had borne, as if to stress that they had fulfilled their maternal role in the marital bargain. In the same way that Katherine Willoughby spoke of the thirteen children Kenelm 'had by her', Anne Chapman was presented in pleadings as a gentlewoman who had provided her husband with a good portion and 'divers children', which together were the 'meanes to have contynued love and lykeinge' between herself and her husband. The suggestion here was that while Anne had completed her side of the contract, her husband had reneged on his.[61] Humfrey Stafford, by contrast, made much of his wife Elizabeth's failure to provide an heir to carry on the Stafford name, saying that he had been 'now left destytute, contrary to his expectacion and truste upon maryage had withe the said Complainant, without issue of his boddy lawfully begotten to inherryt his landes and possessyons'. Perhaps to imply that Elizabeth was unwilling, rather than unable, to bear him a child, Humfrey also reported how one of her lovers, Robert Brown, had confessed that 'yf she were delyvered of a childe, wheche then she and the saide Browne thought her to be withall . . . That the Childe was his the saide Roberts. And that he the said Robert was father thereof. Whereby yt maye well appere that he was well pryvye to the getting thereof.'[62]

Adultery

Humfrey Stafford's allegations about his wife and Robert Brown move the discussion on from economics to sexual infidelity. Questions of parity in wealth and status, of the legal duty of husbands to maintain their wives, and of wives' performance of their roles as household managers, loyal spouses and nurturing mothers, were all of deep importance to the men and women involved in court actions, but rarely did they result in legally sanctioned separation. The same is true of the question of whether or not a union had been blessed with children.

---

[60] *Joane Frenche v. Alice Pynchback*, PRO Req 2/164/60 [m. 4], B.
[61] *John Chapman v. Chrystofer Preston & Anne Chapman*, PRO Req 2/193/16 [m. 1], A.
[62] *Elizabeth Stafforde v. Humfrey Stafforde*, PRO Req 2/166/171.

For a separation *a mensa et thoro*, the church courts required proof of adultery or cruelty, and it is no coincidence that almost every separation case in Requests involved allegations of sexual impropriety.[63] Wives accused their husbands of adultery almost as often as husbands accused their wives. In some cases the accusations appear to have been 'tit for tat', as if the best way to meet a claim of infidelity was with a similar claim. In the Lloyd case, for example, it may be significant that a clause in Anne's bill of complaint accusing Humfrey of, 'lyving a moste loose and licencyous a lief by many monethes past, the detecting whearof were not fytt to be in particulers revealed without greate oblquay and disgrace' was struck out, presumably under advice from the counsel who signed the bill.[64] However, while both wives and husbands accused each other of adultery, the operation of the 'double standard' – the community belief that male fornication and adultery were less threatening to the stability of families and of society than female fornication and adultery (even though most writers believed they were equally sinful) – meant that accusations were invariably more damaging when directed against women, and litigants worded their allegations accordingly.[65]

While many husbands made adultery the linchpin of their arguments, wives were restricted to presenting sexual infidelity merely as further evidence of their husbands' immoral characters. Wives' allegations could be elaborate: Elizabeth Stafford not only described Humfrey's adulterous relations with a maidservant and his fathering of a child, she revealed how he had sacked servants, slandered acquaintances and falsely accused her of infidelity, all in an attempt to hide his double life. Moreover, such accusations appear to have carried considerable weight: husbands went to lengths to deny charges of infidelity, because they recognised the potential of such claims to 'incense the ears of the Judges and so discredit' the accused.[66] However, adultery alone was never sufficient to justify a woman separating from her husband or to ground an order for maintenance. Hence women tied accusations of adultery to other complaints against their husbands, notably violence, and used them to emphasise not only sexual betrayal, but other kinds of betrayal as well. Katherine Willoughby, for example, brought economics into the frame when she accused Kenelm of spending more on women of evil fame than he spent on her, and Elizabeth Stafford raised questions of honour and status when she accused Humfrey of keeping his maidservant mistress 'in apparell and jewells like unto the complainant'.[67]

[63] Exceptions include *Issabell Osmoderley v. William Osmoderly*, PRO Req 2/24/82; *Margery Acton v. Robert Acton*, PRO Req 2/14/53.

[64] *Anne Lloyd v. Humfrey Lloyde*, PRO Req 2/234/61, m. 1; see also *John Chapman v. Chrystofer Preston*, PRO Req 2/185/7, Dem (second demurrer).

[65] On the influence of the double standard, and the critical difference questions of gender made to marriage and marital relations, see Thomas, 'The double standard', pp. 195–216; Gowing, *Domestic Dangers*, chs. 1, 3, 4, 6, 7, 8.

[66] *Elizabeth Stafforde v. Humfrey Stafforde*, PRO Req 2/166/171.

[67] *Katheren Willoughbie v. Kenelm Willoughbie*, PRO Req 2/163/155; *Elizabeth Stafforde v. Humfrey Stafforde*, PRO Req 2/166/171.

Men might evade allegations of adultery, but women usually could not.[68] The power of the accusation of female adultery was such that a single instance of alleged infidelity could provide grounds for separation and the denial of maintenance. Yet, as the Willoughby case demonstrated, most husbands went further and set down a whole catalogue of their wives' adulterous liaisons. The extraordinary volume of accusation suggests that husbands were concerned with more than simply proving transgression. It seems that they wished to shock the court with the scale of their wives' abandon, and so demonstrate that these women were beyond redemption. However, there may be other reasons why men chose to mark out the excessiveness of their wives' sexual appetites. Whenever a husband accused his wife of adultery, he admitted to the world that he was a cuckold. This raised the possibility that his wife had been unfaithful out of frustration at his inability to satisfy her, and husbands may have emphasised the extraordinary nature of their wives' sexuality in an attempt to deflect attention away from their own sexual reputations.[69] When accusing their wives of adultery, some husbands revealed details that in any other circumstances might have been demeaning. Humfrey Stafford, for example, reported how one of his wife's lovers had confessed 'that by his expresse worddes syxe tymes in one nighte to have to doe with her', and Kenelm Willoughby called a deponent who reported an admission by Katherine that she 'could not live without a man'. Husbands set out not only to prove adultery, but to show that their wives were guilty of 'abominable whoredom'.[70]

There were other reasons why husbands devoted so much attention to their wives' supposedly errant sexuality. By suggesting that their wives were shameless not only in their infidelity, but in their willingness to publicise that infidelity, married men called into question their wives' modesty and obedience as well as their chastity. Kenelm Willoughby complained that Katherine 'grewe to that ymodesty and impudent caryage of herself as that she was not onlie noted to be publiquelie infamous with divers lewde base persons, butt also secrettlie harbored them in this defendants howse without the privity of this defendant'. According to one deponent 'shee behaved her self so wickedly towards her husband . . . that many of their good frends and kynredd were greatly ashamed of the plaintiffs company, when shee came to their houses, or by chance mett with her abroade'.[71] According to Martin Spragin, his wife Joan had said that she would rather see him hanged than to forsake the company of her lover and another man, and her open acquaintance with these two men was 'to the greate

[68] Some women responded to allegations of adultery by describing successful defences by compurgation at the church courts; *Elizabeth Stafforde* v. *Humfrey Stafforde*, PRO Req 2/166/171.   [69] Foyster, 'A laughing matter?', pp. 8–10.
[70] *Elizabeth Stafforde* v. *Humfrey Stafforde*, PRO Req 2/166/171; *Katheren Willoughbie* v. *Kenelm Willoughbie*, PRO Req 2/163/155, D, deponent Robert Feilder.
[71] *Katheren Willoughbie* v. *Kenelm Willoughbie & Henry Fenne*, PRO Req 2/286/45, m. 3, A; PRO Req 2/163/155, D, deponent John Walker.

myslyke of the Inhabitants of the sayed towne'.[72] Humfrey Stafford alleged that one of his wife's lovers had committed suicide after confessing his adulterous behaviour to his uncle, yet Elizabeth had admitted in public 'her incontynent lyvinge and with whome and howe often'. Her behaviour at home caused 'great offence to the rest of the household', but her open admissions publicised the scandal and threatened the family name. Humfrey declared that he 'cowlde be in no Company but that eyther openly or by pryvate whyspering the Common fame labored of all her evell behavior in the premysses'. Elizabeth's brazenness, and her refusals to repent, appear to have incensed and shamed Humfrey as much as, or perhaps more than, her alleged adultery. Onlookers suspected, said Humfrey, that 'she hathe some secret comforte other wyise the saide complainant woulde be ashamed so openly to stande to the defense of her manifest and innummerable evells'. Nowhere was this more apparent than in her court actions themselves. Having commenced suit against him in the Court of Arches in London, 'in whiche Cyttye she once blussheth not for lacke of grace to knowe and heare of great numbers that withe open mowthe do talke and tell of her detestable vycyusnes', Elizabeth sued him in other courts 'for the further increase and augmentacon' of her 'comon evell fame'. She was not even ashamed 'to exhibyte her byll of Complaint to the prynce or Sovereigne lady and Mistress' in Requests.[73]

In the same way that some men may have exaggerated their wives' sexual exploits to avert attention away from themselves, others had similar motives for emphasising the scale of their wives' misdeeds and their repeated refusals to repent. For husbands who suggested that their wives were immodest and shameless simultaneously admitted their own failure as governors of their households. In the Willoughby case, for example, Kenelm explained how he had sent Katherine to live with her father, asking him to keep her in an 'honest place to restrayne her from her lewdnesse'. However, Katherine refused to be ordered by her father or her friends and fled to London, where she supposedly fell into her former life and 'fylthynesse'. By demonstrating that Katherine had shown contempt for the authority of her father, not just for himself, Kenelm could implicitly deny his own culpability; the reason he had been unable to control her was that she was simply uncontrollable.[74]

Violence

If the chief concern of husbands was their wives' sexual licence, the sin which wives complained of with the fiercest passion was violence against the

---

[72] *Johane Spraggen v. Martyn Spraggyn et al.*, PRO Req 2/273/67, A; see also *Thomas Reader v. Jane Lambert*, PRO Req 2/262/20, B.
[73] *Elizabeth Stafforde v. Humfrey Stafforde*, PRO Req 2/166/171. Unfortunately, the records of the Court of Arches for this year were destroyed in the Fire of London.
[74] *Katheren Willoughbie v. Kenelm Willoughbie & Henry Fenne*, PRO Req 2/286/45, m. 3, A; PRO Req 2/163/155, I, D, deponents Richard Rogers, Robert Feilder.

body.[75] We saw in chapter 6 how Anne Lloyd said that she had 'endured at her said husbands hands vile and inhumane maner of dealing . . . being day by daie . . . assaulted, beaten and wounded moste pyttyfully'.[76] If a servant had not restrained Martin Spragin he would have broken Joan's neck, alleged a deponent, and on another occasion 'he did break her head with a pestell and break her face and did sell her clothes from her backe. And that he so did often tymes.'[77] This equating of the selling of a wife's clothes with physical violence provides a powerful example of the indignities that a husband could inflict on his wife. The stories of violence are shocking, and they are not uncommon. As the law permitted men to use force to control their households, husbands did not have to deny that they had struck their wives. They did, however, go out of their way to deny beating or harming them. For while the law and some social commentators condoned corrective force, almost everyone, from moralists to the neighbours of battered wives, regarded violence on the scale described by wives in Requests as unacceptable.[78] Governance demanded control, and as Elizabeth Foyster has argued, while the ability to assert authority within the household was a constituent part of male honour, men who exercised their commanding powers too forcefully, or did so as a result of wild anger, risked dishonour.[79] Deponents in the Spragin case, for example, belittled Martin by accusing him of acting out of jealousy, and of beating Joan because she gave him good counsel and did 'persuade hym to be A good husbond and to provide for his servants suche things as were necessary'.[80] Opinions varied about where the line between justifiable and unjustifiable violence should be drawn, but husbands in court battles always rebutted accusations that placed them on the wrong side of this line, regardless of where it lay. Humfrey Stafford, for example, admitted striking Elizabeth 'for the evell government and behavior of her develyshe tongue in uttering many unsemely and Quarylus words', and for 'warninge or reformacion of her mannors and lyef', but he denied that he had ever beaten her with a 'coudgell' or punished her 'in any Rage or fury'.[81]

The Masters of Requests certainly took allegations of violent behaviour seriously. In the Lloyd case, as was shown in chapters 4 and 6, they ended up putting

---

[75] Susan Amussen has observed a similar pattern in separation actions before the church courts; Amussen, *An Ordered Society*, p. 128.

[76] *Anne Lloyd* v. *Humfrey Lloyde*, PRO Req 2/234/61, m. 1, B.

[77] *Johane Spraggen* v. *Richard Levens et al.*, PRO Req 2/275/80, D, deponent Faithe Wynsley.

[78] T.E., *The Lawes Resolutions of Womens Rights*, pp. 128–9; Susan Amussen, ' "Being stirred to much unquietness": violence and domestic violence in early modern England', *Journal of Women's History*, 6 (1994), pp. 71–2, 75–84; Dolan, *Dangerous Familiars*, pp. 34–7.

[79] Foyster, 'A laughing matter?', pp. 15–16; Elizabeth Foyster, 'Male honour, social control and wife beating in late Stuart England', *Transactions of the Royal Historical Society*, 6th series, 6 (1996), pp. 215–24; the following discussion owes much to Foyster's arguments in these articles.

[80] *Johane Spraggen* v. *Richard Levens et al.*, PRO Req 2/275/80, D, deponents William Baynard, Thomas Tyler, Faithe Wynsley.

[81] *Elizabeth Stafforde* v. *Humfrey Stafforde*, PRO Req 2/166/171.

their whole jurisdiction at risk in their efforts to protect Anne Lloyd from her violent husband. Humfrey Lloyd made no secret of the fact that he had hit Anne and he did not appear to regret it, judging by his comment in his demurrer that, 'yt woulde seeme straunge and somwhat hard that the husband for once strickinge of his wife shoulde be injoined to be from his wife', or to pay her maintenance while she lived apart from him. However, he fiercely denied Anne's allegations that he had 'day by daie' beaten and wounded her, and went to great lengths to explain why he had hit her. It is worth reproducing his words here, for they provide a husband's view of the duties and obligations he expected of his wife, as well as showing how Humfrey sought to defuse Anne's allegations of violence by painting himself as a man of patience and self-control. He said that Anne:

haveinge by the space of iii monenthes or therabouts denied unto this defendant to doe any of the offices of a wife, and refuseinge eyther to provide and prepare meats and other nesessaries into the defendants howse, or to suffer any other to doe the same, but in spendinge and lavishinge out of the defendants corne and goods and sellinge the same awaye to her owne use and the use of her former husbands children and other of her friends, and beinge then by this defendant in gentle mannor rebuked, shee the said complainant did give unto this defendant hard words not semely for a wife to doe, callinge him Roge, Rascall and such like and theruppon moved him to that for which he is nowe sorrye, and which if it were to doe againe he would not doe, namelye to stricke her [on] the cheeke or face with the back of his hand.[82]

Humfrey presented himself as a patriarch capable of governing his wife, and as a man of reason capable of governing his emotions, except when faced with unreasonable and sustained provocation.[83] He employed the rhetoric of restraint to minimise any possibility of tension between these two roles, emphasising Anne's failings while all but denying his own anger or fury.[84] He ended his demurrer by promising that he would show even more restraint in the future, despite the provocation he believed he had already endured, saying he 'alwaies was and wilbe reddie to receyve cherishe and maynteyne [Anne] in his owne house and dwellinge places as his owne wyfe without givinge anie offence unto hir *although she shoulde nowe occasion thereof as by this publique act and slaunder she hath donne*'.[85] The Masters remained unconvinced by his arguments, but the fact that he felt able to make them serves to demonstrate yet again the imbalance between the pleading options open to men and to women.

---

[82] *Anne Lloyde v. Humfrey Lloyde*, PRO Req 2/234/61, m. 2, A.

[83] It is interesting to contrast Humfrey's show of control and responsibility with Martin Ingram's finding that in five early seventeenth century cruelty cases from Wiltshire, every husband 'showed signs of mental disturbance or instability'; Ingram, *Church Courts*, p. 183.

[84] When violence resulted in actual murder, such excuses could not be sustained and murderers usually attempted to justify their actions by admitting a total *loss* of reason; Davis, *Fiction in the Archives*, pp. 36–8 (and for her comments on Shakespeare's *Romeo and Juliet*, see pp. 72–6); Dolan, *Dangerous Familiars*, p. 103.

[85] *Anne Lloyd v. Humfrey Lloyde*, PRO Req 2/234/61, m. 3, Dem; my emphasis.

For, as Laura Gowing has noted, 'while women's adultery was the epitome of dishonesty, men's violence could be argued to be honest'.[86]

Wives complained of the violent treatment they had suffered at the hands of their husbands, but they were not themselves immune from allegations of violence, even though such accusations were less frequent and usually took different forms. Rarely did husbands report assaults of the kind suffered by Joan Spragin or Anne Lloyd, presumably because they regarded it as demeaning to admit that their wives had beaten them. Such an admission would confirm that they could not control their wives, and unavoidably align them with the powerful stereotype, found in ballads, jest books and other literary texts, of the weak husband beaten by the strong wife, a stereotype with strong allusions to sexual inadequacy as well as compromised authority.[87] Consequently, attacks attributed to women were almost always life threatening, or they were carried out with the assistance of accomplices. Female violence was rarely presented as a physical response to immediate provocation, more often it was premeditated and often secretive. Husbands, for example, regularly accused their wives of trying to poison them. According to Humfrey Stafford, Elizabeth had told a lover who was contemplating marrying someone else: 'be not hasty. Tarry yow a whyle. For the said defendant ys but a yeres bird. By which wordes yt maye well appere what she ment.'[88] Kenelm Willoughby said that it was his discovery that Katherine was plotting 'by undue meanes to destroy and take away' his life that led him to banish her from his house. A magistrate who deposed on Kenelm's behalf reported that Katherine Willoughby had confessed to him 'Divillish practice to have bin attempted against the mother of the said Kelham [Kenelm] by takinge away her life, the whole Circomstances this deponent forbeareth for modesties sake to utter as things not fitt for chaste eares to heare'. According to hearsay from servants, she had also twice become pregnant by her lovers and on both occasions had sought a midwife and a servant to procure an 'untymely birth by violence to her bodie, and takinge of medicines to the distruction of the frute shee bare'. In the realm of unsubstantiated accusations, women were often calculating and dangerous. When they did not poison people's food, they often poisoned their minds, turning sons against their fathers, or making enemies of former friends.[89]

---

[86] Gowing, *Domestic Dangers*, p. 219.   [87] Foyster, 'A laughing matter?', pp. 11, 15.

[88] *Elizabeth Stafforde v. Humfrey Stafforde*, PRO Req 2/166/171; wives also accused husbands of being poisoners; *Johane Spraggen v. Martyn Spraggyn et al.*, PRO Req 2/275/80, I, D, deponent William Baynard; Bess of Hardwick and her husband both accused each other of using poison; Hogrefe, 'Legal rights of Tudor women', p. 104.

[89] Kenelm said he brought up his children 'untill they were withdrawne by the synister perswasyons of the plaintiff', and he accused Katherine of convincing his own son to murder him. Expressing his fear of her lovers and accomplices, he called her the 'wicked fountayne of all of theis myscheiffs and damnable practizes'; *Katheren Willoughbie v. Kenelm Willoughbie & Henry Fenne*, PRO Req 2/286/45, m. 3, A; PRO Req 2/163/155 [m.5], D, deponent Anne Woodgate; PRO Req 2/63/60, D, deponent George Ryvers.

Wives and husbands attacked each other by holding up for scrutiny behaviour of every kind, damning with rumour and insinuation when they could not damn with provable fact. Their systematic critiques of ideal roles and shattered expectations drew heavily on the wedding vows of the prayer book for inspiration, supplementing these promises with more general characterisations ranging from female modesty and concerns about women speaking, to men's propensity for impassioned violence. In almost every case control and self-discipline were crucial, whether in their observance or in their failure. When providing guidance for how to discern immorality, Angel Day wrote that: 'Whatsoever is furthering to a dissolute living, unbrideled luste, covetous tenacitie, prodigalitie, or detestable excesse. These and such like, as confounders of civilitie and humaine government, are confirmed to be unhonest.'[90] The 'unhonesty' of opponents was taken for granted, but as this discussion has shown, litigants revealed how this 'unhonesty' manifested itself in a complete breakdown of self-control in all matters, whether sexual behaviour, speech or financial dealings. The language parties employed is critical here. To Angel Day's 'unbridled', 'prodigalitie' and 'detestable excesse' can be added a whole lexicon of terms denoting waste, decay, profligacy or incontinence. Litigants accused each other of 'wasting and spending' or otherwise consuming valuable resources, of 'loose living', 'licentiousness' and 'unshamefastness', of being 'careless' and possessing a 'foule & corrupt conscyence', and of being unable to 'purge' themselves of their 'disordered and unquiett livinge'. Anne Chapman's husband 'was a man greatlye decayed by his owne willfullnes and thoroughe the lewde companye with whome he had assosiated hym selfe'.[91] While Joan French had attended her husband's funeral 'as her becommed', her husband's sister entered Joan's house with accomplices: 'And then & there moste violently & rudely they did behave themselves, threateninge & yll behavinge themselves towards the servants . . . and tossinge & tumblinge all the household stuff and goods . . . taking both there pleasures & Inventories thereof.'[92] While defences of character contained metaphors of containment, in attacks the dam wall burst, and modest, 'honeste and sober' individuals became loud, violent, 'unbridled' and 'incontinent'. All sides resorted to this common strategy, but once again women had a different, and usually a more limited, repertoire from which to draw, whether they were defending themselves or attacking the character of their opponents.

Kinship and trust

Passions rarely ran higher than they did in cases between wives and husbands. The intensity of feeling and the richness of detail mark out these pleadings as

[90] Daye, *English Secretorie*, p. 61.
[91] *John Chapman v. Christopher Preston & Anne Chapman*, PRO Req 2/193/16 [m. 1], A.
[92] *Joane Frenche v. Alice Pynchback*, PRO Req 2/164/60, B.

remarkable, but they were not unique. Many of the patterns of pleading identified in marital disputes recurred in other actions. Litigants questioned women's sexual honesty, for example, even in cases where adultery was not obviously an issue. Elizabeth Shipper's suits against Thomas Good concerned property transactions and alleged fraud, yet Good attacked Shipper as 'a woman moste infamous and of yll lyef & lewde behavyor' who had married a man named Baddam, 'he then havynge an other wyf lyvynge & dwellinge together in one howse at Brydstome' in Herefordshire, and lived with him 'most incontinently & ungodlie . . . goyng & coming from place to place'. Good also accused Shipper of luring his brother-in-law into her 'ungodly' house, and encouraging him to live in sin with 'a common strumpett' so that 'by the wickede & lewde company & councell of the sayd complainant' he was 'brought to forsake hys lawful wyf & children & be in the only state of myserye & beggynge'.[93] It should be noted, however, that attacks on women's sexuality, in cases where chastity or fidelity were not directly in issue, were relatively rare. Such claims might undermine a woman's credit, but usually they could do little to answer or discount allegations about bonds, leases, testamentary disputes and the like, and they are far less common in equity court than in church court archives.

A greater number of litigants challenged female opponents by invoking the supposed immodesty of women. In the Banks case, Thomas Gowen called his former servant 'the most slaunderous tongued woman that lyveth', and explained to the Masters that he had sacked her because 'she was soe owtragious in cursinge and soe lewde of behaviour and soe false', adding that he was keen to settle with her so that he could be 'honestly ridd of soe lewd impudent and clamorous [a] woman'.[94] Christopher Symcocks similarly alleged that Dame Mary Cheeke had 'outragiously & publickly used raling & revyling speeches against & to this diffendant', so that it seemed to him 'she beareth her selfe soe bould in her greatnes, as what she lusteth to speake or doe to this deffendant should be for a lawe'. He went on to say that 'yf the very dyvell should be the complainant he could noe more untrewly or slaundrously accuse or belye this defendant'.[95]

The major similarity between marital and other disputes, however, was that plaintiffs and defendants concentrated attention on the duties and expectations that attached to specific relationships. As we have seen, the relationships in question were not always those between plaintiffs and defendants. Christopher

---

[93] True to gender stereotype, Shipper responded to Good's attack on her sexual honesty by questioning his non-sexual honesty, alleging that he had committed perjury and encouraged others to commit it on his behalf; *Elizabeth Shipper* v. *Thomas Good & William Taylor*, PRO Req 2/39/60, m. 16, A.   [94] *Elizabeth Bankes* v. *Thomas Gowen*, PRO Req 2/182/11, A.

[95] *Mary Cheeke* v. *Christopher Symcocks*, PRO Req 2/47/36 [m. 28], A; in another case, Christopher Kenny accused the widow Joan Willyn of 'willfull misbehavior' that led to the breakdown of her marriage. Willyn responded by saying that such allegations were 'to the infamy of this complainant'; *Johan Willyn* v. *Christopher Keny et al.*, PRO Req 2/283/61.

Symcocks, for example, managed to invoke Dame Mary's relationship with her late husband. He told the Masters that he 'thinketh that the spirit of the said Henry Mackwilliam (if the deade knowe what the quicke doe) althoughe it be in hapie state, doth in sorte greeve at this ingratefull dealinge of his said late wyffe, and would that she should desiste and shun this unmeasurable & evell desyre to ransacke his frende'. Whereas her husband had observed his duty to provide hospitality, and been considerate to his trusted employees, Mary's mind was 'fully bent in the ende to praye uppon and wholly to devour this defendant without pitie'. In other words she was failing to live up to the standards of a model widow, and shaming the memory of her husband in the process.[96] The more intimate the relationship, the more intimate the details litigants provided in their pleadings, and the richest material for historians is undoubtedly found in cases between family members; quite simply, they had more stones to throw. Legal actions between parties who were related to one another were not uncommon. Inheritance suits and contests over copyhold interests, like those described in the previous chapter between widows and stepchildren, regularly brought kin into conflict. Furthermore, in a society where trust and credit were essential in financial dealings, kinship often had the effect of heightening levels of trust, leading individuals who needed loans or other kinds of credit to gravitate towards family.[97] When these arrangements went wrong, legal actions might result.

Every combination of kin link can be found in Requests, and almost all of them produced differences between male and female pleading strategies. There is space here to consider at length only one, the relationship between parents and children. Given the nature of inheritance, the restrictions of coverture, and the tendency for wives to outlive their husbands, children were more likely to find themselves in legal conflict with their mothers than their fathers, except, perhaps, in the case of stepchildren. Jane and Elizabeth Thompson sued their stepfather Robert Powe to recover the lease of a messuage in Holborn, and in their pleadings they held up for scrutiny his record as a stepfather, saying that he had contributed nothing at all to their upbringing, 'but in greate extreamyte hath turned them owte of the dores, whereby they have bene dryven to seke relief at the hands of straungers'. Here we have aggrieved children attacking their neglectful, spendthrift stepfather. Powe denied their allegations, saying that he had brought up and apprenticed Jane and Elizabeth at his own cost, he had bound himself to provide them with portions worth £8, compared with the 20s. their natural father had left them, and he said he was 'ready to do them any pleasure according to his abilitie as to a father in lawe appertaineth'.[98]

Cases involving mothers who sued, or who were sued by, their children,

[96] *Mary Cheeke v. Christopher Symcocks*, PRO Req 2/47/36 [m. 28], A.
[97] Tittler, 'Money-lending in the west Midlands', p. 256.
[98] *Jane & Elizabeth Thompson v. William Bradley & Robert Powe*, PRO Req 2/276/33.

stepchildren or children-in-law usually took a slightly different form. Mothers, more than fathers, tended to take up the stance of concerned parents acting in the interest of their family, or of the aggrieved mother betrayed by her ungrateful offspring. The respect that mothers could demand was considerable, and children were usually circumspect when suing their mothers, prefacing criticisms with placatory remarks. When Margaret Kempe complained to the Masters about her son William, who was suing her in Queen's Bench and Chancery, she detailed all of the money and assistance she had extended to him over the years, describing how notwithstanding her generosity and her 'naturall and motherlie care and favoure towards him', William 'verie unnaturallie and uncontionablie exhibited a Bill of complainte' against her in Chancery. In answer, William made a show of his respect, speaking 'of the dewtifull care & loving minde that this Defendant Doth now & allwayes hath & doth beare to this said Complainant being his naturall Mother'. He blamed the pair's falling out on his half-brother, Robert Kempe, who had induced Margaret, 'being an aged woman . . . to thinke hardly of this Defendant without all cawse', and to do him 'open wronge even ageinste her will'. But after confirming his continuing love for Margaret and explaining how she had been led astray, he then poured scorn on her assertion that she was a good mother. He said she had brought him up 'very meanly', at no cost to herself, and made him work for his keep, providing him with no more than meat and drink for his labour.[99]

Mothers had a heightened ability to benefit from the impact of supposed inversions of normal family hierarchies of gender and age, as well as from expectations about how children should treat their mothers. Agnes Haselwood, whose case was described in chapter 5, told the Masters that she had let her daughter Sara take on the administration of her late husband's estate, because she was 'willinge to be a loving & a naturall mother unto' her. When Sara betrayed her, Agnes complained to Requests, and a commission found in her favour, reporting that Agnes 'hathe byn verry motche abused by the sayd Sara her naturall dawghter', who had sold the lease 'contrary bothe to the sayd truste and her dewty towards her mother'.[100] When Dame Eleonora Zouche sued Dame Eleonora Zouche, the Masters ordered 'that the sayd dame Elionor the daughter shall use her self duetifull to the sayd dame Elionor her natyrall mother'.[101] When the lord of a manor argued that he could overthrow estates granted during his infancy by his stepfather, acting in right of his wife, an opponent in Requests said that this proved he lacked 'reverend respecte' for his mother.[102]

However, the position of mothers was fragile. If it was unnatural for children

[99] *Margaret Kempe v. William Franklyn*, PRO Req 2/230/12, m. 5, A; m. 6, B.
[100] *Agnes Haselwood v. Sara Hazelwood et al.*, PRO Req 2/38/20, mm. 1, 6, 11.
[101] *Eleonora Zowche v. Eleonora & John Zowche*, PRO Req 1/15, fol. 407ᵛ.
[102] *Anstice Newman v. John Parham*, PRO Req 2/158/153.

to neglect or to confront their mothers, some observers regarded it as equally, or perhaps more, unnatural for mothers to flout their roles as nurturers and sue their own children. Take, for example, Elizabeth Roche's counter suit against her son-in-law Richard Rothe. Richard, a London fruit merchant, had married Elizabeth's daughter Susan and then immediately commenced common law proceedings to claim her inheritance. Elizabeth came to Requests arguing that Richard had taken advantage of Susan's youth, marrying her 'without the consent of youre saide subjecte or anie other of her ffriendes' merely so he could claim a bequest in her father's will, not due to her until she turned twenty eight. In reply, Richard used conciliatory language – he had hoped 'by his curteous and gentle dealinge to winne her of a foe to be hys frend' – but then audaciously turned Elizabeth's stance as a good parent and mother on its head. He said he had married Susan not for gain, as she had no portion, but 'upon grete good lykinge conceyved of her', and that Susan's father had approved of the match. All sides agreed that a prospective son-in-law should seek parental approval before marriage, but Richard was able to imply that a father's approval was more important than the approval of a mother 'or anie other of her ffriendes'. In his attempt to wrest the moral initiative from his mother-in-law, Richard said he marvelled at Elizabeth's perversity and her 'cruel and more than unnaturall' dealings in seeking to deprive not just Richard but also his wife Susan, 'her owne daughter'.[103] Not only did Elizabeth have less parental authority to assert than her husband, but she was more susceptible to being labelled 'unnatural' for denying her daughter her inheritance.

The suggestions of Margaret Kempe, Richard Rothe and others that it was 'very unnatural' for a son to sue his mother or a mother to sue her daughter, serve as a useful reminder that court actions between family members involved two distinct breaches of trust. Firstly, the breach contained within the transgression which brought the parties into court, and, secondly, the act of going to court itself. Going to court was a public declaration that the bonds of family had split asunder. If wives sued their husbands they publicly challenged their husbands' authority, and could be accused of proving themselves immodest in the process. If parents and children brought suits against each other they publicly admitted the breakdown of their relationship and with it an inversion of natural order, for as William Gouge later wrote, God has 'so fast fixed love in the hearts of parents, as if there be any in whome it aboundeth not, he is counted unnaturall'.[104]

The Masters of Requests shared litigants' distaste for actions between family members and whenever possible they referred matters between closely related

---

[103] Richard ignored Susan's father's will and made his claim for her inheritance under the custom of the City of London; *Elizabeth Roche* v. *Richard Rothe*, PRO Req 2/163/125, m. 3, A; m. 4, B.

[104] Wrightson, 'Infanticide in earlier seventeenth-century England', p. 11.

parties to arbitration, often selecting family members as arbitrators.[105] They regarded it as 'unnatural' not just for mothers and their children, but for *any* close family members, to seek settlement of their disputes by means of decrees in open court. In 1599, for example, they referred a case to arbitrators, declaring that 'the same sute being betwixt the father and the sonne, seemed to her majesties Counsaill of this Court to be very unnaturall'.[106] The records provide a strong sense that court officials and litigants believed that it was 'unnatural' for family members to shatter 'natural' family bonds with court actions, however the number of family disputes which came to court suggest that in practice this ideal could be difficult to sustain.

It should be clear from the cases discussed in this and in other chapters that the key issue in sixteenth century equity cases, as in most equity cases today, was trust. Masters and litigants considered family disputes unnatural because the duties that close kin owed each other were among the strongest imaginable, and breaches of these duties amounted to sacrifices of trust that could easily spark court actions. Once in court, however, these family ties and responsibilities provided litigants with a powerful pleading device for emphasising the scale of misdemeanours, and parties regularly tried to use their sense of kin responsibilities to gain the high moral, and with it the legal and equitable, ground.

Litigants stressed the existence of any kin links and responsibilities they could, often describing more than one relationship. One set of plaintiffs complained that their opponent 'neither regarded the duty of a child to his father, nor the trust reposed in him by the said testator nor the love he ought to beare to his own naturall sisters'.[107] A married couple said their opponent had no regard for his father's promise, 'nor havinge any care of motherlawe nor of her children'.[108] Multiple relationships meant multiple breaches, but any relationship was worth stressing, however remote. Agnes Nowell, it will be remembered, placed her maintenance money during her temporary separation with 'her neare kinseman', but she allowed Thomas Hall to convince her to transfer the money into his hands because he was her neighbour, and 'somwhat of kinred' to her.[109] Other litigants spoke of the 'special trust and confidence' they had in their nephew, in 'a neare kynsman', a 'friend and kynsman', a 'cosyn and frend', or a 'neare kinswoman'.[110] When John Stoughton needed to borrow £50 he

---

[105] Marcus Knight found a similar situation in the Durham Chancery; Knight, 'Litigants and litigation', pp. 454, 459–61.

[106] *Richard Oxenbridge v. John Oxenbridge*, PRO Req 1/19, p. 911; for further examples, see *Thomas Cowchman v. John & Gyles Cowchman*, PRO Req 1/21, p. 62; *Margaret Stanhop & John Lockow v. John Stanhop et al.*, PRO Req 1/21, p. 68.

[107] *Alexander & Dorothy Glover et al. v. Alexander Ratclyff*, PRO Req 2/163/60, B.

[108] *Richard & Elizabeth Browninge et al. v. William Nelme*, PRO Req 2/166/33 [m. 2], B.

[109] *Agnes Nowell v. Thomas Hall*, PRO Req 2/166/134 [m. 4].

[110] *John Chapman v. Chrystofer Preston & Anne Chapman*, PRO Req 2/193/16; *Mathewe & Jane Graye v. Thomas Eyre et al.*, PRO Req 1/19, p. 141; *Jane Goddard v. William Goddard*, PRO Req 2/81/18, D, deponent Edward Wiest.

approached Ferdinando Bawde, because he was 'of kinne, and then in speciall league of amitie' with him.[111] The stress that litigants placed on even the most marginal kin links provides a view of kinship that extends well beyond the confines of the nuclear family. Litigation records suggest that kinship played an important role in the borrowing and lending of money, in the establishment of trusts and uses (especially secret ones), and in the seeking of professional advice. Litigants and lawyers believed that the Masters would find arguments built around kin links convincing, and perhaps they exaggerated their importance, letting hindsight cloud their actual motivations. However, the sense in pleadings that blood was indeed thicker than water, that kinship and trust were closely intertwined, provides an interesting counterpoint to the common suggestion that links with extended kin in Tudor and Stuart England rarely held any significance.[112]

Litigants who were unrelated included less elaborate descriptions in their pleadings, concentrating instead on the particular breaches of trust they had suffered. Once again, however, it is noticeable how often women emphasised their own vulnerability. In fraud cases women stressed the 'special truste and confidence' they had placed in lawyers, trustees, or agents, explaining how this trust resulted from the professional knowledge or power of their opponent.[113] Joan Uphill had 'a moste speciall truste, good opinion and Confidence' in three trustees, until they took advantage of 'the simplicitie of your saied subjecte, beinge redy and apte to be drawen into all myscheeffe and inconvenience, by reason they were men in whome your saied Subjecte reposed suche Confidence as she did not mystruste or dowbted of any fraude, guile or inderrect dealinges'.[114] Even Elizabeth Shipper, by her own reckoning an independent woman with property originally worth more than £300, accused Thomas Good of, 'intending to abuse the simplissetie of your pore subjecte'. She also said that he had evicted her at midnight, leaving her not 'so much as a Littell Linnen out of hir owne chests to shifte hir withall', so that her creditors then 'ymprissoned hir, turnde hir out of hir howse, & compelled hir to lyve in the streets, to hir utter undoing, shame & discredit'. Good refused her any aid in prison, 'yet tooke an occasion seeing your subjecte in great povertie by this last politicke demise to make hir beg

---

[111] *Ferdinando Bawde* v. *John Stoughton*, PRO Req 1/21, p. 194; in inheritance disputes, parties sometimes asked 'of what kindred or howe neare in blud' were certain individuals, or stressed that claimants were 'not of the blood or kindred' of testators; *James & Susan Aske* v. *William & Jane Paine*, PRO Req 2/172/25, I, D, deponents Henry Bristowe, Anthony Barnett; *John & Johan Dawbin* v. *Thomas Howe et al.*, PRO Req 2/196/24, B; some plaintiffs emphasized the strength of opponents by saying they were 'well kynned and allyed' in their counties; *Ellen Greene* v. *Richard Norris*, PRO Req 2/26/38, B.

[112] Keith Wrightson, 'Kinship in an English village: Terling, Essex, 1550–1700', in R.M. Smith, ed., *Land, Kinship and Lifecycle* (Cambridge, 1984); David Cressy, 'Kinship and kin interaction in early modern England', *Past and Present*, 113 (1986), pp. 38–69; Gowing, *Domestic Dangers*, pp. 20–1. [113] *Alice Bawghes* v. *William Knighte*, PRO Req 2/166/14.

[114] *Johanne Uphill* v. *Richard Hole et al.*, PRO Req 2/281/16, m. 1.

hir bread'.[115] Again and again litigants presented the world of bonds, deeds and other documents as a male enclave in which women were regularly disadvantaged through their lack of experience and specialist knowledge.

THE MEANING OF STORIES

The narrative structures, stereotyped images and the style of accusation employed in Requests pleadings are strikingly similar to those found in ballads, plays, debates about women and other forms of contemporary Elizabethan literature. Regardless of whether lawyers sang particular ballads or purchased and read florid tales about adultery, pleading cases in an equity court clearly involved the telling of stories. It is difficult to believe, for example, that married couples attempted to poison each other with the regularity which a literal reading of accusations in pleadings suggests.[116] Yet attempts by spouses to poison their mates or to murder them by other means were common fare in the literature of the period.[117] When it came to fighting a maintenance action, litigants, lawyers and witnesses knew how to describe the conditions of a broken marriage, which facts to include, which arguments to emphasise, which behaviour to justify and how much detail to supply, and Masters or judges knew how to interpret these tales. Just as authors drew on infamous cases for inspiration, especially witch trials, so those involved in litigation borrowed techniques from authors.[118] Or more likely, both groups drew on a common heritage of conventions and stereotypes embedded in the consciousness and culture of literate as well as illiterate society.

If the narrative structures and imagery in pleadings bear the influence of literature, the values they contain are largely indistinguishable from the values propagated in sermons and conduct literature. At first sight the close fit between the values in legal records and moral writings might suggest that the authors of sermons and conduct books were giving voice to common practice, not envisioning possible improvements; that their works were descriptive rather than prescriptive. However, on closer inspection it becomes apparent that the duties and values present in pleadings rarely equated with the standards by which

---

[115] *Elizabeth Shipper v. Thomas Good & William Taylor*, PRO Req 2/39/60, m. 17, B; for further examples, see *Michael Keynton et al. v. Alice Walley*, PRO Req 2/231/24, A; *Agnes Chicke v. Elizabeth Clifton*, PRO Req 2/190/27, B.   [116] See the section on violence above.

[117] See, for example, Ann de Boyse, *A True Discourse of a Cruell Fact Committed by a Gentlewoman Towardes Her Husband* (London, 1599), pp. 6–7; Dolan, *Dangerous Familiars*, pp. 30, 45, 173; Hugh Latimer declared in a sermon preached before Edward VI: 'Alacke, shal poysonning come now hither in to England oute of Italie?'; Hugh Latimer, *A Moste Faithfull Sermon Preached Before the Kynges Most Exellente Majestye* (London, 1550), fol. Bi^v.

[118] John Phillips, *The Examination and Confession of Certaine Wytches at Chensforde the xxvi. Daye of July 1566* (London, 1566); W.W., *A True and Just Recorde of the Information Examination and Confession of All the Witches, at St Oses in Essex* (London, 1582); and see Jardine, *Reading Shakespeare Historically*, 1996), p. 37.

people actually lived their everyday lives. Instead, as I have been arguing, they represented ideals, and there are regular hints in pleadings that litigants were not always offended in life by the transgressions of which they complained so vigorously in court. In many instances, for example, individuals complained long after the event about misdemeanours which they seemed willing to over-look at the time they were committed.

To take just one example, Margaret Dier complained to Requests that she had let Anthony Delonie move into her house after he displayed an intention to marry her daughter, Margaret Rawlines. She described how she had spent considerable sums accommodating and feeding not just Delonie, but also his sister Olive, her two children and a servant, over a period of eight months, as his relationship with Rawlines developed and 'there wanted nothinge but the solemnisinge of the marriage'. During this time, however, Delonie,

not having the feare of god before his eies, in contempte of Lawe and Justice upon ade-velishe minde to satisfie his owne luste, your said subjects daughter very lewdely and dis-honestly by flatterings words and other ungodlie alurements did entice into secret and darke places of your said subjects house, att tymes moste fitt and convenient for his wicked purpose, to abuse the bodie of your subjects daughter and accordinglie obtained his filthie purpose and pleasure and gott the said Margaret . . . with childe.

Delonie was brought before the deputy alderman of the ward for his 'lewde and ungodlie' behaviour, and he promised that he would marry Rawlines. In response, Dier gave him £12 to purchase a lease so that the couple would have somewhere to live, but Delonie put the lease in his own name and then married someone else. As a result, Dier lost her money, and her daughter, 'who before was of honest fame and name and might have matched with his equal before the injury donne her by him', was left carrying a bastard child.

Margaret Dier's anger at Anthony Delonie's behaviour was intense, but from her own evidence it appears that she had encouraged him to live with her daughter while the pair remained unmarried, even after Rawlines became preg-nant. In her desire to see Delonie marry her daughter, it seems that Dier had been willing to pay out considerable sums of money and to condone the couple's sexual indiscretions in the hope that things would turn out well in the end.[119] When they did not, she hurried to Requests to recover her losses and to have Anthony punished, and described the past with a moral indignation which may well have exceeded the feelings she actually experienced at the time.

Rather than perfectly mirroring reality, the duties and values which under-pinned pleadings represented a somewhat artificial code of ideal behaviour, a set of norms which resembled, and doubtless were influenced by, ideal stan-

---

[119] Dier maintained that she never suspected Delonie of 'any such lewde dealinge but only kept him upon hope of the mariage'. As a result of her daughter falling pregnant, Dier said she was 'sharplie punnished as maineteiner and supporter of the daughters follie' and her daughter was 'sore whipped' at Bridewell; *Margaret Dier* v. *Anthony Delonie*, PRO Req 2/99/24.

dards drawn from and echoed in sermons, conduct books and the Homilies. People might appeal to these norms on occasions of social conflict, or when they felt threatened in some way by the failure of others to conform to lesser, everyday standards of reasonable behaviour. A whole variety of different reasons led litigants to take their grievances to court, but once in court they, or at least their counsel, appealed to the standards of this moral code. Like Margaret Dier, many of them used hindsight to muster moral resentment in an attempt to bring their values into line with the values they suspected the Masters embraced.

As this chapter has argued, the archives of English bill courts like Requests have immense value as storehouses of norms and of conventional images of men and women. But given the slippage between norms in pleadings and lived reality, the question of authorship becomes unavoidable. Were litigants or their lawyers instrumental in setting forward these ideals and values? Did litigants join their lawyers in second-guessing their audience of Masters and commissioners, or does the sameness in the structure and phrasing of pleadings suggest that lawyers alone were responsible? Could it be that pleadings did not simply appeal to, but actually embodied, a value system exclusive to gentlemen counsel and Masters and foreign to most litigants? This last possibility seems unlikely for a number of reasons. To begin with, those who drew up pleadings were not all of gentle status. The difference in wealth and social standing between the Masters and senior members of the bar in London and scriveners and attorneys in the localities means that even if such a monopoly of high moral and legal values existed, it covered a considerable expanse of social ground.[120]

It is, moreover, illogical to think that litigants could be so comprehensively excluded from the production of pleadings that bore their names. The richness and urgency of detail in pleadings suggests a considerable input by litigants, however lawyers may have organised and edited the details that their clients provided. Like the tellers of pardon tales in France examined by Natalie Davis, litigants faced the prospect of being cross-examined on their pleadings by Masters or commissioners if their cases proceeded to a hearing, and they had to be actively aware of proceedings. William and Jane Paine showed the pleadings from their case to friends, asking them what they thought of them.[121] Thomas Finch's answer to a bill of complaint in Requests was so much of his making that it led to contempt proceedings for slander. In answer to interrogatories, Finch explained that Mr Ockley of Broxborne in Hertfordshire had prepared

---

[120] On the relatively low status and means of members of the lower branch of the legal profession, see Brooks, *Pettyfoggers*; C.W. Brooks, R.H. Helmholz and P.G. Stein, *Notaries Public in England Since the Reformation* (London, 1991), pp. 5–10, 52–95.

[121] *James & Susan Aske* v. *William & Jane Paine*, PRO Req 2/157/20, D, deponent Robert Smithe.

his answer at his instruction. He had then taken the answer to Mr Dorrell of Grays Inn who had 'set his hand thereto', after Finch assured him that the claims later adjudged slanderous were true and sustainable.[122] The image of Joan and Richard Badger stalking Westminster pretending to be suitors, after the Masters had dismissed their cause, provides evocative evidence of the personal involvement of litigants in their legal affairs.[123] To this evidence can be added the testimony of deponents from all social ranks who rarely espoused values which differed markedly from those expressed by the parties they were supporting. Litigants may have had limited control over the form and language of their pleadings, but these documents nevertheless had to represent their grievances to their satisfaction in a form that they could understand.

It seems likely, then, that Masters, lawyers, litigants and deponents shared a common understanding of equity, fairness and acceptable behaviour, even if they lived their respective lives according to diverging values. Keith Wrightson has identified 'two concepts of order' co-existing in seventeenth century England: the order of the governing majority embodied in legislation and the 'somewhat broader area of behaviour permitted to themselves by a group of villagers'.[124] In the words of John Brewer and John Styles: 'it would seem that the law of patrician society was not the justice of plebeian culture'.[125] As Laura Gowing further points out: 'we cannot assume an unproblematic community whose moral interests and ideas were more or less in accord with those of lawgivers in the spiritual and secular sphere and more or less the same across the differences of age, class, family and gender'.[126] The Requests records suggest that however many divergent concepts of order, and however many moral codes, different social groups embraced, once in court most people knew the correct answers to judges' questions. Litigants put on moral airs, much as they might put on their Sunday best, but the act was convincing because knowledge of the high moral standards demanded in courts of law seems to have been widespread. Historians rightly identify the law as a maintainer of social division within society, a necessary but often unpopular evil that tended, through its concentration on property rights, to favour the wealthy more than the poor. But as well as perpetuating social divisions, it could also cut through the boundaries that separated different groups within society, in a cultural as well as in a legal sense, transporting ideas back and forth between the highest courts in the land

---

[122] *John ffynche v. Thomas ffynche*, PRO Req 2/27/15; Req 2/26/121; PRO Req 1/19, pp. 692, 745; five days after Finch answered the interrogatories put to him, the Masters committed him to the Fleet for contempt; PRO Req 1/19, p. 756.

[123] Letter from Alan Dale to her Majesty's Knight Marshal and his deputies 'attendant at the court', PRO Req 3/33; see chapter 6 above.

[124] Keith Wrightson, 'Two concepts of order: justices, constable and jurymen in seventeenth-century England', in John Brewer and John Styles, eds., *An Ungovernable People: The English and their Law in the Seventeenth and Eighteenth Centuries* (London, 1980), p. 21.

[125] Brewer and Styles, *An Ungovernable People*, p. 15.   [126] Gowing, *Domestic Dangers*, p. 11.

and the humblest subjects in town and province.[127] 'The law', as John Walter has pointed out, 'served as a pivot for the relationship between rulers and ruled in early modern England'.[128]

Litigants in Requests appear to have shared not only a common understanding of elite values and of ideal standards of behaviour, but also a common resort to conventional methods of defending and undermining credit. As we have seen, individuals asserted the probity of their own behaviour and questioned the morality of their opponents' actions, many parties contrasting their own self-discipline with the lack, or loss, of control of their rivals. Whether litigants were male or female, rich or poor, they did everything in their power to fight their corner, and women were as capable as men of manipulating the legal system and using every legal tool at their disposal. But while the general tactics that parties employed varied little across class and gender boundaries, female pleadings regularly differed from male pleadings. As it has already been noted, all parties, including witnesses, were capable of using questions of sexual reputation to undermine both male and female credit.[129] However, such allegations were almost invariably more potent when they were directed at women.

Some differences between male and female pleading styles could work to women's advantage. While it appears that women had less freedom than men to admit the active pursuit of proprietary rights for gain, they could more readily accentuate the betrayals of trust they had experienced, and so appeal for judicial sympathy. The residue of this difference in power persists today. Modern students of courtroom behaviour have distinguished separate styles of characteristic speech employed by women and men, and at least one study of witnesses in criminal actions has identified the use women make of 'powerless speech'.[130] Lawyers may have encouraged their female clients to stress their

---

[127] See Sharpe, 'The people and the law', especially pp. 244–7; Brooks, *Pettyfoggers*, ch. 12; Brooks, Helmholz and Stein, *Notaries Public in England*, pp. 84–9; C.W. Brooks, 'The professions, ideology and the middling sort in the late sixteenth and seventeenth centuries', in Jonathan Barry and C.W. Brooks, eds., *The Middling Sort of People: Culture, Society and Politics in England 1550–1800* (London, 1994).

[128] John Walter, 'Grain riots and popular attitudes to the law: Maldon and the crisis of 1629', in Brewer and Styles, *An Ungovernable People*, p. 83.

[129] A deponent in the *Lewis v. Pleydell* case alleged that the gentleman orchestrating the eviction of Joan Lewis had expressed his desire 'to have the said Joan' and one of her gentlewomen 'at his pleasure', leading the deponent to inform him 'that that was not the way to wyne a woman'; *Johan Lewis v. Thobye Pleydell*, PRO Req 2/164/103, m. 2, D, deponent John Pyttman; and see *Walter Cope v. Henry Archer*, PRO Req 2/51/41, D, deponents Jane Barger, Robert Dodson; *John Graye v. Thomas Spencer et al.*, PRO Req 2/209/47, Dem.

[130] W.M. O'Barr, *Linguistic Evidence: Language, Power, and Strategy in the Courtroom* (New York, 1982), pp. 61ff; for a study which revealed relatively little difference between the treatment of men and women in criminal courts, see H.M. Kritzer and T.M. Uhlman, 'Sisterhood in the courtroom: sex of judge and defendant in criminal case disposition', in K.O. Blumhagen and W.D. Johnson, eds., *Women's Studies: An Interdisciplinary Collection* (Westport, Connecticut, 1978), especially p. 84.

vulnerability, or even sought to enhance women's 'powerless speech' in pleadings, for as Deborah Greenhut has found, male writers in Tudor England clearly observed conventions about the speaking abilities and styles of male and female characters. Comparing Ovid's characterisations in *Heroides* with the characterisations of his Tudor translators, she discovered that female characters in Ovid's original expressed themselves more freely than their counterparts in the Tudor works.[131]

The fact that women, with the aid of their lawyers, thought that they could attract the sympathy of Requests Masters by depicting themselves as vulnerable females, bringing themselves within the rich biblical, literary and humanist tradition of concern for the weak, provides an interesting example of female initiative. However, the nature of the stereotypes they employed prevents this example of female initiative from being equated with female independence. For while the poverty of a plaintiff might attract sympathy, poverty in general was not universally well regarded in the later sixteenth century.[132] When it came to deposition evidence, for example, most sides regarded witnesses without substance as witnesses without credit. A Norwich linen draper suing in Requests denigrated his opponent's main witness by saying she was a 'very pore woman of noe estimacion nor credytt'.[133] As Barnabe Rich quipped in the seventeenth century (with his tongue only partly in his cheek): 'Poverty in this age is the greatest dishonesty that a man can fall into', adding that 'neither can there be a greater blemish to any man's credit, then to be reputed poore and honest'.[134] Furthermore, as it was noted in chapter 5, women accused of being poor or ignorant responded by asserting their independence, and the vehemence of their replies provides further proof of the ignominious relationship between poverty and personal credit.[135] To take an example, one woman said that her foe 'hath no reason to disable or discredit the said defendants estate', for it was 'well knowne to the saide Complainante and many others that shee the said defendante was well able to lende greater somes of money then shee did lend' in this case.[136] Some women may have benefited from crying poor, but they

---

[131] Deborah Greenhut, *Feminine Rhetorical Culture: Tudor Adaptations of Ovid's Heroides* (New York, 1988), p. 163.

[132] When the Masters referred to litigants as 'poor', they were usually admitting sympathy rather than describing poverty.

[133] *Robert Goldyng v. Thomas & Christian Pettons*, PRO Req 2/213/29 [m. 1], B.

[134] Rich, *My Ladies Looking Glasse*, p. 59; for examples of deponents judging credit according to wealth, and the use of the expression poor 'but yet honest', see *Suzanne Ashley v. Thomas Cartwright*, PRO Req 2/159/7, D, deponents John Elsworth, Margarett Marshe.

[135] On the connection between moral and material worth, see Susan Amussen, 'Gender, family and the social order, 1560–1725', in Anthony Fletcher and John Stevenson, *Order and Disorder in Early Modern England* (Cambridge, 1987), p. 212; Erickson, *Women and Property*, p. 95; Gowing, *Domestic Dangers*, p. 50.

[136] *Joane Frenche v. Alice Pynchback*, PRO Req 2/164/60, Rj.

were relying on what observers of modern courtrooms have labelled 'the chivalry factor', judicial sympathy that was ultimately paternal and often condescending.[137]

Conventions in courts such as Requests governed the ways it was felt correct for men and women to express and represent themselves, and in almost every case they left women at a disadvantage. In some cases the differences were slight, but nevertheless it seems that while any individual's credit could be attacked directly – if they had acted dishonestly or fraudulently – women's credit was more open than men's to indirect attack, through allegations about general demeanour. To quote Deborah Greenhut (referring not to litigants but to figures in literature), 'men must prove their honor while women must disprove their dishonor and be silent about their chastity in order to conserve it'.[138] In law courts, as in life, there were rhetorical boundaries it could be difficult for women to cross. This imbalance in pleading options exacerbated the more obvious imbalances present within the law itself, but *both* of these imbalances reflected and sustained more general prejudices and beliefs circulating in wider society. As the author of *The Lawes Resolutions of Womens Rights* remarked, on the question of women's diminished rights, 'the common law here shaketh hand with divinitie'.[139] Society and its laws were inextricably connected, and the temptation to regard them as being somehow distinct from each other, for example to talk about law on the one hand and 'reality' on the other, and to assume that the former was always harsh and the latter always permissive, needs to be resisted.

The methods parties employed to question the credit of opponents and witnesses in Requests often mirrored the methods neighbours from a variety of social groupings used to attack each other's good standing in the community. The language, the conventional images, and the stereotypes, all echoed (if they did not always perfectly reflect) the public attacks on character which in the sixteenth and seventeenth century increasingly led to the mounting of slander, libel and defamation actions. Historians interested in these concerns in Elizabethan and Jacobean England have so far restricted their researches to the records of

---

[137] According to Albie Sachs and Joan Wilson, writing in 1978, 'The "chivalry factor" is the euphemism used to describe the alleged leniency rather than justice that women experience in the courts. It is particularly evident in the criminal justice process where women are seldom viewed as adult persons, but rather as dependent persons who cannot take care of themselves and who must be protected. This largely unconscious paternalism pervades the American legal system and knows no class boundaries'; Albie Sachs and Joan Wilson, *Sexism and the Law: A Study of Male Beliefs and Legal Bias in Britain and the United States* (Oxford, 1978), p. 125.

[138] Greenhut, *Feminine Rhetorical Culture*, p. 163.

[139] T.E., *The Lawes Resolutions of Womens Rights*, p. 6; Lord Chief Baron Hale similarly observed in 1663, 'by the law of God, of nature, of reason and by the Common Law, the will of the wife is subject to the will of the husband'; Margaret Ezell, *The Patriarch's Wife: Literary Evidence and the History of the Family* (Chapel Hill, 1987), p. 2.

these actions, but these echoes demonstrate that evidence for community concerns about social and sexual reputation, and about male and female honour, is not to be found only in cases of libel, defamation and slander. In a court like Requests it can be found in actions of all kinds.

9

Women waging law

Women have no voyse in Parliament, They make no Lawes, they consent to
none, they abrogate none. All of them are understood either married or to bee
married and their desires [are] subject to their husband. I know no remedy
though some women can shift it well enough.

T.E. *The Lawes Resolutions of Womens Rights* (1632)[1]

In *The Patriarch's Wife*, Margaret Ezell posed the rhetorical question: 'was seventeenth-century England a society of submissive, deferential, opinionless females whose quietude was ensured by their ignorance and a hostile legal system?'[2] If we broaden her question to include the sixteenth century, the answer is clearly no. As countless examples in the foregoing chapters confirm, the central courts at Westminster regularly processed cases involving knowledgeable women who were neither submissive nor deferential. The legal system was certainly hostile in the sense that crown, judiciary and parliament each accorded women fewer rights than men, but these bodies never denied women rights altogether, and female litigants went to court in their thousands.

Women's relationship with the law was far from ideal, but it was not as uniformly bleak as some commentators have assumed. A variety of separate courts operated side by side in England, applying principles of equity or administering common law, ecclesiastical law or custom. Even the most male-centred of these jurisdictions provided women with distinctive rights and assistance, as well as burdening them with distinctive obligations and restrictions on their freedoms. Women who were able to pick and choose between jurisdictions, or who had access to legal advisers who could guide them to the legal institutions that best suited their needs, could gain considerable benefit from the legal system. If they were unprincipled they might even exploit the system, just as unprincipled men exploited the system, wasting their opponents' time and money by delaying legal proceedings, by entering suits simultaneously in different jurisdictions,

---

[1] T.E., *The Lawes Resolutions of Womens Rights*, p. 6.
[2] Ezell, *The Patriarch's Wife*, p. 8.

and by responding to unfavourable decisions with appeals to higher courts. The widow Ellen Cole, for example, contracted to marry William Wyett, a member of the Inner Temple, but according to Wyett she lacked 'the feare of god before hyr eyes' and refused to proceed. To prevent him enforcing the contract she staged a campaign of litigation against him at common law, supposedly consisting of bogus or unconscionable actions on the case, which eventually landed him in prison.[3]

Women's legal options were considerable, and their access to litigation improved substantially with the growth of the central justice system between the accession of Elizabeth I and the demise of Charles I. The numbers of women who participated in litigation increased at a rate that outstripped increases in population. In the church courts, Chancery, Requests and the major common law courts, women, like men, were availing themselves of institutional justice in numbers which approach or exceed modern levels of participation in the legal process. This meant more women travelling to court and more women defending their honour and protecting their property, but it also meant more wives publicly challenging their husbands, more women fighting contests against men, and, for a while at least, more poor women challenging their richer neighbours. This rising surge of independent action attracted comment from judges and male litigants, and may have offered inspiration to playwrights and satirists. It may also have contributed to more general feelings of unease about women's independent behaviour, feelings which David Underdown, Susan Amussen, Anthony Fletcher, J.A. Sharpe, Laura Gowing and Bernard Capp have all argued were intensifying at this time. Few historians share Underdown's belief that this unease constituted a 'crisis in gender relations' – Martin Ingram has questioned Underdown's use of prosecutions for scolding as evidence of such a crisis, while Gowing and Lyndal Roper remain sceptical of descriptions of gender relations which identify single periods of crisis, rather than ongoing contests – but most concede that during the sixteenth century debates and concerns about gender became more intense, or at least more visible.[4] Certainly, court orders expelling vociferous women (as well as lawyers) from courtrooms give the impression that women played a more active role in the law suits that

---

[3] William Wyett v. Ellen Colle et al., PRO Req 2/104/5.

[4] David Underdown, 'The taming of the scold: the enforcement of patriarchal authority in early modern England' and Amussen, 'Gender, family and the social order', both in Anthony Fletcher and John Stevenson, eds., *Order and Disorder in Early Modern England* (Cambridge, 1987); Fletcher, *Gender, Sex and Subordination*, especially pp. xvi, 27–9; Sharpe, 'Witchcraft', p. 183; Bernard Capp, 'Separate domains? Women and authority in early modern England', in Paul Griffiths, Adam Fox and Steve Hindle, eds., *The Experience of Authority in Early Modern England* (London, 1996); Martin Ingram, '"Scolding women cucked or washed": a crisis in gender relation in early modern England?', in Jenny Kermode and Garthine Walker, eds., *Women, Crime and the Courts in Early Modern England* (London, 1994); Gowing, *Domestic Dangers*, pp. 28–9, 274–5; Lyndal Roper, *Oedipus and the Devil: Witchcraft, Sexuality and Religion in Early Modern Europe* (London and New York, 1994), pp. 37–52.

bore their names, and were regarded by authorities with greater suspicion, in the sixteenth and early seventeenth centuries, than in later periods when court-rooms tended to be less boisterous and chaotic venues, and when lawyers played a greater role in legal proceedings.[5]

In Elizabeth's reign the total number of women suing and being sued in the central courts was impressively high, for a system that many historians regard as the sheet anchor of patriarchal authority and institutionalised discrimination against women in this period. Women participated as litigants in one third of actions in Requests, and between a quarter and a third of actions in most other Westminster courts.[6] However, optimism about women's participation needs to be qualified, given that women appeared as lone plaintiffs in only one in twelve Requests suits (the equivalent ratio for men was two in three), despite the court's status as a haven for widows, orphans and the poor. Clearly the barriers to participation in law, like the barriers to participation in so many other areas of life, remained higher for women than for men. But what form did these barriers take? The law itself was not solely to blame, for as this study and the studies of Gowing, Erickson and Cioni have shown, examples can be found of single women, widows and married women (with or without their husbands) gaining entry to courts of almost every kind. Before attempting to identify long term patterns in women's changing position at law, it is worth trying to identify these barriers, and to consider the specific conditions in late sixteenth and early seventeenth century England which may explain why the picture is not more optimistic; why even greater numbers of women did not fight their way into courts of law.

BARRIERS TO LITIGATION

Various factors influenced women's ability to assert or defend their rights and interests in court. Resources, for example, were fundamental. Despite the existence of legal aid provisions, in the form of *in forma pauperis* admissions, it cost money to sustain a court action, and money, real property and personal property were disproportionately in the hands of men. This meant not only that women had fewer resources than men with which to fund court battles, but that they possessed less property and fewer interests that might give rise to disputes in the first place. However, if levels of property ownership help to explain why more men than women became litigants, they fail to account for the extent of

---

[5] On the rowdiness of Elizabethan courtrooms, see PRO Req 1/19, p. 302; Req 1/21, pp. 190–1; Prest, *The Rise of the Barristers*, pp. 302–3; on the possibility that authorities regarded women as more threatening in the sixteenth than in the eighteenth centuries, see Dolan, *Dangerous Familiars*, pp. 18, 29; Fletcher, *Gender, Sex and Subordination*, especially ch. 1.

[6] See chapter 2 above.

the discrepancy, given the amount of property women controlled through inheritance, employment, the profits of moneylending and from other sources.

Another impediment that affected women's ability to bring law suits was coverture. As I have sought to show, this doctrine restricted not only married women, by barring them from owning property or from suing without their husbands, it also inconvenienced many widows. The withdrawal and reinstatement of legal capacity that widows experienced over the course of their lives could interfere with their knowledge of important transactions, and leave them without the leases, bonds and other proofs required to mount legal actions. Furthermore, in instances where wives had to wait months or years until they could sue as widows, the time they lost could prove disadvantageous. Opponents might leave the country or dispose of relevant interests, documents could be lost, witnesses might die or find their memories clouded by age.

Economic and legal explanations provide part of the answer for the relative absence of women from law courts, but not all of it. The discovery (in chapters 5 and 6 above) that even well-informed women of means might hesitate before going to law, in many cases waiting until they married or remarried and could bring joint actions with their husbands, suggests that further impediments kept women from the courtroom. Some women may have delayed litigation because marriage was an agreed entry point into adulthood, and they preferred bringing suits as 'mistress' rather than 'maid'. Marriage itself could also trigger legal causes, because legacies often accrued at marriage. However, a significant minority of women appear to have felt wary about going to court, for reasons that appear to be social and cultural in nature as much as economic and legal. When Richard Hooker sought to explain in *The Lawes of Ecclesiastical Politie* the origin of the custom in marriage of the bride being given away by a man, he said that it echoed former times when women without fathers or husbands had tutors. However, he felt that the custom remained useful because 'it putteth women in minde of a dutie, whereunto the verie imbecillitie of their nature and sexe doth bind them, namely to bee alwayes directed, guided and ordered by others, although our Positive Lawes doe not tie them now as Pupils'.[7] Positive laws did not exclude women from court actions, but the prejudice encapsulated in Hooker's remark and the general environment from which it sprang did little to encourage women to sue.

As previous chapters have disclosed, judicial figures as eminent as Thomas Egerton and Anthony Benn were not above expressing prejudice against women publicly in Star Chamber and Chancery. Meanwhile, Edward Coke, one of the foremost common lawyers of his age, is alleged to have kidnapped and beaten his own daughter Frances to make her agree to marry Sir John Villiers,

---

[7] Hooker, *Of the Lawes of Ecclesiastical Politie*, p. 398.

and to have left a battered widow who remarked on his death: 'We shall never see his like again, praises be to God.'[8] Regardless of the personal attitudes of judges, and indeed of the truth or falsehood of the stories told about them, the law was undeniably a male domain. Judges, magistrates, constables, commissioners and trial jurors were all male, it was men who made laws, men who staffed the courts, men who took down the testimony of witnesses and recorded judicial decisions and orders. I have mentioned the practical effects of coverture, but in this context it is worth considering its symbolic effect, for it was a doctrine built on the premise that law (and property) were men's matters, and as Juan Luis Vives put it, 'an honest wyfe shulde be ignorant, what lawes be made or anulled in her countrey, or what is done amonge men of lawe in the courte'.[9]

The commonly held beliefs that coverture somehow made married women immune from the criminal law, and that authorities regarded women as less threatening to public order than men and were therefore less likely to prosecute them, help to account for the participation of women in food riots and protests against unjust laws, enclosure, and radical breaks from custom. Lambarde, for example, believed that 'if a number of women (or children under the age of discretion) do flocke together for their own cause', they were not punishable by statutes forbidding unlawful assembly, 'unlesse a man of discretion moved them to assemble for the doing of some unlawful act'.[10] Bernard Capp has argued that documented incidents of female protest 'raise the question of female attitudes to male authority in the public sphere'.[11] Overall, the number of women who participated in riots, and the number of women-only protests, was relatively modest, but the existence of these popular beliefs (however ill-founded they turned out to be in practice) is revealing. The same can be said of the examples of men who wore women's clothing when protesting. Some men donned women's clothes simply to disguise their identities, some seem to have believed that it lessened their responsibility for unlawful acts (perhaps by marking their actions as community protests rather than purely self-interested

[8] L. Norsworthy, *The Lady of Bleeding Heart Yard* (London, 1935), pp. 11–12, 36–64; Webster, *The Devil's Law-Case*, p. viii; Prest, 'Law and women's rights', p. 171.

[9] Vives, *Instruction of a Christen Woman*, fol. 99ᵛ; and see chapter 3 above.

[10] As quoted in R.B. Manning, *Village Revolts; Social Protest and Popular Disturbances in England, 1509–1640* (Oxford, 1988), p. 96, and see pp. 97–8, 115–16, 281; R.A. Houlbrooke, 'Women's social life and common action in England from the fifteenth century to the eve of the civil war', *Continuity and Change*, 1 (1986), pp. 176–85; John Bohstedt, 'Gender, household and community politics: women and English riots 1790–1810', *Past and Present*, 120 (1988), pp. 88–90, 102, 119; Walter, 'Grain riots and popular attitudes to the law', pp. 62–3; Peter Clark, 'Popular protest and disturbance in Kent, 1558–1640', *Economic History review*, 2nd series, 29 (1976), pp. 365–82; Buchanan Sharp, *In Contempt of All Authority: Rural Artisans and Riot in the West of England, 1586–1660* (Berkeley and London, 1980), pp. 22–3, 35–6, 91, 105–6.

[11] As Capp further points out, 'paradoxically . . . women could sometimes turn their inferior legal and political status to their own advantage' as well as to the advantage of the men in their communities; Capp, 'Separate domains?', pp. 121–2.

crimes), while others probably borrowed this tactic of inversion from popular rituals which played upon the image of the 'unruly' or 'disorderly' woman.[12] Historians have yet to fully explain the symbolism behind female protest and cross-dressing, but at least one plank in the raft of beliefs on which these actions rested appears to have been the understanding that where authority and law were concerned, women were somehow outsiders.[13]

The affidavit books of Requests contain further evidence that certain women felt themselves to be in some sense outside of the law's reach. When process servers attempted to deliver subpoenas bearing the wax impression of the Privy Seal, some defendants or their servants repulsed them using violence. John Pery, for example, supposedly speared a process server in the shoulder, the arm and the leg with a pitchfork, saying that the Privy Seal he carried 'was made under a hedge' and that he was a 'Rascall runagate villaine and scabbe'.[14] However, in many cases it was defendants' daughters or female servants (or if they were male householders, their wives) who set about disrupting official process. When John Bowers fixed a writ of Privy Seal on the door of John Gill's house in Whitford in Devon, Gill's wife supposedly came out with a cudgel in her hands and 'did beate and evill entreate' Bowers, 'aswell with stripes as evill speeches', while her son and two daughters pulled down the Privy Seal 'and did teare yt and caste yt awaye'.[15] Walter Amendeth tried to serve process on John Bowser in his Cambridge shop, but 'the wyef of the said Bowser hurled the said Privie Seale out of the dore'. Lastly, the wife of a Sussex defendant told a process server that her husband was sick, but when this failed to deter him the woman's daughter ripped down the Privy Seal and 'cast it in the duste, and sayd hoggs should eate yt, yt should not hange theare', after which a servant took it and ran after the process server and threw it into a field.[16]

As was seen in chapter 3, dramatists also appear to have gained mileage from the fact that female characters in court scenes could be depicted as being outsiders within a male domain that was largely unfamiliar to them. Playwrights such as John Webster realised that the contrast between an innocent, wrongly accused litigant or defendant and a corrupt legal system (and between a malicious litigant and a just legal system) could often be exposed more effectively using a female defendant rather than a male.[17] Women were largely unrepresented politically, they were less likely to have their cries for justice taken seri-

---

[12] Examples of such rituals include skimmingtons in the West Midlands, 'riding the stang' in the north, charivaris in France, and numerous festivals of fertility across Europe; it is also significant that some convicted rioters were made to wear women's clothes while in the pillory; Sharp, *In Contempt of All Authority*, p. 108.

[13] N.Z. Davis, *Society and Culture in Early Modern France* (Cambridge, 1987), pp. 129–32, 146–50; Steve Hindle, 'The shaming of Margaret Knowsley: gossip, gender and the experience of authority in early modern England', *Continuity and Change*, 9 (1994), pp. 391–419.

[14] Allsebrook, 'The Court of Requests', p. 63.   [15] PRO Req 1/107, p. 1052; and see p. 1062.

[16] PRO Req 1/107, pp. 734, 763, 772, 1052, 1062, 1106; and see the examples of obstructive wives in chapter 6 above.   [17] See Blessing, 'Women and the law', pp. 8, 172–3.

ously, to be accustomed to the ways of the courtroom or to be literate in its languages, Latin and law French. Valeria, the rich and legally experienced heroine in Middleton's *The Widow* (c.1616) declares that 'I'm but a woman, /And, alas, ignorant in law businesses.'[18] Vittoria in *The White Devil* (c.1612) requests that the lawyer 'speake his usuall tongue', despite the fact that she understands Latin. 'By your favour', she says to the judge,

> I will not have my accusation clouded
> In a strange tongue: All this assembly
> Shall heare what you can charge me with.

When she is found guilty by her self-interested accusers she cries 'A rape, A rape', declaring to the judge, 'Yes you have ravisht justice,/ Forc't her to do your pleasure.'[19]

Other explanations for women's reluctance to litigate are suggested by the stereotypes and tactics that litigants and lawyers employed in pleadings directed against women. It was observed in the previous chapter how opponents often sought to undermine women's credit by questioning their social as well as their sexual modesty, depicting them as lewd and loud, greedy and disorderly. The very act of women waging campaigns of law in large central courts brought into question conventional images of female modesty, as well as raising commonly expressed suspicions of women's uncontrolled speech.[20] Litigants such as Richard Puttenham, who labelled his wife Mary a 'clamorous strumpet', drew upon and in turn fired the stereotype of the 'clamorous' litigating woman, described in chapter 3.[21] Most of these attacks were largely rhetorical, one strategy among many that litigants and their legal counsel employed, and judges would have recognised them as such. But the chord which litigants and lawyers were attempting to strike clearly existed. Egerton's suggestion that women with law suits be banned from appearing in person in Star Chamber, it will be remembered, was prompted by his frustration at the outbursts of the 'clamorous and impudent' wife of a plaintiff.[22]

Hugh Latimer and other authors who related the story of the importunate widow in Luke 18: 1–8 forgave this woman her importunity because she was being ignored by an unjust judge. Her example provided churchmen with a useful metaphor for deploring any situation in which the cries of the innocent fell on deaf ears.[23] However, in Requests, as in moral literature, the line between

---

[18] Middleton, *The Widow*, p. 20.   [19] John Webster, *The White Devil* (London, 1632), sig. E4.
[20] Men's uncontrolled speech was also an issue in this period, although most commentators regarded unguarded speech as a worse fault in women; Lodge, *Wits Miserie, and the Worlds Madnesse*, p. 88.   [21] PRO Req 1/14, fols 279[r-v]; see chapter 6 above.   [22] See chapter 3 above.
[23] Playwrights also depicted female characters whose cries for justice fell on deaf ears; Isabella in *Measure for Measure*, for example, vainly implores her father; 'O worthy Prince, dishonour not your eye/ By throwing it on any other object/ Till you have heard me, in my true complaint/ And given me justice, justice, justice, justice!'; *Measure for Measure*, V.i.22–25, in Peter Alexander, ed., *William Shakespeare: The Complete Works* (London and Glasgow, 1951).

the 'deserving' female litigant and the 'clamorous' female litigant could be a fine one. 'Importunate', after all, was a term of disparagement synonymous with tiresome or troublesome.[24]

Depending on the cause, it is possible that some women may have thought twice about going to law for fear of being labelled immodest or clamorous, or more likely for fear of bringing private matters into public view; for fear, in other words, of risking damage to their reputations. As the previous chapter showed, women's perceptions of their honour and reputations were as complex and multi-faceted as men's, an amalgam of the status and occupations of their parents and siblings, the wealth and credit of their current or previous husbands, their independence, their employment, the money they owned or brought to a marriage, their demeanour, the clothes they wore, their treatment of others, their success in conforming to, or exceeding, expected standards of behaviour, and so on. Yet as Laura Gowing has so persuasively argued, the most fundamental component of a woman's reputation, and the component most vulnerable to attack, was her sexual reputation.[25] As the author R.G. remarked in *The Mirrour of Modestie* in 1584: 'Tis a saieng not so common as true, that a woman's cheefest treasure is hir good name, and that she which hath crackt hir credite is halfe hanged; for death cutteth off all miseries, but infamie is the beginning of all sorrowes.'[26] Infamy most often arose from immodesty, and *any* kind of immodesty in women was taken to suggest sexual immodesty.[27]

Law courts, then, were 'public' as well as being 'male', in the sense that they were in public view. It is anachronistic to divide sixteenth century England too sharply into clearly defined public spheres and private or domestic spheres, just as it is dangerous to characterise the former as male and the latter as female.[28]

---

[24] The judge in Luke's gospel heard the widow's case 'to stop her incessant babbling', and in 1530 Leonard Cox wrote that 'Our lybertie is overcome . . . by the importunatnes of our wyves'; Cox, *The Art or Crafte of Rhetoryke*, p. 67; and see, *Margaret Hewett* v. *Thomas Fermor et al.*, PRO Req 1/19, p. 166; *Magdalen Holland* v. *Thomas Wilford*, PRO Req 1/19, p. 827; *Thomas & Margery Beadell* v. *Freemon Jrishe et al*, PRO Req 1/21, p. 61; the word 'importunity' was used against men as well as women.

[25] Gowing, *Domestic Dangers*, pp. 2–3, 52, 107, 129–30, 180, 230, 251.

[26] J.P. Collier, ed., *Illustrations of Old English Literature* (3 vols., New York, 1866; reprinted 1966), vol. 3, p. 19.

[27] As Elizabeth Foyster has shown, men were also deeply concerned about their sexual reputations, but male sexual reputation, especially among married men, was almost always intertwined with the sexual credit and behaviour of women; Foyster, 'The concept of male honour'; Gowing, *Domestic Dangers*, pp. 62–3, 94.

[28] On the complexity of the notion of 'public' and 'private' in different periods of English history, see Patricia Crawford, 'Public duty, conscience and women in early modern England', in John Morrill, Paul Slack and Daniel Woolf, eds., *Public Duty and Private Conscience in Seventeenth-Century England* (Oxford, 1993); Willen, 'Women in the public sphere', pp. 559–75; Gowing, *Domestic Dangers*, pp. 26, 269–70; Bennett, 'Public power and authority', pp. 18–19, 24; Leonore Davidoff, *Worlds Between: Historical Perspectives on Gender and Class* (Cambridge, 1995), pp. 227–64; Staves, *Married Women's Separate Property*, pp. 196–7.

The boundary between public life and private life in this period was blurred, and women and men regularly crossed it both inside and outside their households. But the boundary nevertheless existed, and contemporaries shared a strong sense of which spaces might be deemed public and which private, depending on the activities that took place within them. Law courts were public symbols of the justice and authority of crown and parliament, but they were also public in the sense of publicity. In common with defamation, slander and libel (which by legal definition had to occur in public or be public knowledge) going to court usually involved individuals making matters that were known only to a few people known to many people.[29]

The extent to which making accusations in a public court might involve a different, or more complicated, set of considerations for women than for men can be sensed from the way husbands reacted when their wives decided to sue them. It was noted in chapters 6 and 8 how Humfrey Stafford regarded his wife Elizabeth's suit against him as an affront to his authority that rivalled her adultery in causing him public humiliation. Humfrey Lloyd reacted in a similar way when his wife Anne accused him of assaulting her. He put it to the Masters that:

if she were but halfe soe wise as shee myght Be, or woulde but enter into A due consideracion of her estate and the estate of this defendant, and rightly consider that a house devided in it selfe cannott stand . . . then woulde shee have borne with this defendants infermyties, if any such were in him, . . . and not have published them soe openly to both their Ruines if it should affect as it is expeckted.[30]

Anne Lloyd went to court to escape a dangerous and intolerable marriage, but according to Humfrey in doing so she risked the ruination of her (and his) honour. Other women in sixteenth and seventeenth century England found themselves in similar binds. David Lindley has argued that Frances Howard, Countess of Somerset, had to choose between continuing her deeply unhappy marriage to the Earl of Essex, or risk shame and censure if she instigated divorce or annulment proceedings.[31] Cynthia Herrup has drawn attention to the impossible situation in which the wife of the disgraced Earl of Castlehaven found herself. Although the law Lords deemed her innocent of all of the allegations made against her, and sentenced her husband to death for his appalling treatment of both her and his servants, she could not prevent her reputation being tarnished by public knowledge of the indignities she claimed to have suffered.[32] Just as depressing is the example of Katherine Willoughby, who found

---

[29] Humfrey Lloyd answered his wife's accusations in Requests because, 'a publike defamacion is not to be cleared with a pryvat defence'; *Anne Lloyd* v. *Humfrey Lloyde*, PRO Req 2/234/61, m. 2, A, Dem.   [30] *Anne Lloyd* v. *Humfrey Lloyde*, PRO Req 2/234/61, m. 2, A, Dem.

[31] Lindley, *The Trials of Frances Howard*, pp. 89–93.

[32] Cynthia Herrup, '"To pluck bright honour from the pale-faced moon": gender and honour in the Castlehaven story', *Transactions of the Royal Historical Society*, 6th series, 6 (1996), pp. 137–59; Dolan, *Dangerous Familiars*, pp. 85, 87.

herself faced not with two difficult choices, but with three. According to Katherine and certain deponents, she decided to sue her husband Kenelm on the day that he offered her an impossible ultimatum. He told her that he would be a loyal and loving husband to her forever if she would agree to admit falsely that she had committed adultery with one of his enemies. If she refused, he said he would beat her, desert her and perhaps even kill her. Faced with a choice between physical damage and damage to her sexual honour, Katherine chose a third option and fled from Kenelm's brutal authority to seek relief in Requests.[33]

In all of these examples women came to court. The horrific situations they were seeking to escape far outweighed any worries they might have had about making their domestic lives public. Similarly, a belief that the law was predominantly a male domain was clearly no deterrent to Anne Clifford, Elizabeth Cheeke, and to hundreds of other women who brought actions each year in Requests, Chancery, Common Pleas and Queen's Bench. But it appears that the very same concerns that led scores of women to hurry to the church courts to challenge the slanders of their neighbours may have made some women reluctant to initiate actions in other courts. Mary Browne, Countess of Southampton, for example, wrote to her father about a crisis in her marriage, saying 'good my Lord if it may be, lett it be [heard] & ended by some counsellors & go no ffarder: for very loth I wolde be to have my name come in tryall in open courte'.[34] Other women chose to conduct their legal affairs with, or behind, others. It was observed in chapter 5 how widows sometimes delegated legal authority to their sons, their apprentices or to other male advisors, and studies of private papers and correspondence reveal further instances of women who oversaw legal actions that concerned their own property and affairs, or the affairs of their husbands or sons, although they were not themselves named as parties.[35] To take an example from Requests, *John Kitchen* v. *Arthur Huet* was well under way when both men chanced upon each other in Cheapside, and Huet told Kitchen and his servant that he would refuse to obey any order the Masters made, before adding, 'sett your harte at rest for you shall never have the

---

[33] Kenelm responded by alleging that Katherine had committed adultery with this man; *Katherine Willoughbie* v. *Kenelm Willoughbie & Henry Fenne*, PRO Req 2/286/45, B; PRO Req 2/31/3, I, D, deponent William Dutton; and see chapters 6 and 8 above.

[34] Merton, 'The women who served Queen Mary and Queen Elizabeth', p. 182; when Lady Anne Glenham promised Julius Caesar payment in return for interceding on behalf of a friend, she requested that he 'dispatch this matter with all convenient speed, care and secrecy', saying that she 'would not be named in it for much money'; Lady Anne Glenham to Julius Caesar, November 1604; BL Additional MS 12,506, fol. 331; of course, the fear of adverse publicity and shame could also make men wary litigants; Foyster, 'The concept of male honour', pp. 191, 231.

[35] In the later seventeenth century, Lady Chaytor ran the estates of her disgraced husband and dealt with his creditors on his behalf, without her name appearing on the relevant documents; Craig Muldrew, 'Women, debt litigation and credit in early modern England', paper delivered to the 'Women, Trade & Business conference', University of Exeter, 15–17 July 1996.

bond, yf I lye in prison all the dayes of my lyef'. Kitchen's servant reported this exchange to his mistress (Kitchen's wife): 'And his said mistres sayed, sayeth he so, he shall not keepe my bonde, but my husbande shall have yt from him and I will release my husbande.'[36]

The suggestion that it was more difficult for women to enter courts of law than for men is hardly earth-shattering. What is surprising is the extent to which the fault for this imbalance lay not with institutional rules and legal sanctions but with more general currents of prejudice that ran within wider society. The wall of words that confronted women, the barrage of advice about correct behaviour, the debates about women's worth, the praise and dispraise in rhetorical pamphlets and bawdy ballads, are all well known. Despite incessant calls to stay home, to remain chaste, and to speak only when spoken to, women worked, they went to market, they exerted political influence and exchanged political gossip, they shouted, they cursed, they rioted. As Keith Thomas has noted, the volume of appeals is itself evidence for the failure of those appeals, and scholars such as Kathleen McLuskie believe that they represented a 'consoling fiction', one that tells us more about elite male anxiety about women than about how women actually behaved.[37] But this cannot be the end of the story.

While it is clear that advice literature did not have the effect apparently intended by its authors – it is often easier to find examples of women defying this advice than to find women who conformed to it – this does not mean that these works, and more importantly the well of beliefs and opinions from which they sprang, exerted no influence. The climate of advice and assumptions clearly affected women's language and outward demeanour, if not their actions.[38] This is apparent from the disclaimers or token expressions of humility that many women used to preface their actions or words when they entered traditionally male worlds, whether to litigate, to write or publish, to transact business or to speak in public institutions.[39] In 1564 Queen Elizabeth addressed a Cambridge University audience in Latin, and apologised that 'Although that womanly shamefacedness . . . might well determine me from delivering this my unlaboured

---

[36] *John Kitchen v. Arthur Huet*, PRO Req 1/107, p. 930.

[37] Linda Fitz, '"What says the married woman": marriage theory and feminism in the English Renaissance', *Mosaic*, 13 (1980), pp. 11–12, 18; McLuskie, *Renaissance Dramatists*, p. 225.

[38] Lisa Jardine has argued that women in this period were 'increasingly constrained by an ideology of duty and obedience which removed from them the most elementary possibilities for rebellion against traditional serving roles'; Jardine, *Still Harping on Daughters'*, p. 68; Linda Woodbridge has remarked that 'Renaissance women could not take group feminist action . . . partly because they must have believed what literature said about them'; Woodbridge, *Women and the English Renaissance'*, p. 326.

[39] Ann Jones, 'Nets and bridles: early modern conduct books and sixteenth-century women's lyrics', in Nancy Armstrong and Leonard Tennehouse, eds., *The Ideology of Conduct: Essays on Literature and the History of Sexuality* (New York and London, 1987), pp. 40, 48–52; Anne Larsen, 'Legitimizing the daughter's writing: Catherine des Roches' proverbial good wife', *Sixteenth Century Journal*, 21 (1990), p. 560.

speech and oration before so great an assembly of the learned, yet . . .' and so she continued and delivered a lengthy speech.[40] Anne Locke prefaced her translation of Jean Taffin's *Of the Markes of the Children of God, and of their Comfort in Afflictions* (published in 1590) with a similar expression of feminine modesty:

Everie one in his calling is bound to doo somewhat to the furtherance of the holie building; but because great things by reason of my sex, I may not doo, and that which I may, I ought to doo, I have according to my duetie, brought my poore basket of stones to the strengthning of the walles of that Jerusalem, whereof (by grace) wee are all both Citizens and members.[41]

Further examples can be found in private correspondence and in court records. Maria Thynne began a letter to her husband: 'My best Thomken I know thou wilt say (receiving two letters in a day from me) that I have tried the virtue of aspen leaves under my tongue, which makes me prattle so much, but consider that all is business, for of my own natural disposition I assure thee there is not a more silent woman living than myself.'[42] Elizabeth Hargrave used her rejoinder in Requests to affirm that everything in her answer was true 'Albeit the Complainant opprobriouslie and unseemelie imputeth Audacious bouldnes to this defendant'.[43] Margaret Knowsley confessed the wrongs done against her 'with much discontentment', because she said 'it is against the rule of modesty and womanlike behaviour to publish such like matters'.[44] In 1610 a woman in a defamation case asked: 'Have I had any more lawe than an honest woman should have?'[45] These women commandeered the language of humility to their cause, demonstrating their awareness that failure to explain why they were speaking (or writing, or making accusations at law), when women's speech was incessantly condemned as an indicator of rebelliousness or unchastity, might result in husbands, fathers or male and female onlookers aligning them with 'the monstrous regiment of women'.

The conventions of female speech differed from the conventions of male speech. The ability of certain women to observe the form of conventions while ignoring their substance, and in venues like Requests of joining their lawyers in manipulating images of womanhood and poverty to advantage, does not erase the fact that these conventions placed restrictions on women's freedom to speak and act. The fact that contemporaries were alive to the differences between male and female speech in court is made explicit in drama, especially in plays where playwrights have their characters assume the guise of the opposite sex to speak

---

[40] Maria Perry, ed., *Elizabeth I: The Word of a Prince* (London, 1990), p. 179; and see Jardine, *Still Harping on Daughters*, ch. 6; Deborah Greenhut, 'Persuade yourselves: women, speech and sexual politics in Tudor society', *Proteus*, 3 (1986), pp. 42–8; Fletcher, *Gender, Sex and Subordination*, p. 79. [41] As quoted in Greaves, *Society and Religion*, p. 310.

[42] Alison Wall, ed., *Two Elizabethan Women: Correspondence of Joan and Maria Thynne 1575–1611*, Wiltshire Record Society, 38 (Devizes, 1983), p. 48.

[43] *John Leake v. Elizabeth Hargrave*, PRO Req 2/165/135 [m. 1], Rj.

[44] Hindle, 'The shaming of Margaret Knowsley', p. 410. [45] Gowing, *Domestic Dangers*, p. 132.

in legal settings. Dressed as a judge, Shakespeare's Portia possesses one of the most eloquent legal voices in print. When the character Lorenzo in *Swetnam the Woman-Hater Arraigned by Women* (c.1618) disguises himself as Atlanta to address an assembly of judges, the contrast with Portia could hardly be more striking. Dressed in female garb, he tells the court that it is an honour 'farre beyond my weaknesse' to be accepted, 'I but a woman, before men to plead'. As 'she' goes on to explain:

> Dumbe feare and bashfulnesse to speake
> Bold Orators of State, men grave and wise,
> That can at every breathing pause, correct
> The slipp'ry passages of a womans speech:
> But yet withall my hopes are doubly arm'd . . .
> First, that my bashfull weaknesse claymes excuse,
> And is to speake before such temp'rate Judges,
> Who in their wisdome will, no doubt, connive
> At small defects in me a silly woman.

This speech is doubly ironic because Atlanta is an Amazon, and the lawyers in this comedy remark on the excellence of this rhetorical ploy of claiming weakness to make opponents appear unchivalrous.[46] The knowledge that the author included this episode for its comic effect does not undermine its value as an indicator of the malleability of language, and of the way expectations based upon gender could constrain female speech.

The imagery of pit and pedestal met women at every turn in sixteenth and seventeenth century England. Not just in the pairing of archetypes, such as modest and immodest or chaste and incontinent, but in the all-embracing images of 'good woman' and 'bad woman' from which these dichotomies derived. In the rhetoric of debate literature and ballads, just as in the rhetoric of pleadings, some women were good, but most were bad.[47] The authors of sermons and conduct books reinforced this point by advocating extremely high standards of piety and obedience, setting up ideal images of womanhood which were advertised and sustained in exemplary literature, and contrasting these images with their polar opposites.[48] The Masters of Requests were not above

---

[46] As quoted in Woodbridge, *Women and the English Renaissance*, p. 302; Frances Dolan has shown how the character Elizabeth Arden in *Arden of Faversham*, manipulates male as well as female stereotypes; Dolan, *Dangerous Familiars*, especially pp. 52–3.

[47] As Linda Woodbridge has observed; 'Literature repeatedly took refuge in an unexamined paradox: while one bad woman "shamed her sex" and served as an impetus to general misogyny, one good, strong, self-sufficient woman was dismissed as an exception to the rule'; Woodbridge, *Women and the English Renaissance*, p. 326.

[48] A typical example is William Gouge, who in *Of Domesticall Duties* punctuated calls for good behaviour with counter examples of misbehaviour; e.g., 'Contrary to the forenamed subjection is the opinion of many wives who think themselves every way as good as their husbands and no way inferior to them'; 'Contrarie is their practise, who must and will have all the prate. If their husbands have begun to speake, their slippery tongues cannot expect and tarrie till he have done'; Gouge, *Of Domesticall Duties*, pp. 271, 282, 285.

drawing upon similar stereotypes and dichotomies for the purposes of satire. In *The Rule of Reason*, Thomas Wilson repeated the tired adage that 'a woman hath her name so given her by cause she bringeth wo unto man', and in *A Discourse of Usury*, he had his character the Doctor speak of women's 'myserable and gredie desyres to gett, their aptnes to supersticion, their greatnes of pryde, their lousenes of lyfe' and 'theire ambicious desires, without all reason to have all soverayntie'. Wilson's Doctor excluded, 'in all this my speache againste women', all good women, yet he added that such women 'are very fewe in deede, and maye be easely packed up, al the whole packe of them, in a very small rowme'.[49]

The chasm between the ideals set out in conduct literature and the reality of women's actual life experience did not necessarily represent the failure of the wielders of patriarchal authority to assert their chosen ideals and to subdue women. If nothing else, the creation and perpetuation of constricting standards of feminine behaviour, accompanied by negative references in rhetorical pamphlets and in countless 'harmless' jests, served to undermine women's confidence. As Linda Woodbridge has observed, many of the dangerous stereotypes that hamper women in their daily lives 'have been built up piece by piece like a great mosaic. And the pieces are jokes.'[50] The gap between published ideals and reality may therefore constitute one of the supports that helped sustain patriarchal authority. Just as the church could inspire feelings of guilt in those who failed in their attempts to emulate the purity of Christ, some women might have felt inadequate if they failed to emulate exemplary women like Katherin Brettergh.[51] Was this the thinking of moralists and memorial writers? Failure to live up to good stereotypes could leave women in the position of fearing they might be judged alongside bad stereotypes. If not a pitiable widow then a clamorous widow. If not Mary then Eve.[52]

CHANGING STRUCTURES

What are the implications of the two themes outlined here, women's increasing use of the courts, and the cultural pressures impeding women's participation in

---

[49] Thomas Wilson, *The Rule of Reason, Conteinyng the Arte of Logique* (London, 1551), sig. Dvii^v; Wilson, *A Discourse Upon Usury*, p. 297.

[50] Woodbridge, *Women and the English Renaissance*, p. 32; and see p. 81.

[51] *The Christian Life and Death of Mistris Katherin Brettergh*; Stephen Geree, *The Ornament of Women. Or, a Description of the True Excellency of Women. Delivered in a Sermon at the Funerall of M. Elizabeth Machell* (London, 1639); see also Peter Lake, 'Feminine piety and personal potency: the 'emancipation' of Mrs Jane Ratcliffe', *The Seventeenth Century*, 2 (1987), pp. 143–65.

[52] Vives, for example, remarked that 'The honeste wyves ought to hate and blame the noughty wyves: as a shame and [slander] unto al kynd'; Vives, *Instruction of a Christen Woman*, fol. 61^v; on the possibility that ballads may have had a similar regulative effect, see Foyster, 'A laughing matter?', pp. 5–21, especially p. 18.

legal processes? And what do they suggest about women's legal fortunes over a much longer period, in the decades and centuries preceding and following Elizabeth's reign?

So far, historians have found it difficult to reach a consensus about women's legal status and how it changed over time. There are those who argue that women's legal and social position worsened over the course of the sixteenth, seventeenth and eighteenth centuries.[53] Others, meanwhile, suggest that it improved.[54] The former group can point to precedents from the days when the law was supposedly less rigorously enforced and exceptions to general principles were common. Alice Clark, for example, highlighted the flexible interpretation of coverture embodied in the published customs of the City of London, which in the medieval period allowed married women to ply their own trades and to litigate in courts of Record as if they were *femes sole*.[55] Other examples of this type are not difficult to find. Thomas Egerton, in *Calvin's case* in the early seventeenth century, reminded the judges in Exchequer about Sibbel Belknappe's case (decided during the reign of Henry IV) in which the wife of a judge brought an action without naming her husband as a co-plaintiff, 'and it was adjudged good and she recovered'.[56] The latter group, who argue that women's legal position improved, can point to the increasing sophistication of uses and trusts within marriage settlements, the extension in 1691 of benefit of clergy to convicted female felons, and changes in marriage; prior to this period the lord of the manor could decide who the widow of a tenant should marry, while at the end of the period divorce followed by remarriage was possible without an annulment or an act of parliament to sanction it.[57]

---

[53] Sachs and Wilson, *Sexism and the Law*; Clark, *Working Life of Women*, p. 237; Lawrence Stone, *The Family, Sex and Marriage in England 1500–1800*, abridged edition (London, 1979), p. 202; Charlotte Stopes, *British Freewomen*, p. 121; Roger Thompson, *Women in Stuart England and America* (London, 1974), p. 5.

[54] Cioni, *Women and Law*, pp. i, 2; Glanz, 'The legal position of English women', p. 10; Wright, *Middle-Class Culture*, pp. 465–6, 473; Underdown, 'The taming of the scold', p. 136; though see David Underdown, *Revel, Riot and Rebellion: Popular Politics and Culture in England 1603–1660* (Oxford, 1987), p. 38; Prest, 'Law and women's rights', p. 183; and see Maclean, *Renaissance Notion of Women*, p. 80, n. 55; for the more general debate about the position of women see Amy Erickson's introduction to Clark, *Working Life of Women*.

[55] Clark, *Working Life of Women*, p. 152.

[56] As quoted in Cioni, 'Women and Law', p. 29; on another occasion, in the case of *Stausly* v. *Crosse*, Egerton 'woulde give noe order in Chancery for a wife severed from her husband saying lett the Bishopp call them together and allow her Allymony', however he acknowledged that in the past Chancellor Bacon 'did otherwise in the Case of Crippes'; C.U.L. Gg.2.31, fol. 379ᵛ; see also Holdsworth, *A History of English Law*, vol. 5, p. 311.

[57] John Beattie argues that the extension of benefit of clergy to women was partly the result of out-raged London shop owners lobbying parliament in response to a female crime wave. They believed female offenders were escaping any form of punishment because of a general reluctance to prosecute them when the death penalty would result. The extension therefore reflected a more punitive attitude towards women rather than an increase in sympathy for them; J.H. Beattie, 'Women in the Old Bailey'; paper given to Durham early modern seminar, 12 May 1993.

The divergence of opinion about women's rights results from two main causes, firstly the complexity of the English legal system and the myriad of variables that could influence women's experiences of the law, and secondly the insufficiency of existing knowledge. However, thinking in terms of rises or falls in women's legal fortunes may not, in the end, be very useful. To begin with, this approach suggests a steady progression from past Dark or Golden Ages to better or worse legal pastures, when in practice change was more often haphazard than predictable and linear. As Susan Staves has observed of married women's property rights, 'the same struggles appear to be repeated over and over again with only minor variations of vocabulary, depending on what particular forms of property were important at different historical moments'.[58] More importantly, attempts to chart rises and falls imply that the rights of all women in English society at any given time can be measured and averaged, a proposition that few historians would ever consider for men. The truth is that in the realm of law some women made gains over the course of the so-called early modern period, while others saw their rights or their access to legal process curtailed. And to complicate matters further, some of the rights trumpeted as women's rights pertained as much to women's families, and to the dynastic maintenance of property and honour, as to women themselves (and vice versa).[59] Eileen Power's reflection that the position of women is 'one thing in theory, another in legal position, yet another in everyday life', therefore needs to be extended even further, for the position of women could vary as widely within the confines of the law as it could outside it.[60]

The full story of women's rights under non-criminal law cannot be told without first unpicking the individual threads of justice that made up the English legal system, analysing each jurisdiction in isolation, and then observing how they interacted together. And throughout this process it is essential to remain sensitive to differences in women's experiences of the law caused by, or related to, their social class. These are difficult tasks that require extensive examinations of central and local court records, statutes, case reports, pamphlets, private papers, diaries and the correspondence of litigants, judges, crown officials and members of parliament. At present it is easier to raise questions than to provide answers.[61] However, combining the findings of this study with the little work on women and litigation that historians have so far undertaken, it is possible to make some general observations and to speculate about the effect different changes may have had on individual women. It is difficult to generalise about these matters, for all of the reasons I have just outlined, but

---

[58] Staves, *Married Women's Separate Property*, p. 229.
[59] Although see Erickson, 'Common law versus common practice', pp. 21–39.
[60] See p. 1, n. 1 above.
[61] For an insightful list of such questions where married women are concerned, see Staves, *Married Women's Separate Property*, pp. 203–4.

making attempts when the evidence allows, despite the knowledge that new interpretations will inevitably come to modify or supersede the old, is important, for it ensures that questions about change remain at the centre of ongoing research and debates about litigation and women's rights before the law.

Dividing the legal system into its constituent parts, it seems that women's rights were in flux in the sixteenth and early seventeenth centuries largely because the jurisdictions that extended them rights were in flux. As we have seen, the common law was continuing its steady, but not inevitable, climb to predominance, encroaching on to the territories of most of its rivals. Many of its underlying principles worked against women, especially if they married, but it provided dower rights to widows and regarded women with *femes sole* status as legally competent beings. Single women and widows who possessed written bonds or other agreements could sue defaulters for non-performance, even if married women could do little without the co-operation of their husbands. The church courts, by contrast, recognised married women as competent litigants and admitted a higher proportion of female litigants than any of their competitors, as well as overseeing a system of intestate inheritance that treated sons and daughters equally, in marked contrast to primogeniture. These courts participated in the boom in litigation, but ecclesiastical justice nevertheless lost ground to the common law, as the regulation of personal morality and other matters such as defamation increasingly became matters for secular jurisdictions in the wake of religious reformation in the sixteenth century, the abolition of the court of High Commission in 1641, and the consolidation of centralised secular authority.[62] Customary law, which could be particularly beneficial to widows, was also in decline, in the sense that less and less land in England was held by customary tenures. Nevertheless, it provided a remarkably resilient form of local justice, and many women with customary interests found their options expanded for a time by their increasing ability to bring appeals in Requests, Chancery, the equity side of Exchequer, and later at common law.

The influence of equity grew as caseloads increased in both central and regional prerogative courts, and the refinement in these institutions of equitable devices like the trust provided women with opportunities for combating some of the more damaging effects of coverture. But as the evidence from Requests confirms, the nature of equity was changing, becoming more formal and less flexible or discretionary. Maria Cioni has argued that this change was beneficial for women, because it gave to their rights a certainty that was previously lacking. I would argue that the opposite was the case for many poorer women who came to court seeking justice in their particular cases, rather than certainty or consistency with previous decisions about which they were probably

---

[62] Gowing, *Domestic Dangers*, p. 31; for information on later church court litigation, see Meldrum, 'A woman's court', pp. 1–20.

unaware.[63] Equity costs were also multiplying, for as levels of business grew, procedures became more formalised, fees rose, and the services of lawyers became increasingly essential for the drawing up of complicated agreements and settlements. This situation worsened considerably in the 1640s, when Requests and other prerogative courts disappeared or were abolished, so that after 1660 the increasingly expensive Chancery assumed a virtual monopoly of the equitable jurisdiction at Westminster.[64]

This staccato listing of changes in women's fortunes, and in the fortunes of particular courts, suggests little in the way of any overarching pattern. On the contrary, these movements seem almost arbitrary, the serendipitous result of competition between neighbouring courts. However, many of these shifts can be reconciled if they are considered in the context of more general movements towards the increasing individualisation of property rights and the growing sophistication of organs of justice and government. The period from 1300 to 1800 witnessed what might broadly be described as the rise of private property, especially where land was concerned.[65] Control of real property increasingly shifted into the hands of individuals, as commons were enclosed, feudal tenures like knight socage were abolished and surviving customary tenures like copy-hold increasingly gave way to freehold and leasehold. This led to a reduction in the ancient obligations and dues that attached to many tenures, but it also involved a mental shift from the possession of land organised around the web of personal relationships – between interest holders, tenants and lords – that con-stituted tenure, to a sense that land could be 'owned'.[66] Instead of holding landed interests 'by the will of the lord', for example, more and more rights became transferable and saleable, and freehold and fixed-term leases became the norm.[67] In inheritance, uniform customs and rules (the distribution of land according to the tenets of primogeniture, the distribution of goods according to the custom of 'thirds', and so on) gave way to freedom of disposition.

[63] Cioni, 'Women and Law', p. 12; those who entered the court *in forma pauperis* were not risking their savings on legal fees, and most desired 'her Majesty's accustomed clemency' rather than cer-tainty born of precedent.

[64] Chancery costs were traditionally greater than those of the common law courts; Brooks, *Pettyfoggers*, p. 72.

[65] On the change 'from a world of relatively stable landed property to a world in which land increas-ingly becomes a commodity like others', see Staves, *Married Women's Separate Property*, espe-cially p. 212; on contemporary perceptions and representations of these changes, see Andrew McRae, *God Speed the Plough: The Representation of Agrarian England, 1500–1660* (Cambridge, 1996), especially pp. 7, 14.

[66] Neil Jones describes a similar shift, observable in the language of pleadings, in contemporary perceptions of the trust; 'like seisin, the trust at first exists between two people rather than between a person and a thing'; Jones, 'Trusts', p. 7, n. 9.

[67] Susan Staves has described the possibility of a change in the eighteenth century from owners seeing property as something to use but not to sell or develop (as cutting down a forest to make way for a factory would constitute 'waste'), to them seeing property as something more abstract, transformable and exploitable; Staves, *Married Women's Separate Property*, p. 209.

Increasingly, property owners could decide for themselves how they wished to divide their estates during their lives and at death. From the fourteenth century onwards, landholders had been able to achieve this by creating uses, vesting land in third parties (foeffees) and instructing them about how to distribute interests when vestors died, but into the sixteenth century and beyond, growing numbers of individuals devised increasing proportions of their property, quite literally, according to their 'wills'.[68]

The general move from inheritance imposed by custom to inheritance organised by individuals was mirrored in the changing property entitlements of widows. As we have seen, dower, like primogeniture, was a default mechanism that gave widows rights over a proportion, usually a third, of any land their husbands held in fee during marriage. But over the course of the period fewer individuals relied on dower and more and more turned to jointure. Once again (for reasons that will be discussed in a moment) a uniform procedure lost ground to an alternative that allowed individuals to negotiate rights to property and to tailor them according to their personal wishes and needs.

Concurrent with these changes, the legal system (embodied in parliament, the magistracy and the courts) was expanding in size and sophistication. With improving communications and expanding infrastructures came an increasing uniformity of rules across the country and between centre and periphery. As Cioni rightly pointed out, 'precedent' and 'certainty' came to be watchwords of the legal system, epitomised by the common law and aided by the growth of law reporting, first in manuscript and then in published reports.[69] As the common law waxed, custom and ecclesiastical law waned. As I mentioned a moment ago, equity, which early in the fifteenth century was still a loose term denoting an ill-defined set of principles of natural justice, matured (or hardened) in the seventeenth century into an identifiable system with increasingly fixed rules and procedures. The relative informality of the early Elizabethan Requests and the determination of its Masters to hear each case on its merits (sometimes almost regardless of previous practice), contrasts sharply with the formality of procedure, the published reports, and the business-like consistency of the eighteenth century Chancery.

What were the likely implications of these changes for women? The theoretical possibilities for women undoubtedly improved. Increasingly sophisticated uses and trusts gave women powers over their property, both during and after marriage, that were unknown to their predecessors. But if the potential to

---

[68] The Statute of Wills (1540), passed in the wake of the Statute of Uses (1536), empowered testators to dispose of their real and personal property at their 'will and pleasure'; Baker, *An Introduction to English Legal History*, p. 343; and see pp. 289–94.

[69] The Masters in Requests almost never referred to previous decisions in their judgments, whereas in the twentieth century it is possible to find judges citing precedent cases from the nineteenth, eighteenth, seventeenth and sixteenth centuries.

protect property or extend personal rights grew, so too did the potential for the opposite to happen. While well constructed marriage settlements could safeguard women's property, give them power to make a will, and ensure them a generous share of their husbands' estates, equally well constructed strict settlements could all but disinherit them. The same was true of the move from dower to jointure. As was mentioned in chapter 2, many women preferred jointure to dower because dower did not apply to land that was entailed, or to land that was tied up in uses at the time of marriage, and with more and more landholders vesting their lands in the names of third parties from the thirteenth or fourteenth centuries onwards, by the sixteenth century its effect was considerably diluted.[70] Other women preferred jointures because dower could be difficult to claim. Grace Mildmay complained in her autobiography of the lack of provision her husband had made for her widowhood, saying he 'bound his portion of land by a perpetuity and made me no jointure (but left me to the third which might be troublesome and uncertain)'.[71] Finally, it was the flexibility of jointure that made it attractive. Powerful widows who married two, three or four times could amass considerable amounts of capital through judicious jointures, because the value of a jointure could be set at any level a couple agreed upon. They could also use legal means to maintain control of their interests during marriage, as well as retaining ownership of those interests after marriage should they outlive their husbands.

There were reasons, however, why husbands and fathers might prefer jointure over dower, and why very few jointures exceeded the level that dower would have allowed (had all a man's lands been held in fee). The gradual move from dower to specified lands held jointly by husband and wife, and then to jointures that guaranteed an annuity (an annual money pension), was a move that took lands out of women's control. The same can be said about the trend to replace widow's life interests in lands with interests that lasted, as widow's estate usually lasted, only so long as widows remained 'soule, chaste and unmaryed'.[72] These changes lessened the potential for conflict between widows and heirs, as well as removing uncertainty from the land market. The displacement of dower by jointure represented a further marker on the road to private property, one that allowed husbands more freedom to sell real property without having to consider their wives' interests, and gave men and women more freedom to buy real property without having to fear that vendors' wives might enter writs of dower in the future if they became widows. This freedom was entrenched after a

---

[70] 'By 1500 it could be asserted that the greater part of the land in England was held in use'; Baker, *Introduction to English Legal History*, p. 287.

[71] As quoted in Pollock, *With Faith and Physic*, pp. 14, 33.

[72] Staves, *Married Women's Separate Property*, p. 99; *Johanne Howe* v. *John Blewett*, PRO 2/220/70; *John & Anne Wallgrave* v. *Anne Nashe et al.*, PRO Req 2/291/5, A; *Edward & Anna Moone* v. *Roger Heron*, PRO Req 2/68/22; and see chapter 2 above.

clause in the Statute of Uses (1536) stated that a woman who had a jointure prepared before marriage was forever barred from claiming dower. Eileen Spring has referred to this statute as 'the husband's charter', for this clause removed the widow's right to choose dower over jointure in cases where the former was more generous than the latter.[73]

The apparent decline in women's control of land that came with the move from dower thirds to money jointures (in common with the substitution of money or other equivalents for land in the inheritance of heiresses-at-law) was significant, given the associations of land with actual as well as symbolic power.[74] Furthermore, as argued in chapter 2 above, there is evidence that this shift also brought about a decline in the average value of widows' entitlements. Most elite women's jointures were worth considerably less than the one third interest of dower, and their value appears to have decreased over time.[75] According to one estimate, the average ratio of portions to jointures, the amount a woman contributed at marriage to the amount she might collect each year as a widow, approached four or five to one in 1550, but had sunk to nearly ten to one by 1700.[76] This was partly because the average value of landed estates had increased, so that the changes to widows' entitlements were not as great in real terms as these figures suggest, but it also reflected an increase in the value of portions, and the direction of change remains unmistakable.[77] Amongst women of lesser means, this shift held far less significance, because the difference between the value of lands and of jointures was less stark. And in the many cases where couples possessed no lands of their own, any kind of marriage settlement whatsoever was more beneficial than common law dower.

It seems likely, then, that legal opportunities increased for a minority of

---

[73] Where jointure was arranged after marriage, a woman who was left a widow could choose whether to accept this jointure or rely on dower instead; Spring, *Law, Land and Family*, pp. 42–9; on the precise nature and practical effect of this legal change on the negotiation of jointures in pre-nuptial agreements, and on the further erosions of women's rights that came with the development of a doctrine of 'equitable jointure', see Staves, *Married Women's Separate Property*, pp. 97–103.

[74] As Spring, Staves and Amy Erickson all point out, heiresses-at-law who did not inherit land (due to the operation of marriage settlements or trusts) were almost always compensated with alternative (though almost never equally valuable) forms of property or money; but this substitution usually gave them 'entitlement to profit from capital, but not control over capital itself or the power to alienate capital'; Staves, *Married Women's Separate Property*, p. 222; Spring, 'The heiress-at-law', pp. 273–96.

[75] Barbara Harris, 'Property, power, and personal relations: elite mothers and sons in Yorkist and early Tudor England', *Signs*, 15 (1990), p. 609, n. 7.

[76] Stone, *The Crisis of the Aristocracy*, pp. 643–5; Habbakuk, 'Marriage settlements in the eighteenth century', p. 27; Spring, *Law, Land, and Family*, pp. 49–65; on the difficulty of measuring the ratio between portion and jointure, see Staves, *Married Women's Separate Property*, p. 204.

[77] In many instances the duration of jointure entitlements decreased as well as their value, as jointures for life increasingly gave way to jointures that lasted only as long as a woman remained a widow; Erickson, *Women and Property*, p. 120; Staves, *Married Women's Separate Property*, p. 100.

women. Firstly, for those rare individuals from the ranks of the elites who not only had access to capable lawyers but who could stand their ground in marriage negotiations when bargaining with future husbands and their families. Secondly, for those women from lower down the social scale who managed to use legal and equitable instruments to protect the moneys and moveable goods they had earned or inherited. But the majority of women, who did not have access to lawyers or to the world of documents and courts, or whose access to land was curtailed, saw their legal and property rights eroded. It appears, therefore, that the increasing power of the individual in matters of property favoured men more than women, because those who enjoyed the lion's share of the enlarged freedoms to buy and sell land, to dispose of property and so on, were heads of households.[78] And male heads of households outnumbered female heads throughout this period, by a ratio of between three and four to one.[79]

We must be careful not to assume in these discussions of change, that the actual ownership and distribution of property always extended to their theoretical limits. As mentioned in earlier chapters, Amy Erickson has identified a number of discrepancies between expressed law and opinion and practice: ecclesiastical authorities regularly gave female heirs a greater share of estates than custom dictated, even after the 1670 Act for the Better Settling of Intestates' Estates expressly forbid this practice; the majority of parents appear to have spent as much on the education, upkeep and health of daughters as on sons; many testators either left lands to daughters and younger sons, or else compensated these members of their families with legacies of roughly equivalent value to the lands they left to eldest sons. However, throughout this period women's access to property of all kinds depended to a considerable degree on the benevolence of men, whether husbands, fathers, brothers, administrators, executors, or ecclesiastical court officials, a benevolence that Erickson has pointed out was 'conditional upon women's good behaviour'.[80] And the move towards increasing individual freedom, and away from customary rights and usages and traditional rules of inheritance, enlarged that dependence on male benevolence for a great many women. Most traditional rules were prejudicial (daughters only inheriting land in the absence of sons, and so on), but the level of prejudice was fixed, and it was generally difficult for testators to exceed them. With increasing freedom of disposition came the ability to be more generous, but also *less* generous than tradition allowed.[81]

---

[78] Laurence, *Women in England*, pp. 273–4.
[79] Power was linked to heads of households, and so disproportionately contained in male hands in earlier centuries, but the kinds of freedoms described here were less available to them; Bennett, 'Public power', p. 21; on gender and 'individualism', see Davidoff, *Worlds Between*, pp. 231–7.
[80] Erickson, *Women and Property*, pp. 224–5, 234.
[81] Gampel, 'The planter's wife revisited'; Staves, *Married Women's Separate Property*, p. 98.

A useful way of envisaging the kind of transformations being posited here is to consider once again Barbara Todd's analysis of female property-holding in two Berkshire villages, referred to in chapter 7 above. In the village of Long Wittenham, where custom remained a powerful force in the seventeenth century, Todd found that widows inherited and controlled a greater proportion of land than widows in Sutton Courtney, where customary tenures had lapsed. The majority, therefore, had better entitlements under the 'older' traditions of custom. However, in most cases they were constrained by the needs of future generations, and they managed their interests conservatively. In Sutton Courtney most widows fared less well, and poverty among them was more common, but those women who possessed interests in land had more freedom to manage their interests actively. In the 'newer' economy of the open village, characterised by encumbered title and a more flexible land market, an enterprising minority did more than simply conserve their holdings to pass on to their children and grandchildren; they took risks, lent money, and succeeded in increasing their holdings. In Todd's words, 'in the economy of Sutton Courtenay, as in free enterprise economies everywhere, there was less security for most women, but far greater scope for a few'.[82]

Todd's study is helpful for many reasons. It demonstrates how two different regimes, one that might be characterised as 'old' and another that might be regarded as 'new', could overlap, and in Sutton Courtney and Long Wittenham, could coexist within the same county. It also demonstrates the difficulties involved with evaluating or assessing rights and conditions under different regimes. In which of these two villages, for example, can it be said that widows fared best? To answer that question requires the weighing of resources against opportunities and security against enterprise, and demands the making of comparisons; between the fortunes of wealthy widows and poorer widows in single communities, and between the fortunes of similarly placed widows in different communities. Such calculations are rarely easy, and they serve as yet another reminder of the importance of exposing, rather than trying to average, the variety of individual experience. If, as the example of Sutton Courtney suggests, the move towards increasingly individualised property rights widened the gap between the opportunities enjoyed by a few and the opportunities enjoyed by the many, then further questions arise. What symbolic effect did the example of a select group of women doing well in a community have on the other members of that community? Did the female litigants who made large gains in courts like Chancery serve as models to others, perhaps contributing to the creation of an embryonic rights culture with implications for the eighteenth, nineteenth and twentieth centuries? Or did they merely inspire satirists and dramatists to create figures of fun, like the litigation-obsessed Widow Blackacre

---

[82] Todd, 'Freebench and free enterprise', pp. 196–7, 200.

in *The Plain Dealer*? And as I proposed at the beginning of this chapter, did the steady retreat from the noisy hubbub of litigation in Westminster Hall and the White Hall in the sixteenth century, to the relative calm and decorum of wood-panelled lawyers' offices in the eighteenth and nineteenth centuries, change the whole experience of women going to law? Did the growing professionalism of the legal fraternity reduce the opportunities for women to speak out on their own behalf, and so render female litigants 'safe' in the eyes of courtroom observers?

How women's legal fortunes actually progressed in the decades following Elizabeth's reign only further research will tell. The highly speculative picture sketched here provides a view from the centre, built around the little we currently know about changes in the law and in shifting patterns of business within the highest courts in the land. The effective abolition of Requests, the spiralling increase in the costs of legal actions, a probable decline in legal aid and an apparent decrease in the proportion of women suing in the major common law courts, all suggest that women's access to central justice declined, and that what remained became concentrated in Chancery.[83] However, if women did indeed lose ground in all of the most expensive and prestigious courts in the land except Chancery (and perhaps the equity side of Exchequer), that does not necessarily mean that they withdrew from the justice system altogether. The work of Louis Knafla and Craig Muldrew is beginning to reveal the extraordinary levels of business in the hundreds of cheap local courts that dotted Kent and the rest of Britain in the seventeenth century and beyond, and their findings indicate that women's participation in litigation remained considerable at most levels of society. Muldrew has calculated that in the 1690s, the Palace Court in London (formerly known as the Court of the Verge and before that the Court of Marshalsea) was hearing 20,000 plaints a year, involving upwards of 60,000 plaintiffs and defendants, at a time when the population of the area it served probably amounted to little more than 125,000. And women appear to have been involved in 36 per cent of actions, and to have made up 15 per cent of plaintiffs.[84] In a changing economy, women may have had less access to real property, but these figures suggest that they were quick to defend the property they did possess, pursuing their claims more rarely in the central courts and more often in the burgeoning tiers of local jurisdictions below.

---

[83] Henry Horwitz has calculated that women made up just over 14 per cent of litigants suing in Chancery in 1627, rising to just over 21 per cent in 1818–19, and that contrary to expectations, the proportion of litigants of gentry status or higher decreased over the same period, from 31.4 per cent to 18.6 per cent; Horwitz, *Chancery Equity Records and Proceedings,* table 8, p. 38.

[84] The Palace Court was a small claims court with a catchment area that extended around London to a distance of twelve miles from the monarch's lodgings; Muldrew, 'Women, debt litigation and credit'; Knafla, ed., *Kent at Law.*

LEGAL RECORDS AND LEGAL RIGHTS

This book has been as much about court records as about women and litigation. There are dangers associated with using the records of litigation as a source for social history. First of all they provide an inherently biased view of the world, because they deal almost exclusively with dispute and social breakdown, almost never with harmony and social cohesion; trying to determine the quality and nature of legal rights and human relations by looking solely at the records of law courts, is akin to trying to determine the health of a community by looking solely at the records of its hospitals. Secondly, they can give a deceptive impression of reliability, authority and authenticity that can be seductive to historians interested in recovering the actions, thoughts and speech of individuals from the past. Despite these shortcomings, the archives of law courts remain rich storehouses of information about events, individuals, attitudes, and norms, which can be unlocked if legal actions are studied according to the relationship of the litigants involved, their sex, their wealth and their social status, not simply according to the subject of their disputes.

Lawmakers concern themselves with conflict and law courts provide the venues for the playing out and the settling of conflicts. For women, the conflict of law extended outside the courtroom and the lawyer's office into the workplace, the street, the household. The cases that fill the pages of this book provide an idea of the independence some women achieved and the hardship and oppression others endured. Many women had to fight for their rights, rather as tenants had to wrestle to uphold, or to advance, their rights under custom. The balance of power on manors was in the lords' or the ladies' favour, but tenants could on occasion gain the upper hand if their landlords were absent or negligent. The balance of power within the law was weighted against women, but those who had sufficient drive and opportunities, and who pushed aside public anxiety about the correctness of women going to law, could gain relief in a variety of different courts. The balance of power within marriage was weighted in favour of husbands, but wives with strong personalities could carve out pockets of independence, even if to go to court they had to confront their husbands, whether by persuading, duping or leaving them, before they could consider confronting the law. And in the community, beyond the gaze of judges and jurists, some married women escaped the restrictions of coverture. They bought and sold their own clothes as well as household goods. They kept moneys 'in sekeret' and lent moneys to sisters, brothers, aunts, uncles and neighbours for safe keeping, just as single women and widows lent and borrowed money and engaged in financial and commercial dealings that never found their way into court. To get to the heart of women's relationship with the law, therefore, it is necessary to look beyond the lives of the women who gained entry to large Westminster courts like Requests, to the lives of the many women who did not.

GLOSSARY

acquittance: written acknowledgement of the settling of a debt

administratrix/administrator: a woman/man appointed by a court to administer the estate of a deceased person who did not leave a valid will or name an executrix/executor

alienate: to sell or otherwise grant away land or other rights

amerce: to punish with a discretionary fine

answer: a defendant's written response to a plaintiff's bill of complaint

assizes: courts held in major towns within six assize circuits outside London twice a year, at which circuit judges had a royal commission to hear and determine civil and criminal cases

attach: to arrest a person, or to seize property, under a writ of attachment

attorney: an officer of a court with the authority to act on behalf of a litigant. Distinct from a barrister; but similar to a modern solicitor

Benefit of Clergy: a privilege, originally granted to clerics but later extended to laymen, allowing felons convicted of certain crimes to evade execution if they could demonstrate an ability to read (usually the 'neck verse', Psalm 51:1). Extended in 1624 to women convicted of larceny of goods worth not more than 10 shillings, and in 1691 to all women

bill of complaint: initial pleading in a civil action in an equity court, in which plaintiffs or complainants set out their grievances and the remedies or responses they required from the court

bill of revivor: a bill to continue a court action after an original party had withdrawn or died. Courts required widows to enter such bills to continue actions begun jointly with their husbands, but widowers needed no such bill to continue actions begun jointly with their wives

bond: a written obligation between two or more people setting out legally enforceable conditions, usually with a penalty for non-compliance

chattels: 'chattels personal' included moveable goods and property other than interests in land (real property), while 'chattels real' included rights connected to land, such as leases

civil law: law other than criminal law; or Roman law as taught in the universities, in contrast to common law taught in the Inns of Court. Masters in equity courts such as Requests and Chancery were often 'civilians' trained in civil law

commission of *dedimus potestatem*: 'we have given power'; a commission granted to magistrates or other gentlemen, typically to take the sworn answer of a defendant unable to travel to Westminster

commission of *oyer* **and** *terminer*: a commission granted to assize judges, magistrates or other commissioners authorising them to 'hear' and 'decide' specified civil or criminal cases

copyhold: a tenure of land either at the will of the lord or lady or according to the customs of a particular manor; so named because tenants received a copy of the court roll entry describing their interests

counter: a debtors' prison, or a prison attached to a city or mayor's court

Court of Chancery: court presided over by the Chancellor and by Masters of Chancery, dispensing equitable relief and remedies

Court of Common Pleas: central common law court specialising in civil cases between subject and subject. Secondary to Queen's Bench in authority, but not in size

Court of High Commission: prerogative court(s) created to deal with ecclesiastical matters arising from the Reformation

Court of Queen's Bench/King's Bench: the most important common law court in England, with an extensive criminal (and by Elizabeth's reign a growing civil) jurisdiction

Court of Requests: a prerogative equity court with a reputation for dealing with the claims of widows, orphans and the poor, presided over by Masters of Requests

coverture: under the doctrine of 'unity of person' the common law regarded husband and wife as one person for most civil and some criminal purposes. A wife was therefore seen to be under the 'cover' or protection of her husband

Curtesy: a husband's common law right to a life interest, even if he remarried, in all of his wife's lands that he was seised of (in control of) at her death, provided the marriage had produced a child born alive capable of inheriting the lands (which otherwise reverted to her heirs)

custumal: written record of customs, usually held and maintained by a manor's steward

deed: a written agreement or instrument signed, sealed and delivered by the party/ies concerned. Required as proof of most transactions at common law

defamation: a general term for the damaging of someone's reputation by the making of a defamatory statement. Such statements constituted libel if they were written and slander if they were spoken

demesne: under the feudal system of tenure, a tenant was seised 'in his/her' demesne, while a lord was seised 'in service'; also, the lands of a manor held by the lord or lady themselves, rather than by tenants

demise: a grant, particularly of lands, for a term of years

demurrer: a plea by one party rejecting another party's plea as insufficient on technical legal grounds, because even if it could be proved true, it would not succeed in that court

deposition: witness statement made on oath, usually in response to interrogatories, written down for use at later court proceedings

divorce *a mensa et thoro*: under canon law the marriage bond was normally indissoluble, but the church courts granted separations 'from bed and board' on the grounds of adultery, cruelty or abandonment, allowing couples to live apart but not to remarry

divorce *a vinculo matrimonii*: divorce 'from the bond of marriage' allowing remarriage, achievable only by annulment or (after the Reformation) by private Act of Parliament

dower: common law right of a widow to a life interest in a share of her late husband's lands (usually a third)

dowry: property given to a woman and/or to her husband on marriage, usually by members of her family. Not to be confused with dower

entail: the same as fee tail, and in contrast to fee simple. An entail directed that land would pass to a particular class of heirs, rather than to heirs generally. Testators often devised entails that excluded daughters from inheriting, even in the absence of sons

equity: a body of principles developed in contrast to common law and statute law predominantly by Chancellors in the court of Chancery. Originally a flexible system used to compensate for deficiencies caused by the strictness of common law; in the seventeenth century it developed its own complicated and equally rigid rules

Exchequer: a judicial as well as a financial body, initially concerned only with revenue cases, which by the later sixteenth century had developed extensive common law and equitable jurisdictions

executrix/executor: woman/man appointed in a will to administer a testatrix's/testator's property and carry out the terms of that will

fee: an estate in land inheritable by the holder's heirs. The fullest estate possible, approaching the modern sense of 'ownership', was fee simple; for fee tail, see entail

felony: a serious criminal offence such as murder, rape, burglary, wounding, arson or robbery

feme covert: a married woman; see coverture

feme sole: an unmarried woman, including widowed and divorced women

feoffees to uses: persons granted lands to hold for the use of another

feoffment: the creation or transfer of a freehold interest in land, requiring 'livery of seisin'

Fleet: an ancient London prison located near the Fleet river; by the sixteenth century used primarily to house debtors and those convicted of contempt of court

forms of action: by the sixteenth century the common law described its remedies in terms which required litigants to enter writs aligned to existing classifications or 'forms of action', such as trespass, ejectment, debt and actions on the case

freebench: see widow's estate

freehold: under feudal tenure, the freest, and usually the most desirable, estate in land. Freehold estates, whether fee simple, fee tail or an estate for life, all had uncertain duration, in contrast to leasehold, where land was held for a specified term of years

Gavelkind: customary law and tenure in Kent, in particular the equal or partible inheritance of lands by sons; in contrast to primogeniture

heriot: a tenant's 'best beast' or equivalent, due to the lord or lady of the manor at the transfer or surrender of a copyhold interest

homage: jury of tenants in a customary court; also the ceremony associated with feudal tenures by which tenants swore fealty (or loyalty) to their lord

in forma pauperis: the right of litigants with less than £5 in goods, or 40 shillings annual income from lands, to request free legal representation and exemption from court costs

indenture: a deed between two or more people, written on a single sheet of parchment or paper which was cut into two (or more) pieces along a wavy line. The pieces could later be realigned with each other to prove they were genuine

Inns of Court: four London societies for the training of lawyers, especially barristers; Lincoln's Inn, Inner Temple, Middle Temple and Gray's Inn

interrogatories: written questions prepared by litigants and their counsel to be answered by witnesses or deponents in connection with court cases

intestate succession: the transferral of property at death in cases where the deceased person did not leave a valid will or name an executrix or administratrix

inventory: a list of personal property at death, exhibited in the ecclesiastical court by a deceased person's executrix or administratrix

jointure: either a joint interest in property in the name of a husband and wife, under which the surviving spouse would enjoy the property, or an agreed annuity to be paid to a wife if she survived her husband. In general the former, 'legal' jointure was actionable at common law, while the latter, 'equitable' jointure (usually set down in a marriage settlement) was actionable in courts of equity

justice of the peace: a magistrate appointed by royal commission to act in a particular county; usually a barrister or country squire

leasehold: an estate in land for a fixed term of years or lives

legal fiction: a convenient assumption employed by courts or lawyers, often to facilitate change in the law. The idea that husband and wife were one person was a legal fiction

letters of administration: the authority a church court granted to a person to act as administratrix of the estate of a person who died without naming an executrix

libel: see defamation

litigant: a party to a civil suit

livery of seisin: the formal delivery of possession of land under the process of feoffment, often marked by the handing over of a symbolic clod of earth with a twig in it

mark: 13s. 4d. (i.e., two thirds of a pound)

marriage settlement: a written agreement entered into at the time of marriage setting out a wife's rights during marriage and her entitlements after marriage, often made with the assistance of a third party or parties acting as trustee/s; see also strict settlement

Master: a judge in the Court of Requests or in Chancery

messuage: a dwelling house and the lands, gardens or buildings immediately surrounding it. A capital messuage was the chief dwelling house on an estate

moveable property: property that can be owned, such as pots and pans and livestock, as opposed to real (or immoveable) property, such as lands and buildings, that can only be possessed

nisi prius: 'unless before'; the trial or hearing of civil (as opposed to criminal) pleas referred from Westminster courts to assize judges in the counties where the suits arose

personal property: all property other than interests in land (real property)

portion: a woman's dowry; or, a child's share of inheritance not including land

prerogative courts: courts that relied on the royal prerogative for their existence and authority, including Star Chamber, the courts of High Commission and the Court of Requests (although the status of Requests as a prerogative court was contested)

primogeniture: inheritance of land by the eldest surviving son, and in the absence of sons by daughters in equal shares (partible inheritance)

Privy Seal: a royal seal below the Great Seal; used, among other things, to provide authority for all process issued out of the Court of Requests

probate: the process of proving a deceased person's will and registering it in an ecclesiastical court

real property: technically property recoverable by means of a real action at common law, but generally a reference to land, usually freehold land, in contrast to personal property

rejoinder: a pleading in a civil suit; a defendant's response to a complainant's replication

remainder: an estate in land which would pass (possibly, if the remainder was contingent, or definitely, if the remainder was vested) to another individual after the present estate ended. In other words, one person's interest in property currently held by another

replication: a pleading in a civil suit; a complainant's response to a defendant's answer

seisin: the justifiable possession, occupation and use of land, usually referring to freehold estates in land. At common law a person in effect 'owned' land if they could show a better right to seisin than anyone else

sequestration: the judicially approved confiscation of property, often from parties who refused to comply with a previous court judgment

slander: see defamation

spiritual court: ecclesiastical or church court, administering canon law

Star Chamber: a prerogative court in London empowered to deal with offences threatening the state. By Elizabeth's reign it enjoyed a civil and a criminal jurisdiction, specialising in riot, conspiracy, forgery, libel, fraud, and the maintenance of public order

stare decisis: a doctrine which binds judges to follow, not simply to be guided by, previous decisions on the point in issue by an equal or higher court. It did not apply during Elizabeth's reign

Statute of Uses: see 'use'

strict settlement: a settlement designed to keep land in a family passing through the eldest male line and to prevent individual heirs from alienating it. Provision in strict settlements was made for younger sons and daughters in the form of money portions

surety: a person pledged to ensure another's fulfilment of an obligation; for example, to appear in court or repay a debt, with a money penalty for default

tenement: anything that could be held in tenure, including lands and profits derived from lands

tenure: originally a reference to the relationship by which a tenant held land from the lord or lady of the manor, but general shorthand for the means by which land was held

testate succession: the transferral of property at death in cases where the deceased person left a valid will

testatrix/testator: a deceased woman/man who left a valid will

trust: after the Statute of Uses (1536) and the Statute of Wills (1540) made many uses ineffectual, lawyers developed trusts to replace them. To the lay observer the two devices are almost indistinguishable, as both operated by separating legal from beneficial ownership of property, allowing one person (a feoffee or a trustee) to hold and manage property on behalf of another (a '*cestuy que use*' or a beneficiary)

trustee: a person who holds property in trust on behalf of another

use: in a use, one person held property for the use or benefit of another. The holder, the 'feoffee', was the nominal owner of the property at law, while the '*cestuy que use*' was the beneficial owner, in the sense that they possessed an interest which equity courts were willing to protect; the arrangement allowed persons to avoid taxes and other feudal 'incidents of tenure', or wives to keep their property separate from their husbands. The Statutes of Uses (1536) and Wills (1540) collapsed this distinction by transferring legal possession in most uses from feoffee to beneficiary

widow's estate: widows' customary right to an interest (between one third and the whole) in customary lands her husband held at his death, either for life or for widowhood

BIBLIOGRAPHY

1 UNPUBLISHED PRIMARY SOURCES

BRITISH LIBRARY

Additional Manuscripts
Lansdowne Manuscripts

CAMBRIDGE UNIVERSITY LIBRARY

C.U.L. Gg.2.26
C.U.L. Gg.2.31
C.U.L. Hh 2.6.(c)

PUBLIC RECORD OFFICE

C2	Chancery Proceedings
C3	Chancery Proceedings
CP40/1187	Common Pleas plea roll
KB27/1194	Kings Bench plea roll
Req 1	Court of Requests Court Books
Req 2	Court of Requests Proceedings
Req 3	Court of Requests Miscellaneous Documents
S.P.12	State Papers Domestic, Elizabeth I
STAC 5	Star Chamber Proceedings, Elizabeth I

2 PRINTED SOURCES

A Breefe Discourse, Declaring and Approving the Necessarie and Inviolable Maintenance of the Laudable Customes of London (London, 1584) [*S.T.C.* 16747]

Agrippa, Henricus Cornelius, *Of the Nobilitie and Excellencie of Womankynde*, trans. Thomas Clapham (London, 1542)

Anger, Jane, *Jane Anger her Protection for Women. To Defend Them Against the Scandalous Reportes of a Late Surfeiting Lover* (London, 1589)

Beaumont, Francis; see Fletcher, John

Billingsley, Martin, *The Pens Excellencie or the Secretaries Delighte* [London, 1618][*S.T.C.* 3062]

Blackstone, William, *Commentaries on the Laws of England* (London, 1765) de Boyse, Ann, *A True Discourse of a Cruell Fact Committed by a Gentlewoman Towardes Her Husband* (London, 1599) [*S.T.C.* 3469]

Bracton, Henry of, *De Legibus et Consuetudinibus Angliae*, trans. Samuel Thorne, *Bracton on the Laws and Customs of England* (Cambridge, Mass., 1968)

Brathwait, Richard, *The English Gentlewoman* (London, 1631)

Burton, Robert, *The Anatomy of Melancholy* (Oxford, 1621)

Caesar, Julius, *The Ancient State, Authoritie, and Proceedings of the Court of Requests* (London, 1598)

Calendar of State Papers, Domestic Series, of the Reign of Elizabeth, Addenda, 1566–1579, ed. M.A.E. Green (London, 1870–1)

Calendar of State Papers, Domestic Series, Elizabeth, 1601–1603; with Addenda, 1547–1565, ed. M.A.E. Green (London, 1870)

Calendar of State Papers, Domestic Series, of the Reign of Edward VI, 1547–1553, rev. edn, ed. C.S. Knighton (London, 1992)

Callis, Robert, *The Reading . . . Upon the Statute* (London, 1647)

du Castel, Christine [Christine du Pisan], *The Boke of the Cyte of Ladyes*, trans. B. Anslay (London, 1521)[*S.T.C.* 7271]

Chamberlaine, Bartholomew, *A Sermon Preached at Farington in Barkeshire, the Seventeene of Februarie, 1587* (London, 1591)[*S.T.C.* 4952]

The Christian Life and Death of Mistris Katherin Brettergh (London, 1612)

Coke, Edward, *The Compleate Copy-Holder* (London, 1641)

    The Second Part of the Institutes of the Laws of England, 3rd edn (London, 1669)

    The Fourth Part of the Institutes of the Laws of England (London, 1797)

Cox, Leonard, *The Art or Crafte of Rhetoryke* (London, 1532)

Croke, George, *The First Part of the Reports of Sir George Croke*, trans. Harbottle Grimstone (London, 1661)

Crompton, Richard, *Star-Chamber Cases. Shewing What Causes Properly Belong to the Cognizance of that Court* (London, 1630)

Daye, Angell, *The English Secretorie. Wherein is Contayned, a Perfect Method, for the Inditing of All Manner of Epistles and Familiar Letters* (London, 1586)(Facsimile edition; Menston, Yorks., 1967)

Dictionary of National Biography, eds. Leslie Stephen and Sydney Lee (63 vols., London, 1885–1900)

E., T., *The Lawes Resolutions of Womens Rights* (London, 1632)

English Reports (176 vols., Edinburgh, 1900–30)

Fisher, R.B., *A Practical Treatise on Copyhold Tenure, with the Methods of Holding Courts Leet, Court Baron and other Courts* (London, 1794)

Fletcher, John, with [and without] Beamont, Francis; *The Woman-Hater* (1606), *The Coxcomb* (1609), *Four Plays in One* (1612), *The Nightwalker, or the Little Thief* (1614), *The Laws of Candy* (1619), *The Spanish Curate* (1622), *The Queen of Corinth* and [with Ford, Massinger and Webster?], *The Fair Maid of the Inn*; all in *Fifty Comedies and Tragedies Written by Francis Beaumont and John Fletcher*, 2 parts (London, 1679)

Fraunce, Abraham, *The Lawiers Logike, Exemplifying the Præcepts of Logike by the Practise of the Common Lawe* (London, 1588) [*S.T.C.* 11343]

(G., A.), *The Widdowes Mite, Cast into the Treasure-House of the Prerogatives, and Prayses of Our B. Lady, the Immaculate, and Most Glorious Virgin Mary, the Mother of God* (London, 1619), [*S.T.C.* 11490]

G., R., *The Mirrour of Modestie* (London, 1584), in J.P. Collier ed., *Illustrations of Old English Literature*, vol. 3 (New York, 1866, reprinted 1966)

Garter, Thomas, *The Commody of the Moste Vertuous and Godlye Susanna* (London, 1578)

Geree, Stephen, *The Ornament of Women. Or, a Description of the True Excellency of Women. Delivered in a Sermon at the Funerall of M. Elizabeth Machell* (London, 1639) [*S.T.C.* 11763]

Gouge, William, *Of Domesticall Duties* (London, 1622) (Facsimile edn; Amsterdam, 1976)

Greene, Robert, *The Second Part of Conny Catching* (London, 1592)

    A Disputation, Betweene a Hee Conny-Catcher, and a Shee Conny-Catcher, Whether a Theefe or a Whoore, is Most Hurtfull in Cousonage, to the Common-Wealth (facsimile edn; Edinburgh, 1966)

Hake, Edward, *Epieikeia: A Dialogue on Equity in Three Parts*, ed. D.E.C. Yale (New Haven, 1953)

Hargrave, Francis, *A Collection of Tracts Relative to the Law of England, from Manuscripts* (London, 1787)

Hawarde, John, *Les Reportes del Cases in Camera Stellata 1593 to 1609*, ed. William Baildon (privately printed, 1894)

H[eywood], T[homas], *A Curtaine Lecture: as it is Read by a Countrey Farmers Wife to Her Good Man* (London, 1637)

Hooker, Richard, *Of the Lawes of Ecclesiasticall Politie* (London, 1617)

Jonson, Ben, *The Staple of News*, ed. D.R. Kifer (London, 1975)

Jordan, Edward, *A Disease Called the Suffocation of the Mother* (London, 1603)

Knox, John, *The First Blast of the Trumpet Against the Monstrous Regiment of Women* (Geneva, 1558)

Lambarde, William, *Archeion or, a Discourse Upon the High Courts of Justice in England* (London, 1635)

Latimer, Hugh, *A Moste Faithfull Sermon Preached Before the Kynges Most Exellente Majestye* (London, 1550)

    Twenty Seven Sermons Preached by the Ryght Reverende . . . Maister Hugh Latimer (London, 1562)

Lodge, Thomas, *Wits Miserie, and the Worlds Madnesse: Discovering the Devils Incarnat of this Age* (London, 1596) (Menston, Yorks, 1971)

Lodge, Thomas and Greene, Robert, *A Looking Glasse for London and England*, ed. Tetsumaro Hayashi (Metuchen, New Jersey, 1970)

Middleton, Thomas, Jonson, Ben, and Fletcher, John, *The Widow*, in W.R. Chetwood, *Memoirs of the Life and Writings of Ben. Jonson . . . to Which are Added, Two Comedies . . . The Widow, and Eastward Hoe* (Dublin, 1756)

The Mirror of Justices, ed. W.J. Whittaker, Selden Society vol. 7 (London, 1895)

Moryson, Fynes, *An Itinerary Written by Fynes Moryson Gent. First in the Latine Tongue, and then Translated by Him into English* (London, 1617) (facsimile edn; Amsterdam, 1971)

Nashe, Thomas, *The Anatomie of Absurditie* (London, 1589), in J.P. Collier, ed., *Illustrations of old English Literature*, vol. 3 (New York, 1866) (reprinted 1966)

    Christs Teares Over Jerusalem (London, 1593)

Overbury, Thomas, *His wife: With Additions of New Characters, and Many Other Wittie Conceits* (London, 1627)

The Parliamentary History of England, from the Earlier Period to the Year 1803 (London, 1806)

Phillips, John, *The Examination and Confession of Certaine Wytches at Chensforde the xxvi. Daye of July 1566* (London, 1566) [*S.T.C.* 19869.5]

Powell, Thomas, *The Attourneys Academy or, the Manner and Forme of Proceeding Upon Any Suite* (London, 1623)

Pyrrye, C., *The Praise and Dispraise of Women* (London, 1569?)[*S.T.C.* 20523]

Rich, Barnabe, *My Ladies Looking Glasse* (London, 1616)

Ridley, Thomas, *A View of the Civile and Ecclesiasticall Law* (London, 1607)

Robinson, Richard, *A Briefe Collection of the Queenes Majesties Most High and Most Honourable Courtes of Recordes*, ed. R.L. Rickard, Camden Miscellany, vol. 20 (London, 1953)

Shakespeare, William, *A Midsummer Night's Dream* (c.1595), *The Merchant of Venice* (c.1596), *Much Ado About Nothing* (1598), *As You Like It* (c.1599), *Measure for Measure* (c.1603), *Othello* (c.1604), *King Lear* (c.1605), *The Winter's Tale* (c.1609), *Cymbeline* (c.1610), *King Henry VIII* (1613), in Peter Alexander, ed., *William Shakespeare: The Complete Works* (London and Glasgow, 1951)

Smith, Thomas, *The Common-Wealth of England, and Manner of Government Thereof* (London, 1601)

Stubbes, Phillip, *The Second Part of the Anatomie of Abuses* (London, 1583)

  A Cristal Glasse for Christian Women. Containing an Excellent Discourse of the Life and Death of Katherine Stubbes (London, 1591)

Taffin, Jean, *Of the Markes of the Children of God, and of their Comfort in Afflictions*, trans. Anne Locke, (London, 1590)

Udall, Nicholas, *Ralph Roister Doister* in William Tydeman, *Four Latin Comedies* (Harmondsworth, 1984)

Vives, Juan Luis, *A Very Fruteful and Pleasant Boke Callyd the Instruction of a Christen Woman*, trans. Richard Hyrde (London 1541)

W., W., *A True and Just Recorde of the Information Examination and Confession of All the Witches, at St Oses in Essex* (London, 1582) [*S.T.C.* 24922]

Walton, Izaak, *The Lives of Dr. John Donne, Sir Henry Wotton, Mr. Richard Hooker, Mr. George Herbert, and Dr. Robert Sanderson* (London, 1825)

Watkins, Charles, *Treatise on Copyholds* (London, 1797)

Webster, John, *The Devils Law-Case. Or, When Women Goe to Law, the Devill is Full of Businesse* (London, 1623)

  The White Devil (London, 1632)

Wilbraham, Roger, *The Journal of Sir Roger Wilbraham*, ed. H.S. Scott, Camden Miscellany vol. 10 (London, 1902)

Wilson, Thomas, *The Rule of Reason, Conteinyng the Arte of Logique* (London, 1551)[*S.T.C.* 25809]

  A Discourse Upon Usury: By Way of Dialogue and Orations, for the Better Variety and More Delight of all Those that Shall Read this Treatise, ed. R.H. Tawney (London, 1962)

Wriothesley, Charles, *A Chronicle of England During the Reigns of the Tudors, from A.D. 1485 to 1559. By Charles Wriothesley*, ed. William Hamilton, Camden Society, new series, vol. 11 (two vols., London 1875)

Wycherley, William, *The Plain Dealer* (London, 1676)

3 SECONDARY SOURCES

Abbott, L.W., *Law Reporting in England 1485–1585* (London, 1973)

Allen, C.K., *Law in the Making*, 7th edn (Oxford, 1964)

Amussen, Susan, 'Gender, family and the social order, 1560–1725', in Anthony Fletcher and John Stevenson, eds., *Order and Disorder in Early Modern England* (Cambridge, 1987)

An Ordered Society: Gender and Class in Early Modern England (Oxford, 1988)

'"Being stirred to much unquietness": violence and domestic violence in early modern England', *Journal of Women's History*, 6 (1994), pp. 70–89

Aston, T.H. and Philpin, C.H.E., *The Brenner Debate: Agrarian Class Structure and Economic Developments in Pre-Industrial Europe* (Cambridge, 1987)

Baker, J.H., 'The Dark Age of English legal history, 1500–1700', in D. Jenkins, ed., *Legal History Studies 1972* (Cardiff, 1975)

An Introduction to English Legal History, 3rd edn (London, 1990)

Baker, J.H., ed., *Legal Records and the Historian* (London, 1978)

The Notebook of Sir John Port, Selden Society vol. 102 (London, 1986)

Reports From the Lost Notebooks of Sir James Dyer, Selden Society, vols. 109–10 (London, 1993–4)

Baker, J.H. and Yale, D.E.C., *A Centenary Guide to the Publications of the Selden Society* (London, 1987)

Barnes, T.G., 'Star Chamber litigants and their counsel, 1596–1641', in J.H. Baker, ed., *Legal Records and the Historian* (London, 1978)

List and Index to the Proceedings in Star Chamber for the Reign of James I (1603–1625) in the Public Record Office, London Class STAC 8 (Chicago, 1975)

Barry, Jonathan and Brooks, C.W., eds., *The Middling Sort of People: Culture, Society and Politics in England 1550–1800* (London, 1994)

Bateson, Mary, *Borough Customs*, Selden Society, vol. 21 (2 vols., London, 1906)

Bayne, C.G., *Select Cases in the Council of Henry VII*, Selden Society, vol. 75 (London, 1958)

Beard, Mary, *Woman as Force in History: A Study in Traditions and Realities* (New York, 1946)

Beattie, J.M., *Crime and the Courts in England 1600–1800* (Princeton, 1986)

Bell, H.E., *An Introduction to the History and Records of the Court of Wards and Liveries* (Cambridge, 1953)

Bennett, Judith, 'Feminism and history', *Gender and History*, 1 (1989), pp. 259–63

'History that stands still', *Feminist Studies*, 14 (1988), pp. 269–83

'Public power and authority in the medieval English countryside', in Mary Erler and Maryanne Kowaleski, eds., *Women and Power in the Middle Ages* (Athens, Georgia and London, 1988)

Bennett W.L. and Feldman, M.S., *Reconstructing Reality in the Courtroom* (London, 1981)

Benston, Alice, 'Portia, the law, and the tripartite structure of *The Merchant of Venice*', *Shakespeare Quarterly*, 30 (1979), pp. 367–85

Bentley, Gerald, *The Profession of Dramatist in Shakespeare's Time 1590–1642* (Princeton, New Jersey, 1971)

Berg, Maxine, 'What difference did women's work make to the Industrial Revolution?', *History Workshop Journal*, 35 (1993), pp. 22–44

Bettey, J.H., 'Manorial custom and widows' estate', *Archives*, 20 (1992), pp. 208–16

Blatcher, Marjorie, *The Court of King's Bench, 1450–1550: A Study in Self-Help* (London, 1978)

Bohstedt, John, 'Gender, household and community politics: women and English riots 1790–1810', *Past and Present* 120 (1988), pp. 88–122

Bonfield, Lloyd, 'Affective families, open elites, and strict family settlements in early modern England', *Economic History Review*, 2nd series, 39 (1986), pp. 355–70

Brant, Clare and Purkiss, Diane, eds., *Women Texts and Histories 1575–1760* (London and New York, 1992)

Braunmuller A.R., and Hattaway, Michael, eds., *The Cambridge Companion to English Renaissance Drama* (Cambridge, 1990)

Brennan, Elizabeth, ed., John Webster, *The Devil's Law-Case* (London, 1975)

Brewer, John and Styles, John, eds., *An Ungovernable People: The English and their Law in the Seventeenth and Eighteenth Centuries* (London, 1980)

Brooks, C.W., 'The common lawyers in England, *c.* 1558–1642', in W.R. Prest, ed., *Lawyers in Early Modern Europe and America* (New York, 1981)

  Pettyfoggers and Vipers of the Commonwealth: The 'Lower Branch' of the Legal Profession in Early Modern England (Cambridge, 1986)

  'Interpersonal conflict and social tension: civil litigation in England, 1640–1830', in A.L. Beier, David Cannadine and J.M. Rosenheim, eds., *The First Modern Society: Essays in English History in Honour of Lawrence Stone* (Cambridge, 1989)

  'The place of Magna Carta and the ancient constitution in sixteenth-century English legal thought', in Ellis Sandoz, ed., *The Roots of Liberty: Magna Carta, Ancient Constitution, and the Anglo-American Tradition of Rule of Law* (Columbia, 1993)

  'The professions, ideology and the middling sort in the late sixteenth and seventeenth centuries', in Jonathan Barry and C.W. Brooks, eds., *The Middling Sort of People: Culture, Society and Politics in England 1550–1800* (London, 1994)

Brooks, C.W., Helmholz, R.H. and Stein, P.G., *Notaries Public in England Since the Reformation* (London, 1991)

Brooks, C.W. and Lobban, Michael, eds., *Communities and Courts in Britain 1150–1900* (London and Rio Grande, 1997)

Brucker, Gene, *Giovanni and Lusanna: Love and Marriage in Renaissance Florence* (Berkeley, 1986)

de Bruyn, Jan, 'The ideal lady and the rise of feminism in seventeenth-century England', *Mosaic*, 17 (1984), pp. 19–28

de Bruyn, Lucy, *Woman and the Devil in Sixteenth-Century Literature* (Tisbury, Wilts, 1979)

Bryson, W.H., *The Equity Side of Exchequer: Its Jurisdiction, Administration, Procedures and Records* (Cambridge, 1975)

Cahn, Susan, *Industry of Devotion: The Transformation of Women's Work in England, 1500–1660* (New York, 1987)

Callaghan, Dympna, *Woman and Gender in Renaissance Tragedy: A Study of King Lear, Othello, The Duchess of Malfi and The White Devil* (London, 1989)

Capp, Bernard, 'Separate domains? Women and authority in early modern England', in Paul Griffiths, Adam Fox and Steve Hindle, eds., *The Experience of Authority in Early Modern England* (London, 1996)

Carroll, Berenice, 'On Mary Beard's *Women as Force in History*: a critique', in Berenice Carroll, ed., *Liberating Women's History* (Urbana, 1976)

Champion, W.A., 'Recourse to law and the meaning of the great litigation decline, 1650–1750: some clues from the Shrewsbury local courts', in Christopher W. Brooks and Michael Lobban, eds., *Communities and Courts in Britain, 1150–1900* (London and Rio Grande, 1997)

Charles, Lindsey and Duffin, Lorna, eds., *Women and Work in Pre-Industrial England* (London, 1985)

Churches, Christine, '"The most unconvincing testimony": the genesis and historical usefulness of the country depositions in Chancery', *The Seventeenth Century*, 11 (1996), pp. 209–27

Cioni, Maria, 'The Elizabethan Chancery and women's rights', in D.J. Guth and J.W. McKenna, eds., *Tudor Rule and Revolution: Essays for G.R. Elton from his American Friends* (Cambridge, 1982)
 Women and Law in Elizabethan England with Particular Reference to the Court of Chancery (New York and London, 1985)
Clark, Alice, *Working Life of Women in the Seventeenth Century* (London and New York, 1992)
Clark, Peter, 'Popular protest and disturbance in Kent, 1558–1640', *Economic History Review*, 2nd series, 29 (1976), pp. 365–82
Clugstone, George, ed., *A Looking Glasse for London and England by Thomas Lodge and Robert Greene: a critical edition* (New York and London, 1980)
Cohen, Thomas and Cohen, Elizabeth, *Words and Deeds in Renaissance Rome* (Toronto, 1993)
Collier, J.P., ed., *Illustrations of Old English Literature* (3 vols., New York, 1866; reprinted 1966)
Collinson, Patrick, *The Birthpangs of Protestant England: Religious and Cultural Change in the Sixteenth and Seventeenth Centuries* (London, 1988)
Crawford, Patricia, 'From the woman's view: pre-industrial England, 1500–1750', in Patricia Crawford, ed., *Exploring Women's Past* (Sydney, 1984)
 'Public duty, conscience and women in early modern England', in John Morrill, Paul Slack and Daniel Woolf, eds., *Public Duty and Private Conscience in Seventeenth-Century England* (Oxford, 1993)
Cressy, David, 'Kinship and kin interaction in early modern England', *Past and Present*, 113 (1986), pp. 38–69
Cust, Richard and Hughes, Ann, eds., *Conflict in Early Stuart England: Studies in Religion and Politics 1603–1642* (London, 1989)
Dabhoiwala, Faramerz, 'The construction of honour, reputation and status in late seventeenth- and early eighteenth-century England', *Transactions of the Royal Historical Society*, 6th series, 6 (1996), pp. 201–13
Davidoff, Leonore, *Worlds Between: Historical Perspectives on Gender and Class* (Cambridge, 1995)
Davies, Kathleen, 'Continuity and change in literary advice on marriage', in R.B. Outhwaite, ed., *Marriage and Society: Studies in the Social History of Marriage* (London, 1981)
Davis, N.Z., *Fiction in the Archives: Pardon Tales and their Tellers in Sixteenth-Century France* (Cambridge, 1987)
 Society and Culture in Early Modern France (Cambridge, 1987)
Dickens, Charles, *Oliver Twist* (Harmondsworth, Middlesex, 1966)
Dolan, Frances, *Dangerous Familiars: Representations of Domestic Crime in England 1550–1700* (Ithaca and London, 1994)
Dolan, Frances, ed., Renaissance drama and the law', *Renaissance Drama*, new series, 25 (1994)
Dusinberre, Juliet, *Shakespeare and the Nature of Women*, 2nd edn (London, 1996)
Dyer, Christopher, 'Changes in the size of peasant holdings in some west Midland villages 1400–1540', in R.M. Smith, ed., *Land, Kinship and Lifecycle* (Cambridge, 1984)
Elton, G.R., *Star Chamber Stories* (London, 1958)
 England 1200–1640 (London, 1969)
 The Tudor Revolution in Government: Administrative Changes in the Reign of Henry VIII (Cambridge, 1969)
 The Tudor Constitution: Documents and Commentary, 2nd edn (Cambridge, 1982)

Erickson, Amy, 'Common law versus common practice: the use of marriage settlements in early modern England', *Economic History Review*, 2nd series, 43 (1990), pp. 21–39

Women and Property in Early Modern England (London and New York, 1993)

Everitt, Alan, 'The marketing of agricultural produce' in Joan Thirsk, ed., *The Agrarian History of England & Wales* (Cambridge, 1967), vol. IV, pp. 466–592

Evershed, Raymond, *Aspects of English Equity* (Jerusalem, 1954)

Ewan, Elizabeth, 'Scottish Portias: women in the courts in medieval Scottish towns', *Journal of the Canadian Historical Association*, new series, 3 (1992), pp. 27–43

Ezell, Margaret, *The Patriarch's Wife: Literary Evidence and the History of the Family* (Chapel Hill, 1987)

Finin-Farber, Kathryn, 'Framing (the) woman: *The White Devil* and the deployment of law', *Renaissance Drama*, new series, 25 (1994), pp. 219–45

Finkelpearl, Philip, *John Marston of the Middle Temple: an Elizabethan Dramatist in his Social Setting* (Cambridge, Mass., 1969)

Finn, Margot, 'Women, consumption and coverture in England, *c.* 1760–1860', *The Historical Journal*, 39 (1996), pp. 703–22

Fitz, Linda, '"What says the married woman": marriage theory and feminism in the English Renaissance', *Mosaic*, 13 (1980), pp. 1–22; see also Woodbridge, Linda

Fletcher, Anthony, 'The Protestant idea of marriage in early modern England', in Anthony Fletcher and Penny Roberts, eds., *Religion, Culture and Society in Early Modern Britain: Essays in Honour of Patrick Collinson* (Cambridge, 1994)

Gender, Sex and Subordination in England 1500–1800 (New Haven and London, 1995)

Fletcher, Anthony and Stevenson, John, eds., *Order and Disorder in Early Modern England* (Cambridge, 1987)

Foyster, Elizabeth, 'A laughing matter? Marital discord and gender control in seventeenth-century England', *Rural History*, 4 (1993), pp. 5–21

'Male honour, social control and wife beating in late Stuart England', *Transactions of the Royal Historical Society*, 6th series, 6 (1996), pp. 215–24

Fraser, Antonia, *The Weaker Vessel: Woman's Lot in Seventeenth-Century England* (London, 1985)

Freedman, Sylvia, '*The White Devil* and the fair woman with a black soul', in Clive Bloom, ed., *Jacobean Poetry and Prose: Rhetoric, Representation and the Popular Imagination* (Basingstoke, 1988)

Friedman, Arthur, ed., *The Plays of William Wycherley* (Oxford, 1979)

Frost, David, *The Selected Plays of Thomas Middleton* (Cambridge, 1978)

Gampel, Gwen, 'The planter's wife revisited: equity law, and the Chancery court in seventeenth-century Maryland', in Barbara Harris and JoAnn McNamara, eds., *Women and the Structure of Society* (Duke, North Carolina, 1984)

Gardiner, Samuel, ed., *Reports of Cases in the Courts of Star Chamber and High Commission 1631–1632*, Camden Society, new series, vol. 39 (1886)

Gatrell, V.A.C., *The Hanging Tree: Execution and the English People 1770–1868* (Oxford, 1996)

Geis, G., 'Lord Hale, witches and rape', *British Journal of Law and Society*, 5 (1978), pp. 26–44

Gibb, Frances, 'Lawyers criticise slow arm of the law', *The Times*, 14 January 1992, p. 5

Goody, Jack, *The Logic of Writing and the Organization of Society* (Cambridge, 1986)

Goody, Jack, Thirsk, Joan and Thompson, E.P., eds., *Family and Inheritance: Rural Society in Western Europe, 1200–1800* (Cambridge, 1976)

Gowing, Laura, 'Gender and the language of insult in early modern London', *History Workshop Journal*, 35 (1993), pp. 1–21

'Language, power and the law: women's slander litigation in early modern London', Jenny Kermode and Garthine Walker, eds., *Women, Crime and the Courts in Early Modern England* (London, 1994)

Domestic Dangers: Women, Words, and Sex in Early Modern London (Oxford, 1996)

'Women, status and the popular culture of dishonour', *Transactions of the Royal Historical Society*, 6th series, 6 (1996), pp. 225–34

Gray, Charles, *Copyhold, Equity and the Common Law* (Cambridge, Mass., 1963)

Greaves, R.L., *Society and Religion in Elizabethan England* (Minneapolis, 1981)

Greenberg, Janelle, 'The legal status of the English woman in early eighteenth-century common law and equity', *Studies in Eighteenth-Century Culture*, 4 (1975), pp. 171–81

Greenhut, Deborah, 'Persuade yourselves: women, speech and sexual politics in Tudor society', *Proteus*, 3 (1986), pp. 42–8

Feminine Rhetorical Culture: Tudor Adaptations of Ovid's Heroides (New York, 1988)

Gurr, Andrew, *Playgoing in Shakespeare's London* (Cambridge, 1987)

Guy, J.A., 'The development of equitable jurisdictions, 1450–1550', in E.W. Ives and A.H. Manchester, eds., *Law, Litigants and the Legal Profession* (London, 1983)

The Court of Star Chamber and its Records to the Reign of Elizabeth I, PRO Handbook No. 21 (London, 1985)

Haaker, Ann, 'The plague, the theater, and the poet', *Renaissance Drama*, new series, 1 (1968), pp. 283–306

Habakkuk, H.J., 'Marriage settlements in the eighteenth century', *Transactions of the Royal Historical Society*, 4th series, 32 (1950), pp. 15–30

Haigh, C.A., 'Slander and the church courts in the sixteenth century', *Transactions of the Lancashire and Cheshire Antiquarian Society*, 78 (1975), pp. 1–13

Hailsham, Lord, ed., *Halsbury's Laws of England*, 4th edn (London, 1975)

Hanawalt, Barbara, ed., *Women and Work in Preindustrial Europe* (Bloomington, Indiana, 1986)

Harris, Barbara, 'Property, power, and personal relations: elite mothers and sons in Yorkist and early Tudor England', *Signs*, 15 (1990), pp. 606–32

Hay, Douglas, 'Property, authority and the criminal law', in Douglas Hay, Peter Linebaugh, John Rule, E.P. Thompson and Cal Winslow, eds., *Albion's Fatal Tree: Crime and Society in Eighteenth-Century England* (London, 1975)

Heinzelman, Susan, 'Women's petty treason: feminism, narrative, and the law', *The Journal of Narrative Technique*, 20 (1990), pp. 89–106

Heinzelman, Susan and Wiseman, Zipporah, eds., *Representing Women: Law, Literature and Feminism* (Durham and London, 1994)

Helmholz, Richard, *Marriage Litigation in Medieval England* (Cambridge, 1974)

Herrup, Cynthia, 'Law and morality in seventeenth-century England', *Past and Present*, 106 (1985), pp. 102–4

The Common Peace: Participation and the Criminal Law in Seventeenth-Century England (Cambridge, 1987)

'"To pluck bright honour from the pale-faced moon": gender and honour in the Castlehaven story', *Transactions of the Royal Historical Society*, 6th series, 6 (1996), pp. 137–59

Hill, Bridget, *Women, Work, and Sexual Politics in Eighteenth-Century England* (Oxford, 1989)

Hill, Christopher, *History and the Present* (London, 1989)

The English Bible and the Seventeenth-Century Revolution (London, 1993)

Hill, L.M., *Bench and Bureaucracy: The Public Career of Sir Julius Caesar, 1580–1636* (Cambridge, 1988)

Mistress Bourne's Complaint (forthcoming)

The Ancient State Authoritie, and Proceedings of the Court of Requests by Julius Caesar (Cambridge, 1975)

Hindle, Steve, 'The shaming of Margaret Knowsley: gossip, gender and the experience of authority in early modern England', *Continuity and Change*, 9 (1994), pp. 391–419

'Custom, festival and protest in early modern England: the Little Budworth wakes, St Peter's Day, 1596', *Rural History*, 6 (1995), pp. 155–78

Hogrefe, Pearl, 'Legal rights of Tudor women and the circumvention by men and women', *Sixteenth Century Journal*, 3 (1972), pp. 97–105

Holdsworth, W.S., *A History of English Law*, 3rd edn (London, 1923)

Holmes, Clive, 'Drainers and fenmen: the problem of popular political consciousness in the seventeenth century', in Anthony Fletcher and John Stevenson, eds., *Order and Disorder in Early Modern England* (Cambridge, 1987)

'Women, witnesses and witches', *Past and Present*, 140 (1993), pp. 45–78

Holmes, Clive, review of D.J. Guth and J.W. McKenna, eds., *Tudor Rule and Revolution: Essays for G.R. Elton from his American Friends* (Cambridge, 1982), in *Law and History Review*, 2 (1984), pp. 153–6

Honeyman, Katrina and Goodman, Jordan, 'Women's work, gender conflict, and labour markets in Europe, 1500–1900', *Economic History Review*, 2nd series, 44 (1991), pp. 608–28

Hopkins, Lisa, *John Ford's Political Theatre* (Manchester, 1994)

Horwitz, Henry, *Chancery Equity Records and Proceedings, 1600–1800: A Guide to Documents in the Public Record Office* (London, 1995)

Houlbrooke, Ralph, *Church Courts and the People During the English Reformation, 1520–1570* (Oxford, 1979)

'Women's social life and common action in England from the fifteenth century to the eve of the civil war', *Continuity and Change*, 1 (1986), pp. 176–83

Howell, Cicely, 'Peasant customs in the Midlands, 1289–1700', in Jack Goody, Joan Thirsk and E.P. Thompson, eds., *Family and Inheritance: Rural Society in Western Europe, 1200–1800* (Cambridge, 1976)

Hoyle, R.W., 'An ancient and laudable custom: the definition and development of tenant right in north-western England in the sixteenth century', *Past and Present*, 116 (1987), pp. 24–55

'Tenure and the land market in early modern England: or a late contribution to the Brenner debate', *Economic History Review*, 2nd series, 43 (1990), pp. 1–20

Hull, Suzanne, *Chaste, Silent and Obedient: English Books for Women 1475–1640* (San Marino, 1982)

Hutson, Lorna, *The Usurer's Daughter: Male Friendship and Fictions of Women in Sixteenth-Century England* (London and New York, 1994)

Ingram, Martin, 'Communities and courts: law and disorder in early seventeenth-century Wiltshire', in J.S. Cockburn, ed., *Crime in England 1550–1800* (London, 1977)

'"Scolding women cucked or washed": a crisis in gender relation in early modern England?', in Jenny Kermode and Garthine Walker, eds., *Women, Crime and the Courts in Early Modern England* (London, 1994)

Church Courts, Sex and Marriage in England, 1570–1640 (Cambridge, 1987)

Innes, Joanna and Styles, John, 'The crime wave: recent writing on crime and criminal justice in eighteenth-century England', *Journal of British Studies*, 25 (1986), pp. 380–435

Ives, E.W., 'The common lawyers in pre-Reformation England', *Transactions of the Royal Historical Society*, 5th series, 18 (1968)

Jardine, Lisa, *Reading Shakespeare Historically* (London and New York, 1996)
    Still Harping on Daughters: Women and Drama in the Age of Shakespeare, 2nd edn (London, 1983)

Jones, Ann, 'Nets and bridles: early modern conduct books and sixteenth-century women's lyrics', in Nancy Armstrong and Leonard Tennehouse, eds., *The Ideology of Conduct: Essays on Literature and the History of Sexuality* (New York and London, 1987)

Jones, W.J., *The Elizabethan Court of Chancery* (Oxford, 1967)

Jordan, William Chester, *Women and Credit in Pre-Industrial and Developing Societies* (Philadelphia, 1993)

Kagan, Richard, *Lawsuits and Litigants in Castille 1500–1700* (Chapel Hill, 1981)

Kanner, Barbara, ed., *The Women of England from Anglo-Saxon Times to the Present: Interpretative Bibliographic Essays* (London, 1980)

Kay, W. D., *Ben Jonson: A Literary Life* (Basingstoke and London, 1995)

Kermode, Jenny and Walker, Garthine, eds., *Women, Crime and the Courts in Early Modern England* (London, 1994)

Kerr, Heather, 'Thomas Garter's Susanna: "pollicie" and "true report"', *Journal of the Australasian Universities and Literature Association*, 72 (1989), pp. 183–202

Kerridge, Eric, *Agrarian Problems in the Sixteenth Century and After* (London, 1969)

Kiralfy, A.K.R., *A Source Book of English Law* (London, 1957)

Kiralfy, A.K.R., ed., *Potter's Historical Introduction to English law and its Institutions*, 4th edn (London, 1958)

Kittel, Ruth, 'Women under the law in medieval England 1066–1485', in Barbara Kanner, ed., *The Women of England from Anglo-Saxon Times to the Present: Interpretative Bibliographic Essays* (London, 1980)

Knafla, Louis, ed., *Kent at Law, 1602* (London, 1994)

Kornstein, Daniel, *Kill All the Lawyers? Shakespeare's Legal Appeal* (Princeton, New Jersey, 1994)

Kritzer, H.M. and Uhlman, T.M., 'Sisterhood in the courtroom: sex of judge and defendant in criminal case disposition', in K.O. Blumhagen and W.D. Johnson, eds., *Women's Studies: An Interdisciplinary Collection* (Westport, Connecticut, 1978)

Kuehn, Thomas, 'Reading microhistory: the example of Giovanni and Lusanna', *The Journal of Modern History*, 61 (1989), pp. 512–34

Lacey, K.E., 'Women and work in fourteenth and fifteenth century London', in Lindsey Charles and Lorna Duffin, eds., *Women and Work in Pre-Industrial England* (London, 1985)

Lake, Peter, 'Feminine piety and personal potency: the 'emancipation' of Mrs Jane Ratcliffe', *The Seventeenth Century*, 2 (1987), pp. 143–65

Larsen, Anne, 'Legitimizing the daughter's writing: Catherine des Roches' proverbial good wife', *Sixteenth Century Journal*, 21 (1990), pp. 559–74

Laslett, Peter, 'Mean household size in England since the sixteenth century', in Peter Laslett and Richard Wall, eds., *Household and Family in Past Times* (Cambridge, 1972)

Laurence, Anne, *Women in England 1500–1760: A Social History* (London, 1995)

Le Roy Ladurie, Emmanuel, *Montaillou: Cathars and Catholics in a French Village 1294–1324*, trans. Barbara Bray (Harmondsworth, 1978)

Leadam, I.S., ed., *Select Cases in the Court of Requests: A.D. 1497–1569*, Selden Society vol. 12 (London, 1898)

Lee, Sidney and Stephen, Leslie, eds., *Dictionary of National Biography*, 63 vols (London, 1885–1900)

Leech, Clifford, *Christopher Marlowe: Poet For the Stage* (New York, 1986)

Levack, Brian, *The Civil Lawyers in England 1603–1641: A Political Study* (Oxford, 1973)

Lindley, David, *The Trials of Frances Howard: Fact and Fiction at the Court of King James* (London and New York, 1993)

Loengard, Janet, 'Legal history and the medieval Englishwoman: a fragmented view', *Law and History Review*, 4 (1986), pp. 161–78

MacDonald, Michael, ed., *Witchcraft and Hysteria in Elizabethan London: Edward Jordan and the Mary Glover Case* (London and New York, 1991)

Maclean, Ian, *The Renaissance Notion of Women: A Study in the Fortunes of Scholasticism and Medical Science in European Intellectual Life* (Cambridge, 1980)

Mahood, M.M., ed., *The Merchant of Venice* (Cambridge, 1987)

Maitland, F.W., ed., *Select Pleas in Manorial and Other Seigniorial Courts*, Selden Society vol. 2 (two vols., London, 1889)

Manning, R.B., *Village Revolts; Social Protest and Popular Disturbances in England, 1509–1640* (Oxford, 1988)

Marchant, Ronald, *The Church Under the Law: Justice, Administration and Discipline in the Diocese of York, 1560–1640* (Cambridge, 1969)

McLuskie, Kathleen, *Renaissance Dramatists* (Hemel Hempstead, 1989)
Dekker and Heywood: Professional Dramatists (London, 1994)

McRae, Andrew, *God Speed the Plough: The Representation of Agrarian England, 1500–1660* (Cambridge, 1996)

Meldrum, Tim, 'A women's court in London: defamation at the Bishop of London's consistory court, 1700–1745', *The London Journal*, 19 (1994), pp. 1–22

Mendelson, Sara, *The Mental World of Stuart Women: Three Studies* (Brighton, 1987)

Merchant, W.M., 'Lawyer and actor: process of law in Elizabethan drama', *English Studies Today*, 3rd series, 3 (1962), pp. 107–24

Miles, Rosalind, *Ben Jonson: His Craft and Art* (London and New York, 1990)

Milsom, S.F.C., *The Historical Foundations of the Common Law*, 2nd edn (London, 1981)

Muldrew, Craig, *The Economy of Obligation: The Culture of Credit and Social Relations in Early Modern England* (Basingstoke, forthcoming)

Newman, Karen, *Fashioning Femininity and English Renaissance Drama* (Chicago and London, 1991)

Norsworthy, L., *The Lady of Bleeding Heart Yard* (London, 1935)

O'Barr, W.M., *Linguistic Evidence: Language, Power, and Strategy in the Courtroom* (New York, 1982)

Oldham, James, 'Truth-telling in the eighteenth-century courtroom', *Law and History Review*, 12 (1993), pp. 95–121

Outhwaite, Brian, *Clandestine Marriage in England, 1500–1850* (London and Rio Grande, 1995)

Parker, Patricia, *Literary Fat Ladies; Rhetoric, Gender, Property* (London and New York, 1987)

Perry, Maria, *Elizabeth I: The Word of a Prince* (London, 1990)

Philips, J.F., 'Arbitration', *Litigation*, 1 (1982), pp. 239–43

Phillips, O.H., *Shakespeare and the Lawyers* (London, 1972)

Plucknett, Theodore, *A Concise History of the Common Law*, 4th edn (London, 1948)

Pollard, A.F., 'The growth of the Court of Requests', *English Historical Review*, 56 (1941), pp. 300–3

Pollock, Frederick and Maitland, F.W., *The History of English Law Before the Time of Edward I*, ed. S.F.C. Milsom, 2nd edn (Cambridge, 1968)

Pollock, Linda, '"Teach her to live under obedience": the making of women in the upper ranks of early modern England', *Continuity and Change*, 4 (1989), pp. 231–58

With Faith and Physic: The Life of a Tudor Gentlewoman Lady Grace Mildmay 1552–1620 (London, 1993)

Poole, Eric, 'West's *Symboleography*: an Elizabethan formulary', in J.A. Guy and H.G. Beale, eds., *Law and Social Change in British History: Papers Presented to the Bristol Legal History Conference, 14–17 July 1981* (London, 1984)

Powell, C.L., *English Domestic Relations 1487–1653* (New York, 1972)

Power, Eileen, *Medieval Women*, ed. M.M. Postan (Cambridge, 1975)

Prest, W.R., 'Law and women's rights in early modern England', *The Seventeenth Century*, 6 (1991), pp. 169–87

The Rise of the Barristers: A Social History of the English Bar 1590–1640 (Oxford, 1986)

Prest, W.R., ed., *Lawyers in Early Modern Europe and America* (New York, 1981)

Prior, Mary, 'Women and the urban economy: Oxford 1500–1800', in Mary Prior, ed., *Women in English Society, 1500–1800* (London, 1985)

'Wives and wills 1558–1700', in John Chartres and David Hey, eds., *English Rural Society, 1500–1800: Essays in Honour of Joan Thirsk* (Cambridge, 1990)

Public Record Office Lists and Indexes, no. 21, 'List of proceedings in the Court of Requests preserved in the Public Record Office' (New York, 1963)

(supplementary series), no. 7, 'Proceedings in the Court of Requests' (New York, 1966)

Quaife, G.R., *Wanton Wenches and Wayward Wives: Peasants and Illicit Sex in Early Seventeenth Century England* (London, 1979)

Roberts, Michael, '"Words they are women, and deeds they are men": images of work and gender in early modern England', in Lindsey Charles and Lorna Duffin, eds., *Women and Work in Pre-Industrial England* (London, 1985), pp. 122–80

Roberts, Simon, 'The study of dispute: anthropological perspectives', in John Bossy, ed., *Disputes and Settlements: Law and Human Relations in the West* (Cambridge, 1983)

Roper, Lyndal, *Oedipus and the Devil: Witchcraft, Sexuality and Religion in Early Modern Europe* (London and New York, 1994)

Ross, Charles, 'Shakespeare's *Merry Wives* and the law of fraudulent conveyence', *Renaissance Drama*, new series, 25 (1994), pp. 148–9

Royal Commission on Legal Services, Final report (1979)

Rushton, Peter, 'Women, witchcraft and slander in early modern England: cases from the church courts of Durham, 1560–1675', *Northern History*, 18 (1982), pp. 116–32

Sachs, Albie and Wilson, Joan, *Sexism and the Law: A Study of Male Beliefs and Legal Bias in Britain and the United States* (Oxford, 1978)

Sanders, G.W., *Orders of the High Court of Chancery* (London, 1845)

Scott, H.S., ed., *The Journal of Sir Roger Wilbraham*, Camden Miscellany vol. 10 (London, 1902), p. 95

Searle, C.E., 'Custom, class conflict and agrarian capitalism: the Cumbrian customary economy in the eighteenth century', *Past and Present*, 110 (1986), pp. 106–33

Seaver, Paul, 'A social contract? Master against servant in the Court of Requests', *History Today*, 39 (September, 1989), pp. 50–6

Sexton, Joyce, *The Slandered Woman in Shakespeare*, English Literature Monograph Series, No. 12 (University of Victoria, 1978)

Sharp, Buchanan, *In Contempt of All Authority; Rural Artisans and Riot in the West of England, 1586–1660* (Berkeley and London, 1980)

Sharpe, J.A., *Defamation and Sexual Slander in Early Modern England: The Church Courts at York*, Borthwick papers no. 58 (York, 1980)

'The history of crime in late medieval and early modern England: a review of the field', *Social History*, 7 (1982), pp. 187–203

'"Such disagreement betwyx neighbours": Litigation and human relations in early modern England', in John Bossy, ed., *Disputes and Settlements: Law and Human Relations in the West* (Cambridge, 1983)

Crime in Early Modern England, 1550–1750 (London, 1984)

'Debate: the history of violence in England: some observations', *Past & Present*, 108 (1985), pp. 206–15

'The people and the law', in Barry Reay, ed., *Popular Culture in Seventeenth Century England* (London, 1985), pp. 244–70

'Witchcraft and women in seventeenth-century England: some northern evidence' *Continuity and Change*, 6 (1991), pp. 179–99

Sheail, John, 'The distribution of taxable population and wealth in England during the early sixteenth century', *Transactions of the Institute of British Geographers*, 55 (1972), pp. 111–26

Shoemaker, Robert, *Prosecution and Punishment: Petty Crime and the Law in London and Rural Middlesex, c. 1660–1725* (Cambridge, 1991)

Sisson, Charles, '*Keep the Widow Waking*: a lost play by Dekker', *The Library*, 8 (1927–8), pp. 39–57, 233–59

Lost Plays of Shakespeare's Age (Cambridge, 1936)

Sommerville, Margaret, *Sex and Subjection: Attitudes to Women in Early-Modern Society* (London and New York, 1995)

Spring, Eileen, 'The heiress-at-law: English real property law from a new point of view', *Law and History Review*, 8 (1990), pp. 273–96

Law, Land, & Family: Aristocratic Inheritance in England, 1300 to 1800 (Chapel Hill and London, 1993)

Spufford, Margaret, *Contrasting Communities: English Villagers in the Sixteenth and Seventeenth Centuries* (Cambridge, 1979)

Statutes of the Realm (London, 1819)

Staves, Susan, *Married Women's Separate Property in England, 1660–1833* (London, 1990)

Stenton, Doris, *The English Woman in History* (London, 1957)

Stone, Lawrence, *The Crisis of the Aristocracy 1558–1641* (Oxford, 1965)

The Family, Sex and Marriage in England 1500–1800, abridged edition (London, 1979)

'Interpersonal violence in English society 1300–1980', *Past and Present*, 101 (1983), pp. 22–33

The Past and the Present Revisited (London, 1987)

Road to Divorce: England 1530–1987 (Oxford, 1990)

Stone, Lawrence and Stone, Jeanne, *An Open Elite? England, 1540–1880* (Oxford, 1984)

Stopes, Charlotte, *British Freewomen; Their Historical Privilege*, 3rd edn (London, 1907)

Stretton, Tim, 'Social historians and the records of litigation', in Sølvi Sogner, ed., *Fact, Fiction and Forensic Evidence. Tid og Tanke. Skriftserie fra Historisk Institutt, Universitetet i Oslo*, No. 2 (Oslo, 1997)

Sugarman, David and Rubin, G.R., eds., *Law, Economy & Society, 1750–1914: Essays in the History of English Law* (Abingdon, Oxon., 1984)

Tanner, J.R., ed., *Tudor Constitutional Documents A.D. 1485–1603 with an Historical Commentary* (Cambridge, 1951)

Taub, Nadine and Schneider, E.M., 'Perspectives on women's subordination and the role of law', in David Kairys, ed., *The Politics of Law: A Progressive Critique* (New York, 1982)

Tawney, R.H., *The Agrarian Problem in the Sixteenth Century* (London, 1912)

The Parliamentary History of England, from the Earliest Period to the Year 1803 (London, 1806)

Thomas, Keith, 'The double standard', *Journal of the History of Ideas*, 20 (1959), pp. 195–216

'Age and authority in early modern England', *Proceedings of the British Academy*, 62 (1976), pp. 205–48

'The puritans and adultery: the act of 1650 reconsidered', in Donald Pennington and Keith Thomas, eds., *Puritans and Revolutionaries: Essays in Seventeenth-Century History Presented to Christopher Hill* (Oxford, 1978)

Thompson, E.P., 'The grid of inheritance: a comment', in Jack Goody, Joan Thirsk, E.P. Thompson, eds., *Family and Inheritance: Rural Society in Western Europe, 1200–1800* (Cambridge, 1976)

Customs in Common (London, 1991)

Thompson, Roger, *Women in Stuart England and America* (London, 1974)

Tittler, Robert, 'Money-lending in the west Midlands – the activities of Joyce Jefferies, 1638–1649', *Historical Research*, 67 (1994), pp. 249–63

Todd, Barbara, 'Freebench and free enterprise: widows and their property in two Berkshire villages', in John Chartres and David Hey, eds., *English Rural Society, 1500–1800: Essays in Honour of Joan Thirsk* (Cambridge, 1990)

'The virtuous widow in protestant England', in Sandra Cavallo and Lyndan Warner, eds., *Widowhood in Medieval and Early Modern Europe* (Longman; forthcoming)

Travitsky, Betty, 'Husband-murder and petty treason in English Renaissance tragedy', *Renaissance Drama*, new series, 21 (1990), pp. 171–98

Travitsky, Betty, ed., *The Paradise of Women: Writings by Englishwomen of the Renaissance* (Westport, Connecticut, 1981)

Tucker, E.F.J., *Intruder into Eden: Representations of the Common Lawyer in English Literature 1350–1750* (Columbia, South Carolina, 1984)

Underdown, David, 'The taming of the scold: the enforcement of patriarchal authority in early modern England', in Anthony Fletcher and John Stevenson, eds., *Order and Disorder in Early Modern England* (Cambridge, 1987)

Revel, Riot and Rebellion: Popular Politics and Culture in England 1603–1660 (Oxford, 1987)

Fire from Heaven: Life in an English Town in the Seventeenth Century (London, 1993)

Waage, Frederick, *The White Devil Discover'd: Backgrounds and Foregrounds to Webster's Tragedy* (New York, 1984)

Wales, Tim, 'Poverty, poor relief and the life-cycle: some evidence from seventeenth-century Norfolk', in Richard Smith, ed., *Land, Kinship and Life-Cycle* (London, 1984)

Walker, Garthine, 'Expanding the boundaries of female honour in early modern England', *Transactions of the Royal Historical Society*, 6th series, 6 (1996), pp. 235–45

Wall, Alison, 'Elizabethan precept and feminine practice: the Thynne family of Longleat', *History*, 75 (1990), pp. 23–38

Wall, Alison, ed., *Two Elizabethan Women: Correspondence of Joan and Maria Thynne 1575–1611*, Wiltshire Record Society vol. 38 (Devizes, 1983)

Walter, John, 'Grain riots and popular attitudes to the law: Maldon and the crisis of 1629', in John Brewer and John Styles, *An Ungovernable People: The English and their Law in the Seventeenth and Eighteenth centuries* (London, 1980)

Watt, Tessa, *Cheap Print and Popular Piety, 1550–1640* (Cambridge, 1991)

Whittaker, W.J., ed., *The Mirror of Justices*, Selden Society vol. 7 (London, 1985)

Willen, Diane, 'Women in the public sphere in early modern England: the case of the urban working poor', *Sixteenth Century Journal*, 19 (1988), pp. 559–75

Wilson, Adrian, 'The ceremony of childbirth and its interpretation', in Valerie Fildes, ed., *Women as Mothers in Pre-industrial England: Essays in memory of Dorothy McLaren* (London, 1989)

Wood, Andy, 'Custom, identity and resistance: English free miners and their law c. 1550–1800', in Paul Griffiths, Adam Fox and Steve Hindle, eds., *The Experience of Authority in Early Modern England* (Basingstoke, 1996)

Woodbridge, Linda, *Women and the English Renaissance: Literature and the Nature of Womankind 1540–1620* (Urbana, 1984)

Woolf, D.R., 'Speech, text, and time: the sense of hearing and the sense of the past in Renaissance England', *Albion*, 18 (1986), pp. 159–93

Wright, L.B., *Middle-Class Culture in Elizabethan England* (Chapel Hill, 1935)

Wrightson, Keith, 'Infanticide in earlier seventeenth-century England', *Local Population Studies*, 15 (1975), pp. 10–22

'Kinship in an English village: Terling, Essex, 1550–1700', in R.M. Smith, ed., *Land, Kinship and Lifecycle* (Cambridge, 1984)

'Estates, degrees, and sorts: changing perceptions of society in Tudor and Stuart England', in Penelope Corfield, ed., *Language, History and Class* (Oxford, 1991)

'Two concepts of order: justices, constable and jurymen in seventeenth-century England', in John Brewer and John Styles, eds., *An Ungovernable People: The English and their Law in the Seventeenth and Eighteenth Centuries* (London, 1980)

Wrightson, Keith and Levine, David, *The Making of an Industrial Society: Whickham 1560–1765* (Oxford, 1991)

Yale, D.E.C., *Lord Nottingham's 'Manual of Chancery Practice' & 'Prolegomena of Chancery and Equity'* (Cambridge, 1965)

4 UNPUBLISHED THESES

Allsebrook, W.B.J., 'The Court of Requests in the reign of Elizabeth' (University of London M.A., 1936)

Beattie, J.H., 'Women in the Old Bailey', paper given to Durham early Modern Seminar, 12 May 1993

Bensel-Meyers, Linda, '"A figure cut in alabaster": the paradoxical widow in Renaissance drama' (University of Oregon Ph.D., 1985)

Blessing, Carol Ann, 'Women and the law in the plays of John Webster' (University of California, Riverside Ph.D., 1991)

Foyster, Elizabeth, 'The concept of male honour in seventeenth century England' (University of Durham Ph.D., 1996)

Glanz, Leonore, 'The legal position of English women under the early Stuart Kings and the Interregnum' (Loyola University Ph.D., 1973)

Hindle, Steve, 'Aspects of the relationship of the state and local society in early modern England, with special reference to Cheshire c. 1590–1630' (University of Cambridge Ph.D., 1992)

Ingram, Angela, 'Changing attitudes to "bad" women in Elizabethan and Jacobean drama' (University of Cambridge Ph.D., 1977)

Jones, Neil, 'Trusts: practice and doctrine, 1536–1660' (University of Cambridge Ph.D., 1994)

Kaiser, C.R.E., 'The Masters of Requests: an extraordinary judicial company in an age of centralization (1589–1648)' (University of London Ph.D., 1977)

Knight, Marcus, 'Litigants and litigation in the seventeenth century Palatinate of Durham' (University of Cambridge Ph.D., 1990)

Knox, D.A., 'The Court of Requests in the reign of Edward VI, 1547–1553' (University of Cambridge Ph.D., 1974)

McIntyre, Bronwyn, 'Legal attitudes towards women in England 1558–1648' (University of New Brunswick M.A., 1972)

Merton, Charlotte, 'The women who served Queen Mary and Queen Elizabeth: ladies, gentlewomen and maids of the Privy Chamber 1553–1603', (University of Cambridge Ph.D., 1992)

Muldrew, Craig, 'Credit, market relations and debt litigation in late seventeenth century England with special reference to King's Lynn' (University of Cambridge Ph.D., 1991)

   'Women, debt litigation and credit in early modern England', paper delivered to the 'Women, Trade and Business conference', University of Exeter, 15–17 July 1996

Stretton, Tim, 'Women and litigation in the Elizabethan Court of Requests' (University of Cambridge Ph.D., 1993)

Warner, Lyndan, 'Printed ideas about "man" and "woman" in France, 1490–1610' (University of Cambridge Ph.D., 1995)

INDEX

Cambridge Studies in Early Modern British History

Titles in the series